NEW MOONS FOR SAM

Becoming Kiwi

Life of a New Zealand Diplomat

PETER HAMILTON

Published by Mawhitipana Publishing

Contact: newmoonsforsam@outlook.com

ISBN 978-0-473-58027-8 (paperback)

ISBN 978-0-473-58028-5 (EPUB)

A catalogue record for this book is available from the National Library of New Zealand.

Mo te Whanau Katoa

Rachel, Chris, Fiona, Alexander, Coen, Isla and Isabella

CONTENTS

PART III

REPUBLICANISM, RATIONALISM AND (MAYBE) OPTIMISM

INTRODUCTION

Summer has left the island today and gone north for a season. In exchange, the north wind and squally rain blow across the Gulf and up the valley, signalling a return to winter. There is thunder in the clouds. The rain beats on the window panes of the cottage and the raw wind whistles through the ill-fitting door frames.

From the warmth and cheerfulness of summer, the captivating trilling of the tui and the exuberant dance of a kereru on a thermal updraught, a prosaic and grey mood descends on the island. The days are shorter and colder and night comes earlier. Gone for the moment are the long still evenings and gentle sunsets. With the sound of the waves crashing and foaming on the beach below, everything now is in rough motion.

There is an aching beauty in this island, no matter the season. It is easy to overlook the scars on the landscape. In places the vista is of an undisturbed nature, as the island must have been before *Homo*, not always *sapiens*, discovered it and began to diminish it. Winter is a time for reflection and there is time enough for that. Far out to sea, it is difficult to see the horizon. Sky and sea seem to merge indistinguishably.

We walk a difficult path in this life and there are good and bad times. We are blessed when a new child joins the family and we contemplate in humility life's mystery. But darkness follows the day, like winter the summer. Often it is a darkness we ourselves have created.

It is wrong to damn a whole nation for the sins of some, but there are those who have ceaselessly waged war, built the concentration camps and the gulags, let loose the killing fields, profited from arms sales and, without compassion, have countenanced the death even of children.

We never seem to learn the lessons of the past, which is why history is so important when we risk knowing less and less about more and more. In the midst of unspeakable horror, there are the courageous few, the resisters, like Sophie Scholl and her brother Hans in Nazi Germany, who refused to kowtow to evil. Sophie was a bit younger than me when I was a student in Germany, 33 years after she was cruelly murdered, at the young age of 21, by a corrupt regime.

When I first heard Sophie's story, I was filled with admiration for her courage. Doing the right thing when most others had taken the easy route by acquiescing in barbarism. There have been countless others through the ages who have been equally brave. A younger generation must learn from them and must guard against a lazy indifference and complacency.

It is reassuring to look out to sea from the vantage point of this island and to feel thankful. The optimist in me knows things can get better, but the pessimist, who is never far away, sees the uncertain and degraded world our children inherit.

We will be affected in many different ways by those we encounter. Nothing is so painful as losing loved ones and companions. Except we can draw comfort from the knowledge that we have known them and loved them and that they too have been on life's journey with us.

There have been many who have influenced me, family and friends, and the many individuals I narrate in this story whom I have met in 70 years:

- my maternal grandfather, satisfied with the daily routine of country life on his small farm in Somerset, a no-nonsense, plain-speaking, rough but loving man, who had little education but great wisdom;
- my maternal grandmother, a love of family, a skepticism for established religion, a disinclination, despite an outward politeness, to kowtow to inherited privilege;
- my paternal grandparents, a dour and narrow outlook which can cloud appreciation of family life;
- my father, a sense of humour to demolish life's false airs and graces, to carry one through the tough times, but, as well, a shyness and stubbornness;
- my mother, optimistic perseverance in whatever we undertake and a generous and forgiving nature;
- Edith Baker, my teacher at the age of nine, dramatising the story of King Alfred of Wessex burning the cakes at Athelney in Somerset over a thousand years ago, which made me realise what fascinating characters had been on life's road before me;
- Fordy, my teacher at high school, an appreciation of the timelessness of everything and our own insignificance and yet the grandeur of it all;
- and those, like Sophie Scholl, who inspire by their selfless example.

PART I

BECOMING KIWI

CHAPTER 1

THE EARLY YEARS

THERE ARE 39 PLACES IN THE WORLD CALLED WELLINGTON, 47 called Hamilton and five called Christchurch and Dunedin. There are even two Aucklands.

But there is only one Stogursey. Most people have never heard of Stogursey, population about 1600. It is a little village in West Somerset, nestling at the foot of the ancient Quantock hills not far from the Bristol Channel. As English villages go, there is nothing very special about it, apart from its lovely Norman church. It has the required ruined castle, a non-descript pub, a squat Victorian-era stone school, a couple of little shops and a sports field for cricket.

Stogursey is a corruption of 'Stoke Courcy', indicating that the ancient Norman family of de Courcy held land in the area after the Norman conquest. At the time of the conquest in 1066, the land was owned by a Saxon thane called Brixi. He was rudely dispossessed.

If you drive north from the church, up through the village past long rows of pastel-coloured houses and past the pub and school, after about a kilometre you come to Little Water Farm and its imposing two-storey farmhouse set at right angles to the country road.

I was born in this farmhouse on Thursday, 28 June 1951, early in the morning. The next day, 29 June, was my father's 25th birthday, so I assume I was a welcome birthday present. Sixty-four years later, in 2015, Dad would decide to cement this connection by dying on my birthday, just a few hours short of his 89th.

My mother gave birth to me in my grandparents' bedroom, the same room in which she had been born on 21 December 1927. I am told that electricity was switched on at the farmhouse the same day. I guess for the family my arrival was a doubly auspicious occasion.

The farmhouse, with slate roof and whitewashed exterior walls, dates back to the 16th century, possibly earlier as it had a 'cruck arc' internally. This signified that it was originally a medieval yeoman's cottage, before it was enlarged in the late 18th or early 19th century to make it a 'gentleman's' cottage. Its small rooms had low ceilings and metre-thick stone walls.

It had four bedrooms of varying sizes upstairs, each with a small latticed window. Downstairs there were a small dining room, scullery, pantry and two small lounges. A cold, narrow bedroom lay hidden, almost forgotten, under the stairs. A toilet and a large bathroom with a cast-iron bath were recent additions. The toilet had until very recently been in an outhouse. When my mother was a child, bathing and washing had to be done in a moveable tin bath brought into the kitchen, before running water was installed.

In front of the house was a small patch of lawn where afternoon tea could be taken in the summer sun. Behind an adjoining wall my grandfather had his small kitchen garden which in season produced fresh vegetables. A short white pebble footpath led up from the Stogursey road to the cumbersome front door. Here the postman would deliver his letters.

A rear entrance on the road side of the house was meant for tradesmen. This fell into disuse over the years and was kept locked. Mum recalls that one visitor arrived at the tradesmen's entrance in late September 1938 announcing that the Prime Minister, Neville Chamberlain, had just returned from Munich with a piece of paper signed by Hitler to guarantee 'peace in our time'. The threat of war must have been an ever-present reality in her childhood until it actually broke out in September 1939, when she was eleven.

Little Water Farm

A long, narrow bread oven, long out of use, was set deep into the back wall of a freezing-cold pantry. This small room had an uneven flagstone floor and flagstone benches. The coldest room in the house, it served in the absence of electricity as a refrigerator, keeping meat and vegetables fresh, as well as milk and cream for making butter. It had rows of jars of preserved fruit, kitchen utensils and other kitchen bric-a-brac. It was deeply uninviting.

The small dining room was the warmest room in the house because it had a coal range for cooking and heating. Here people congregated. It had an early 19th century grandfather clock that my grandfather would rewind each night before he went to bed. Its ponderous 'tick-tock' measuring life's moments was the only sound that filled the house when all else was silent. I was entranced, in the quiet of night, by its relentless rhythm and its booming metallic chimes on the half and full hour. A second grandfather clock stood at the foot of the stairs leading to the upper bedrooms. They were rarely in sync.

A massive 17th-century high-backed wooden settle, or seat, was the main piece of furniture in the dining room. It was so rigidly uncomfortable that no one sat on it for long. This settle might have come straight out of a Dickens novel, like *Pickwick Papers*, with Sam Weller's 'Old 'un', the coachman Tony Weller, sitting on it in his greatcoat, enjoying a warming draught of scrumpy.

A crude and cumbersome wooden dining table sat six comfortably, or eight with a squash. My grandmother always sat alone at the head of the table, with her back to the lattice window, so she could oversee proceedings. Nearby my grandfather's old armchair was strategically placed next to a small oil heater for warmth in winter. The adjoining scullery had a small sink, once running water was installed, a tiny refrigerator, a hot-water cylinder and a large rough-hewn, wooden storage cupboard.

A small dark, dank, dingy room, full of cobwebs, with holes in its tiled roof, led off the scullery. This was used to store coal and wood for the open fires in the two sitting rooms. It was a cold and creepy place.

The door stud in the cottage was low, just under two metres, indicating that people had been much shorter when the cottage was built 400 years ago. It was a good idea to stoop when passing through any doorway to avoid banging your head. The thick walls of the cottage and flagstone floors ensured it was always freezing cold in winter and chilly in summer. When the wind was howling outside on a dark night, as was often the case, it sounded like my idea of *Wuthering Heights*.

Little Water Farm milked about 10 or 12 cows, which today would not constitute a viable farming unit. It formed part of the large Fairfield Estate owned by the Acland-Hood family. About a kilometre away was Fairfield House, a large E-shaped Elizabethan mansion. Here the estate owner, Lord St Audries, a confirmed bachelor, resided in comfortable domesticity with his two unmarried sisters, Audrey and Maudy, as my grandmother called them, but who to their faces were addressed as Miss Audrey and Miss Maud. They used to drive around in a pony and trap but then progressed to a little car.

My grandparents always referred to Lord St Audries, behind his back, as 'Lordy'. When my mother was a child, Lordy's mother, Lady St Audries, was still alive. As a little girl, Mum had refused her mother's injunction to curtsey to Lady St Audries when they happened to meet her one day in the village. I guess my egalitarian instincts are inherited from my mother. Despite this outward politeness, my grandmother would have laughed at Dr Samuel Johnson's vapid doctrine of 'subordination', meek acceptance of one's place in the social hierarchy.

When my grandmother May Dyer, or Granny as we called her, left the farm in 1994 at the age of 94 to live with her daughter, my Aunty Betty, Little Water Farm had been in the family for over 90 years. My grandparents paid rent all that time for their meagre land holding and had never been able to own either the farm or the house. I blame it all on those rapacious land-grabbing knights, like Sir William de Courcy, who came over from Normandy with William the Conqueror in 1066 and established the peculiar system of English land tenure. But my grandparents were happy and uncomplaining.

Granny Dyer was born on 4 November 1900, a late Victorian and an early arrival in the new century. She came from a large family and grew up in Honiton in East Devon. Her father, my great-grandfather, James Oliver Watts, had been a baker and farmer in the tiny Devonshire village of Gittisham. This had enabled him to live comfortably and provide for his family of nine children. He gambled away the family fortune and, in reduced circumstances, ended up as publican of the Railway Arms Hotel in Williton. Williton is the administrative centre for West Somerset so that is where my birth was registered. Granny lived a long and full life, dying on 15 November 1996.

A photo of her family in 1904 shows my maternal great-grandmother, Caroline Jemimah Watts (her maiden name was Hayman), looking gaunt and tired from all the family troubles and from giving birth to nine children. Great-grandad James Oliver, with his big bushy moustache, looks quite upright and self-satisfied. His friends called him J.O. Granny is the little four-year-old wearing a white pinafore, with the inquisitive pout. She was the youngest but one of the nine children. I got to know all three of her older sisters, Annie, Lily and Daisy, strong and colourful characters, as well as her brother Fred Watts.

My maternal great-grandparents, James and Jemimah Watts, with their nine children (1904). Clockwise left: George (seated on the ground); May, aged 4 (Granny Dyer, white pinafore); Annie, (the oldest sibling) Lily, Fred; Daisy; Jim; Sidney (seated on the ground); Henry (the youngest, on his mother's lap).

Fred died in 1989 shortly after we celebrated his 100th birthday. An older brother, Jim, emigrated to Canada as a young man and joined the Mounties (the Royal Canadian Mounted Police) in Edmonton. Another brother, George, died at the end of the First World War of a tropical illness caught in Burma. This tragedy, surviving the war but dying of an illness just as he was about to be demobbed, so upset my great-aunt Annie, the oldest sibling, that she never went to any church again. The fourth brother, Sidney, spent most of his life in the

British Army. The youngest brother, Henry, was gassed in the First World War but survived the ordeal into later life.

Fred and Henry permanently fell out with each other when Henry objected to Fred describing their father, James, as fond of 'fast women but slow horses'. There was, though, some justification for this criticism. Great-grandad James, described to me by one of his descendants as a 'randy old man', fathered a son with pretty Letty Davis. This caused a huge scandal which the family sought to bury, for the most part successfully. The child was put up for adoption. James' son Sidney later married poor Letty and James' daughter Lily married Letty's brother, Jack Davis. Somewhere in England, I have, or had as he no doubt died long ago, a great-uncle about whom I know nothing. Great-grandad James died in 1947, aged 87 and at rest from his labours is buried at St Decuman's Church in Watchet, where Great-grandma Caroline, who pre-deceased him, is also buried.

Great-uncle Sidney, who had done his father a great favour by marrying poor Letty Davis, is remembered in the family as 'eccentric in the extreme'. He spent over 25 years in the British Army, including in Egypt during the First World War. When asked what rank he had attained after 25 years of active service, he replied proudly: 'A full-blown private, sir'!

Great-grandad James held none too high an opinion of his sons-in-law, describing Aunty Annie's husband, Frank Stevens, as 'mean', Aunt Lil's husband, Jack Davis, as 'lazy' and Aunty Daisy's husband, Fred Besley, as 'needing to be horse-whipped'. What, I wonder, might be a suitable description for Great-grandad James himself? I never knew him.

My maternal grandfather, William James Dyer, known to his friends as Billy and to his few detractors as Cockey Dyer, was born on 4 February 1897. He was a tenant dairy farmer on the Fairfield estate. Grandad Dyer had a distinct Somerset accent, earthy common sense, a calm and normally patient, no-nonsense approach to life. But on the rare occasion he was riled, he could shout and swear like a trooper. My grandmother did not escape the occasional outburst when his patience was sorely tried, but it was sound more than fury. He escaped being called up in the Great War because agricultural workers were deemed essential for food production. His main relaxation was to puff on an old pipe in his free moments. I loved collecting his discarded tobacco tins which still had a delightful aroma of tobacco leaf.

Grandad Dyer, whom I did get to know and love, had little education and rarely socialised outside his home. The Dyer family had lived in the parish for centuries, according to Stogursey Church's baptismal and marriage records. Like my mother after him, Grandad attended Stogursey village school before the First World War. Years later, my mother visited her old school and was shown the school's punishment book. One entry recorded that her father, Billy Dyer, had been punished in 1907 for being absent. He had absconded to go bird-nesting.

His parents owned the little grocery shop in Stogursey. His father, my great-grandfather George Dyer, used to make frequent trips to nearby towns, Bridgwater or Taunton, in a horse and cart for his supplies. He took over the tenancy of Little Water Farm shortly before the First World War and that provided full-time employment for my young grandfather. They still kept the village store, however, which was run by my great-grandmother, Mary Dyer, whose family name was Richards. She was a buxom, homely matriarch. Her world view did not extend beyond the village.

When Grandad Dyer married young May Watts in 1926, he took her to live at Little Water Farm, which became her home for the rest of her life. Life was hard for my grandparents who had to raise two little girls, Joan and Betty, as well as pay rent to Fairfield House, living off a meagre milk cheque and any money earned from lodgers or from the sale of a pig or two.

Every morning before school, my mother, Joan, would help milk the cows by hand. At school in Stogursey she received a solid primary education. Nothing much happened there except, she recalls, a visit to the school one day in 1938 by Emperor Haile Selassie of Ethiopia, the 'Lion of the Tribe of Judah'. After Mussolini's invasion of his homeland, Haile Selassie was living in temporary exile in Bath, Somerset, in a place called Fairfield House. Perhaps he had wanted to see the other Fairfield House in Stogursey.

Years later, in 1974, I thought of Haile Selassie again, after he was deposed in an army mutiny in Ethiopia and ignominiously carted off in a little Volkswagen to a final exile and death. How odd to think that an Emperor had visited Stogursey village school. New Zealand was one of only six countries, along with the US, China, the USSR, Spain and Mexico, which did not recognise Italy's brutal invasion and annexation of Ethiopia. Even Britain and France eventually abandoned him, in a fruitless endeavour to avoid a breach with Mussolini. Somewhere on file is a letter Haile Selassie wrote to the New Zealand Government thanking us for our support.

Granny Dyer was an intelligent, vivacious and homely woman who worked hard to make ends meet. Her home was always open to family and visitors. Her life experience too did not extend much beyond her large family and the village. There was always a suggestion on her side of the family that she had married beneath her by marrying a tenant farmer. In her lifetime, she made only two trips out of the UK, the first at the age of 76 when she visited us in New Zealand and the second, aged 85, when she visited my wife Louise and me, and her great-grandchildren, Rachel and Christopher, in Ottawa, Canada.

Grandad Dyer was a shy man and was quite content to enjoy and live by the slow rhythms of the countryside. He had only a few friends and, since my grandmother did everything for him in terms of home comforts, he had no real need of any. He would often refuse to accompany my very sociable grandmother to village dances or social events, to her intense disappointment, putting his foot down with a gruff 'I shan't be there, May'! This became a favourite family saying whenever any of us did not want to do something.

I used to see him standing alone at the barn door in his baggy and ill-fitting corduroy trousers, gazing wistfully into the distance towards the rolling hills. He loved rural Somerset and knew intimately every inch of the Quantock Hills. The poet Coleridge referred to them as 'the silent hills'. I was fascinated to hear Grandad talk of evocative places like Crowcombe, Aisholt, Holford, Seven Sisters, Bagborough and Dead Woman's Ditch. I never knew who this dead woman was but her ditch is a well-known landmark on the Quantocks.

During the Second World War Grandad was made a special constable in the Home Guard. His duties included ensuring the security of the Stogursey neighbourhood. I imagined this must be like the great TV series *Dad's Army* but I am told that the Home Guard was in fact a very effective national defence operation.

A young Italian prisoner of war, captured during the North Africa campaign, was sent to assist my grandfather on his farm. Perhaps he had come from those 'acres' of Italian POWs captured in Egypt, as the British Army had described them when there had been too many to count. His name was Esposito Pascal and he came from a poor family in Naples. I am told that he had a lovely tenor singing voice.

I was amazed that a POW had been billeted with my grandparents and allowed to roam around relatively unsupervised but there was never any real concern about security. The military authorities at the nearby prisoner of war camp would have kept a close eye on him. Esposito, who was referred to as 'Pos', was unlikely to run away and being well fed and housed on the farm probably thanked his lucky stars that he was not still fighting in Mussolini's army with his compatriots. Like other Italian prisoners of war, Pos was required to have a round orange patch sewn on the back of his uniform so he could be easily identified. He slept in that cold, narrow bedroom under the stairs.

There was of course a major language barrier with my grandfather. Whenever Grandad failed to make himself understood, he resorted to the well-tried device of shouting at Pos even more loudly. Pos could be heard complaining to whoever would listen: 'Boss, he shout too much'. Pos formed a rather strong liking, reciprocated evidently, for my mother's first cousin, Frances, who was later my teacher.

After the war Pos returned to Italy. He endeavoured to keep in touch with the family. I have seen a postcard in Italian which he sent to my mother from Naples in June 1946, written in careful printing, asking how everyone in the family was and saying that he was waiting for news from Little Water. After that he was never heard from again. How strange the prisoner of war experience must have been, both for my grandparents and for Pos.

One particular friend of my grandfather was Jack Burge, a large imposing man who, with his wife Molly, lived all his life in Stogursey village. Like Grandad, Jack loved fox hunting and always had a small fox terrier with him. He used this little critter to unearth foxes on hunting days when the hounds had driven a fox to ground. I regarded it as a nasty, nippy sort of animal but it was Jack's pride and joy.

Molly was a warm-hearted, rotund, jolly and outgoing person who would often bring a freshly baked fruit cake or sponge cake, dripping with cream, to Little Water for afternoon tea and a gossip. Molly and Jack spoke with strong Somerset accents and were very well fed thanks to Molly's excellent and very rich cooking.

Mrs Cridge, a red-faced woman who lived in a little cottage up the road to Fairfield House, came once a week to help with the family washing. This she did in an old tin tub placed on the kitchen table.

Another friend was Bill Nurton whose nickname was Fourpence. He lived next door in a little cottage. Fourpence's wife, Mrs Nurton, helped my grandmother with house cleaning and she became a lifelong friend of the family. We called her Nurtney. When we returned to the UK from New Zealand for the first time in 1971, Fourpence was very ill. I visited him in his sick bed but he died a few days later during the night. For some reason I was the first one to tell Grandad that his old friend had just died. I will never forget the look of surprise and sadness on his face as I told him the news.

Grandad died in October 1972, aged 75, of a massive heart attack. He had stepped outside after afternoon tea and collapsed opening a farm gate near the road. His crumpled body was found a short time later in the gateway. My grandmother told me she always regretted that the last words he spoke to her, just before he went outside, were to complain, only half in jest, about how much cake she had eaten for her afternoon tea.

Grandad was spotted by some members of a film crew who happened to be walking past Little Water Farm. They were in the area on location to film *The Belstone Fox*, which starred Eric Porter, a well-known British actor at the time. One of them went inside to keep my grandmother company while another went to fetch her daughter, my Aunty Betty, who lived just up the road at Colepool Farm.

The Belstone Fox, released in 1973, tells the poignant story of a huntsman (Eric Porter) who befriends an orphaned fox and then faces the dilemma of whether or not to kill it when it is the cause of death and destruction to his prized pack of hounds. The film was directed by James Hill, who also directed *Born Free*. It was shot in West Somerset using the West Somerset Vale Hunt hounds and riders as extras in the film. My uncle Terry Chidgey, Aunty Betty's husband, was one of the Masters of the Hunt at the time, so he, like many of the Stogursey villagers including Grandad, made a cameo appearance in the film.

To make ends meet my grandmother used to take in long-term lodgers, called PGs, or 'paying guests'. She would cook their meals and essentially operate her home as a small hotel. A long-term PG, just after the war, was Miss Aggie Rees, a confirmed spinster who was the daughter of a local vicar. She taught at Stogursey school, riding her bicycle there and back each day. Miss Rees always tied her long hair in plaits which she would carefully wind around the top of her head.

A young William Hamilton, my father, at the time courting my mother, did place a dead rabbit in Miss Rees's bed one evening. Her reaction is not recorded.

Mum resented having paying guests living in her home as they were always a distraction and, she felt, a burden for her mother despite the welcome additional income.

The longest-staying PG was Lordy's close relative, the Hon Dorothy Hood, a venerable spinster who had been a well-known socialite in the London of the 1930s. She escaped war-time London and the Blitz for the tranquillity of rural Somerset and then made Little Water her home for her declining years. She was well cared for by my grandmother. To me there was always something mysterious about the Honourable Dorothy.

The Honourable Dorothy Violet Hood had been born in 1877, daughter of the 4th Viscount Hood of Whitley. Except to her face, Miss Hood was known in the family as 'Dottie'. Granny was always polite and courteous to her but she had no truck with anyone who displayed airs and graces. It was never clear to me why Dottie wasn't living in the great mansion with her relatives at Fairfield House. As her three relatives there were also quite elderly, this was possibly not a realistic option.

At Little Water, Miss Hood slept in the small upstairs bedroom with low beams at the far end of the creaking passageway. Downstairs she had use of one of the small sitting rooms where she ate her meals on a tray brought in by my grandmother or by Nurtney. Whenever my grandmother wanted to summon Miss Hood from her bedroom for her meals, she would ring a little bronze bell fixed to the wall by the staircase. I still have that bell.

To make a bit of extra money Granny hit upon the idea of serving cream teas to passers-by, until Lordy put a stop to it. Overt commercial activity of this sort was evidently not permitted to tenant farmers. Hosting his relative, the Honourable Dorothy, clearly did not constitute commercial activity.

When there were family gatherings Granny would open up the larger sitting room at the roadside end of the house. There was no more amusing and touching sight than to watch the four elderly sisters Annie, Lily, Daisy and my grandmother May engrossed in a round of cards, rummy being their preferred game. Their gossip could be merciless about other members of the family.

In this sitting room, a little log fire in winter threw out its cheerful heat and was cozy and comforting. Soon the whole room would warm up and create a stuffy fug. If it was too cold outside to have any of the windows open, it could be quite unpleasant when the room was full of people.

The room could fit up to 15 with a comfortable squash. I recall several family occasions when everyone would be talking excitedly at once and over each other, creating a loud cacophony. The unexpected silences would be truly deafening.

Granny had her own chair to the right of the fireplace and was the centre of attention. She wore knee-length skirts and was always able to show off her fine slim legs to good effect. These, it is true, had borne the years well. She was always very proud of her legs, even into her nineties, and with false modesty was delighted whenever anyone complimented her on them.

Granny was indeed a little vain. She was short-sighted but on outings to the village she refused to wear her spectacles. Not infrequently she would fail to recognise acquaintances in the street and ignore them. This gave rise to an unfortunate reputation for being rather aloof, an attitude that did not sit well with the villagers.

When vexed, Granny could on occasion display a spiteful side. She could be very unkind about people she disliked or who had annoyed her. She had no time for religion and only went to church on special occasions such as weddings (not funerals, not even her husband's). She kept her views on religion to herself.

Grandad, too, lived his life completely unconcerned with religion although the village vicar was always made welcome with a cup of tea and a scone whenever he paid a pastoral visit. Granny and the rest of the family were however very proud of Sonny Stevens, Aunty Annie's son, who became an ordained Anglican Minister and spent many years in pre-independence Uganda as a teacher.

Sonny's daughter Jane continued the link with the Anglican Church by marrying an Irishman, George Cassidy. George became Archdeacon of London and from 1999 to 2009 was Bishop of Southwell and Nottingham. George was an ex officio member of the House of Lords, the Upper House of the British Parliament. Lordy too was a member of the House of Lords because of his barony.

Grandad tolerated rather than accepted his wife's large family. For the most part he acquiesced in Granny's wish to keep in close contact with her siblings. Grandad had only one sister, my great-aunt Evelyn.

Granny's oldest sister, Annie, ran the Hood Arms Public House in Kilve village, at the foot of the Quantock Hills, at first with her husband Frank Stevens from 1909 and then when he died, on her own until 1962. She could on occasion be loud and bossy, not helped by her increasing deafness.

We are not sure what occasioned it but when Annie was living for a while at Little Water Farm, her daughter Marjorie (Sonny's younger sister) threw Grandad a hefty punch. Apparently, Grandad in his rather intolerant manner had tried to lay down the law to her mother. Thereafter Marjorie and Grandad never spoke. Granny in no way let this altercation interfere with her own close relationship with her oldest sister and with Annie's children.

Grandad did not like to engage in protracted debate on any topic and soon became impatient. To close off discussion, he would say dismissively that if someone went ahead and did something of which he disapproved, then that would be 'their own funeral'. As indeed it would be.

My paternal grandfather was William Henry Hamilton, whom everyone, including me, called Father. His parents, Diana and

Francis Hamilton, had three children, Francis, Jack and my grandfather William. We have a rare photo of my great-grandparents riding at the Gap of Dunloe in County Kerry in July 1912 (just three months after the *Titanic* had sunk). Great-granny Diana is riding side-saddle and looks very prim. I know little about them.

My paternal grandmother was Louise Josephine Rann before she married my grandfather. He called her Lou and her own children called her Mother. We, her grandchildren, always called her Mimi. She had upper-middle-class aspirations and tended to look down upon the Dyers as Somerset country folk. This made life difficult for my mother when for many years she had to live in close proximity to her mother-in-law.

Mimi came from Stranraer in Scotland. Her parents, Joseph and Margaret Rann, had six children. I never knew any of them except her sister Rene and her husband Alf Roper, who stayed with us in New Zealand for some months in 1963. They were visiting their only son Michael, my dad's cousin, who had emigrated to New Zealand several years before us.

Mimi's brother Bill Rann served in the First World War. He was a baker and emigrated to Canada after the war, where he opened a little bakery shop in Biggar, west of Saskatoon in Saskatchewan. Biggar has a famous sign outside the village which says 'New York is big, but this is Biggar!'

Mimi's family had grown up in the late Victorian and Edwardian eras and were insular in their middle-class outlook and values. How could it have been otherwise in the days before mass communication and social media? Mimi was very house-proud. An early instance of this was her placing newspaper on the floor in her home for me, aged one, to crawl about on, to avoid dirtying the place.

My aunty Josie was their oldest child, followed by my father William and his three brothers, John, Colin and Peter.

The Hamilton family lived in a large house called Springcroft, located in Plaxtol, Kent. Every work day Father Hamilton would cycle to Wrotham Station to catch the train to London. There he worked in the British Forestry Commission until he retired in 1952. One of his tasks was to arrange the annual Trafalgar Square Christmas tree, a gift from the city of Oslo as a token of gratitude for British support to Norway during the war. As a young man he had seen service in the British Army in Mesopotamia, modern-day Iraq, during the First World War, we think as a hospital orderly. He never talked about his experience there but it can only have been horrid.

During the Second World War, Father Hamilton's position at the Forestry Commission was temporarily transferred out of London to Bristol. They lived in the nearby village of Tickenham. Dad attended the Bristol cathedral school and was a choirboy. His younger brother John was sent off to naval college and began a very successful career in the British Navy. Dad remembers watching a dogfight between British and Nazi fighter aircraft during a bombing raid by the *Luftwaffe*.

Mimi always referred to my father as Billy although everyone else called him Bill. He had no middle name. He was a rebellious youth, often getting into trouble. His mother was furious with him one day when he had been given responsibility to look after his younger brother Colin. Bored with the task, Dad tethered his brother to a tree, like a horse, so that he could run off and play with his friends.

Dad did not like school. After leaving at age 15, he undertook a farming apprenticeship at his father's expense, on Mr Triggol's farm near Fiddington, not far from Stogursey. He didn't much like old Mr Triggol who appears to have been tight-fisted and distant. Dad did enliven proceedings one afternoon by surreptitiously releasing some mice on to Mrs Triggol's afternoon tea table. Placing mice and dead rabbits in strategic places appears to have been one of his hobbies.

Dad first met Mum in 1942 at a village dance in Nether Stowey while he was working at Mr Triggol's farm. He was checking tickets at the entrance to the dance hall when a young Joan Dyer came along. He was 16 and she was 14. From then on, they stayed in touch even during the war years when he joined the army.

On 9 December 1942, aged 16, Dad was confirmed as an Anglican in Fiddington church by the Bishop of Taunton. Although in later life he would accompany Mum to Anglican church services, I do not recall him ever discussing his religion or indeed any religion, apart from an occasional anti-Catholic remark that was more traditional than considered on the part of many Protestant English. To this day I have no idea what he really believed about God and the metaphysical. It is possible that he saw no point in reflecting on such matters in too much depth.

After his unhappy stay on Mr Triggol's farm, Dad moved to his second and far more enjoyable farming apprenticeship, with the Sillifant family at East Peake Farm, Tetcott, near Holsworthy in Devon. He stayed here until August 1944, when, aged 18, he enlisted in the Coldstream Regiment of Foot Guards. After training he went off to Palestine as a lance corporal just as the war ended, to help keep the peace between the Arabs and Jews. Despite Jewish terrorist attacks on the British administering authorities during the Palestine Mandate, Dad had a lifelong admiration for the Israelis.

The Coldstream Guards is the oldest regiment in the British army in continuous service. It was founded at Coldstream, Scotland, by Colonel George Monck in 1650 as part of Cromwell's New Model Army. Dad was always proud of his time as a Guardsman and could recite to us the regimental motto: *'Nulli Secundus'* (Second to None), the only Latin he knew.

Dad as a Coldstream Guard, on leave in Beirut, 1947

As Monck had also been awarded the Order of the Garter by King Charles II, after Monck was instrumental in recalling the Stuarts to the throne of England, Dad could also cite the motto of the Garter: *'Honi Soit Qui Mal Y Pense'* (Evil Be to Him Who Evil

Thinks), the only French he professed to know. The Coldstreams were present at many of Britain's great battles, including Dettingen, Waterloo, Sevastopol, Ypres and the Somme.

We have a certificate which says: 'This is to inform the relatives and friends of William Hamilton that he is serving his King and Country as a soldier No 2668166 in the Coldstream Guards. Signed: Headquarters, Coldstream Guards, Birdcage Walk, London SW1, 25th August 1944.' I hope the King was pleased with his service. We never knew.

But among his papers after he died, I found this fine testimonial from his commanding officer: 'A very quiet, well-spoken and well-mannered man. Although young he has been promoted (to Lance Corporal) because of his ability to control men, and to get them to work for him. He is sober, honest and trustworthy and will always finish a task set him without supervision. He has proved himself efficient, and is liked by his comrades. He is a man of integrity and of the highest character.'

He must have formed some attachment to a Jewish family in Tel Aviv as one day a box of delicious Jaffa oranges arrived at his mother's home in England, special delivery from Palestine. He rarely talked about his experiences in the Guards but in later years he and Mum could be heard laughing about Jungle Mary, who was a prostitute in Tel Aviv frequented by British soldiers. There was never any suggestion that Dad had sampled.

After twenty months in the army, he was released in April 1946, on the grounds that his occupation as an agricultural worker was deemed of 'national importance'. He returned to East Peake Farm where he remained until 1949.

The Sillifant family became his home away from home. In 1971 I met Grandfer Sillifant, the head of the family, for the first time. He had been very kind to my father during his apprenticeship and quite possibly had become a surrogate father figure.

Grandfer was now 101, bedridden and very frail. I was fascinated to meet someone who had been born so long before, during the time of the land wars in New Zealand. When Grandfer was born in 1870, Te Kooti was being actively pursued by Ropata Wahawaha, two legendary Maori leaders, and Louis Napoleon was being deposed as French Emperor in Paris as a result of Bismarck's machinations.

Grandfer's life had been spent almost entirely on his farm in Devon. I asked him about his experiences as a child and what he thought of Queen Victoria. He told me what a great admiration and respect everyone had had for her. He cannot, of course, have known very much about her. He died soon after our visit. I liked to imagine that, as a young boy, he listened to stories told by old men who had served in Wellington's army at the Battle of Waterloo in 1815, or by old soldiers who had fought against Russia in Lord Raglan's army during the Crimean War in 1853.

The surrender of Germany in early May 1945 was celebrated far and wide. Mum and her cousin Evvie Watts, both attractive 17-year-olds, eagerly went to the celebratory dance at Kilve Hall in a village not far from Stogursey. Aunty Annie had said they could stay the night with her at her hotel, the Hood Arms, afterwards. They met two handsome American GIs at the dance, Vinny and Lenny, just back from the war and staying at the nearby army camp. Vinny and Lenny were very good kissers, but somehow Aunty Annie got wind of what they were up to and was outraged at their behaviour. She scolded Mum and Evvie severely for acting like two village girls. Mum and Evvie always wondered what happened to Vinny and Lenny in later life.

Another GI, a very handsome Russian-American, walked the five miles from the army camp to visit Mum at Little Water Farm. He came a couple of times until Grandad Dyer sent him packing.

After leaving grammar school and while Dad did his farming apprenticeship, Mum undertook a domestic science degree for three years at what is now the University of Bath. Although her tuition was free, enabling her to go to university would have been a big financial burden for my grandparents.

While he was still working at East Peake Farm, a nervous Billy Hamilton invited my mother to come to Kent to meet his parents. The stated occasion was to celebrate his 21st birthday. Dad and his father were supposed to pick her up from the local railway station but they missed her. Mum made her own way to the Hamilton family home, Springcroft, by taxi. Mimi was home alone and, surprised, let her in.

It was an uncomfortable hour while they sat rather formally and waited for Dad and my grandfather to return. Tired after her long journey from Somerset, my mother was not offered any refreshments. Mimi did however offer to share with her some cherries she had been eating while she regaled my mother with stories about how well one of her other sons, John ('my Johnny', as she called him), was doing in the Royal Navy.

My parents were married in Stogursey Church on 27 May 1950. Mum's sister, Betty, was a bridesmaid. Dad's parents were present as was his brother John, his best man resplendent in naval uniform.

My parents' wedding day, May 27, 1950, one of the few occasions both sides of the family met. Dad's brother John (naval uniform) was best man; Mum's sister Betty was bridesmaid. At Little Water Farm.

Other than the wedding, the two sides of the family had little in common. Granny Dyer told me later what a trial it had been to accommodate my father's parents in her home for the wedding. During the night, Mimi went downstairs to stop the grandfather clock at the foot of the stairs. The regular chimes were keeping her awake.

Stogursey's small but magnificent Norman church was built about 1100 by one of William the Conqueror's henchmen, William de Falaise. He sent monks over from the Abbey at Lonlay in Falaise, Normandy, to establish a Benedictine priory church. It is believed to be on the site of an earlier pagan temple.

My own connection with Stogursey Church goes no further than baptism at the ancient stone font. It is now a special place as so many of our family are buried there, Grandad and Granny Dyer, Grandad's sister Aunty Evelyn, my mother's sister Betty and her husband Terry, near the little stream which runs through the churchyard. It is a quiet and silent place.

After we emigrated to New Zealand it was always a special occasion to come back to Little Water Farm to stay with my grandparents. I was particularly grateful that our children Rachel and Christopher, on visits from Ottawa and Geneva, had been able to stay at Little Water and got to know their great-grandmother. They never knew Grandad Dyer.

On the last occasion I stayed at Little Water Farm, my grandmother was about to leave and the house revert to Fairfield Estate. It was the end of our family association with this grand old home so I took a few minutes to stand alone in the spartan room I had been born in. Here was the lumpy old poster bed, the washstand and tall china water jug, a night commode, a huge cumbersome closet for clothes, smelling of camphor and stuffed with Granny's hats, and the rough-hewn, creaking floorboards. From the bedroom window one had a clear view of the country road and of anyone passing by.

In this little room, my grandparents had slept all their married life, here my mother and I had been born, here so many people before me had lived their lives over hundreds of years. Here as a young boy of six I had crept into my grandparents' bed early on a cold morning to share a mug of tea and some of Granny's delicious biscuits. What stories this farmhouse can tell.

CHAPTER 2

CHILDHOOD FREEDOM ON A DEVON FARM (1952–1958)

I HAVE NO MEMORY OF OUR FIRST HOME WITH MY PATERNAL grandparents at Springcroft in Kent. My father had been asked by his parents to 'come home' with his wife and new baby to help out when his mother was sick. I was never sure why it was my dad who had to fulfil this task.

When Father Hamilton retired from the British Forestry Commission in 1952, he seriously considered taking his family, four sons and a daughter, to Kenya, presumably to buy a farm. The advent of the Mau Mau 'rebellion' in 1952 convinced him that this was not a good idea — as indeed it was not. It is interesting to me that he ever gave any thought to this possibility. My grandmother, who never journeyed outside the UK except for a short holiday in France, would have hated every minute in colonial Africa.

Instead, he bought Speccott Barton, a large farm in North Devon not far from the historic medieval town of Torrington. The aim was to have my father run the farm assisted by his younger brother Colin. John was still in the Royal Navy — he spent some time on secondment to the fledgling New Zealand Navy in the mid-1950s. Dad's sister Josie married Kenneth Jelly and did not live at home. Dad's youngest brother, Peter, who was only seven years older than me, had survived a nasty bout of polio. He was my main leader into temptation on the farm before he went away to boarding school.

Speccott Barton had an even older history than Little Water Farm and is mentioned in the Domesday Book. It is named after a Lady Jane Speccott but who she was and when she lived, I never knew. The farm was a magnificent property with large rolling meadows, hedgerows and fields, all with individual evocative names, like 'Broad Close', 'Barn Meadow' and 'Mud Lane'. It had a large farmhouse in which my grandparents lived. This house was rumoured to conceal a priest's hole, a 17th-century hiding place for Roman Catholic priests escaping capture during the time of religious persecution.

The Farmhouse at Speccott Barton

We lived in a small adjoining cottage, clean but spartan. It had originally been the servants' quarters attached to the main farmhouse. It had a row of little bells, long out of use, on a high beam in the sitting room, so that the servants could be summoned whenever they were needed in the main house.

My parents and I had the place to ourselves until my brother Stuart joined us on 2 May 1954. When my father informed his mother that Mum was expecting her second baby, Mimi's only reaction was to say 'how sad'. It is a comment no one since has been able to comprehend.

Speccott Barton was intended to be Dad's opportunity to work towards owning his own farm. It milked about 30 Friesian cows but, as his father controlled the purse strings and would not invest in the business, my father became increasingly disenchanted. His paycheck of £8 a week was just enough for essentials. Tensions built up over a period of five years before they reached breaking point.

I was an inquisitive child and there was much to explore. In my pre-school years I was given extraordinary latitude to wander unsupervised over the farm, exploring the hedgerows, meadows and streams, watching the cows being milked, hay and silage being made, the fields being ploughed or just chasing and cuddling the chickens. There is something very special about discovering a bird's nest hidden in a hedgerow with a clutch of three or four tiny eggs and beating a silent retreat so as not to disturb it.

I would often watch my father cool the milk over the milk cooler in the shippen before it was put into churns. I never heard anyone use the word shippen again after we left Speccott but when I learnt German, 10 years later, I came across the word 'Schuppen', which means barn. Clear proof of some long-forgotten linguistic connection.

Mimi took me for long walks when we would pick primroses — my mother's favourite flower — from the hedgerows. In season I loved to pick hazelnuts and crunch the hard shells in my poor teeth. I helped my grandmother collect the eggs from the henhouse and then, standing on a little stool, would carefully wash them at her kitchen sink. I remember thinking what a lot of chicken shit some of the eggs had on them.

Mimi loved children, perhaps because in her eyes some of her own proved difficult as they got older. She refused to use the name my parents had given me but called me Sam, because I loved the *Sam Pig* stories of Alison Uttley, as well as *Rupert Bear* stories. One of my favourite fictional characters was the loveable *Mr Whoppit*, a teddy bear who featured in the comic magazine *Robin*, which I pestered my mother to buy each week.

I was often a naughty boy. My grandfather, a keen gardener, had potted out a large number of chrysanthemums to propagate, each one with its lollipop stick for identification. Thinking it would be a great help, I carefully extracted all the labels and presented him with a handful of sticks. His propagation exercise ruined, I was the occasion for some heated words with my parents, no doubt about parental control. But he grew the most delicious raspberries I have ever tasted and to be offered a slice from his apple while he worked in the orchard was a real treat.

An occasion of dissension occurred when, at the age of four, I tried to set fire to the hayloft above the milking parlour. My grandfather was working just below the loft with his ladder reaching up to it. A keen pipe smoker, he left his cigarette lighter on a rung of the ladder and, distracted, did not see me take the lighter and go up into the loft. I remember starting quite a nice little fire in the hay before my grandfather rushed up the ladder and, in a fury, pushing me aside, frantically tore off his jacket to beat out the fire which fortunately had not too strong a hold. This led to another 'blazing' row on the need for my parents to exert better control.

Another time I clambered onto the tractor parked at the top of a slope which we called Mud Lane. Dad would kick-start it more easily on a cold morning by letting it run down the slope. I managed to disengage the brake and the tractor started rolling nicely down the hill before my father jumped frantically onto the tractor beside me and reapplied the brake. Disaster averted.

A piece of mischief on my part, when no one was looking, was to unscrew the cap of the petrol tank on top of the tractor and to breathe in the petrol fumes. I did this on several occasions and felt pleasantly light-headed. Since it was my one and only instance of substance abuse, I guess I should not be too hard on myself. I was not about to injure myself intentionally and I did acquire a strong sense of personal freedom which has coloured my whole attitude to life.

Several people from the little village of Merton, about three kilometres away, helped on the farm. Maybel Drayton came to char for my grandmother. She was a diminutive, simple, roly-poly lady with a heart of gold which I think my grandmother took advantage of.

Her husband, Walter, dug by hand the farm ditches and trimmed the hedgerows. I liked following Walt about and loved the smoke of his burning hawthorn fires. I shared his morning break ('elevenses' we called it) and was amazed when he dunked his thick sandwich into his enamel mug of tea. Ever after I have always

Speccott Barton, meeting the locals

dunked my biscuits in my tea or coffee and, undeterred by any disapproving looks, say a silent 'thank you' to Walter Drayton.

Mr Smaile came sometimes. His work was carpentry and he did some work in the house for my grandmother. He lived in one of the little cottages which lined Merton Square near my school. I never knew if there was a Mrs Smaile, but I loved the sound of his name — *Smaile*. For a brief moment, our lives intersected.

Speccott Barton was situated about half a kilometre down a bumpy, gravel track leading off the A386, the Torrington–Okehampton road. A highlight of the day was the mail delivery when Frankie Leverton came bouncing along on his bicycle in all weathers, wearing his postman's uniform. He would hand a sheaf of letters from his mailbag to my grandfather, pass the time of day briefly and then pedal off. The expectant shout 'Frankie's coming!' was a daily ritual. Very rarely, Frankie would give the letters to me and I always loved the smell of his bundle. I am not sure what the scent was but ever after it has signified 'Royal' Mail.

The fact that Frankie was delivering 'Royal' Mail meant that he must be a person of standing. Most of the letters were for my grandfather, although an altercation did occur when he accidentally opened a letter meant for my father. Letters addressed to W.H. Hamilton, my grandfather, and W. Hamilton Esq, my father, were easy to confuse. As Dad had no middle name, he was 'William Hamilton'. The designation 'Esq' or 'Esquire' has thankfully fallen out of fashion and was not used in New Zealand, but it indicated then a young gentleman with no other title, such as Dad was.

In springtime I watched my father sowing seed by hand with a fiddle, a device which scattered the seed in front of him as he strode along. It reminded me later of the characters sowing seed by hand in the magnificent medieval manuscript of '*Les Très Riches Heures*'.

In the warm sun I wandered around the farm in my ragged old coat, tied with a piece of string for a belt, a hand-me-down from my uncle Peter. I would lie in a hollow of a newly ploughed field with its smooth clay furrows and fall asleep. When it came time to make silage, I watched the tractor trying to compress the grass in the huge silage pit, with my uncle Colin driving, often in a wildly dangerous manner, up on the grass mounds to compact it. When no one was looking I would stick my fingers into the molasses barrel. Thick molasses was used as an additive for the silage and tasted delicious, just like toffee.

Some mornings I would accompany Colin on the back tray of the tractor when he took the 10 or 12 milk churns up to the concrete milk stand at the top of the side lane for collection by the milk lorry. One morning as he was unloading the churns a man came grinding along the road in a horse and cart. I had not seen one before and even in those days it was something of a rarity. The driver was wearing a cap and huddled in a greatcoat. Pointing rudely and shouting loudly at him, I received a hefty punch in the stomach from my uncle which had the excellent effect of shutting me up. When I took my son Christopher for a walk down this side lane many years later, it was no longer used and was completely overgrown.

At the bottom of the farm there was a railway line, with a stop at Dunsbear Halt nearby. I loved waving to the train driver and sometimes got a toot as it puffed on by. One day to my surprise I saw my grandmother waving back at me from a carriage as she returned from a shopping trip to Bideford or Barnstaple.

One summer's day, Peter took me along the railway track a few miles to visit the clay pits near Peters Marland. Our aim was to ask if we could go down into the mine. The answer was unfortunately no, so we decided to help the miners out by pushing the small rail trucks to their siding once they had been filled with the sliced clay. I am surprised we were allowed anywhere near the place but I remember one worker running fast, after a truck we had pushed too hard threatened to run off the end of the rail track before it could be switched to its proper siding.

Speccott Barton, with my grandmother, Mimi, sitting on a hay bale

This was my one and only experience of train wrecking. I guess my mother believed that Peter was taking good care of me that day. The line closed in 1965 and Dunsbear Halt is no more.

Our nearest neighbours were the Gomans. I never went to their home. Mimi, who tolerated but did not enjoy rural isolation, certainly never invited them to visit. They spoke with a broad Devonshire accent, so 'thickey' for 'this' and 'I bain't' for 'I am not' and 'I do mind' for 'I remember'. I marvelled at their manner of speaking.

The earliest memory that I can date is 4 or 5 May 1954 when I was nearly three. This was the day my mother returned from Torrington

Hospital with my brother Stuart. I can still see her in a long cotton frock standing in the hallway of my grandparents' house holding this little bundle in her arms. I often ask myself why I have such a vivid recollection of Stuart's homecoming. I guess I had a vague notion that from then on things would be different.

Apart from the chore of washing eggs at the kitchen sink I was rarely in my grandparents' home. One Christmas there we made paper chains to decorate the Christmas tree and lit wax candles to put on the tree. Placing large candles with naked flames all over a Christmas tree indoors would nowadays be regarded as a huge fire risk.

My grandfather bought 45 rpm vinyl records of easy-listening music. He ordered them from a little catalogue. I saw him unpack some new records in their crisp brown paper sleeves — perhaps Frankie had delivered them. I loved their acetone smell and was fascinated by the little dog sitting next to a gramophone on the HMV label. Father liked the light classics with Mantovani and His Orchestra. I used to believe that Mantovani was the *only* person who knew how to conduct an orchestra.

Mimi loved bagpipe music and Scottish folk songs, in particular the songs of Kenneth McKellar and Sir Harry Lauder. As we washed the eggs, she would sing along with Sir Harry as he coughed and spluttered '*I Love a Lassie*' or '*Roaming in the Gloaming*' or '*Keep Right On to the End of the Road*'. I was told that this last song was one of Churchill's favourites in the dark days of the war. Years later I bought an LP with all of Sir Harry Lauder's songs just to remind me of my grandmother. Some of the recordings go back to 1907 so are part of music recording history. But my mother can't listen to Sir Harry now without it conjuring up the difficult days of her life at Speccott Barton, 65 years ago.

I have never visited Scotland but thanks to my grandmother, and my family name, I have always felt that there is a part of me that would be at home there.

My grandparents did not seem to have a close or particularly happy marriage despite their five children. They slept in separate beds, my mother told me, as she often helped with the cleaning in the larger house. Father was a shy, quiet but stubborn man, prone to grumbling when annoyed. Mimi, aside from being house-proud, was firm and determined in her own way too. Every afternoon my grandfather used to go into voluntary exile for an hour or so to have a nap in a deck chair in the warmth of the generator shed. As the farm still had no mains electricity, the electricity supply came from a diesel generator which we called the 'BB motor'.

Much later I found out this must stand for Brown-Boveri, the Swiss electrical engineering firm. The BB motor shed was always warm and cosy despite the strong smell of grease and diesel. I ventured there one day and was amazed to see my grandfather fast asleep in his deck chair, snoring, mouth wide open, oblivious to the rumble of the generator. He must have been about seventy. Evidently, he preferred to nap in such a place than to hazard going indoors in his old farm clothes. Years later we would joke with my own father, to general hilarity, that it was time for him to 'go to the BB motor shed' for his nap.

Our little cottage had a kitchen and a small lounge downstairs. Upstairs, there were two small bedrooms and a bath. My bedroom seemed a roomy space, right above the kitchen. Until Stuart arrived, I had it all to myself. Outside was a big oak tree. An owl lived in it and at night its hooting would frighten me.

My parents' bedroom was a little way from mine, along a narrow passageway which we called the 'landing'. The landing had a window looking out over the farmyard. I was petrified if I ever had to walk past it in the dark because it was obvious that evil things lurked there at night. I can still remember the awful ache I felt when I had to negotiate this ghosts' lair. In my bedroom I could see 'nasty things' sitting on the wall just under the ceiling. One childish nightmare I have never forgotten involved a lump of dough on the ceiling which would expand all the way down to my bed and smother me.

In the winter it was fascinating to look out of the landing window and see the big icicles that formed under the gables, as there were no gutters on the cottage roof. In springtime the icicles disappeared and the swallows, bit by bit, built their little mud nests under the gables, defying gravity in their ability to make their nest strong and stick to the walls. Those swallows taught me some valuable lessons: to be focused, goal-oriented and patient in dealing with life's many challenges.

The kitchen had an old-style Rayburn stove for heating and cooking. Baking day was always a treat as we would demand to lick the sweet and creamy mixture left in the bowl. My mother would hum to herself a little ditty which was nonsense to me: *'the Esso sign means happy motoring'*. I realised later that this must have been a piece of very successful 1950s radio advertising by a petrol company. If I got in the way, I would be described as a *'meddlesome Matty'*. I never knew what this meant until I recently discovered that Matty was an overly inquisitive and mischievous child featured in a pre-war comic strip.

The Rayburn stove was most unkind to my little army of plastic toy soldiers when I put them on it. Within seconds they melted and were ruined. I am not sure what I thought I was doing placing the army of Wellington on a hot plate.

Just inside the front door of our little cottage was another door which led down into a smaller room that my grandfather had turned into a pigeon loft. In London he had been a well-known pigeon breeder and judge of pigeon competitions. My mother hated these noisy birds always cooing, flapping and crapping everywhere. Another point of dissension.

I protested vigorously at being put to bed in midsummer when it was still bright sunlight outside. Nothing my mother said could convince me she was not unreasonably foreshortening my day.

I had no special pets at Speccott. One day my mother's cousin Marjorie (Aunty Annie's daughter, the one who later would punch Grandad) came to visit us with her husband Ivor Williams. Ivor was a Commander in the British Navy and had served on the famous *Ark Royal*. Marjorie and Ivor brought me a tortoise as a present. Dad painted a white line on its back for ease of identification but it soon wandered off and was never seen again.

It was some time before Stuart was able to join me in adventures on the farm. On a sunny day, before he could walk, he would be strapped into a large pram and taken outside to a meadow near our house. Mum is horrified now to think that she left a baby alone in his pram for several hours. But there was never a problem. Stuart relished the fresh country air and always slept soundly.

Stuart enjoys the open air in his pram at Speccott Barton

Each cow in the herd had a name, not a number like now. Dad had one favourite good-tempered Friesian cow named Bonny, which had been gifted to him by Grandad Dyer. We made a fuss of her. Another cow, which had a single crumpled horn and so was named Horn, was very bad tempered. One day Horn took a particular dislike to two-year-old Stuart in the farmyard. She hooked her horn under his little jacket belt and started butting him up against a wall.

Stuart might easily have been killed. Dad intervened just in time to stop her. Horn paid the price which, tied up in a cow bale, involved a violent whipping from my father. Whether she in her cow's mind made any connection between the two events is unknown. I realised in later years that Dad could have a dreadful temper but he hid it well and, as the years advanced, he mellowed.

One of my less pleasant memories is of Stuart and me hiding behind a wall waiting for my grandmother Mimi to come out of her front door to sweep the forecourt. Stuart and I bobbed up and down poking our tongues out at her and making faces. She must have seen us and it was a very hurtful thing to do but it probably reflected the tensions building up between Dad and his parents and the arguments my own parents used to have.

I think my mother made us apologise but I don't remember doing so. Mimi's habit of sweeping the forecourt each day became the object of some unsubtle fun when one Christmas my father presented her with a nicely wrapped new broom-head. I doubt that she found it at all funny.

John Elliott ran a farm near Dunsbear Halt. He became a lifelong friend of my father. Given the growing difficulties on the home front, Dad would escape when he could to visit John, whose family always made us welcome. John lived with his aunt Gladys in a big and terribly cold farmhouse. He married only some years later.

One day I was wandering alone in the Elliotts' orchard when to my horror I came across a dead sheep in the long grass. It had been dead some time, was terribly fly-blown and maggoty, and stank. This was my first experience, aged about six, of death. I always wondered why they hadn't bothered to bury it.

We once visited John Elliott's relatives on an isolated farm at Horns Cross near the A39, almost on the Bristol Channel. This gloomy farmhouse scared the living daylights out of me. Cold, dark and spooky, its hallway had many stuffed animals mounted on the walls, foxes, deer and boar, which gaped down at me in accusing silence, baring their fangs and teeth. I half expected Sir Francis Drake, who was born not far from Speccott at Tavistock, or some other pirate of old, to come barging in.

Many years later, when we visited Miss Elliott in her own little cottage at Dunsbear, she referred to me as 'young Master Hamilton' which I found both quaint and endearing. She also referred to the congregation of the Methodist Church just up the road from her house as the 'non-Conformists'. How long memories are of religious differences.

I was five before I went to my first village school, Merton, and interacted with other children. My first day at school was a rude shock. Mr Bull in his little bus would pick me up from the end of our lane on the main road so I always had to hurry each day to catch it. It probably carried six or eight of us.

Merton School no longer exists. It was a drab 19th-century stone building with two little classrooms for perhaps 30 children. My first teacher was a kind, rotund, mothering sort called Mrs Bamsey. The following year I was taught by Mrs Spicer, a younger, strict and much less endearing mistress. We children used to hum the rhyme 'Mrs Spicer likes micer', my introduction to nonsense poetry. Why do we remember such trivia?

My first school, Merton

My first school friends were all very different people. Kathleen Smolden lived in a run-down cottage at the top of our lane. I begrudged the fact that Kathleen did not have to walk far to catch the school bus. She was a pretty little thing but she picked her nose and ate the booger a little too frequently for my liking. Andrew Tithecott, a true Devonian, lived along the road from Kathleen, not far from Great Potheridge.

Potheridge — a lovely sounding name — was the birthplace in 1608 of General George Monck, later the Duke of Albemarle, of English Civil War fame. As I have said, he restored Charles II to the English throne in 1660 after the death of Oliver Cromwell. As Monck had been the founder of the Coldstream Guards regiment, Dad liked living just down the road from his birthplace.

John Subbertig was a close friend. He lived on a farm on a bend in the main road about a kilometre from us. I roamed the countryside with John who taught me how to roast potatoes in the embers of the fires which burned the hawthorn hedge clippings. The potatoes, burnt to a crisp, were the most delicious I ever tasted.

When my uncle Peter went off to boarding school, I inherited his little bicycle and loved to ride it around the farmyard. Disaster struck just before my seventh birthday when I fell off riding down our bumpy lane and grazed both my chin and knees. They soon healed but were very scabby. This was enough for me to insist on a postponement of my birthday party as I was in no fit state to host guests, certainly not girls.

For the first few years, my parents had no car of their own. Dad was allowed to use his parents' Austin for special events like the weekly shopping trip to Torrington. The car always had to be returned in tip-top condition. Sometimes I would see Mimi being driven in the car as she came back from her own visit to town. She liked to sit in the back seat while her son Colin drove.

There seemed to be only one grocery shop in Torrington. The grocer was a jocund middle-aged man whom we knew only as Mr Sutton. In his brown grocer's smock, he would greet us warmly and wag his finger at us in humorous greeting. I was fascinated as he cut off a slice of cheese with a wire cutter which slid effortlessly and cleanly through his big block of cheese. He then weighed the slice and wrapped it in greaseproof paper. Plastic wrapping had not yet been invented.

At Speccott Barton my mother felt isolated from her Stogursey family. No one made it possible for her to attend her sister Betty's wedding in Stogursey Church. There was never any suggestion that Dad's parents would make their car available for the trip.

Later when Grandad Dyer's sister, Aunty Evelyn, died after a short illness, my parents were able to buy a small car with her £200 legacy. But not before Father Hamilton had vetoed my father's first choice. Dad chose one that looked more like a van. My grandfather felt that a van was not the appropriate image for a young farmer. Dad had to take it back to the dealer.

With our own car we could now make the occasional trip to Stogursey to visit my Somerset grandparents. One day, as we drove down a steep hill at Withypool on Exmoor, we saw three old ladies vigorously beating a carpet hanging on their washing line. They must have been spring cleaning. We called them the '*Three Old Maids*' and ever after, when we passed their house, we would look out for them. It took well over two hours to drive the less than 60 miles to Stogursey.

Dad's frustration with the set-up at Speccott Barton grew over the years. Many factors contributed to the eventual rupture with his parents. The main one, as I have mentioned, was his anger at not being able to manage the farm as he thought necessary. When Mr Goman wanted to sell an adjoining field that would have enlarged Speccott considerably, Father refused to buy it.

His relationship with his mother also deteriorated. Mimi made little effort to help her son and his young wife. In due course she barely spoke to my mother. One day Peter, aged 11, stood at the door of our little cottage while my mother was on her hands and knees scrubbing the concrete floor and said innocently: 'My mother says you are a slut'. He did not realise that his brother, my father, was standing behind him so this remark earned him some boxed ears. My mother became annoyed too that Mimi would buy things, like clothes, for Stuart and me that she herself could not afford.

On another occasion as I was washing eggs at her sink, Mimi said to me, 'Your daddy is a very naughty boy'. I did not think much about it at the time as I was always being called a naughty boy for one transgression or another but, in later years, I thought what a terrible remark that was to have made to a small boy. I never repeated it to my father as I am sure it would have been painful for him.

Symptomatic of the growing tensions and family arguments, for no reason at all I would suddenly throw the most violent tantrums and lose all self-control. I remember my mother trying to deal with this little monster on several occasions and failing miserably. My mother says she has no memory of it now. Perhaps it is something she prefers to forget. My tantrums ceased at the age of seven the moment we left Speccott Barton.

At some point in 1958, Dad decided to leave Speccott. Grandad Dyer offered him a job on his farm at Little Water. A little truck came to pick up our meagre possessions and headed off to Stogursey. This truck was just like Lance Corporal Jones' old delivery van in the TV series *'Dad's Army'*.

I don't remember much about leaving Speccott or even if we said goodbye to my grandparents. En route to Stogursey we broke our journey at a tea shop in South Molton. Sitting in the shop, I was surprised to see the little truck go rattling by with all our possessions on board. It was so odd to think it contained my bed, my clothes, my few books and toys. Another truck came and took Bonny away as well, as she was Dad's own cow. Horn stayed behind.

Speccott Barton was sold soon after we left. The family consensus is that Father Hamilton badly handled the whole enterprise at Speccott. Because he had no knowledge of farming, he had interfered too much in day-to-day operations instead of leaving it to my father. Speccott Barton would have been a profitable business if Dad had been able to manage it in the way he wanted and believed he had been promised.

For many years, I was the only one who wrote to my grandmother, Mimi, even after we went to New Zealand. The rupture at Speccott poisoned Dad's relationship with his siblings. It was not until some eight years later in 1966, when my Uncle Peter brought his wife, Mary, to New Zealand and got in contact with his brother that the ice started to thaw. Peter and Dad became very close, as did Dad and John.

Many years later, we went to see Walter Drayton at his home at Pretty Top near Merton. We were saddened to hear that Maybel had died but Walt greeted us warmly. I could not help noticing, despite the warmth of his welcome, that he lived in near poverty in a run-down house, with old newspaper for a tablecloth. It taught me a valuable lesson that one could be poor and still be the most genuine and dignified of human beings. We knocked on Mr Smaile's door and had a brief word with him.

In 1986, when I visited Speccott Barton again, the farm was owned by a family called Williams, the pigeons had long flown the coop and their room turned into a comfortable additional sitting room. There seemed to be no sign of Mr Owl in the big tree outside my bedroom, or the ghost on the landing. But the hayloft was still standing.

The farm has passed through several owners since we left. It was once a Christian Bible Camp and is now a rural retreat offering upmarket holiday accommodation bookable on the Internet.

CHAPTER 3

STOGURSEY VILLAGE IN
SOMERSET (1958-1960)

THE MOVE FROM SPECCOTT BARTON IN DEVON TO STOGURSEY IN
Somerset was a relief for my parents and an adventure for me. I was
seven and Stuart was four. My Stogursey grandparents were
delighted to have us nearby. The family tensions so evident between
Dad and his parents had been lifted but had left a bitter taste.

We moved into a cottage about a kilometre from Little Water Farm,
in the hamlet of Knighton. Our house was semi-detached. It had a
red picket fence in front and was called 'Knighton Cottage'. It had
two small rooms and a kitchen downstairs and two bedrooms and a
bathroom upstairs. It was a bright summer's day when we moved in.
Despite its emptiness and spartan décor, the house was light and airy
and the bare concrete floors warm, with last autumn's dried leaves
swirling about the kitchen. It must have been empty for some time.
Even now, I can recollect the excitement I felt at moving into this
cheerful little cottage.

Outside the back door was a little garden and lawn. The grass, tall
and untidy, smelt sweet, with lots of summer flowers but also tall
stinging nettles. Dad soon took a long-handled scythe to cut the
nettles.

Our immediate neighbours were the Sharp family. Little Peter and Michael Sharp, aged two or three, would peer inquisitively over the low garden wall that separated our two houses and watch with keen interest whatever we did in our garden.

My father went to work on the farm at Little Water. Grandad made him welcome but the farm was small and hardly big enough to support one family, let alone two. And it gave my father no opportunity to further his own farming ambitions. My mother, having set up home at Knighton Cottage, went to work in the mornings helping Aunty Annie, Granny's oldest sister. Annie was then still publican of the Hood Arms in the village of Kilve, about 6 km west of Stogursey.

In the evenings my mother got a job supervising the cleaners at the huge Hinkley Point nuclear power plant, then under construction beside the Bristol Channel. Sometime later she obtained a full-time position teaching domestic science at Westover Secondary Modern School, in Bridgwater. This involved a daily drive of some 15 km for her. She was delighted to have the opportunity to put her domestic science training into practice. The additional income was very welcome. It did rankle with my father that she was always able to earn more than him.

Stuart and I were enrolled at East Quantoxhead School, which lay on a slight rise on the Bridgwater–Minehead road, about half a kilometre west of Kilve village. East Quantoxhead School no longer exists but was another Victorian-era, Dickensian, squat stone building, cold and foreboding. It had 20 pupils and two teachers: the principal, an elderly spinster, Miss Miriam Hughes, and my mother's first cousin, Frances Napper. Because Frances was a relative, Mum knew that the move for me from Merton to East Quantoxhead would be relatively painless. This was my brother Stuart's first school.

Aunty Frances was the daughter of Granny's older brother Jim Watts, the one who had gone to Canada and become a Mountie. Frances had two sisters, Audrey and Evvie and a brother Edwin.

Frances as a very young girl had witnessed the tragic death of her mother, Harriett, who died in a fire in the kitchen of their Edmonton home. Jim could not look after his four children on his own, so the whole family came back to England. The children were billeted with various members of the extended family.

Great-uncle Jim was traumatised by these events. Despite a relatively happy second marriage to Hilda, he ended his days in a mental asylum. Frances never mentioned this tragedy which scarred her own life. She remained always warm, kind, self-effacing and loving, strong in her Christian faith. She would never think badly of any person. She had one daughter, my cousin Ruth, and lived all her life happily in Old Ham, Kilve, with her farmer-husband, Walter Napper.

Just up the road from our home at Knighton Cottage lived another family friend of my grandparents, Peter Reid and his wife Joyce. They had the unusual distinction of living in a little bungalow, a single-storey house which was unusual in England but of course is the norm in New Zealand. Pete, who wore large spectacles, was a civil servant in the small town of Williton. His daily drive to work took him right past our school. When my mother had to travel to Bridgwater each day in the opposite direction, he kindly agreed to take Stuart and me to school. There was no public or school bus.

The daily drive with Pete, in his little black Austin, was a fun experience. He would amuse us with stories, tales and verbal games. We were amazed when his car backed out of his driveway in the morning with no hands on the steering wheel. To make the ride more interesting, we each had a pseudonym: Pete became 'Rotten Rat', Stuart became 'Stinky Stoat' and I was 'Porky Pig' (continuing, for me, the porcine connection begun by my grandmother). We had to use these names while we were with him in the car.

Aunty Frances taught us to count money by holding paper coins of different denominations in her hand and then asking us to tell her the value of what she held. I made good progress learning to read and write in her class. *Janet and John* books were my favourite. Frances would reward good work with silver and gold stars which she would stick at the bottom of the page in our workbooks. Sometimes, if we did not merit a star, we would receive the written comment '*Well Tried*'. It was always a competition to see who could get a gold star for any piece of work. It was deeply satisfying to be given one.

My best friend at East Quantoxhead school was Raymond Pearce, who lived in the village of Kilve and remained there throughout his working life. He became a mechanic. Raymond had an uncle who had journeyed to Hong Kong or who may have worked there. I had no idea where Hong Kong was but it sounded a very exciting place, especially when Raymond showed me some of the gifts his uncle had brought back for him.

At East Quantoxhead School

I was quite interested in two girls called Marlene Sweet and Veronica Davis. But the one I really liked was little June Bissett. I snatched a discreet kiss from her one day when we played outside in an old tractor tyre. I was eight.

After a time in Aunty Frances' class, I moved 'up' to Miss Hughes' class. Cooked school lunches were provided about midday from an adjoining kitchen and were served to us at our desks — the old-style wooden sort, with lids that opened upwards. On the top was an inkwell for ink to fill our pens when we wrote. One lunch is particularly memorable as I was sitting next to Roger Clark, eating some deep-fried battered fish, peas and mashed potatoes. Roger was the son of the local policeman.

Suddenly Roger violently spewed up his fish lunch and, in the process, sprayed me and my desk. This caused such a severe psychological reaction on my part that from that day forth I have not been able to eat anything from the sea, fish or seafood, without feeling quite unwell. Even the smell of fish makes me feel ill. Later on, I had no problems catching fish on a rod or line, even gutting them, as there is usually no strong smell but I could never eat what I caught.

At East Quantoxhead I must have been — still — a naughty boy. One day we noticed a small turd floating in the bowl of the boys' toilet. We engaged in a childish witch-hunt to discover the offending party. Every boy, including Peter Pole, was interrogated but one in particular, a meek lad, Christopher Routley, fell under suspicion. To my great shame we tried to bully him, verbally, not physically, into a confession which to his credit he stoutly refused to make.

I thought nothing further of the incident until the next day I saw a big black car pull up at the school gates. A tall, thin, unsmiling man with a moustache emerged with Christopher in tow and marched off stiffly to see Miss Hughes. I had a sinking feeling the two events were linked. Miss Hughes took me in hand and was very firm with me for a few days but she did not smack or beat me.

Although Pete Reid would drop us off at school, Mum would come to pick us up in her own car after she had finished teaching in Bridgwater. As it was sometimes necessary for us to wait an hour or so after school before she would arrive to collect us, Stuart and I would walk the little way from school to see Aunty Annie at the Hood Arms Hotel.

Aunty Annie, the oldest child in the Watts family, born in 1883, was 17 years older than Granny Dyer. Not that I could tell the difference as they all looked incredibly old. Annie would make us welcome and give us something to drink. As it was a public house, we would arrive just as she was preparing the evening meal for any guests staying at the Hood Arms. This would be steaming away merrily on the Aga stove in her kitchen. She used to boil the hell out of the cabbage which must have been quite tasteless afterwards.

Being quite deaf Aunty Annie would put her hand down inside the front of her dress to fiddle with the volume of her hearing aid. Her loose-fitting dentures rattled when she spoke. She had frequent need of a helping hand at the Hood Arms. Family members including Aunt Lil and Aunty Letty would, like my mother, help out when they could.

I recall seeing Great-aunty Letty, the widow of Granny's older brother Sidney ('A full-blown private, sir'), pouring out the tea. I was amazed to see her hand shake violently as she held the swaying teapot. Many years later I realised that Letty must have suffered from Parkinson's disease, although in her case it was undiagnosed. I knew nothing at the time of her relationship with my great-grandfather James.

Annie, Lily and Letty were well-known in the surrounding community as the three widows who ran the local pub. Aunty Annie had the reputation of being a difficult and at times cantankerous landlady. They earned for themselves the epithet '*Queens of the Quantocks*'. There is no doubting, though, that Annie was '*prima regina inter pares*'.

Aunty Daisy also spent some years helping her sister Annie at the Hood Arms. She frequently stayed overnight with her husband, Great-uncle Fred Besley. One evening Fred popped his head around the bar-room door and said to his wife: 'I am going to bed, Daise. Are you coming or shall I take on a book'? Ever after, we have wondered how much reading poor Fred Besley was obliged to do alone at night.

Little Water Farm was only a short 10-minute walk from Knighton Cottage. We often called in for a few minutes to see Granny and Grandad on the way home from school. Sometimes I would bump into the Honourable Dorothy, who never seemed to go out anywhere although her relatives from Fairfield would visit her. Lord St Audries turned up one day with a single peach from his garden nestling in a little basket. He presented it proudly to my grandmother. I thought at the time that it was a nice wee 'thank you' gift for my grandmother but the peach, I am told, was meant for the delectation of the Honourable Dorothy.

Not far from Little Water, I stumbled one day upon a very pretty girl sitting alone on the fence of a cow pen up the Fairfield Road. We overcame our shyness and she told me her name was Margaret Sully, she lived nearby and that her father, Billy Sully, worked as a handyman on the estate. Margaret and I became firm friends and every free weekend we would roam the countryside together.

Little Water had a two-storey outhouse building, opposite the milking parlour, which we called the malt-house. No one quite remembers its original purpose but I recall the corn being bagged and stored there in summer. It had gradually fallen into disrepair. A listed building, it couldn't be pulled down but there was no requirement to stop it falling into ruin.

On the second floor of this malt-house, reached by a steep and broken wooden stair, there was a little room, dark, rat-infested, smelling of corn and very dusty. The broken tiles on the roof let in some light but also the rain. Here Margaret and I decided to set up shop with help from my brother Stuart. Over succeeding weeks, we collected used and discarded cartons, packaging, tins and other grocery items and launched a profitable little grocery enterprise on a wooden plank. Anyone visiting Little Water was invited, and earnestly encouraged, to visit our shop where the visitor would be served by Margaret, Stuart and me.

An invitation to visit was extended to the Honourable Dorothy but none of us imagined that she would accept it. To our astonishment one afternoon, who should be struggling up the steep rickety steps but Miss Hood herself. She showed great interest in our enterprise and made several purchases. This was the only time a member of the British aristocracy visited our little shop and it was the talk of our family. When the second storey of the malt-house became too dilapidated for us to play there any longer, or we lost interest in the business, we unceremoniously dumped all our inventory down a dark bottomless shaft. Perhaps in 2000 years' time, some archaeologist will unearth them, like Roman letters lost in the mud at Hadrian's Wall, and wonder who had tipped them there.

In summer Miss Hood could be seen sitting alone quietly in an old deck chair on the front lawn, a rumpled aristocrat, wearing a large sun hat and taking tea or reading a book. One evening, she asked Nurtney to find her something light to read from her bookcase. Nurtney chose a small book off the shelf which she thought might do the trick and handed it to Miss Hood. 'No, Mrs Nurton', said Miss Hood, 'I would like something lighter'. Nurtney, weighing the book in her hand, said she did not think she could find a book much lighter than the one she was holding.

My encounters with Miss Hood were not always positive. Little Water had a single toilet with a cast-iron, wall-mounted cistern and clanky chain. I barged in one day, the door was not locked, and to my horror there was Miss Hood — in full splendour — on the seat. Her baggy white bloomers were down around her ankles and she raised her hands in sudden surprise. I beat a hasty retreat muttering some words of apology. I think my grandfather made the very valid point that if Dottie did not want to be disturbed in this manner, then she had better remember to lock the door.

One day Dad offered to drive Miss Hood on a visit to some relatives, I forget where. She needed to stop en route to go to the loo but when she came out Dad noticed that Miss Hood, walking in front, had tucked her skirt into her baggy knickers. These were now on display over a rotund bum. Dad tried deftly to pull the skirt out without her knowing but of course Miss Hood could feel someone was touching her bottom. She turned around to my father and demanded peremptorily: 'What are you doing, William?'

Miss Hood was an avid reader of the *Illustrated London News* and filled scrapbooks with clippings she found of interest. She knew personally many of the people who filled its pages. She also wrote a remarkable book, *London is Invincible*, a history of the London she had known in her childhood. She also wrote a biography of the Hood family. How I wish I could talk to her now about her life.

Miss Hood died in 1965. Thinking the scrapbooks were of no interest to anyone, my grandmother threw them all out. Not exactly the same as Mrs Burton destroying, after his death, all of Richard's personal letters from Africa, but a loss of what would now be regarded as a very interesting historical collection.

If you walked on past our cottage at Knighton for a kilometre or two through the surrounding farmland, you would eventually reach a beach on the Bristol Channel. Or sometimes we would go to nearby Lilstock beach for a picnic. I say beach but there was no sand and the strong muddy Channel tides made it almost impossible to swim. The beach was just a steep rocky incline with large stones and shingle, scoured by the daily tides, but the bracing and tangy sea air did us good. Sometimes we would discover fossils in the rocks.

In the far distance you could see the coast of Wales and Cardiff on a clear day. Not far offshore was the little island of Steep Holm. I imagined Sir Walter Raleigh or some other buccaneer sailing magnificently up the Channel in his great ship. Much later I read that, in the early 17th century, Barbary corsairs had reached Lundy Island off north Devon and raised the flag of Islam. These pirates had plundered the Cornish and Devon coasts, sacked towns and taken local inhabitants away as slaves. His Majesty, seated comfortably in London, had not been able to prevent this outrage perpetrated against his West Country subjects.

We were happy at East Quantoxhead School but the transport arrangements were not exactly convenient for my mother so she transferred us to primary schools in Bridgwater. I was enrolled at West Street School and Stuart at East Street School, around the corner from mine. I am not sure why we did not go to the same school. From now on we would travel each day to and from school with my mother.

West Street School was another grim and grimy brick building from the 19th century. It had five or six classrooms and a small asphalt playground enclosed by a high brick wall next to a small stream. Inside, the classrooms had high-gloss green plaster walls. It was demolished long ago to make way for a housing estate. I could discover the site of the school from the little stream which ran adjacent to it. The move from a country school to a town school was unsettling and I remember little of the year or so I spent there.

I did not live in the town so it was not easy to form lasting friendships. We used to eat our cooked lunches in a school canteen seated around large Formica tables. There was one odd individual who wore huge spectacles. He disliked his lunches and insisted on rolling his boiled potato across the table, as if it were a mini soccer ball. I had not encountered such bad table manners before. His surname was Fish, which was another reason for me to be suspicious of him.

Mr Jarvis was the principal. A bearded Mr Baird was my class teacher. One day I told him our family would be leaving England to emigrate to New Zealand. I said I had heard (goodness knows from where!) that in New Zealand children of my age, nine, wrote like seven-year-olds in England. 'Ah well, you will be all right then', he said, 'because you write like an eight-year-old'.

This was my first experience of that nasty characteristic, which in retrospect seems so English, the quick-witted but sarcastic put-down. I never forgot it. Billy Connolly described a similar experience from his own early school days: 'To humiliate someone is a desperately bad and wrong thing. Humiliation is forever. It takes you so long to get over it'.

Mrs Edith Baker taught us history. From her I first heard of the Anglo-Saxons and the Viking invasions and how King Alfred of Wessex, fleeing in disguise from the Vikings in the 9th century, had burnt the cakes in the kitchen of his refuge at Athelney in Somerset.

I developed a lifelong interest in history, thanks to Mrs Baker. She became a family friend and for 10 years after I went to New Zealand, we corresponded by letter. Our family visited her in her little cottage which was called 'Newgara', on the edge of Bridgwater, when we returned from New Zealand in 1971. Physically she bore a remarkable resemblance to my grandmother, Mimi, which may have been why I liked her so much.

Mrs Baker asked me one day if I had any hobbies. I said that in the garage at home I had a large and interesting collection of birds' nests assembled on my travels around the neighbourhood. I did not know at the time that there was a very respectable precedent for this hobby in the form of Grandad Dyer over 50 years earlier. Mrs Baker looked slightly disapproving and said 'Well, you should save stamps'.

She gave me the first stamps of what became a great hobby and a great aid to my geographical awareness. For many years, Mum's cousin, Evvie Watts, the sister of my teacher Aunty Frances, would send us first-day covers of every new stamp issued in the UK.

Bridgwater is a small Somerset rural town on the banks of the muddy River Parrett. We used to visit the dentist in this town, which is why I never really liked it. I did though like to watch the tidal bore that twice a day would race up the Parrett all the way from the Bristol Channel.

In 1937, British Cellophane built a major factory in Bridgwater to produce cellophane. The factory converted to producing war munitions and Bailey bridges for the planned invasion of Europe, returning to cellophane production again after the war.

I disliked the smell from the factory that pervaded the town air. By the 21st century, demand for cellophane as a packaging was declining and there were growing concerns at the polluting side effects of the production process. The factory closed in 2005. Bridgwater now focuses on, among other industries, providing accommodation for construction workers at the huge Hinkley Point nuclear power station expansion project.

One day Stuart and I were walking from Knighton Cottage to Little Water Farm when a little Ford Zephyr Zodiac pulled up beside us. To my amazement, inside were my grandmother Mimi and my uncle Colin who was driving. She said they were doing a tour of the area and, as luck would have it, we just happened to be walking along the road as they drove by. I hadn't seen her since we had left Speccott Barton, several years earlier.

We got into the car and had a nice chat about what we were doing now at school. She looked disapprovingly at my fingernails and said 'Always push the nails back, Sam, so the moons are visible'. I never forgot this sage piece of advice.

I asked Mimi if she would come into Little Water to say hello to everyone, but she uttered some excuse about not having enough time and after dropping us off, they drove on. It was over 10 years before I saw her again. I thought nothing of the fact that she had declined to call in at Little Water, but it certainly occasioned some discussion there when I told everyone who we had just seen.

I saw Mimi and Father for the last time when we visited England in 1975. They were then living in retirement with Peter and his wife Mary on a farm near Pickering, Yorkshire. It was a strained if civil enough occasion but no one could quite let the past go by. My wife Louise and I took my grandparents for a drive across the Yorkshire moors. It was quite hard to sustain a conversation. But to my grandmother, I was still Sam.

Just across the road from Grandad's farm he had a small sloping field which he called Yoné. Being 'over Yoné' meant he was out and about on the farm. It had a little stream, Bayley's Brook, which flowed through it and a small concrete bridge over the brook. This became our favourite place for playing Pooh Sticks. Bayley's Brook, further upstream, formed a ford at the hamlet of Shurton. One day, taking the child of some war evacuees, then staying at Little Water, for a long walk in a pram, my mother tipped the baby into the brook as she tried to navigate the stony ford. The baby wasn't any the worse for the soaking apparently. When I visited the concrete bridge again much later, the brook was much degraded and no longer able to host games of Pooh Sticks.

Bayley's Brook would flood after heavy rain. It was not unusual for the stream to inundate the road outside Little Water and come up the pebble path into the main front door of the house, flooding Granny's hallway and sitting room. When it became clear the water was about to enter the house, there would be a mad scramble to lift the carpets out of the way.

Milking times were always interesting. If the cows had been all day in an adjacent field, Grandad had merely to open the gate of the field, stand aside and start shouting 'Hup Hup'. The cows would know it was milking time and would slowly amble their way to the milking shed without any fuss. For years I thought he was shouting 'Hope, Hope' and wondered what on earth 'hope' had to do with his cows.

If little else was happening on the farm, we could play in the hay barn and build secret igloos. Sometimes we could help turn the handle of the mangle machine which cut up mangles given to the cows as supplementary feed. I loved the crunchy sound as they were sliced.

Aged nine, feeling the need for some form of independence, I announced that I wanted to build my own house in the field under the Morgan apple tree. Morgan apples, a famed Somerset cider apple, were juicy and delicious and I knew I would not go hungry. Given permission to construct my dwelling, I dug a foundational trench about two metres long in the field, but to my intense disappointment, the project stalled as no one else showed any interest in it and I really hadn't thought through the intricacies of residential construction.

One day one of Grandad's cows was taken into the shed to calve. I asked to watch as she gave birth but my father told us to go away. Stuart and I were left to peer in unobtrusively through a small side window. The right approach would have been to give us ringside seats to watch. But in fairness to my father, he was preoccupied with the animal and the shed was very small.

Sometimes horses would be grazing in the nearby fields but Grandad no longer had his loyal cart horses, Prince, a chestnut, and Damsel, a blackie. They had been made redundant when Grandad bought a small Massey Ferguson tractor to plough the fields and cart the hay and corn.

Grandad no longer had a farm dog either. That was in large part my fault. When I was about two, he had a much-loved shaggy collie called Scamp. I used to play with Scamp until one day, sitting on his back, I pulled his hair too hard and he bit me deeply on the lower lip. This required a stitch or two from the doctor and left me with a small permanent scar. But the sad thing was that Grandad felt he had to put Scamp down because he had bitten me.

I got on well with my grandfather, who rarely rebuked me. One time that he did was when I threw the cat out of the upstairs bedroom window. I guess I had heard that cats always land on their feet and have nine lives and I had wanted to find out if this was true. Grandad was not amused.

Grandad Dyer relaxes on the lawn at Runnymede, one of the few occasions he travelled outside Somerset

My mother's only sister, Betty, lived with her husband Terry Chidgey at Colepool Farm, two hundred metres up the road from Little Water. This farmhouse had two storeys, with four bedrooms upstairs and several rooms and a kitchen downstairs. It was impossible to keep warm in winter and to me was always freezing cold. Wood fires downstairs helped to keep individual rooms warm but once away from the fire, you froze. The warmest place was the kitchen which had a Rayburn oven. Like Little Water, this was where people congregated.

Colepool Farm had a muddy duck pool in front by the road. I was often chased and hissed at by a gaggle of nasty geese who lived around its banks. Aunty Betty also kept a plump of ducks and reared goslings to produce a steady flow of duck eggs for sale.

Terry was a tenant farmer on the Fairfield estate like my grandfather. He didn't enjoy having his mother-in-law living so close to him and Granny Dyer could on occasion be interfering. He always addressed her as Mrs Dyer, as did my father. Their relationship was polite and correct if not exactly warm. Terry did not visit Little Water more often than he had to. Granny knew only too well that Terry had a wandering eye.

Terry's passion was fox hunting and he became a Master of the West Somerset Vale Hunt. The hunt's hounds were at that time housed near Stogursey. He was a noted horse breeder and people would bring their mares to Colepool to mate with his stallions. This must have been a very nice side earner for him.

Terry's parents had worked the farm before him and had both died in their early sixties as a result of their hard lives. I saw his mother and father not long before they died, propped up in their sick beds in the downstairs lounge, being cared for by my Aunty Betty. Terry swore that he would not work himself into an early grave as they had done.

He did therefore tend to neglect his farm. Huge dung heaps at the entrance to Colepool confronted visitors. These piled up after the sheds which housed his horses had been cleaned out and became home to dozens of frolicking rats. This did not please his neighbours.

My cousin Sarah, their only child, was born in 1958 and became a very capable rider. Aunty Betty suffered a nasty accident one hunting day when she fell off her horse, hurt her neck and wasn't able to ride again. She remained a keen follower of the fox hounds all her life, even after hunting foxes was banned in England, a ban the Somerset hunting folk strongly opposed.

Grandad had an old black 1930s Austin 6 car, registration DYC 390, which had running boards and a little yellow indicator arm that used to extend from the side of the car to signal when turning. On cold mornings, the car needed to be cranked in the front to get it started. I got into strife with Aunty Betty one time when she was driving the car. I leaned over from the back seat and turned off the ignition key. The car came to a juddering halt in the middle of the road.

We had lots of adventures in this car. One day Grandad tried to drive up Porlock Hill, a notoriously steep incline beyond Minehead. The Austin struggled and shuddered, then jarred to a halt and refused to go any further. Grandad had the ignominy of having to back all the way down the hill to take the far longer route. He was not a happy man.

Granny, when annoyed, could be feisty. During one outing in the car to the nearby Dunster Show, Grandad, an impatient driver, slightly dented the fender of another car. A policeman duly arrived at Little Water to investigate and was shown into the kitchen/dining room. Granny, most alarmed at this turn of events, kept interrupting her husband, repeatedly saying 'Don't tell him anything, Dad!' Greatly embarrassed by this 'uxorial' interference, the policeman and Grandad removed themselves to the hay barn outside, to continue their conversation in private.

Just before we left England in 1961, Grandad sold this car and bought a much smaller Morris Minor. I recall seeing DYC 390 one last time, sitting in a car sales yard in Williton, looking very unloved. Granny never learned to drive. Seeing her sitting diminutively in the little Morris, wearing a new hat after an excursion to Taunton, was quite endearing.

There was a little brook just down the road from Knighton Cottage. We used to spend hours there fishing for sticklebacks, little silvery fish which have no scales. We put them in jam jars but of course they did not survive long in such a confined environment. This brook was also the scene of a decapitation, namely that of my teddy bear. Ted accidentally fell into the water and in subsequent rough play his head came flying off. Nothing I did could reattach Ted's head and I think from that moment my interest in teddies started to wane.

Shortly before his demise, Ted accompanied me on a journey of discovery when, after a serious altercation with my mother, I decided to leave home and seek my fortune. I packed a small suitcase and with Ted headed off up Knighton Road. I guess I had gone about 100 metres as far as the corner when it began to dawn on me that leaving home at the age of nine just before dinner time was not such a good idea. I slunk back home and was readmitted. Nothing further was said, until years later we all laughed about it.

During these years our world was peopled by all sorts of interesting characters. Freddie Chilcott, an old man like Walter Drayton, lived near our cottage and could often be seen marching down the road with a little basket of something on his arm. I never knew what was in it, probably eggs to sell. Directly across the road, in an ivy-covered, dark and dingy cottage, lived an old woman whom we never spoke to and who kept to herself. I called her the witch and, in my ignorance, I supposed that she must be one.

With my younger brother Stuart, at Knighton Cottage, 1960. Two English boys about to embark on a great adventure.

Halfway from our cottage to Little Water, one had to pass the hamlet of Burton which once had a blacksmith. I remember the smithy shoeing horses but he is long gone now. Above the forge were a couple of cottages. Walking past them one day, to our great surprise an upstairs window was suddenly flung open. Madge Wilcox popped her head out, called out to us and threw a large handful of coins down on the road for Stuart and me to gather up. We scrambled to collect them and felt very fortunate that day.

Mr Ellis turned up every few weeks in his little jeep, towing a small round caravan from which he sold fresh fish. Whenever he came, Granny would be eager to buy some fresh plaice or haddock (or 'shrimps, please, if you have any!') and I would be detailed to buy it. I liked talking to Mr Ellis but was completely indifferent to his product.

If Granny wanted a beef roast, pork chops or sausages, this required a trip to the village, where Mr Fawn had his little butcher's shop. I was fascinated to see his various cuts of meat on display, his huge oak chopping stump with sawdust all over the floor and his instruments of butchery arrayed. Mr Fawn wore a white overall, splattered with blood and gore. I imagined that Henry VIII's torture chambers would have looked somewhat similar.

The little village shop in Stogursey, once owned by Grandad's parents, provided some very welcome additional groceries during the war years of rationing. Grandad's sister, Aunty Evelyn, worked in the shop and eventually took it over when her parents died. She would regularly bring the food items to Little Water but for some strange reason always used the tradesmen's entrance. Granny never paid for this food. The cost must have been absorbed by the business.

Aunty Evelyn never married. She did at one point have a 'beau', a certain Mr Fling who would cycle over from a nearby village and sit quietly with Aunty while she served in her shop. It was hardly a fling with Mr Fling and he never popped the question. Or perhaps he did and she turned him down.

Aunty Evelyn died while we were at Speccott Barton, as I have mentioned. Her shop was taken over by Ralph Sealy. I loved going into his shop with Granny for a treat. We would buy a bag of sticky toffee sweets, which were called 'humbugs', from one of his huge glass sweet jars. The only problem with humbugs was that they were so sticky they all stuck together and were impossible to extract individually from the paper bag which soon tore. When Mr Sealy moved to a bigger shop in the village, Aunty's shop, as we called it, became a hair salon. A weekly trip to the hair salon was one of Granny's few indulgences, except when she made the longer journey to Bridgwater or Taunton to buy a new hat.

One of the few long outings we made during those years was a day trip to Southampton in 1960, to welcome home Evvie Watts, Mum's dancing partner with Lenny and Vinny. She was returning from a year's teaching exchange at Los Gatos in California. She and Mum have always been close. Evvie, who never married, was travelling on board the RMS *Mauretania*. This was my first experience, but not my last, of a great ocean-going passenger liner. Later Evvie would return to Canada, to rediscover the country of her childhood, teaching for four years in White Rock, near Vancouver, British Columbia.

CHAPTER 4

VOYAGE TO NEW ZEALAND
(FEBRUARY–MARCH 1961)

I DON'T RECALL WHEN OR HOW I FOUND OUT THAT WE WERE
going to emigrate to New Zealand. Sometime in 1960 it became an
accepted part of our daily life that we would be leaving England. My
father saw no future for himself farming in England and, despite
Grandad Dyer's generosity in having him on the farm at Little
Water, it was not without its tensions.

Dad came across an advertisement in the UK *Farmers Weekly*
magazine which caught his eye. It was recruiting young farmers to
help New Zealand develop its own agriculture and farming
industries.

My parents went to an interview at the New Zealand High
Commission, held in Bristol. In due course Dad was accepted for an
assisted immigrant's passage to New Zealand. We were to leave on
the P&O liner *Orcades* on 18 February 1961, from Tilbury Docks.
The cost of the trip was met officially by the New Zealand
Government, with the proviso that if Dad did not stay in New
Zealand for a specified period, he would be responsible for the cost
of the journey back to the UK.

My mother was none too keen on the idea of uprooting herself and
her family to go to New Zealand, as far away from Stogursey as it

was possible to get. My father made it abundantly clear that he wanted to go, even if on his own. In effect he gave my mother something of an ultimatum, which she had little choice but to accept. Granny Dyer was heartbroken that my father was proposing to remove the family from England. There were tearful discussions along the lines of 'it is so far away, why do you have to go?'

When it had been decided that we would emigrate to New Zealand, I asked the lorry driver who picked up Grandad's milk churns if he could guess where we were going that started with 'New'. He tried New York and some other places but failed to guess New Zealand, as I expect he had no idea where it was.

I don't remember much about packing up and leaving Knighton Cottage. At some point my marvellous collection of birds' nests was unceremoniously disposed of. My parents sold their little Anglia car and managed to squeeze our few possessions into several tea chests, trunks and suitcases, particularly clothing, bedding and one or two of my books. I don't recall any of the goodbyes, which would have been painful for my mother who was happy with her teaching position in Bridgwater and family life in Stogursey. My father was happy to be going.

The four of us took the train from Taunton to London and stayed a night or two at the home of Aunty Rene (Mimi's sister) and Uncle Alf Roper in Canterbury, before taking a taxi to Tilbury and boarding the ship. Although my father had fallen out with his own parents, he still occasionally saw his Aunty Rene who had a son, Mike Roper. As I have said, Mike had gone to New Zealand several years earlier and was to meet us on arrival in Auckland.

Mike Roper was not the only member of Dad's family to have migrated to New Zealand. Dad's sister, Josie and her husband Kenneth Jelly had gone to New Zealand in 1958. Kenneth was a school teacher and they lived for a year in Grey Street, Hamilton. For reasons unclear to us, Kenneth could not find a teaching position anywhere in the North Island to his liking, or perhaps they were unable to adapt to life in a new country. They left after a year and returned to England.

After Speccott Barton was sold, Father Hamilton sent Dad's younger brother Colin to New Zealand at the same time as his sister Josie to investigate the possibilities of farming. It seems Father Hamilton was still attracted to the notion of migrating from England, despite having dropped the idea of a move to Kenya several years earlier. For some incomprehensible reason, Colin recommended against a move to New Zealand. He came back to the UK and Father bought another farm.

This farm was West Cross Side, at Knowstone near South Molton on the Devon-Somerset border. Colin was to manage this farm. It was not a successful venture and was sold after a few years. I never visited it. Father Hamilton and Mimi then gave up any further idea of family farming. Colin and Dad's youngest brother, Peter, in due course went farming in England on their own, while the other brother, John, continued his career in the navy.

At the time, Dad was not close to his sister Josie or brother Colin so it is unlikely their experience of New Zealand would have been discussed with him before he decided to emigrate. Mum did receive a letter from Josie in New Zealand who complained that she could not get good coffee there. This was probably true enough — she would, however, be amazed at the coffee choices available in New Zealand today.

I vaguely recall boarding the *Orcades*. Aunty Rene and Uncle Alf were allowed to come on board for lunch with us before the ship departed. At some point, a message came over the intercom that the ship was about to sail and all non-passengers were required to disembark. As the *Orcades* slipped out of Tilbury Docks into the Channel, we saw the diminutive figures of Aunty Rene and Uncle Alf, as prearranged, standing on the river bank waving us goodbye.

The SS Orcades, our home for six weeks on the voyage to New Zealand

We were allocated a small Second Class cabin on E Deck (E254), which must have been deep in the bowels of the ship. It contained two double bunk beds, a small wardrobe, small shower, toilet and wash basin. This cramped room was to be our home for the next six weeks. Fortunately, none of us suffered from claustrophobia. The room had no natural lighting and the stuffy air mixed all the smells of the ship, especially the nauseating food odours vented down from the dining room way above.

By today's standards a relatively small liner at 28,000 tons, the *Orcades* could carry 1500 passengers in two classes. At that time, it had a yellow livery and was part of the P&O fleet which took emigrant families to Australia and New Zealand. It was filled with young men, women and children similar to our own family, sailing off into the unknown to make a new life in the Antipodes.

The ship was an exciting place to explore. As there was little prospect of our becoming lost or falling overboard, we could, within reason, wander about as we wished except in the First Class areas. There was a movie theatre and a small outdoor swimming pool. The problem with the unstabilised swimming pool was that the water would slosh about dramatically once the ship rolled on the high seas, giving us mouthfuls of very salty water. Meals for Second Class passengers were taken in a communal dining room on round tables with white tablecloths. Several sittings were needed to feed everyone.

Within a few hours of departure, we were warned to expect some rough weather in the Bay of Biscay off the coast of Spain. The boat did roll about a bit but I was not seasick. The first port of call was Gibraltar and the great Rock towered up as we came into port. The view from the top of the Rock was breath-taking. We spent a day wandering the streets and were glad to get back to the ship after a tiring excursion.

Six weeks off school for a lad who, according to Mr Baird, badly needed to improve his writing skills, was an exciting prospect. As the weather got warmer the further south we sailed from England, Stuart and I were enrolled in daytime classes held in the open air on an outer deck. These were taken by some teachers also emigrating. Mine was Miss Laura Carkeek, who was going to a new life in Australia. The lessons were not particularly structured but it did ensure that, after the first few days on board, we did not become too bored with the confinement and daily routine.

The next port was Naples. We spent a magical day driving through the streets of Napoli, with the colourful washing hung out to dry between the apartment blocks. No one gave a thought to Pos, the Neapolitan POW who had spent his war years working at Little Water Farm.

At Pompeii. I was captivated by the story of how this ancient town had been engulfed in the eruption of Mt Vesuvius in AD 79. We walked its uneven stone streets, visited the houses and dwellings of the poor and rich citizens and saw the awful plaster casts of men, women and children caught at the moment of their death.

From this visit sprang my fascination with ancient Rome. As I later learnt, the Elder Pliny had died in this eruption. That rolls of priceless ancient texts, otherwise lost to humanity, might still be preserved in a carbonised but likely recoverable state at the Library of the Papyri at Herculaneum, is a tantalising notion.

After the visit to Pompeii we went to Sorrento, that beautiful town overlooking the Bay of Naples. Here my mother bought a music box that ever after played the lovely tune 'Return to Sorrento'.

By the time we reached Port Said in Egypt and sailed down the Suez Canal, the temperature had risen significantly. Only five years before, the Canal had been the scene of bitter fighting at the time of the misguided and failed British and French invasion of Egypt, with Israeli connivance, to bloody the nose of Gamal Abdel Nasser, the Egyptian nationalist leader. It was this foolish invasion of Egypt that led to the political demise of Britain's Tory Prime Minister, Anthony Eden. Ships sunk during the invasion had only recently been removed from the waterway.

The sandbanks either side of the Canal seemed very high. I was on deck at school when I looked up and saw a man leading four or five camels along the sandy ridge, silhouetted against the blue skyline. I had never seen a camel before and was fascinated by its jerking movement as it padded on by.

It would be 45 years before I would again be at the Canal, drinking tea in an Egyptian military camp at Ismailia, with our ambassador to Egypt, Rene Wilson. Standing on the banks of the Canal, I wondered about that young boy on the *Orcades*. I watched spellbound as every few minutes huge ships appeared out of the sand, one after the other, at first a tiny dot and then looming ever larger from the Timsah Lake, heading north to the Mediterranean Sea, steaming past us, relentless and unstoppable. What struck me was how narrow the Canal was and how there was no margin for error in navigation. (The accuracy of this observation was reinforced graphically in March 2021 when the giant container vessel, *Ever Given*, lost control while navigating the canal and blocked it completely for over a week).

After sailing down into the Red Sea, we spent a day in Aden, then a British Protectorate but now the scene of a bitter civil war in Yemen. Aden was a dusty, dirty place and had little of interest for tourists, except for me as I was allowed to buy a battery-operated tin drummer. This toy was '*Made in Japan*', an early indication of Japan's emerging economic strength. Selling low-quality Japanese consumer goods to passing emigrant ships was no doubt a good source of income for Aden shopkeepers. The tin drum was poorly made ('tinny', as we would say later) with dangerously sharp edges. It soon broke, but I loved it.

My parents bought a new camera in Aden, one that produced 36 colour slides. This meant I could be given their old black and white box camera, which could take about 12 pictures before the film roll had to be replaced. They also bought a copy of D.H. Lawrence's *Lady Chatterley's Lover*, which in 1961 was still banned in the UK as indecent. Nowadays it is hard to see what all the fuss was about. What would the UK censorship authorities of the time make of the pornography freely available on the Internet today?

Once out of the Red Sea we crossed the Indian Ocean to Colombo, the capital of Ceylon, or Sri Lanka as it is called now. When I had nothing else to do, I would go down to the lowest deck of the ship and watch fascinated as the little portholes filled and then emptied with ocean water in time with the ship's rocking motion. I used to wonder what would happen if there was no glass separating me from the sea. Years later, I saw the film *Titanic* and imagined that it was the *Orcades* and that it was me running down the narrow corridors as the seawater rushed in.

Colombo was a magical place too. On the street we came across a snake charmer whose cobra swayed up out of its basket in time with his pan flute music. This particular charmer was called 'Gulli Gulli'. He doubled as a magician because to everyone's amazement he suddenly produced an egg from the bottom of my brother Stuart's trouser leg.

Ceylon was hot and humid. The pungent aroma of the tea plantations was overpowering but in a delightful sort of way. We had a very pleasant lunch at Mount Lavinia Hotel. For the first time I walked along a tropical beach and saw a coconut tree. As I wandered about the hotel grounds, a voice called to me from the undergrowth. A young boy held out a coconut in his hands and urged me to ask my parents to buy it from him for 6d.

In his fascinating book *The Secret War*, Max Hastings records the role Mount Lavinia played in the war against Japan, as the headquarters in South Asia of the British *'Special Operations Executive'* (SOE). This was a secret spy and signals intelligence agency, guarded at the time by New Zealand soldiers.

I have not been back to Sri Lanka. It is on my bucket list. In November 1995, when New Zealand hosted the Commonwealth Heads of Government Meeting in Auckland, I was asked to escort the head of the Sri Lankan delegation. Sri Lanka did not send its Prime Minister to the meeting because of the ongoing civil war so its Foreign Minister, Lakshman Kadirgamar, represented his country. There were pro-Tamil, anti-government demonstrations on the streets of Auckland but Kadirgamar, himself a Tamil, ignored them.

We talked about how he ensured his own security in war-torn Sri Lanka. He told me his secret was always to have numerous unmarked cars travelling around with him in convoy so that no one could know which car he was actually in.

He bought some items for his family at the Body Shop in Queen Street. His visit was otherwise uneventful apart from an incident when, rushing to catch his flight at the airport, the New Zealand Army driver driving our limo at speed smacked into the back of the escorting police car in front, hurtling Kadirgamar forward from his seat almost into the driver's lap. He was not wearing a seat belt but he did not complain. He had insisted on sitting on the right side of the vehicle behind the driver, leaving me to sit on the left side, which is usually where a VIP visitor would sit in an official car. I laughingly told myself that perhaps he figured that if anyone was going to take a pot shot at him in Auckland, they might aim at me first.

I was sorry to learn though, some 10 years later, that he was assassinated at his home in Colombo by a sniper.

The next leg of the journey involved an uninterrupted four-day voyage across the Indian Ocean from Colombo to Australia. This meant crossing the equator. According to tradition, King Neptune came on board ship and ceremoniously summoned us children for inspection, found us not to his liking, smothered us in flour and chucked us into the ship's swimming pool.

Halfway across the Indian Ocean, we passed the SS *Oriana* returning north to Europe after its maiden voyage to Australia. One of the last of the Orient Steam Navigation Company's ocean liners, she was built in 1959 and scrapped in 2005. There was something very special in those few minutes when our two ships passed each other, a few kilometres apart, ships' horns blasting a greeting in the middle of nowhere. It was reassuring to see such a beautiful gleaming vessel pass by and head off into the distance. We were not alone on that great expanse of ocean.

Within a few days we started arriving at the Australian ports, Fremantle, Adelaide, Melbourne and Sydney. As these cities represented the final destination for many on board, the *Orcades* began gradually emptying out. Each time we left an Australian port, there was the colourful spectacle of hundreds of paper streamers which departing passengers threw to those left on the quayside, accompanied by the song 'Waltzing Matilda' blaring from loudspeakers. It was exciting to see whose streamer would be the last to break as the ship edged away from the wharf.

In Sydney, the longest stopover of three days, the foundations of the new Opera House were just visible. We walked across the Harbour Bridge. Somewhere my parents' signatures appear in the visitors' book for late March 1961. We visited Bondi Beach, Taronga Zoo and drove up to the Blue Mountains. We saw the famous 'Rotolactor' in Wollongong, a prototype milking machine that could milk cows continuously while they stood on a revolving platform. Such platforms are now in widespread use on New Zealand and Australian dairy farms.

One afternoon, our parents left Stuart and me in the care of one of the pursers while they slipped off the ship and went to a Sydney cinema to see the newly released movie *Ben Hur*, starring Charlton Heston.

After leaving Sydney, our excitement mounted. It was only a short three-day voyage across to Auckland where we tied up at Queen's Wharf. It was 27 March 1961.

We were sad to leave the *Orcades*, which ever after has been a part of our lives. She was launched in 1947 to great fanfare and named the '*Orcades*', the Latin name of the Orkney Islands. After long service carrying many thousands of emigrant passengers to Australia and New Zealand, she was later a cruise ship before being broken up in Taiwan in 1973.

As we disembarked, we were greeted by Dad's cousin Mike Roper and his friend from Hamilton, Basil Burt. How all six of us and our luggage managed to squeeze into Basil's little car for the three-hour drive south to Otorohanga, in the King Country, is a mystery.

We arrived mid-afternoon on a warm sunny day at the Woods' farm on Puketarata Road, about 10 km north of the small town of Otorohanga. We were greeted warmly by Colin and Pam Brooks. They had two small children, Susan and Michael. Colin had offered Dad a farming job and had therefore made the whole migration possible for us. As our own house was not yet ready to move into, we slept the first nights in New Zealand on mattresses laid out on the Brooks' living room floor.

CHAPTER 5

A NEW LIFE IN THE KING
COUNTRY (1961–1962)

THE FARM WHERE MY FATHER WAS TO WORK WAS OWNED BY
Walter Woods, whom everyone called Wally. He and his wife, Faith,
had given their lives to breaking in the farm from the swamp land
they had purchased, or possibly it was one of the ballot farms
allocated to enterprising returned soldiers as a means of opening up
rural areas and turning them into productive dairying country. The
farm carried 50 or 60 Jersey cows but still had a large area of wet
peat land at the bottom of the farm which was gradually being
brought into production. Piles of swamp timber and ever-
smouldering peat fires signalled that the task of turning the peat into
grassland was not yet complete. There was no thought given to the
environmental impacts of destroying this wetland. In the distance
rose the extinct volcano of Kakepuku, which one day we would
climb.

Colin Brooks was a sharemilker. Under New Zealand's unique
farming arrangements, he was entitled to 28% of the milk cheque in
return for managing and running the farm. Had he owned either the
land or the herd, he would have been entitled to 50% of the milk
cheque. Colin and his family were also recent immigrants from
England.

In offering my father a job as a farm worker, Colin had to pay Dad's
wages from his share of the milk cheque. What Colin himself earned
each year could vary considerably, depending on international dairy
market prices.

Wally was in his late sixties. He had decided to call it a day on the
farm and was building a retirement home for Faith and himself in
Otorohanga. The original plan was that our family would move into
Wally's farmhouse when he vacated it. The problem was that his new
house in Otorohanga was already several months behind schedule
and Wally had not moved out.

This presented a conundrum. Where were we to live? After the first
nights sleeping on the floor of the Brooks' home, we were introduced
to our temporary home, which was a short distance from Wally's.
This was a small dilapidated weatherboard cottage — the original
homestead on the farm which Wally and Faith had lived in eons ago
when they first took over the land. It had been unoccupied for years,
was in a bad state of repair and due for demolition, but we would
have to make do with it for the foreseeable future. It had a central
open space which was both the dining and living room, a double
bedroom at one end, two single bedrooms at the other end, a small
kitchen with gas stove, a bathroom with a huge stone bath, and
crumbling bare wooden floorboards throughout. The toilet was a
long-drop outhouse down the garden path.

That this near ruin was to be our first home in New Zealand would
have been a great shock to my parents. The day after we arrived,
they went into Otorohanga to open a bank account and to buy some
basic furniture: a small Formica dining table and four chairs, a
double bed and two single beds, two easy chairs and a small
bookcase for my books. Fortunately, we had arrived in late summer
so the house was pretty dry. A mouldy crop of potatoes stored on the
floor in one of the rooms was removed so that Stuart could have a
bedroom.

While they were opening their bank account at the ANZ bank, the
bank manager nonchalantly pushed some tobacco leaf across the

table to my father and invited him to 'roll his own'. He then casually asked my mother what she did — I guess he meant other than raise two children and set up home in a new country. She explained that she was a trained domestic science and home economics teacher, whereupon he telephoned the principal of Otorohanga College and my mother had a full-time teaching position at the college before she left the bank. But her teaching was not limited to domestic science. She taught Maths, Biology, English and other subjects, such was the need for teaching staff in those days.

Our shipped effects arrived a day or two later from the *Orcades*: a large sea chest, a couple of tea chests and a few large suitcases. This meant we had sheets and blankets for the beds and a few basic kitchen utensils. My little corner bedroom had faded blue wall paper which was glued to rough sacking cloth. The wind would seep through the cracks in the weatherboards and the wallpaper would heave in and out noisily. It felt like the walls were alive. There was no heating, so on a winter's morning the rooms were freezing cold.

There were no creature comforts either, no TV, no telephone and no refrigerator. A little wooden cupboard, which we called the 'safe', was used to store perishable food items like milk, butter and meat. This was cooled by an air vent that led to the outside of the house. It was fine if the weather was cool, but in the heat of summer food items did not stay fresh for long.

Negotiating the outside toilet at night was a challenge and best avoided, as there was no lighting of any sort. I soon learnt that this was the 'dunny'. The house was rat-infested and before long one large demented rodent fell off the rafters and plopped onto the floor of the bathroom just as Stuart and I were having a bath. It had clearly been poisoned. My mother screamed, abandoned us and beat a hasty retreat to get help to remove it. Wally's teenage son, Leslie, helpfully obliged.

There is a photo of my mother sitting in the sun on the doorstep of this dilapidated house soon after our arrival. She looks tired and stressed. The scene could have come straight out of the US Midwest

Dust Bowl during the depression years. Smoking was her one indulgence, Benson & Hedges cigarettes. My father had given up smoking long since — he had not accepted the ANZ bank manager's invitation to roll his own.

The Brooks had enrolled Stuart and me at Kio Kio Primary School, about five kilometres from the farm, on the main Te Awamutu–Otorohanga road. The Brooks' children also went there. This was a little rural school with one main wooden building, encompassing two classrooms and a small room for the principal's office, and two relocatable 'prefabs'. It had a shallow rectangular concrete swimming pool and a large field for sports.

Our first day at school was a cultural shock. Dressed in shoes and socks and a shirt and tie, looking for all the world as if we were still off to school in Bridgwater, we were the object of intense scrutiny. At lunch time we sat outside on the grass to eat our packed lunch, surrounded by most of the school who wanted to find out who these strange children were with funny accents.

The novelty quickly wore off and next day we reappeared minus the ties. Our first major adjustment to life in New Zealand. Why Mrs Brooks had not given my mother some sage advice about primary school dress code, I never understood.

Don Hudson, one of the four teachers, drove the school bus, a normal practice for teachers in New Zealand's rural schools. He would pick us up from the farm gate each morning in a little yellow bus.

My father went to work on the farm. My mother caught the school bus with us to Kio Kio and then transferred to an Otorohanga College school bus. My parents had brought a little money with them from England, described as 'overseas funds', which were as valuable as gold in those days when New Zealand struggled with its international finances. After six months on a waiting list, they were able to buy another little Anglia car, which my mother drove each day to school. One day, we encountered Mrs Woods in Otorohanga who, espying our new car, quipped 'My, aren't you flash!' Not having heard this expression before, my parents thereafter always laughingly repeated it, whenever any of us sported something new.

It was a bit of guesswork which class I should be placed in at school. For the first few days I was placed in Standard Three. It became clear that I was repeating much that I had already learned at West Street School. I was moved to Standard Four. Mr Baird might have been surprised.

We hated living in that derelict cottage and could not wait until Wally's house in Otorohanga was finished. The short lane from his farmhouse to the road was lined with peach and nectarine trees and these produced the most delicious fruit on which Stuart and I gorged ourselves. The garden also had a strange vine called Chinese gooseberry. We had not come across this fruit before and did not think much of it. Later it was renamed 'kiwifruit'.

There were a number of swan plants, or milk weeds, which hosted the beautiful monarch butterfly. I had never seen a butterfly chrysalis before and had no idea how this miracle of nature worked. Initially I thought the chrysalis must be some unnatural dangling protuberance of the swan plant.

In rotting timber, we discovered some large white grubs, which I was told were the larvae of the huhu, a longhorn beetle endemic to New Zealand. That these grubs could be eaten raw, or cooked in an earth-oven hangi, as a source of fat in one's diet, was a perplexing notion.

Apart from an old radio set which we had brought from England — it had to be tuned to '*Hilversum*' to pick up any local New Zealand station — our only source of outside news was the *Waikato Times*, published in Hamilton, about 40 km away.

This newspaper was delivered each day about 4.30pm by a car which drove past at speed. At the end of our lane by the road was a water-filled cattle stop. The driver chucked the paper, tied in a roll with an elastic band, towards our house. Many times, the paper landed bullseye into the cattle stop so I brought home a very wet newspaper which had to be dried out before it could be read. The driver had to deliver dozens of newspapers in a short time on his rural delivery so was none too interested in where the rolled newspaper actually landed.

One weekend, as we were sitting having lunch at the table in our old house, Wally walked by the open window and peered in, announcing with a crestfallen face that Annabel had slipped her calf. I had no idea what he meant but it was clear that Annabel had done something that she was not supposed to. Annabel was Wally's primary milk producer and his top cow. Breeding from her was a desirable endeavour.

Wally did have a couple of mean Jersey bulls which he kept for breeding purposes. The most important was his pedigree bull, Corfu. I don't know why it was named after a remote Greek island. My father had to beat a hasty retreat on one occasion when one of these brutes took a dislike to him and charged him.

Until we got to Wally's farm, I did not know what 'bloat' was. Bloat is a form of indigestion in cows caused by excessive accumulation of gas in the rumen, which cannot be belched away. It usually happens in springtime when the cows gorge themselves on new pastures with a high clover or lucerne content. If a cow becomes bloated, its abdomen swells up like a balloon and it will quickly die a painful death unless the gas is eliminated. In extreme cases, this would be done by sticking a long knife into the stomach of the cow so that the gas could escape. I saw Colin Brooks sticking several cows in this way. I watched in awe as a giant arc of stinking, foaming grass and hot gas shot out from the side of the cow, such was the pressure.

By this means there was a good chance of saving the cow, once the stomach had been stitched up. When bloat struck a herd, many cows could be affected and if they were not caught in time, they would die. Those that did were dragged unceremoniously from the field behind the tractor and dumped on the side of the road. A truck took the carcasses to the works to turn them into blood and bone fertilizer. The sight of numerous dead cows lining the roadside, their bellies horribly distended, all four legs pointing upwards and stinking to high heaven, was then an accepted rural phenomenon. Pastures are now routinely sprayed with anti-foaming agents and cows likely to be affected by bloat could be drenched with anti-bloat capsules. Of course, now the focus is on the climate-changing methane gas which is belched out.

Eventually we moved out of the ruin into Wally's big farmhouse. The Woods took off on a once-in-their-life time retirement trip to Europe which included a brief stay at Little Water. We heard later from Granny that she found these first antipodean visitors 'a little unusual'.

I now had a nice little bedroom of my own which was clean and tidy. The house exterior was made of flimsy Fibrolite and was showing signs of age, but the kitchen had an early version of an electric dishwasher, which I had never seen before. The Woods clearly had had all the mod cons in their home. There was an antiquated wall telephone which shared a party line with about eight other users along our road. Our number was 398R. When you wanted to use the phone, you had to pick up the receiver, turn the handle to signal you wanted to use the line and then ask 'Working?' If anyone was on the line at that moment they would say 'Yes' so you would hang up the receiver and wait for a while before trying again.

We could identify incoming calls intended for us as the phone would ring an 'R' in Morse code (a short ring followed by a long ring followed by a short ring). As mischievous as always, when no one was around, I loved to listen into private conversations on the line but often other users could tell when someone else had picked up a receiver and they would ask 'Who's there?' I didn't listen in for long.

Drainage on the farm was very important so drains were often being dug or cleaned out to take the run-off from the swamp land and new fields. I was amazed to watch the drag-line machine, with its tank tracks, dig out the ditches and dump its wet mass of oozing mud on the side of the field. It was a far cry from Walter Drayton's ditch-digging by hand. I wanted to have a go at driving it but never dared to start it up when no one was looking. What particularly interested me were the dozens of large, slimy, writhing eels which suddenly found themselves ejected.

Calf Club was a community competition where we could enter a calf in the local A&P Show. Colin Brooks gave each of us a Jersey calf to care for. I called mine Lorna, after a girl on the *Orcades* that I had been quite fond of. I loved brushing and grooming her after school each day. I was disappointed that Lorna only won third prize, but she came home with a nice green ribbon.

Don Hudson tried to interest me in playing rugby, the default sport for all Kiwi boys, but I was too lazy to learn the rules and saw no point in tiring myself out running up and down the field chasing an egg-shaped ball that never came into my possession. At the age of 10, I was already a late starter on the rugby field. In England there had never been an opportunity to play organised sport. Sport was generally referred to as 'games' in the English school curriculum. By the time I got to New Zealand, I was well behind the play when it came to rugby.

Tom and Evelyn Jerry were a Maori brother and sister who came to our school. They were the first Maori I met. They were both tall and wore no shoes, my introduction to the New Zealand habit of going barefoot. Sitting together on the school bench at lunch time, Evelyn would cut a loaf of bread to make a sandwich for them each. Kio Kio School made no concession to any linguistic or cultural needs they might have had. It was a purely monolingual, Pakeha environment. We learnt a few songs and phrases of French when I started in Form One the next year (*'Sur le Pont d'Avignon'* and the like) but not a single word of Maori. I am glad to see that has changed.

Mrs Hoffman was the relieving principal when I first arrived and then Mr Abbott came. He had a son, Max, who was a bit younger than me. Like many of the boys, including me, Max was very smitten by pretty little Andrea Cullen whose father was a local farmer. To enliven proceedings one day, I took my old black and white box camera to school so that, as I said, I could take photos of Max and Andrea and anyone else who wanted to be in them.

The possibility of us all being photographed caused a near riot at playtime as most of the school wanted to be in the pictures. I shot off several snaps and everyone had great fun. A few days later people began asking me when the photos would be ready. I managed to put them off until eventually everyone stopped asking and forgot about them. I never had to admit that the camera had no film in it in the first place.

One of the strangest occurrences at the school involved my introduction to the word 'intercourse'. Working away on a group project with three girls, they began twittering and laughing each time one of them mentioned the word 'intercourse'. I had never heard this word before but guessed it must be significant.

Just then a woman passed by our classroom and headed off towards Mr Abbott's office. One of the girls asked casually of the others: 'I wonder what she wants?' To be helpful and to inject myself into the conversation, I suggested 'Perhaps she has come for intercourse!' Stunned silence from the girls who then went a-chirping and a-twittering again as if I had committed a major sin.

One of them stupidly told our teacher who told Mr Abbott and the next thing I found myself alone with Mr Abbott in his office for a firm telling-off for using untoward language. Up to that point he had always been very pleasant to me but now he was clearly very annoyed. His hairy moustache vibrated as he spoke. Frustratingly though, his telling-off did not involve any explanation of the meaning of the word which my female peers clearly understood but about which I had not the foggiest idea.

I left his office having been roundly sanctioned but without any clue whatsoever as to the meaning of the word which had ruffled so many feathers. You can imagine my puzzlement at the whole episode. It was years later before I found out its meaning. How silly Mr Abbott had been to have rebuked me without having first ascertained whether, at the age of 11, I had any inkling of what the word meant.

To give themselves some peace and quiet in the weekends my parents hit upon the idea of sending Stuart and me to Sunday School, which was held for an hour or two every Sunday afternoon at Kio Kio School. Wally Woods agreed to pick up children from the district and take them to the school in the back of his old cattle truck.

On Saturday afternoons, in preparation for the pick-up, Wally would clean out the back of his truck with a high-pressure hose to remove all the shit from the floor and sides left by the cows he had just been transporting. He would then place two form benches in the back for us to sit on. Totally unsecured seating and no thought given to child safety. Stuart and I were the first on the pick-up run. The truck would hold about 10 of us.

Stuart and I went to Sunday school two or three times before we flatly refused to go any more. Sunday School was taken by a jocular, portly character called Mr Luffett. He had got religion in an inspired way. In addition to lustily singing songs like '*Jesus loves me this I know, for the Bible tells me so*', which I thought was a pretty slim basis for knowing anything about someone else, we did drawings and colouring of biblical scenes. It was all so horribly boring. I protested strongly that my Sunday afternoon should be frittered away in this manner, when we could be outside playing on the farm. I never went to any religious instruction again.

One morning, 17 April 1962, the Governor-General, Lord Cobham, visited the school. His big black limousine swung into the school grounds. Out he hopped, mingled a bit and then planted a tree. A portly, avuncular gentleman, he reminded me of Lord St Audries, the only other Lord who had crossed my path. His tree is now fully grown and the central feature of the school grounds. But the *pièce de résistance* was his departing gift, a day off school in honour of the occasion.

The pupils of Kio Kio School were then bussed into Otorohanga College, where His Excellency was to make an afternoon visit. I am not sure why it was considered necessary for us to be there, since we had just had the pleasure of his company. Perhaps all the schools in the region had been instructed to attend. We were delighted when, as per his usual script, he gave us all a day off school in honour of his visit. We children felt we were justly entitled to two days off school, not merely the one he had given us at Kio Kio, but I don't recall that we were successful in obtaining this.

For a new Kiwi who had never heard of Captain Cook, I loved singing the Willow Macky ballad '*Young James Cook was a sailor bold, he was brave, he was good, he was clever. He rose to be captain in the king's navy and commanded the good ship Endeavour*'. It sounded exciting and romantic to an 11-year-old. If it sounds hackneyed now, we should not underestimate Cook's achievements as a navigator. As well, we should commemorate the great Maori navigators, who came first to Aotearoa, for their amazing feats of seamanship.

Shirley King and her relative Joe Flay were particular friends. One day we were allowed to walk over the big hill from their farm near Kio Kio School all the way to Puketarata Road. This meant climbing up and over the hill after which Puketarata Road is named, i.e. the 'Hill with the Tarata Tree'. We stole and ate a few turnips from a nearby field. At the top of the hill was reportedly a sacred Maori burial site, an urupa, so we approached that area with particular caution. We could see Wally's farm and our homestead shimmering in the distance below. As it was midsummer, we had a great amble down the hillside in the warm sunshine. I snatched a quick kiss from Shirley behind a gorse bush.

Dad's cousin, Mike Roper, came to stay while we were at the Woods' cottage and introduced us to his fiancée, Jenny Turner. She came from a pioneering sheep-farming family at Porewa, outside Hunterville. Mike and Jenny were the only family visitors we had while we were at the Woods' farm.

The community did occasionally get together socially at the Kio Kio hall. My mother was initially puzzled by the invitation which stipulated 'Ladies, a plate please'. She soon discovered that this was New Zealand shorthand for 'please bring a plate with you with lots of food on it to share with everyone'.

In early 1962, our class undertook an exchange with Mellons Bay Primary School in Auckland. This was my first experience of city life. I was billeted with a nice family and went with the son, Roger, for a week to his school. Daily excursions to Auckland city involved a visit to the Auckland War Memorial Museum and the planetarium which in those days was attached to the museum. My first experience of the night sky.

We went to the Ford motor factory in Newmarket to watch cars being assembled from imported componentry. The factory is now long gone and the site is a car sales yard. I embarrassed myself by crashing Roger's bike, riding too fast down a hill near his home and bent the front forks. I was fortunately unscathed. In a return visit, Roger came to stay with us at the Woods' farm for a week to get a taste of rural life.

At some point in late summer 1962, Colin Brooks informed my father that he would have to cut his wages as a result of a reduction in international milk returns. Dad would not accept this. In any case he had decided that he did not much like farm labouring, New Zealand-style, and was not enamoured of the whole set-up at Puketarata Road. He decided to leave the farm.

Both houses have since been demolished and not a trace remains of our first two homes in New Zealand. The site is now grassland once again. We moved into a spartan school house in town across the road from Otorohanga College. Mum had managed to rent this house because of her teaching position at the college.

Stuart and I still went to Kio Kio School but now bussed in each day from Otorohanga. Dad took on one-off farm labouring jobs while he sought out more permanent employment. He looked at working for radio in Hamilton, working on a programme on rural affairs hosted by Fred Barnes, who in 1966 founded the popular TV series *Country Calendar*. But Dad didn't quite have the fluency needed for a job where the speaking voice is all-important.

Kakamutu Road (originally number 28 but long since renumbered) was our home for only a short time. We were there for my 11th birthday, on 28 June 1962. My expectation of a whole lot of birthday presents was rudely shattered when my parents instead gave me a birthday card with a cheque inside, 'to spend as you want'. They had been too preoccupied to think about buying birthday presents. I was most upset.

I made my final break with rugby after trying to join a rugby team in Otorohanga but earning for my tribulations some hearty family laughter at my pathetic attempts to keep up with the ball.

Helen Milson, aged 20, came to stay with us at Kakamutu Road. She was about nine years older than me and was a close friend of Jenny Roper. We had met her at Mike and Jenny's wedding at Porewa, near Hunterville, when Helen was a bridesmaid and Dad was Mike's best man. Helen would become a close family friend and for over 60 years we shared fun times and tragic times together.

British immigrants formed a significant part of the New Zealand demography in the 1960s. It was a sign of New Zealand's growing maturity as a nation, if still not fully developed, that the descendants of earlier British migrants often resented the attitude of newer immigrants from 'the old country'. New Zealanders generally were uncomfortable with the notion that the traditional British social hierarchy might be imported into Aotearoa. Any hint of social or cultural superiority, or suggestion that they 'knew better how to do things', would be roundly condemned in New Zealand's more egalitarian society. The term 'Bloody Pom' to describe newer British migrants who had, for any reason, upset the locals, was often heard. The term has all but disappeared now that New Zealand has opened its borders to migrants from many countries besides the UK.

CHAPTER 6

ON THE MOVE AGAIN

OUR NEXT MOVE WAS TO HAMILTON CITY TO A DILAPIDATED cottage on Knighton Road (another Knighton!), built on land that was subsequently taken over by the University of Waikato. At the time it was still one of the dairy research farms attached to the well-known Ruakura Animal Research Centre. I often cycled to the cow shed on the farm to collect a pail of milk as our neighbour, Mr Parker, was in charge of the farm. This cow shed later became the student common room at the University of Waikato.

Because it was a research centre, the shed housed cows which had had 'window' holes opened up in their sides so that scientists could peer inside the cows' stomachs and extract material to examine the digestive process. The holes were stopped up by round leather plugs. It had something to do with research into the causes of bloat. It must have been very painful for the poor animals.

My father undertook a number of agricultural-related jobs about which I knew very little but my mother quickly got a teaching position at Fairfield College.

At the age of 11, I was about to start my fifth primary school and was enrolled at Peachgrove Intermediate. Stuart was enrolled in

Knighton Road Primary School. Once again, we were not at the same school.

I arrived at Peachgrove Intermediate in time for the final third of the year in Form One. This school had several hundred pupils and I found it intimidating. My teacher was Mr Freyer, who drove about in an old American V8. For the first time, but by no means the last, I experienced school life in a draughty prefab building. This was a low-cost relocatable building on piles, part of the government's cunning solution to housing the country's growing school population without the expense of building permanent accommodation.

It was late winter when I first arrived because I remember how important the potbellied stove was for heating the classroom. I would cycle the mile or so from home each day, parking my bike in one of the many bike sheds provided by the school.

One Monday morning there was great excitement when one of the boys discovered a discarded condom lying in the grass near our classroom. I had not seen anything like it before but was soon told that this was a 'Frenchie'. No one knew exactly how it came to be there.

In 1963, I started in Form Two, the last year before high school, and was taught by a teacher called Nathaniel Dickey. He was a red-faced young man and very strict. He drove about in a Czech Škoda, which stood out because it was so unusual. Although I now have a negative memory of him for reasons which will become clear, his classes were fun.

For the first time, I had a teacher who used to read aloud to us on Friday afternoons, for pleasure, as a reward for a good week's work. The class was captivated as he read a chapter each Friday from *The Oregon Trail*, the true story about 14-year-old John Sager and his family journeying the Oregon Trail by wagon in the early 1840s.

Mr Dickey also taught us country dancing. This was great fun as we got to dance with girls we particularly liked, while he tapped the floor with a large wooden T ruler in time to the music. We had more French lessons from Miss Rouse in the next classroom. She taught us *'Frère Jacques'* as well as a German ditty, my first experience of German. Mr Dickey and Miss Rouse clearly had a liking for each other, as they married soon after.

In February 1963, Queen Elizabeth paid her second visit to New Zealand, or as it was referred to at the time, the 'Dominion' of New Zealand (there was no mention of 'Aotearoa'). To enable young Kiwis to develop an affection for the British monarchy, the government alighted upon the excellent idea of bussing children to a location which the Queen would be visiting so they could wave at her as she drove by. Two children were chosen from each primary school class in our region and were taken by bus on a day trip to the Tauranga Domain.

I have no idea why I, as a recent migrant from the UK, was chosen as one of the two representatives of our class, but I duly found myself with several thousand others on a sunny day as we lined up in rows in the Tauranga Domain to await the Queen's arrival. She had sailed to Tauranga on board the Royal Yacht *Britannia*, which could be seen in the distance tied up in the port. Several years later, we found out that my father's brother, John, was one of the Commanders on the Yacht at that time but because he was estranged from his brother he did not contact us.

A shiny green Land Rover eventually turned up driven by a nervous-looking chauffeur in a cap. Standing upright at the open back, holding on to a railing with her left hand, was a young woman wearing a smart dress and long white gloves. Her husband stood beside her. She waved at us with her other hand in a peculiar manner which I later came to know as the 'royal wave'. We all cheered and waved back.

It lasted all of a minute and she was gone. I did have some film in my box camera this time and took one or two quick snaps. It would be over 40 years before I would meet her again and I did not mention our first encounter. I am not sure what report I made to the class on my return to school. I came to see it as a nice, but rather quaint, excuse for a day off.

In 1963, I briefly joined the Hamilton East Boy Scouts, with my friend Russell Hawken. Unlike my brother Stuart I was never very good at scouting. One particular adventure got me offside with Mr Dickey. Our troop leaders decided we would make a day's hike into the Kaimai Ranges, near Tauranga, to search for the wreckage of a DC3 aircraft belonging to the National Airways Corporation, the forerunner of Air New Zealand. This aircraft had crashed on 3 July 1963 into the ranges as it failed to clear a ridge coming into land at Tauranga Airport. All 23 people aboard were killed. We had a difficult hike up the slopes of the ranges but eventually we found the crashed aircraft and I took photos of it.

When the photos had been developed, I showed them to Mr Dickey thinking he would be very interested in our scouting expedition, but he was horrified by the whole idea that we had visited the crash site. He took particular exception to a photo of me holding up a broken tailpiece of the aircraft. He never said anything but his looks darkened and his mood changed and I knew I had made a big mistake showing them to him. In fact, the crash site did become too much of a hiking excursion for the inquisitive. Sometime later the wreckage was buried by the SAS.

While we were living in the Knighton Road cottage my parents bought a quarter-acre section around the corner at 226 Old Farm Road and made plans to build a house. This was home number nine and I was still only twelve. Old Farm Road was then surrounded by farmland belonging to the Ruakura Animal Research Centre but it is now very much suburbia. The prospect of moving into a home of our own after only three years in New Zealand was exciting and an interesting comment on how much easier it was in those days for a young family to be able to build and own their own home.

Helen Milson came to stay with Stuart and me whenever my parents wanted a night out somewhere. We loved being with this vivacious young woman. Over 60 years later, she still had the effrontery to introduce herself to others as my 'babysitter'. Helen enjoyed coming to visit us, as a home away from home, because her own parents were conservative and quite strict.

For an extended period, Aunty Rene and Uncle Alf Roper came to live with us in our cottage. They had sold up their home in Canterbury, England, to come to New Zealand to live with their son Mike and his wife Jenny. They were unhappy in New Zealand and had decided to return to England. Stuart and I decided to give Aunty Rene a nice surprise one evening by jumping out at her from behind the door. The poor woman nearly died of fright but we thought it was a great joke. Eventually they caught a boat back to the UK from Invercargill and we did not see them again. They lived frugally so Aunty Rene took her plastic bucket with her back to England.

Jeffrey Mitchell was a good school friend. We rode our bikes together far and wide in the weekends and collected discarded beer bottles from the ditches and parks around Hamilton. These we sold back to the DB Brewery in Hamilton for a penny a bottle. Some weekends I would make three or four shillings in pocket money, a lot of money for me in those days.

Jeffrey's family was Mormon. From Mr Mitchell I heard about the dangers of drinking tea and coffee because of the negative effects of caffeine on the heart rate. It was not a stricture I ever took to my heart. Jeffrey belonged to a scout troop run by the Mormon church and was very keen for me to join his pack. I was on the point of doing so when my parents, on sober reflection, vetoed the idea. I guess they feared membership of the scout pack would be the first step to getting me signed up to the Mormon church.

We weren't particularly religious as a family and I never went to church but I suppose if anyone had pressed me, I would have said I was an Anglican. This was a convenient label that suited me for years and enabled me to avoid any protracted discussion about my lack of religious conviction.

Lawrence Southon was widely regarded as the brainiest kid at school and earned general respect for it. He was a quiet, introverted boy with large spectacles and was a keen Esperantist. I had never heard of Esperanto before but Lawrence explained how the world needed a common language and this Esperanto sought to do. It was made up of words taken from several languages so when you learned Esperanto some words would already be familiar, like 'birdo' which meant 'bird'.

There is no doubting the nobility of thought that lay behind the concept of Esperanto but it was based heavily on words originating in European languages. It still has a good following today, but English has to a large extent filled the role of an international language and I saw no point in learning an artificial one.

I loved buying my lunch from the school canteen because the buttered sandwiches, made with fresh bread and a filling of baked beans or spaghetti, were delicious, especially when washed down with a bottle of fresh milk provided free of charge, courtesy of Her Majesty's New Zealand Government.

One incident during metalwork class gave rise to an inquisition. The metalwork teacher, whose name I have forgotten, to his horror found that someone had bent right back a pair of tin snips and effectively destroyed them. This item was school property. Such an act of vandalism was not about to be tolerated. Class proceedings were stopped and the *Riot Act* was read aloud. The culprit was earnestly enjoined to identify himself but after lengthy questioning the vandal remained a mystery.

This caused an escalation in the investigative proceedings. I wondered if one of us had broken the tin snips in our work without realising it. The vandal was never unearthed. I was never sure one existed in the first place. I could not be sure that the act of vandalism had not been committed by another class at another time. It seemed to me an awful lot of angst was caused all for the sake of a pair of tin snips, but I guess if you let a Vandal loose in your classroom, there is no knowing where it might end.

Another school friend was Dimitri Edmonds. His father owned a large farm near Putaruru, about 70 km from Hamilton. In order to go to school in Hamilton he, his mother and an older sister lived in a flat near us during the week. Mrs Edmonds was Greek and had met her husband when he was in the New Zealand Army during the war years. On one visit to Dimitri's home, we went out shooting on the farm and I have to admit, to my intense shame, that I shot a fantail, not knowing that it was a protected bird.

Forever after I have loved those inquisitive little creatures and have always striven to protect them. I developed an intense loathing of hunting in all its forms, especially of those hunters like patrician Brits who shoot grouse, or go to Africa to shoot a lion or an elephant for fun. The fantail was the only creature I have knowingly killed, apart from farm pests such as rats. The experience, and my later guilt feelings, turned me into something of a Greenie when it came to protecting fauna and flora.

While we were waiting for our new house in Old Farm Road to be completed, we moved temporarily into a small flat in Beale Street in Hamilton East. The Anglia was sold and Dad bought a shiny new Cortina station wagon. I loved the smell of the inside of this new car.

Helen Milson married Len Cannon. Stuart and I were not invited to the wedding as Mrs Milson, her mother, didn't want children complicating proceedings. Soon after Helen and Len, in their little Ford Prefect, took Stuart and me on our first ever day outing to Auckland, which I had not been to since the school trip at Kio Kio school.

Walking up Queen Street, I was able to buy some brand-new colouring pencils, which cost 7/9 (seven shillings and nine pence) at a bookshop — a lot of money for me. I was most annoyed to find the very same pencils on sale for 7/6 at the next shop so I went back to the first shop and asked if I could sell my pencils back to them. The shop assistant looked puzzled and asked me why I now wanted to sell them back, having just bought them minutes before. I said it was because in the next shop the pencils were three pence cheaper. Deciding on a quick solution to this major dilemma, she gave me the three pence and sent me on my way.

While I was living in Beale Street, a new newspaper made its appearance, the *Sunday News*, published in Auckland. I got a job as delivery boy and early every Sunday morning I would do my delivery rounds on my bicycle. It was also my job to go around at a later time to collect payment. Each copy cost nine pence. This was a high price to pay for what I personally thought was a pretty flimsy newspaper. But the boss man who came every so often to our house to collect the payments from me was very happy with my work. I was paid one penny for every paper I delivered so earned just less than two shillings a week.

I also took on lawn-mowing jobs and earned ten shillings a time. One lady gave me a glass of cold Coca-Cola on a very hot afternoon. I had never drunk Coca-Cola before and was amazed at how delicious and refreshing it tasted. I did not know at the time that Coca-Cola would become one of the world's major environmental polluters with its plastic bottles, which is why I don't drink the stuff now!

One evening a travelling encyclopedia salesman knocked on the door. After his persuasive sales pitch, my parents agreed to purchase an array of very interesting children's encyclopedias and science books. Dad gave him a cheque as a deposit and I went to bed feeling very excited at the forthcoming large addition to my library. The next evening the salesman popped back as he had discovered an error in the cheque which needed to be corrected. Dad took the cheque back and cancelled the whole purchase order. It wasn't just the travelling salesman who was very disappointed at this unexpected change of heart.

One Saturday morning I was out collecting payment for the newspaper when I came across a classmate who gave me the astonishing news that President Kennedy had just been assassinated. This was 23 November 1963. I raced home to tell my parents but they had just heard the news on the radio.

CHAPTER 7

TEENAGE YEARS AND HAMILTON BOYS' HIGH SCHOOL (1964–1968)

IN EARLY FEBRUARY 1964 I STARTED IN THE THIRD FORM AT Hamilton Boys' High School. It had been barely three years since we had arrived on the *Orcades*, yet it felt like we had been in New Zealand forever. The new house in Old Farm Road was not yet ready so we were still living in the cramped two-bedroom flat in Hamilton East. It was only a short ride to school on my bike past the landmark Riverina Hotel (long since demolished). Here in 1962, I had lined up to see the King and Queen of Thailand arrive for a reception during their State visit to New Zealand. I remember how beautiful the young Queen Sirikit looked.

On that first day at high school it was not long before some senior oaf had grabbed the red school cap off my head and bitten out the knob on the top. Having a cap with a knob in it marked one out as a fresher and caps with knobs just weren't allowed. None of the masters, as we called our teachers, cared a jot for this sartorial outrage. The senior boys could frequently be overbearing towards the juniors but at least the English practice of schoolboy fagging had not caught on in the more egalitarian New Zealand.

Early on in the school year we were required to do military drill. This was a hang-over from the not-so-distant days of the Second

World War, against the backdrop of the then escalating Vietnam War. To defend our country from a surprise enemy attack, perhaps a resurgent Japan or a communist China, it was deemed essential by the government in Wellington that young high school boys spend several days being knocked into shape and turned into men. We marched in endless circles around the football field, in honest formation, shouldering rifles which were actually First World War standard issue with the bolts deactivated. Major McKenzie who was, it seems, both a real major as well as one of our teachers had us wheeling and marching all over the place in the summer sun.

I can't say that we were an effective fighting force as a result of our drilling but I enjoyed being outside in the sunshine. When the Major wasn't available, we were commanded by a gangly senior student who had evidently done some training as an NCO (non-commissioned officer) during his summer holiday in a military camp somewhere. Now for his efforts he got the chance to give orders to the other boys on the school parade ground.

It all seemed pretty pointless to me as no one had bothered to inform us who the enemy was against whom we would have to defend New Zealand. I do remember our young Napoleon barking at us on repeated occasions 'Don't anticipate my orders!' when lines of ill-disciplined teenage boys threatened to lumber forward and become a rabble. I can still see him now, barking out his orders all alone on the sports field, some sort of baton under his arm, with the *Grande Armée* lined up in front of him. From then on I was always very mindful that a cardinal virtue of any self-respecting teenage soldier must be to 'never anticipate orders'. Military drill for schoolboys was discontinued sometime later.

My poor maternal grandparents at Little Water Farm had not spoken to us for nearly four years because telephone calls were too expensive. Letters were the only way to keep in touch. By Christmas 1964, when we were in our new home in Old Farm Road, Dad agreed that Mum could telephone her parents. This involved booking an international telephone call to Little Water via the international toll operator. We had a five-minute slot booked to make the call on Christmas morning. At the appointed time, the operator rang our number, Hamilton 69415, and, lo and behold, Granny's faint voice could be heard at the other end of the line.

The call cost the huge sum of £1 a minute. As my mother spoke, Dad knelt beside the phone and held up his fingers to indicate how many minutes she had left. We all said a few hurried words and the call ended almost as soon as it had begun. But everyone felt uplifted that we had been able to speak to Granny and Grandad and yet sad that they were so distant. It would be another seven years before we would see them again.

Despite its reputation for academic and sports excellence, Hamilton Boys' High School did not have the facilities to accommodate a growing school roll. It was a bit of a shock to find my class, known as '3L2', or the second third form Latin class, was to be housed in yet another prefab classroom. I had confidently expected that I would be leaving such rudimentary accommodation behind at Peachgrove Intermediate. My subjects were English, Latin, French, Social Studies, Science and Maths.

The headmaster was Aubrey Baigent, a short, dumpy, tense and stern disciplinarian with a little moustache, who earned the nickname Budge. There is no doubting his love for, and great pride in, the school but he had no hesitation in using the cane if need be. The most frightening thing for any of the masters was a surprise visit from Budge to check out a particular teacher, mid lesson.

He used to conduct morning assembly in the school hall when we would all sing with gusto a hymn for the day from the Anglican songbook, be given the occasional pep talk and hear school notices. Michael Christie, a fellow pupil, whose father taught biology at the school, pounded away on the school grand piano when we sang our songs. I, who never had any musical ability, marvelled at his skill.

Assemblies involved all the masters sitting on the stage behind Budge who conducted proceedings like a maestro at his lectern. It was rare that any other teacher had a role to play in an assembly which was Budge's personal *tour de force*. Assemblies involved sitting on the hard, wooden floor, no chairs for juniors.

On one occasion, Budge derided the unkempt appearance and unruly behaviour of the Beatles, who were then touring New Zealand. He didn't like their hairstyle and was not about to condone its appearance in his school. I wondered if, in later years, he came to realise just how neat and tidy the Beatles had looked when compared to later hairy adventurers.

Budge tried to help us prepare for important exams. We should not, he intoned, work too long at swotting without taking regular breaks. To illustrate his point, he demonstrated to the assembled exam-hopefuls, contorting his own face, some very useful head massage techniques to stimulate the grey cells. These exercises proved invaluable in later years.

On important occasions we would be required to sing the school anthem: *'Forty Years On'*. Written in 1872, there was nothing to link this song with New Zealand as it was borrowed from Harrow School (the most celebrated Harrovian being Winston Churchill). The lyrics were meant to give us some idea of what school life would be like when we return after 40 years. I can still sing the main lyrics but I have to confess that I now find it hackneyed. And for me it was 50 years before I returned.

The chorus has a line in it: *'Follow up, follow up, follow up, till the field ring again and again, with the tramp of the twenty-two men'*. This appeared to be a reference to two cricket teams but as Hamilton Boys' High was more a rugby sort of place, like New Zealand generally, Budge hatched the idea of changing the lyrics to 'the tramp of the thirty true men', a reference supposedly to two rugby teams. It got rather confusing. The notion that we schoolboys could in any manner be described as 'men' struck me as delusional.

This school song was just another borrowing from the 'old country' at a time when New Zealand's self-consciousness as an independent nation was slowly emerging. I liked the school motto though: *'Sapiens Fortunam Fingit Sibi'* — a wise person carves his own fortune.

One Monday morning, as the masters were filing onto the stage for assembly, the whole school started enthusiastically clapping when one of them, Mike Minogue, made his entry. Mike had been elected Mayor of our city in municipal elections that weekend. Budge was not about to allow this to undermine proceedings and he quickly reasserted control. I don't think he made any mention of Mike's electoral success. Minogue had taught me some English lessons but he soon left school to pursue a political career.

After serving as Hamilton's mayor from 1968 to 1976, Minogue was elected to Parliament in the Hamilton West electorate for the conservative National Party. He quickly fell out of favour with the party bosses and the then Prime Minister, Robert Muldoon, not least for his relentless pursuit of more openness in Government. He was a leading inspiration for what became the Official Information Act, which now requires that government information be released on request to the public, unless there are valid reasons as defined in the Act for withholding it, as opposed to the then general practice of withholding information unless there were good reasons to release it.

Every time I had to grapple with an OIA request in my later career in the Foreign Ministry, I gave a silent 'thank you' to Mike, sometimes tongue-in-cheek if the request was a particularly curly one. His role in achieving more open government in New Zealand is not as well recognised as it should be.

I had no idea what Latin was but my mother had encouraged me to take Latin at high school as she had done at her grammar school in England during the war. This was despite Mr Dickey's dismissive comment to her the year earlier, at Peachgrove Intermediate, that I stood no chance of being accepted into the academic Latin stream at high school. Young Mr Dickey appears to have formed an early dim view of my capabilities. 'The Latin stream would be too hard for Peter', he told my parents. Dickey later became an object of derision for such heresy and I used to congratulate myself: 'Thank God we didn't listen to Mr Dickey'.

That is not to say that learning Latin was easy. There were long evenings of frustrating homework trying to sort out tenses and accusative, genitive and dative cases with the ablative thrown in to add to the joyful confusion. Not to forget the vocative case: Why, I wondered, would any language want a special word case just to say 'O God' or 'O Caesar' or 'O pupil' or 'O teacher'? But I persevered and once I had got beyond *'amo, amas, amat'* ('I love, you love, he /she loves') in the first few days and *'ad tabernam festino'* ('I am hastening to the pub' — a very useful little phrase), Latin became a lifelong pleasure to read and study, although I never studied it at university. Here was the language spoken by those unfortunates buried alive in Pompeii when Mt Vesuvius erupted in AD 79, whose streets I had walked as a nine-year-old. It made history come alive.

A knowledge of Latin made it possible to appreciate the great richness of the English language, a point often overlooked by those who say learning Latin is a waste of time. A later unexpected bonus was that having studied Latin grammar, German grammar held no mystery.

Our Latin teacher, William (Bill) Roche, used to gush around the school, brisk and crisp, in a magnificent long black gown, seemingly always in a hurry. Tall, dark, handsome and of slim build, he spoke in a husky voice and liked the Beatles. He wore a very chunky ring on his finger. He was an early example, we sensed, of a flamboyant teacher, unconventional in dress and thought, unlike some of the other teachers whose experience of life had been forged in the Second World War. To generations of HBHS students, he became known as 'Ringo Roche'.

We tried hard to please him and breathed in his very strong after-shave aroma whenever he leaned over us to correct some arcane point of grammar. I did well in his classes but not brilliantly. One day he slipped two lovely stamps from Aden onto my desk — as he knew I was a keen stamp collector — although he probably didn't know I had spent a day in Aden after leaving the Suez Canal on board the SS *Orcades* in early 1961.

After I left school, I heard nothing further of him until some 25 years later I happened to meet him on the Auckland to Waiheke ferry. By that time he had retired and had no doubt taught many thousands of other pupils. But he was still the same flamboyant Ringo Roche, if much older. Not surprisingly, he didn't seem to remember me. He died in 2012, sadly from the effects of injuries sustained in an unfortunate bus accident in Auckland.

Years later, after Bill had passed away, I met his wife, Collene, who had been a well-known singer in her younger days and in later life was principal for many years of Carmel College, a large Catholic high school for girls in Auckland. She told me that her husband had been strong in his Catholic faith, was quite conservative, and was a staunch royalist. I knew nothing of this when he had been my teacher. He would, I am sure, be most upset to learn now of my republican and rationalist views.

Our social studies teacher was PJ Fordyce, or 'Fordy' as he was affectionately known. He was English and had done many things in life before becoming a teacher but we never found out exactly what. There was a rumour (I think in fact he may have told us) that he had once worked on the railways in the UK. Somehow he had lost a rib, which seemed to explain why he always had a slight lean to one side and never stood vertically. That alone was enough to fascinate us.

William Roche, my Latin teacher at Hamilton Boys High School, painted by Gaston de Vel, my art teacher (Portrait courtesy of Collene Roche, private collection)

Fordy was a slim-built man, balding and gaunt, with a small thin face, smooth tight skin and a wandering, slightly protruding eye. 'Boys!' he would boom, fixing the class with a withering stare whenever he wanted to regain control of his charges, which was often enough. I could never be sure whether Fordy was really looking at me or

Donald Ross, or Victor Agnew or Nigel Vanner, or Denis Graham or John Waugh, or Rhys Mathias perhaps. That was the great advantage of having a wandering eye: he could eyeball two or more of us at once. It was most unsettling, but very effective. Although he could sometimes be disorganised, his passion for teaching was very evident. Unlike the other masters, he never wore a gown.

His main subjects were Social Studies, French and History. He was fond of quoting Voltaire — or Arouet as he called him — and Descartes (*'Cogito, ergo sum'*). It was Fordy who first made us aware of the Enlightenment. Everyone loved his lessons. One memorable day Fordy tried to place human history in relation to time in general. 'Boys', he said, 'try to think of time, infinite and endless. Then think how long we humans have existed'. It was impossible to grasp. 'To give you an idea, watch!'

Turning to the blackboard, Fordy picked up a piece of chalk, his favourite teaching aid whenever he was not personally holding forth. He began drawing a chalk line around the four walls of the prefab classroom, just below the ceiling. The line was thin, continuous, endless. We watched spellbound as he struggled down the first side wall, banging into the desks, arm stretched up high holding his piece of chalk, then stumbling along the back wall, finally returning to the front above the blackboard to finish at his point of departure.

'Imagine', he said, 'that this chalk line represents how long the world has been in existence'. It was an awfully long line. Fordy turned back to his line just above the blackboard and on it drew two small parallel lines which bisected it, about 10 cm apart. 'And that', he said triumphantly, 'is human history'.

Ten centimetres for human history and all four walls of the prefab for the age of the world! Here was graphic proof of our own place in the universe, small, infinitesimal, yet not completely irrelevant. Well, we might be late arrivals, in comparison to the whole four walls of Fordy's chalk line, but we were there now and that's all that really mattered.

Since that day, I have learned that time is not exactly linear but Fordy's chalk line was a seminal moment and has been a great help to me in ordering the great events of history. Thinking about this in later years, with the earth's population around six billion, it occurred to me he might also have said: 'Go out and spend one whole year with each and every person alive in the world today and at the end of it, that will be how old the earth is'.

Fordy introduced us to 17th-century Stuart history and imparted a lifelong fascination for the Gunpowder Plot, the English Civil War, the Restoration and the 1688 Revolution. I could relate to this personally as at Speccott Barton we had lived not far from the manor house of Great Potheridge, where General George Monck had been born in 1608.

Fordy was quite religious but also liberal. Just how liberal dawned on me when I recalled how he had tried to explain King James I's fascination for young boys and men. We had never come across the word 'homosexual' before and the word 'gay' was not then in use. Endeavouring to explain to the class what a homosexual was, Fordy decided to take a practical example close at hand. 'It may be', he said 'that one of you finds Mr Hartstone here particularly attractive, instead of a girlfriend'. Titters all round in our male-only classroom. Paul Hartstone was a beefy rugby player and not at all likely to be an object of sexual attraction to the other boys. But Fordy had made his point, without being too explicit.

One day when I was six or seven, while we were still in England, we made a day's outing to Stonehenge. Apart from the magnificent Henge itself, the day was notable because for the first time I heard a couple speaking in a language I did not understand. Until that point I had no concept of a foreign language since I assumed English was what everyone spoke. I was told they were visitors from France and spoke French.

Six years later, I started learning French. Our first teacher was Monsieur Dederian, a rotund, jovial Frenchman who would not have looked out of place playing an accordion on the Champs-Élysées or riding a bicycle through the French countryside in summer, wearing a beret. Monsieur Dederian disappeared after the first term with no explanation, at least to us boys. We were delighted when Fordy taught us French as well as social studies.

Dr Herbert Ales taught both French and German in the senior school and was the main reason I took up German in the last two years of high school, little realising it would be my university major. There was an air of mystery about Doc Ales, which we never fathomed. Slightly deaf and often fingering his hearing aid like Aunty Annie, he was clearly an intellectual. There was a rumour that he might have been involved with the Czech partisans in the war, which was a tantalising notion but one he never elucidated. He never shared any memories of his wartime experiences. Perhaps these were too painful. Doc Ales often shouted at us. I wished that he would turn up the volume of his deaf aid so that he could hear us, and himself, more clearly.

English lessons in 3L2 were usually boring. The grammar book was written by someone called Pendlebury, so 'Open your Pendlebury' indicated the start of a lesson. Many years later I saw that wonderful movie *Dead Poets Society*, starring Robin Williams. The English grammar textbook the students had been studying, until Robin tells them to start tearing pages out of it, was written by J Evans Pritchard. 'No more J Evans Pritchard', Robin intones. They had been studying Pendlebury! Unfortunately, at the end of the movie it is J Evans Pritchard that is back on their desks again after Robin is dismissed as their English teacher.

I enjoyed studying *The Merchant of Venice* and in our last year at school, *King Lear*. Thanks to Lear I learnt the meaning of hubris, something I was to encounter many times in later life. I read several of Charles Dickens' novels for the first time, especially *Pickwick Papers*. This is one of the funniest books I have read as it follows the trials and tribulations of the naïve, innocent and bumbling Mr Pickwick.

I have since read all of Dickens' novels, and *Pickwick Papers* several times. I know that Dickens is now no longer read as much as he once was, but he is the creator of some immortal characters such as Oliver Twist, Mr Dick, Uriah Heep, Fagin, Mr Bumble, Wilkins Micawber ('something will always turn up'), Mr Peggotty, Betsey Trotwood, Wackford Squeers and many more.

Lord of the Flies was the subject of a major study in English class. At first, I thought it was a thoroughly boring and silly book until our teacher began unravelling its allegorical importance. It then took on a whole different meaning for me.

Our art teacher was Gaston de Vel who not only taught art but was a highly regarded artist in his own right, with exhibitions of his works at art galleries around New Zealand. Gaston was Belgian and had spent many years in the Belgian Congo before political events there caused him to migrate to New Zealand in 1960. None of this interesting background was shared with his pupils. Art was his passion but teaching it was not his forte. His English was far from fluent and he had difficulty controlling the class. His favourite instruction was 'each to his own', an injunction to us to focus on our own work.

Gaston's control of the class struck disaster one day during an art history lesson. I enjoyed his photographs of *'objets d'art'* from the famous museums of the world but a slide of the Venus de Milo proved the tipping point. The Venus de Milo, in the Louvre, is a marble statue from ancient Greece, the torso of a beautiful woman naked from the hips up and missing her arms. Not used to being exposed to the plump and feminine breasts of a woman, even if only a marble statue, Rhys Mathias, for I am sure it was him, began poking fun at her. The reaction was contagious and the class gradually fell into noisy disorder. Gaston, puce with rage, fled the classroom.

We all wondered where he had gone but in a few minutes we found out. In came Budge, with Gaston trailing behind. Budge, his long black gown flowing, looked mad as hell and black as thunder. Budge gave us all a stern dressing down during which Gaston could be heard complaining plaintively: 'No longer I teach this class'. Budge, put off his stride, turned to Gaston and to our astonishment snapped at him: 'That is something you will have to discuss with ME!' We were threatened with three hours of detention every week, forever.

Our English teacher, Richard Newnham, a kind and generous man, helped to settle ruffled feathers over coming days and I recall that Gaston did teach us again. I for one always enjoyed his art history lessons as there was never any prospect that I would be able to draw or paint anything. I liked it when he spoke to me in French outside the classroom. He died in 2010. His obituary made no mention of his time as a teacher and certainly no mention of his efforts to promote the beauties of the Venus de Milo to a gang of pubescent boys.

Barry Fell was the music teacher and we devoted one period a week to him. As I could not hope ever to learn to play a musical instrument, for me it was an opportunity to develop an appreciation of music. A lifelong passion for classical music began in Mr Fell's classes although I am ashamed to admit that I was 21 before I first heard and was captivated by Mozart's *The Magic Flute*, thanks to Dr Alice Strauss at Auckland University.

AG Turnell taught us algebra. He was quite elderly, a good teacher who made a boring subject interesting. I have to admit to enjoying his lessons. We knew nothing about him and never found out what 'AG' stood for. He had no nickname. I saw him one day walking down Victoria Street in Hamilton, wearing a pair of baggy old trousers that looked like his gardening attire. It was a shock to realise that masters did not dress formally on all occasions.

I was always very poor at maths but I enjoyed science and later, in the fifth form, did chemistry, biology and physics. Our first science teacher was Geoff Dolby, who introduced himself to us in a deep voice with the words 'My name is Dolby', with the emphasis on 'Dolby'. Not 'Mr Dolby' or 'Geoff Dolby', just 'Dolby'. I was struck by this, as of course the masters all called us by our surnames too so it was always 'Hamilton', never 'Peter', but we didn't imagine that Geoff actually wanted us to call him 'Dolby'.

In an early science lesson, he tried to explain the atomic structure of matter, with a neat, two-dimensional, blackboard diagram of atoms, electrons and neutrons whirling around everywhere. 'This is the current theory', Geoff intoned and 'it will be changed'. I was struck by these words. How could he be so sure? And why should we bother to learn something if it was soon going to be redundant? I think what Geoff was trying to get across to us was that science was dynamic and theories were always being added to or modified in the light of new knowledge. As far as I know, his basic blackboard diagram has stood the test of time pretty well.

I could never get to grips with the Periodic Table but the chemistry textbook was so nice and glossy with great illustrations that I wanted to do well in the subject. Our chemistry teacher was a tall lanky man whom we called 'Noddy'. His surname was MacDonald. I remember thinking that if science could find some way of transferring all Noddy's knowledge of chemistry from his brain to mine without my having to exert myself, I should be very satisfied.

An early chemistry experiment to count the number of atoms present in a chemical substance involved Noddy releasing a small dose of some chemical with a pungent odour, while we boys arrayed ourselves around the classroom to determine when we could smell it. Once we had all got a whiff of it, we calculated the number of cubic inches in the classroom space to work out the number of atoms that must have been contained in the chemical if we assumed each cubic inch of the classroom had been penetrated by at least one atom of the chemical. Noddy enjoined that no one should fart during the experiment lest that upset the atom count.

One of Noddy's striking aphorisms was that people used only 10% of their brain capacity, leaving fully 90% unutilised. This was a very astute observation.

A youngish Mr Gibbs was the physics teacher. I never understood his subject, which is why I still can't fathom Einstein, but he at least regarded me with patience and some kindness. He was very helpful when I reached that awful fork in the road in the fifth form, when we had to decide whether to go the 'science' route or the 'arts' route. This was an important decision as it would affect the focus of our future studies.

I could see that all sorts of career options could open to those with a science bent. But I was poor at maths and struggled with science topics. It was clear that science was not about to discover some marvellous mechanism that would allow me to plunder Noddy's chemistry brain with no effort on my part. It was a rather natural choice to go the arts route.

I had no idea where this decision might lead. I was at one stage interested in joining the navy or merchant marine and even went to one careers information session. But I soon realised my motivation was primarily to travel overseas. The navy seemed a cost-effective means of doing so. Recalling my experience of military drills on the summer sports ground, I knew that, unlike my father's brother John, I would not like the discipline that goes with being a soldier on water.

On a later visit to Wellington, I looked at the possibility of a career in meteorology and was warmly received by the weathermen at the Kelburn Weather Station. They gave me a very interesting tour of their meteorological premises. At some point during my high school years, I wondered about a career in the diplomatic corps (or 'core' as I wrote in my diary) but I seemed to have put this notion out of mind.

One day, to our great surprise, Mr Gibbs announced that he would now call us by our first names, not our surnames. He was the only master to do so. We greatly appreciated this. My diary described his action as 'decent'. Mr Gibbs was one of the few teachers who could relate to us on a personal level. I liked my teachers as, unlike Mr Baird at West Street School, they rarely used sarcasm to control their classes.

Woodwork and metalwork classes were pleasant distractions. With no skill whatsoever I made some useful little articles like a small wooden bookcase, a small three-legged table which was never stable, a lamp stand, a metal fishing-rod holder and two ashtrays with animal faces which I still have. The woodwork teacher was Eric Luker, a red-faced man whom we dubbed 'Eric the Red'.

The metalwork teacher was Mr A de Blois, clearly French or Belgian in origin — we never knew his first name. De Blois was a dumpy, taciturn and pugnacious little man who excelled at metalcraft but was indifferent to his less gifted protégés. We named him Dabs.

Dabs was a connoisseur of boxing. One day we were ushered into his dimly lit metalwork shop. But that day there was to be no class. Dabs closed the door behind us furtively and for some reason closed the window curtains too. Then, in deepest secrecy, ignoring us boys who just stood around uselessly, he turned on his transistor radio and tuned into the world heavyweight championship fight between Cassius Clay (later Muhammad Ali) and Sonny Liston, held in May 1965 in Maine.

I had no interest in boxing and never developed one but was impressed by the extraordinary measures Dabs had instigated to feed his boxing addiction. We felt privileged to be in on the act, although in later years I wondered about the need for such secrecy. The fact was that the match was being broadcast, Dabs had a class to run at the same time and he wasn't going to let that get in the way of his passion for pugilism. I guess, though, if Budge had flounced in on some unexpected classroom inspection, the sound of Clay and Liston punching the life out of each other, instead of hammers beating metal, might have been difficult to explain.

In addition to periodic incursions by Budge, our teachers would be subjected to visits by the school inspectors who came to examine their performance in class, a nerve-wracking and unsettling experience. Usually, the inspectors would be former teachers. I recall one particular inspector who came to our French class. He relished the opportunity to improve our pronunciation of French. A rather plump man with a rotund red face, he had us repeating after him the French for 'am I?' or 'suis-je?' I have never forgotten the oleaginous manner in which the words 'suis-je?' flowed off his lips. That was all we practised with him, just these two words.

I stood amongst the crowd again at the Riverina Hotel in Hamilton East in 1967 as a 16-year-old to see Marshal Nguyen Cao Ky, the dynamic Prime Minister of the US-backed South Vietnamese military junta, arrive for a reception. It was a fleeting handshake but I felt I had at least seen something of the Vietnam War. He was in New Zealand to drum up support for the South's war against the communist North. He seemed to have matters well in hand which made me wonder why we needed to do military drill at school. I remember Marshal Ky saying on TV during his visit that his main objective was to give his countrymen 'a few more bowl of a rice each day' which, to an impressionable teenager, seemed a laudable objective, until I learnt a bit more in later years about the origins of the civil war.

After the collapse of the South Vietnamese regime in 1975, Marshal Ky ended up as a refugee in the US, running a liquor store in California, a great fall from the heady heights of power he had known. I wondered if he was able to secure his own 'bowl of a rice each day' now that he was a refugee in a foreign country. In later life he apparently did come to believe the war had all been a great mistake, caused by outside interference, meaning by France and the US. Years later, it was a sobering experience for me to visit the Presidential Palace, now a museum in Ho Chi Minh City (Saigon), to see where Marshal Ky had worked so hard but in vain during the final years of the Vietnam War.

History lessons on Italian unification, the First World War, the rise of Nazism and Communism were set against the current backdrop of the Vietnam War and the Arab-Israeli conflict. My own views on international conflicts such as these were unformed and rather monochrome, supporting the Israelis and, thanks to Marshal Ky, the US intervention in Vietnam. Much later I began to realise that such conflicts are never black and white.

Leaders such as Nasser and Ho Chi Minh were often a nationalist reaction to colonial interventions. While no supporter of Communism, I could see that the Vietnam conflict was more a civil war than a Chinese attempt, according to the prevailing domino theory, to roll out Communism through South East Asia. The problem arose when such leaders then entrenched themselves and became bloody dictators, like Idi Amin in Uganda, Gaddafi in Libya, Saddam Hussein in Iraq, or Mugabe in Zimbabwe and many more, usually making them much worse than the colonial rulers they displaced.

With the Cultural Revolution under way in China, I liked listening to China's English language propaganda broadcasts from Radio Peking. The refrain of any broadcast was always '*A long, long life to Chairman Mao*'. I used to wonder why he needed this to be repeated endlessly. I was fascinated by the sheer mindlessness of the propaganda. I was also angered by apartheid in South Africa in a helpless sort of way, as I had no real understanding of what was actually going on in that country. I liked to listen to Radio Noumea and was pleased when I could understand more and more of what was being said in French.

I had a great appetite for world news and information. It was difficult to form an accurate view about world events with so little hard information available. One diary entry noted my conundrum: 'Sometimes I think about something and try to form a considered view on the subject but then my opinions are shaken when I listen to other people's opinions which seem much better than my own'.

In 1966, two 'foreign' boys started coming to school. This was a new phenomenon: two boys from Thailand who had been sent by their well-to-do parents to study at HBHS. I remember their names because they were so unusual: Yod Boonyatchai and Pradap Pibulsongkram. I didn't really get to know them as they were both in a more senior year. Pradap later graduated in political science from Auckland University. Pibulsongkram is a household name in Thailand as Pradap's relative, Field Marshal Plaek Pibulsongkram, was Prime Minister of Thailand from 1938 to 1957, apart for a time during the dark days of the Second World War when Thailand's leaders sought to steer their country through the shoals of an alliance with Japan to preserve Thai independence.

For over 20 years I gave no further thought to them until one day in 1990, when I was in Bangkok with Alastair Bisley, also an HBHS alumnus, to encourage the Thai government to support a new round of GATT Multilateral Trade Negotiations in Geneva, who should be sitting behind the Trade Director's desk in the Thai Foreign Ministry but Pradap! Our paths crossed again in 2004 when we both were our country's ambassador to Switzerland, he resident in Bern, me in Berlin. We greeted each other like old friends.

One day two boys began taking special classes on their own to study the Maori language, te Reo. This was a new development, too, teaching Maori in schools. Later I wondered why we had not all been offered an opportunity to learn Maori as that would have given us a far better appreciation of our country than hours of military drill. I had to wait another 10 years before an enlightened Director of Personnel in the Ministry of Foreign Affairs acceded to my request that I undertake a six-week full-time Maori language course at Wellington Polytechnic.

I did not much enjoy the weekly gym periods as I was not interested in sport and was not athletic. Mr Gilbert, the gym teacher, bore this with equanimity, if not bemused disdain. He did, however, in my school report, inscribe the comment: 'Weak'. I never understood if this was intended as a gloss on my poor exam result or an observation on my physical prowess. I felt he should have been clearer on this point.

During gym classes, as we clambered up the gym wall bars like nimble monkeys, I got to know a fellow student, David Atkin, who seemed to be as disinterested in the whole exercise as I was. I liked David and was devastated when he fell sick after swimming in a Rotorua hot pool and died of meningitis. I had never heard of this disease before. He was only sixteen. It was a humbling experience and forced me to think about the meaning of life.

On occasion, if one of our masters was absent, Budge's wife, whom we knew only as Mrs Baigent, would hold the fort. Clearly, having received advance intelligence as a result of Gaston's experience of the pitfalls of dealing with our class, Mrs Baigent ruled us with an iron rod that was longer even than her husband's. In her classes, we were as meek as lambs.

One day in our sixth form year, Budge gave our class a very frank and open talk about sex and sex life, to alert us to some of the pitfalls. Budge was a man of many parts and I developed a great respect for him. A diary entry in 1967 says 'he always talks great sense, common and moral and it is a pity people don't heed him'.

I was not a school prefect and I wasn't in the First rugby XV or First cricket XI. Evidently, I showed no leadership potential at school. I was, however, a member of the School Council in my last year. The council was established by Budge to enable us to discuss issues of current moment. I can't recall that we were other than totally ineffectual. I enjoyed the school debating club and first learned to have confidence delivering a speech on a particular topic.

I was though a 'sub-prefect', an odd grouping of volunteers, signifying we were the B team, not the A team of prefects. Our tasks included morning gate duty to check on late arrivals, hand out detentions and do other useful tasks assigned to us. Sometimes we would oversee classes of junior students on rainy days, when lunch was eaten inside or other times when a teacher was unexpectedly absent. I enjoyed meeting the younger students in this way and talking to them about their subjects. But one class, 3M, persisted in being unruly even when I admonished them. I began to appreciate how Gaston might have felt.

My closest friend at high school was Donald Ross. When Donald got his learner's licence before me, he took me for a spin in his parents' old Vauxhall Wyvern car. Barrelling down steep Teddy Street in Hamilton, the road near his house, Donald lost control of the car and I had visions of us rolling over into the Waikato River a short distance away. Fortunately, he regained control. It was an unsettling experience.

Mr Ross, his father, a proud Scot, was the first atheist I met, or at least that I knew to be an atheist. He declaimed assertively to me: 'I don't give a damn how the grass grows up out of the ground'. The implication was that an Almighty had precious little to do with it. I liked Donald's unconventional zest for life and his musical talent which I could not emulate. I was entranced by his playing of the accordion and in later life, he became a noted artist on the accordion in London.

Following his parents, Donald was a convinced and dogmatic atheist, whereas I was still at that juncture keeping an open mind on religion. I could see it had had some benefits in the course of history but I was perplexed by the evident downsides, including bigotry, intolerance and blinkeredness. I looked at theosophy as an alternative to Christianity but that led to an intellectual dead-end. I was particularly incensed by the infallibility asserted by the Pope, refusing to countenance birth control but then offering no answer to the resultant poverty experienced by large poor families.

Another close friend was Victor Agnew. Both Donald and Victor later abandoned New Zealand for the 'old country'. Victor's parents were Irish. School was a competitive environment with the constant pressure on us all to do well and study hard. Victor was often too insistent in wanting to know the results of my test or exam scores. Either he would gloat when he had done better than me or be very upset when he hadn't. But both Donald and Victor were good and generous friends.

About this time too, I began to question New Zealand's constitutional set-up. I could still see advantages in having the British monarch as our Head of State, a view I would radically alter later, but I questioned even then the merits of using the British honours system to recognise public and community service in New Zealand. Fortunately, New Zealand does not have hereditary titles and no House of Lords. There is no indigenous Lordy in New Zealand.

Years later, I saw the magnificent 13th-century Winchester Round Table, a large, colourful table top hanging in Winchester Castle in Hampshire. It has inscribed on it the names of the main knights in King Arthur's Court. There were places at the table for a maximum of 25 people. I wondered what sort of undignified scramble there would be if the scores of knights in Her Majesty's New Zealand realm all tried to find a seat at it.

After seven years in New Zealand, I was beginning to feel I belonged, although the old country still exercised a strong pull since so many family members were still there and it held a fascination because of its history. Having lived in nine different homes and attended six different schools, I was used to upheaval. There would be plenty more of it later.

High school years involved an endless routine of study, homework and preparing for exams. It could be physically very exhausting. We played Fives at school for relaxation, using our bare hands to hit a tennis ball against a three-walled court. For a diversion, I began to study Japanese through evening classes at the Girls' High School, but I was so perplexed by the Kanji and Hiragana script that I gave it up after six months.

Despite Mr Gilbert's observation, I was awarded the class prize three years running. Then in my fourth year, the class prizes dried up as subjects became much more difficult and complex. I did though receive the Alliance Française prize as well as one from the Goethe Institute for French and German in my last year.

My English teacher in my last year was Don Duff. We enjoyed a mutual dislike, perhaps because Don had once dated a friend of my parents so I knew more of his personal life than he had wished. He did say at one point that all parents should chuck their kids out of the home when they reach the age of eighteen. This was a very wise observation although, perhaps subconsciously, he had wanted to chuck me out of his class.

On our last day, dear old Doc Ales pretended to cane us all and kick us up the backside. He shook our hand and wished us all luck. For the first and only time, he called me Peter.

As a general rule, the masters were strict and focused closely on their subject curriculum. They were good teachers but gave away very little about themselves so we did not, in most cases, get to know them as individuals.

The curriculum was rigid — only the subjects decreed by the Department of Education. In the last year, we were permitted to undertake a liberal studies course but we studied little about civics, the structure of our government, how to be a citizen with rights and responsibilities, how to cast a vote, the origins of the Vietnam War or New Zealand's own history. Budge did accede to a request in our senior year for a course on comparative religion so that we could understand more of the basic tenets of Christianity, Judaism, Islam and Buddhism. They were thoroughly enjoyable discussions with outside experts. We could never get enough of the wider dimensions of life beyond the narrow confines of our core subjects.

One hundred and eighty years after the signing of the Treaty of Waitangi, it is good to see that New Zealand's education authorities have realised that it might be worthwhile teaching school children something of the history of their own country. Some of the prime movers for this were students from my mother's old school, Otorohanga College, who wanted to know more about the history of the Waikato.

We forget most of what we learn at high school but that is not important: what school should foster in us, as HBHS did, is a lifelong passion for learning, for being inquisitive and questioning, for not accepting anything at face value and an ability to set out on life's great trek with determination and enthusiasm, no matter what, and with a sense of humour.

Our Family Life

Dad's friends during the early years in New Zealand were his work colleagues, or men like himself who had served in the British Army. He joined the New Zealand Association of former British Guardsmen and was presented to the Queen on one of her visits to New Zealand.

When TV arrived in our own home, it became a huge time-waster, as we eagerly watched the latest programmes like *Rawhide* featuring a young Clint Eastwood, or *The Man from U.N.C.L.E.* or Dad's favourite, *Dad's Army*. It is hard to believe that we would waste so much time watching whimsy like *Thunderbirds* or Eddie Albert and Eva Gabor's *Green Acres* on a warm Sunday afternoon, when we could have been doing something more sensible outside the house.

We did listen a lot to the radio. On Thursday evenings, we religiously followed the long-running British radio soap programme *The Archers*, depicting life in rural England, which is no doubt why we liked it. One character was a crusty old farmer called Walter Gabriel, who spoke with a pronounced country accent. His solution to any problem was that 'the answer lies in the soil', as good an answer as any, I guess. Mum treated herself to a little record player and would play The Seekers, or Tchaikovsky's *1812 Overture* when she came home from a hard day at school.

The year 1966 was when the Hamilton ice field started to thaw. Dad's youngest brother, Peter, my leader into temptation at Speccott Barton, and his wife Mary, made a point of looking my parents up when they came on a trip to New Zealand after working for several months in Australia. Not sure what sort of welcome he would receive, Peter wrote to them at Old Farm Road. He knew our address because I was still writing to my grandmother, Mimi, who every year for my birthday sent me a very welcome crisp British £1 note. When Peter and Mary showed up at Old Farm Road with their backpacks, they were invited into the sitting room, where for several minutes everyone sat stiffly, not knowing what to say.

I broke the ice, uttering in embarrassment an expletive critical of my father's silence and promptly left the room. I am amazed to this day that he did not admonish me. Thereafter long conversations were held between my father and his brother to come to terms with the past. These had a good cathartic effect on both sides. Dad was delighted to find his youngest brother again and forged a close and lasting relationship. We were grateful that Peter had made the first move, which enabled my father to meet up with his other siblings and eventually with his parents. The bitterness of the Speccott years did not evaporate, but at least they were now in the past and everyone could move on.

Despite the manner in which she had been treated by her mother-in-law at Speccott Barton, my mother never discouraged me from staying in contact with my grandmother, an indication of her generous and forgiving nature. Having grown up in a warm and loving family environment at Little Water, she could only regret that my father had not experienced the same warmth and love in his own childhood. I wondered too why my mother did not bear a grudge against young Peter for his very hurtful remark to her at the doorstep of our cottage at Speccott Barton. As he was only 11 at the time, perhaps she accepted that that, for him, would have been his own 'intercourse' moment.

CHAPTER 8

APPLYING FOR VOLUNTEER
SERVICE ABROAD

I AM NOT SURE HOW THE IDEA OF BECOMING A VOLUNTEER
teacher with Volunteer Service Abroad first arose. During my last
year at high school the notion of not going straight to university but
undertaking what would now be called a 'gap year' gained in
attraction. In part it was a reflection of an innate wish to travel
overseas, like my naïve initial fascination with a possible career in the
navy or merchant marine. I obtained the application forms for VSA
from Mr Baigent's office. My mother helped me to fill them in and
encouraged me to persevere in my application. I am forever grateful
that she did so. Budge kindly provided a testimonial for VSA to go
with it but I never knew what it said.

A preliminary interview on my suitability as a school leaver
volunteer was held at Waikato University. I appeared before a panel
of two or three examiners tasked to conduct the interviews for VSA.
VSA is akin to VSO in Australia and the UK, or the Peace Corps in
the US. In the late 1960s, New Zealand VSA did recruit volunteers
straight from high school for the South Pacific and South East Asia
to fill a severe teaching shortage, on the basis that even untrained
volunteers were a better option than leaving classes in many cases
with no teacher at all. As teaching standards developed, the school
leaver programme was phased out and only volunteers fully trained

in their chosen field were sent overseas. I was fortunate that the school leaver programme was still operating when I developed my first burst of wanderlust.

There were two of us from Hamilton Boys' High School who applied for VSA that year. I knew the other boy in passing as he was a member of the First XV rugby team. The interview panel quizzed me about my life, my personality, my school subjects, my interests and hobbies. I tried to answer the questions carefully but opened a trap for myself when I said history was my favourite subject. At which point one of them asked encouragingly what I thought of Arnold Toynbee's work.

I had to admit that I had never heard of him. Clearly, he must be an historian of some note or she would not have asked the question. I rectified this awful lacuna many years later by reading some of his works. I felt sure my ignorance would be held against me and I wondered why Fordy had never mentioned Toynbee in our history classes. Coupled with the fact that I was not a member of any of the school's sports teams, I felt sure my chances of a trip overseas with VSA had just evaporated.

A while later, a letter arrived in the mail to say that I had made the first cut of the VSA selection process and was now required to undertake a further interview and assessment, along with my colleague from the First XV. This time the interview process would last nearly a full week during the August school holidays and be held in the capital, Wellington. The August holidays duly came and I prepared to travel there. I had never been to Wellington before. More to the point, I was to travel by an old National Airways DC3 from Hamilton Airport. This was my first ever flight. I was seventeen. It was very exciting.

The inter-island ferry *Wahine* had sunk during a storm in the entrance to Wellington harbour a few months previously, on 10 April 1968, with the tragic loss of over 50 lives. My first memory of that visit to Wellington was seeing the exposed hull of the sunken vessel lying in the harbour entrance.

The VSA interview process was conducted at Weir House, one of the halls of residence for students at the Victoria University of Wellington. There were perhaps 80 of us. It consisted of a series of psychological and aptitude assessments to determine our ability and suitability to handle the challenges of working as a volunteer in a South Pacific or South East Asian country. I don't remember, at this distance, much about that week.

One embarrassing moment was when each of us was required to give a solo presentation, a speech or some item of our own choosing, to all the assembled others at a concert evening. This was to test our ability to handle ourselves in a public context. I, for the life of me, could not decide what to do that was in any way original so in desperation I sang '*O Tannenbaum, O Tannenbaum*', that lovely German Christmas song. I quite surprised myself and am happy to say it was not a total disaster.

As a break in proceedings one afternoon, we were taken to a gully near the university, overgrown with weeds and dead trees and were asked to do the university a favour by helping to clean it up. We set to with enthusiasm, cutting weeds, hacking bushes, carting timber and generally giving the place a good tidy-up. I wondered at the time who in VSA had thought such activity would constitute a nice break for us. I could think of better ways of relaxing.

Years later, I realised that clearing up the gully was not the point of the exercise at all. The real point was to examine how, as individuals, we handled a common task. We had been closely observed by the VSA selectors. There were those of us who put their heart and soul into it and completely ignored their colleagues in their eagerness to complete the chore and have done with it. And there were those who worked collaboratively as part of a team effort and made the task more enjoyable, even fun, even if it took slightly longer. There is no doubting what VSA was looking for in a volunteer.

One major international event happened while we were at Weir House: news came from Prague that the Soviet Union and the Warsaw Pact countries had invaded Czechoslovakia and had put down the Prague Spring of Alexander Dubček. I liked what I had read about Dubček and thought the invasion was a terrible blunder by the Russians who had no business overturning the wishes of the Czechoslovak people. Eating my breakfast as I read this terrible news that August 1968, I had no inkling that in 2003 I would be New Zealand's Ambassador to Czechoslovakia, which by then had not only thrown off its communist and Russian fetters, but had also split into two separate countries, the Czech and Slovak Republics.

Some weeks after my trip to Wellington I received an instruction to visit Budge in his office. I had never been invited to his office before. Usually those who had the privilege of entering it, exited with a painful posterior as a reminder of the encounter. I could not think of any recent action on my part which merited his personal attention so I was unsure why I had been asked to see him. The last time I had been in a headmaster's office was my perplexing and baffling 'intercourse' interview with Mr Abbott at Kio Kio Primary School, six years earlier.

Imagine my surprise, then, when Budge told me that I had been accepted as a VSA volunteer. My elation at this piece of good news was matched only by Budge's evident surprise, not that I had passed the selection process, but that my colleague from the First XV had not. Rather than congratulating me, Budge offered some words of apparent bafflement of his own at this unexpected turn of events.

He did however mention my selection for VSA in a subsequent assembly. I received a clap and many of my friends and colleagues congratulated me. I knew they would be a year ahead of me at university after I returned from VSA but I was not too worried by that.

My last six months at high school were focused on preparation for the end-of-year university scholarship exams. I studied hard for them although I was never satisfied with the effort which I put in. Our kind neighbour, Elizabeth Toxopeus, kept me supplied with cups of coffee and lunches during study days at home.

I was disappointed with my overall exam results as I failed to win a scholarship. Instead, I received the lesser award of an 'A bursary', which would still help towards meeting my costs when I did eventually enrol at university. I applied for and was granted a teaching studentship, with the aim of becoming a teacher. My disappointment was tempered by the knowledge that I would soon be heading off on a year's assignment as one of 26 school leaver teachers in the Kingdom of Tonga for 1969.

Before we left for Tonga, we were required to spend another week in Wellington preparing for the assignment and learning about the language and culture of the country we would be living in. It was summer, I had finished high school and I enjoyed every minute of the assignment preparation. Two Catholic nuns who had worked in Tonga as missionaries taught us our first words of the Tongan language including: *'Malo e lelei'* (Hello), *'Oku ke fefe hake?'* (How are you?), *'Oku ke 'alu ki fe?'* (Where are you going?) and much more. I knew little Maori so this was my first exposure to a Polynesian language. It sounded so bright and interesting.

On the last day, the volunteers were invited to Parliament for a special afternoon tea with the Prime Minister, Keith Holyoake. A large man, dressed in the conventional pinstripe suit, he stood at the door shaking our hand as each of us filed past. I don't remember much of his speech to us except his hallmark plummy accent and his words of introduction. 'Boys and girls,' he said, for that is how he addressed us, 'think of me as your father'. These were endearing words and I am sure they fitted well with his notion of himself as the father of the nation.

When Keith died in 1983, I was working in the Prime Minister's Department in the Beehive and would be instrumental in assisting his wife, Lady Norma Holyoake, to attend the Service of Remembrance for him at St George's Chapel in Windsor, as Keith, like General Monck, had been a Knight of the Garter.

Before leaving for Tonga, I drove to Fordy's house to return some books and to say goodbye to him. By then I had obtained my driving licence, after two attempts. Like Ringo Roche and Doc Ales, Fordy had been an important part of my school years. I never forgot them. That evening, to my great surprise, Victor had organised a farewell party, with a large bonfire in a paddock. Donald serenaded everyone on his accordion, while we sang along, ate sausages and chops cooked on the bonfire and capped it off with beer and champagne. At the end they sang '*For He's a Jolly Good Fellow*' and '*Auld Lang Syne*'. I certainly didn't feel like a jolly good fellow, as I was only too well aware of the magnitude of the task that lay before me. But as I noted in my diary that evening, friends are the best thing in the world!

There were hurried preparations for my departure, packing up my gear, buying some clothes for a tropical climate, medical injections (including cholera and a big hepatitis jab in the bum), organising some money to take with me and freighting my bicycle to Tonga so I would have something to get around the island on. I needed some new specs too, as since the fifth form I had had to wear glasses for short-sightedness, something I blame on Granny Dyer.

I met several other volunteers bound for Tonga at Auckland Airport and said goodbye to my parents, and my brother Stuart. My first international flight was from Auckland to Nadi in Fiji, as in those days there were no direct flights to Tonga.

We spent a sleepless night at the Tanoa Hotel in Nadi, before catching our flight very early next morning to Nausori near Suva and then our connecting flight on to Tonga. I was struck by the awful humidity, by the scent of the frangipani, the brown grass, the huge frogs and the insects and bugs as they sizzled and burned loudly as they flew into the hot outdoor lights. For a moment, I wondered if I was going to be able to live is such a climate for a whole year and thought that perhaps I had made a terrible mistake. But a cool midnight swim in the hotel pool, floating on my back looking at the myriad bright stars in the sky, immediately refreshed me.

From Nausori, we flew over deep blue lagoons and small islands sparkling in the sea. Any fears I might have had soon disappeared once we arrived at Fuaʻamotu Airport on the main Tongan island of Tongatapu. The plane bounced and bumped onto the grass landing strip — having aborted the first landing. A throng of Tongans stood around the airport building, as a plane landing was always an event worth watching. An over-eager customs officer proceeded to make me open my bulging suitcase, looking for narcotics apparently, but was told by a more senior officer that we were 'VSA', so he desisted. We had arrived.

CHAPTER 9

VSA IN TONGA — PART ONE
(1969)

I<small>N</small> <small>MY LAST TWO YEARS AT HIGH SCHOOL AND DURING MY</small> VSA year in Tonga, I kept a diary of my daily life, the only time I have done so. I re-read the diary for the first time in nearly 50 years to write these two chapters. That year was such an important part of my life and my first year away from home. I am sure I gained far more in terms of personal development than I was able to contribute.

I was assigned to teach English and Geography at Tupou College (in Tongan, the 'Kolisi ko Tupou'), which was a weekday boarding school for about 600 boys run by the Free Wesleyan Church. The college had been founded in 1866 by a Methodist missionary, the Reverend James Moulton, and claimed to be the oldest secondary school in the Pacific Islands. It was located in the bush on a large estate known as Toloa, not far from the airport and about twelve kilometres by road from the capital, Nuku'alofa.

Land in Tonga is owned by the king and administered on his behalf by a small group of nobles who form the societal upper class. Individual Tongans may be given a grant of land for family use, but with a growing population, there was insufficient land available to meet demand. Methodism is the state religion and was closely connected to Tonga's monarch, King Taufa'ahau Tupou IV, the son of the famous Queen Salote. Tupou College, as a Methodist church school, was therefore part of the Tongan establishment. Miss Elliott's description of Methodists as 'non-Conformists' did not apply in Tonga.

I was joined by another volunteer, John Dunckley, from Dunedin, who would focus on science subjects. John and I would spend the next year working and living together, sharing a small two-room wooden cabin especially renovated for our arrival, located close to the school classrooms.

I was dead tired and thirsty after the early-morning start in Fiji. We were met at the airport by the Reverend Jeff Cummins, principal of Tupou High School, the senior sister school to Tupou College, located in Nuku'alofa. We were taken to meet the principal of Tupou College, the Reverend Clive Skewes, and his wife Margaret, who were on assignment to the Free Wesleyan Church in Tonga from Australia.

The Skewes lived in a large, colonial-style, wooden house on a hillock overlooking the college grounds. Here we spent our first few days in Tonga while renovation of our own accommodation was completed. They made us very welcome and do not seem to have begrudged the intrusion of two teenage boys from New Zealand. Clive, a hard-working, serious and deeply religious man, with a mischievous sense of humour which he did not often deploy, told us what classes we would be expected to teach when school resumed after the Christmas holiday.

Clive had three hyperactive dogs, Coffee, Domino and Ginger. As in much of Polynesia, packs of dogs roaming free are sometimes a curse, especially at night, but at least Clive's were well fed and were not mangy.

The first drink Margaret served us was iced passionfruit. I had never tasted quite such a delicious beverage before. Breakfasts of pawpaw or 'lesi', with a touch of lemon juice, were divine, as were the large ripe mangoes.

John and I were the first school leaver volunteers to be assigned to Tupou College. No doubt VSA and the college would both have been wondering just how useful it would prove to be to have us there. There were two adult VSAs already at the college, Eric and Pat Calvert. Eric had retired as a farmer in New Zealand and was tasked with developing the Church's agricultural programmes for young Tongans. Pat taught English at the college.

Hard-working, no-nonsense, with a very New Zealand 'can do' mentality — but often frustrated at his inability to get things done the way he wanted — Eric was immediately likeable, despite his occasional pessimism. He reminded me of that kindly Jed Clampett in the then popular TV series, *The Beverly Hillbillies*. John and I were fortunate that Pat was able to mentor us as we settled into our roles and began taking classes. Pat and Eric left mid-year and were replaced by Clive and Cath Kenyon from Katikati.

While we were at Toloa, several Peace Corps joined us including Steve Gray, the son of a church minister, in Utah I think, and Sandy and Judy MacIntosh from New York. The Peace Corps volunteers had spent much longer in preparing for their assignments so spoke much better Tongan than we did, to our embarrassment.

Early on we met Siupeli Taliai, the head tutor (and later principal of the college). Siupeli was the scion of a prominent Tongan military family and had married an Australian, Helen. I quickly came to like him despite his rather austere and firm manner, especially with the students. He was deeply religious and as I came to realise, his political convictions were decidedly anti-establishment. Siupeli took John and me on a tour of the large estate, Toloa, which had many hectares of bananas, coconuts, manioc, taro, yam, kumara, watermelons, cattle and pigs and areas laid out for farm experiments.

I familiarised myself with the school layout. The library had thousands of books sitting in useless piles, donations to the school from overseas which had never been catalogued. Siupeli and his wife gave John and me a lovely feast of welcome which enabled us to meet the other staff. Manisela Tonga, one of the tutors, was amazed to find out I was only seventeen.

John (far right) and I with Reverend Siupeli Taliai and his wife Helen

In our first week, we stayed at the Official Residence of the Reverend and Mrs Harris in Nuku'alofa, while we undertook a VSA orientation course for all the school leaver volunteers assigned to Tonga that year. The Reverend George Harris was the king's personal chaplain and head of the Free Wesleyan Church. If I came late to a meal, I was expected to say my own grace before eating. They were very welcoming although I felt somewhat overawed by living in their home.

There was no mains electricity at the college so the electricity supply depended on oil-fired generators which were expensive to run. Our little cottage ('fale' in Tongan) had an outhouse kitchen ('peito'), toilet and shower room. There was no hot water but as the temperature was always around 28 degrees Celsius outside, cold showers were much to be preferred and were lukewarm in any case. The house was divided into a shared bedroom, with two steel-sprung mattress beds, and a lounge with a table and two wooden chairs. Helen Taliai put up some nice curtains and mats in our fale so it was very comfortable.

The kitchen had not yet been painted but several tutors, including Malakai Pomana and George Pahulu, came by to help out with the painting. The problem was that hundreds of insects would get stuck to the paint before it dried. Our home was spartan perhaps, but it was my first home away from home. There was no mosquito netting over the windows so at night we were bitten alive. One evening, I killed 20 mosquitoes. John had thoughtfully brought several cans of Pea Beu insect repellant from New Zealand, something which had not occurred to me. These were liberally deployed but they quickly ran out. I seemed to develop an immunity to mosquitoes and after a while they didn't really bother me.

Next to our fale was the college's little store which sold basic necessities — bread, butter, Hellaby's canned beef, toothpaste, kerosene for cooking and lighting, toilet paper and ship's cabin biscuits. These biscuits were so hard you could break your teeth on them but they were always a good snack when you were hungry. Often supplies, like flour or toilet paper, would run out and we would need to wait until the next monthly shipment from New Zealand. The store was run by a portly and jocular teacher, Siua Helu, whose permanent broad smile revealed several missing teeth. His mischievous and conspiratorial laughter was infectious. Our neighbour on the other side was Semisi Siu, the school's art teacher and his wife, Seini (Jane). They were always most kind and generous to us. They had two delightful little girls, Ma'ata and 'Ana, aged about five or six. The girls would often visit us to play last card ('pele faka'osi'), sitting alone for hours on the cool flax mats of our cabin.

Clive said we would be assigned one or two college students to help us around our little cottage, to keep it tidy and do a bit of cooking for us. There was always keen competition from the schoolboys to be house boys in the homes of the teaching staff, not least because the food they received was far better than the mediocre fare served up in the school's communal dining hall.

Clive had a house help, Viliame, one of the college students, who was very friendly to us when we first arrived. He proposed that he transfer to our house to assist us with household chores. I thought this was a very generous suggestion. Clive however vetoed the idea and I wondered why. Later I learnt that Viliame was a fakaleiti, or 'lady-boy', a common phenomenon in Polynesia of a boy or man who lives as a woman.

Although Viliame was readily accepted at an all-boys' school, Clive evidently felt that John and I, as naïve teenagers from New Zealand, should be assigned other boys to assist us. We had several students to help us during the course of the year, especially Tevita (David) Tupou, Naʻasoni Tuiʻileʻila and Tevita Vaʻivaka. The latter Tevita became a good friend into adulthood and I got to know his family. I was very sorry to learn, many years later, that he died at the relatively early age of fifty-eight.

Each school day I taught English to four or five classes of 30 to 40 boys whose ages ranged from 12 to twenty-two. Some were much older than me. Sometimes I was asked to tackle a geography lesson. The classrooms were big and airy but sparsely furnished. At the start of the year some lacked desks so the boys sat on the hard, rough wooden floor. One classroom I had was divided into two with no partition so there was always another noisy class being conducted right next to mine.

I began to enjoy the daily lessons and interacting with my students, most of whom were very eager to learn. The college charged a fee for attendance. It was a huge financial burden on parents and community to raise the necessary school levies. I was soon asked to help out with English lessons at the nearby primary school. Often these lessons were held in our little fale, with the boys and girls sitting on mats on the floor. They were always bright-eyed and very attentive.

The school bells sounded at 5.45am. I say bells but they were actually hollow metal cylinders struck with metal bars which resounded for miles around the estate. There was absolutely no way any boy could innocently claim he hadn't heard the bell. After breakfast, the boys would march to the church for morning service, or 'lotu', at 7.15am. This was compulsory. I often found it difficult to get up in time and have my own breakfast beforehand, until Clive made it clear that we should make an effort to take part. But even then, I didn't always make it. I used to enjoy the harmonious singing and tried to improve my Tongan by deciphering the words of the sermon.

The boys attended class from 9am until about 1pm. After a meagre lunch they spent the afternoon working in the large gardens on the estate where they grew most of the food used in the school kitchens. They all had large machetes for gardening and bush clearing which made them look like a band of armed marauders. After working in the gardens, the students would have an evening meal and then do study in their dormitories by the light of a very weak lamp or kerosene lantern. The school provided a bland diet, mainly carbohydrates supplemented on occasion with mutton flaps, called 'sipi', or Hellaby's tinned corned beef imported from New Zealand. Despite the vast ocean that surrounded the island, fish was rarely on the menu.

There was never any discipline problem in the class. The main issue was fatigue from the poor diet and the vigorous physical regime of gardening. School sports were uniformly rugby or athletics and every inter-school event created a great sensation. The school had an excellent brass band, known throughout Tonga, led by Tevita Kamitoni. It would rise to every important occasion in the school calendar and would lead the whole school as it marched in uniform and formation.

I had to learn quickly how to prepare lessons and how to hold the interest of my classes. I soon learnt that things went best if I was well prepared, but I did not always succeed. My form class was 7B — they were 12 or 13 years old. I liked them a lot but 12C was the most attentive and engaged. They were boys my own age or even older. They loved having class debates on such topics as whether one should get married or whether Tonga should be influenced by other cultures. Their English was not always correct but their enthusiasm was first rate.

I sometimes became frustrated if a class had not done its homework, but laziness was not always the reason. The boys could easily be distracted by other tasks. One class, 9C, received a detention from me but the detention had to be cancelled because the allocated time was required to be spent looking for rhinoceros beetles on the estate — a major threat to the coconut trees and a major pest, like rats. One time Siupeli interrupted my class to say the boys were required to prepare for a hurricane then threatening Tonga. On another occasion, classes were cancelled so the boys could be given their TB injections.

On Friday afternoons, a convoy of menacing-looking army trucks would suddenly appear at the college. In other countries, their arrival might herald a coup d'état. The trucks took the boys back to their home villages for the weekend, where they would help their families, including by doing further gardening. Only a few remained at the college, those from other islands who did not have family on the mainland they could stay with.

On Sunday afternoons they would all return to school in the same army trucks, for an evening assembly and church service. The school uniform was a white cotton shirt and black vala, a lightweight Tongan skirt akin to a kilt. On Sundays for church, the boys wore a blue tie and a smart white vala. Around the waist they wore a ta'ovala, a waistband of plaited flax, tied with brown coconut fibre, or sennit, which is the Tongan equivalent of being properly dressed.

The Sunday service was held in the huge wooden and thatch church, cool and dry in the evening twilight. The outside humidity was sometimes stifling, especially just before a thunderstorm. Being inside the church during a torrential downpour was magical. No sound could be heard except the heavy pounding of the rain on the thatch roof. Even the words of the preacher, the faifekau, would be drowned out. This magnificent thatch church caught fire some years later and was destroyed, to be replaced by a more permanent, but far less imposing, concrete building.

Sermons were by definition long, on the basis that if you preached a short sermon you were not really being serious about religion. They were for me tedious. Once he got into his pulpit, however, there is no doubting the preacher's passion. The audience would be mesmerised by his fluency and poetry. I imagined this might have been exactly how Samuel Marsden had preached to the crowd at Oihi Bay in the Bay of Islands in 1814, the first sermon delivered in New Zealand, the Maori crowd, like me, not understanding a word of his message, despite Ruatara's interpretation, but being mightily impressed by the delivery.

A faifekau, as a man of God, enjoyed high standing in the community and lived well. It was the ambition of many a young boy to become a preacher. The Mormon church was at that point making inroads into Tonga and the main churches saw this as a threat to their primacy. The greater economic benefits offered by the Mormon church proved irresistible, providing the opportunity for many Tongans to live and work in the US. Even Tevita Va'ivaka, our student house help, would eventually go to the US this way. Tongan villages were often divided between the Catholics and the Wesleyans and frequently the bright, white, gleaming Mormon churches would appear in their midst. The Anglicans had always been unenthusiastic missionaries. Their influence in Tonga was limited.

Our colleagues on the teaching staff were all men ranging in age and experience. Lea'aepeni Ma'amaloa — whose name meant 'writing of the pen' in English — was the music teacher and my Toloa equivalent of Fordy. He had a shiny bald pate and was often the object of light-hearted teasing. It is important to bear in mind that, unlike my experience of Mr Baird in England, Tongans would never openly laugh *at* anyone, only *with* them.

We got to know many of the tutors well and they became firm friends, including Lopini Felisi and Mohenoa Puloka, both of whom in later life would go on to become school principals and have senior roles in Tongan public life. Lopini was Tongan for Robin and as he had a flamboyant character and liked to joke, his nickname was Robin Hood. Tevita Unga was in charge of the poultry farm attached to the school. He worked in collaboration with Eric Calvert and was affectionately known as 'chicken-man'. I was invited to his wedding to his blushing bride, held in the college church. Faiva Uhila was in charge of farm implements and equipment.

Tevita Talakai was another tutor who became a good friend. He invited us to his family fale for a meal prepared by his beautiful young wife. One day Tevita asked to borrow the flashlight torch that I had brought from New Zealand. It was very useful to me getting around the unlit college at night and I was miffed that he failed to return it. It was some time before I understood that in Tongan culture there was no obligation on him to do so.

After the hustle and bustle of a school week, the departure of the boys for the brief weekend meant an unusual calm descended over the college. John and I would often be invited to a Tongan celebration, marriage ceremony or dance event. A traditional Tongan feast would be set out for the guests on a long platter of banana leaves laid on wonderful woven Tongan mats. Guests would sit in long rows eating either side of the platter, or 'pola' in Tongan. These feasts were sumptuous, with suckling pigs, roast chicken, baked yams, sweet potatoes, bananas, watermelon, fish and 'lu' — a delicacy of fish, mutton or beef cooked in coconut oil and wrapped in young banana leaves.

The food was cooked in the traditional 'umu', or earth oven and to me tasted delicious, far less smoky than the Maori equivalent, the hangi. If, on occasion, I was the chief guest at a family meal, I would be expected to stand up at the conclusion and deliver an impromptu speech of thanks to the host. From this developed an ease with public speaking.

I also took part in my first kava circle, or 'fai kava', the traditional Tongan kava ceremony. I was asked what I thought of kava. I said I thought it tasted like potato peelings, whereupon someone asked how I knew what potato peelings tasted like. I grew to enjoy kava, and the informal drinking ceremonies would often last late into the night. Many years later I would find myself advocating in Brussels and Berlin for the lifting of import restrictions on exports of Pacific Islands' kava to the markets of the European Union.

One morning Clive came to our cabin and said 'A piece of junk has just arrived'. My old school bicycle from home had made it to Tonga. John and I could choose how we spent the weekend. We both had bicycles so we would often cycle the 10 or 12 kilometres into Nuku'alofa to catch up with other VSAs working in the capital. Three VSAs, Mairi McPhee from Maraekakaho, Dorothy Williams from Kaitaia and Pat Moir from Auckland, shared a house. Mairi and Dorothy were trained teachers. Pat was a school leaver like John and me. They lived near two Australian volunteers, Jeff Hocking and Glen Carruthers, who kindly let John and me sleep Saturday nights on their living room floor, with only a pillow and no bedding. I have never slept so well in my life.

Often Clive or Margaret, or sometimes Eric, would drive us into Nuku'alofa to do our weekly shopping or to catch up with the other VSAs. The drive to Nuku'alofa was an obstacle course in itself, with Clive weaving all over the road, using his car horn at every opportunity to try to avoid the people wandering about, the many horses and carts, the buses and lorries and pigs. Clive's car, a battered old Holden, served him well but was prone to breakdowns and punctures. On one trip we had two punctures so of course, as there was no second spare, the outing was ruined.

The main street of Nuku'alofa had a tumble-down movie theatre, the 'HauHau 'o Taufa'ahau'. In it we could while away a pleasant hour or two. Nuku'alofa was populated by interesting characters. One, an old lady named Mele Mata'ele, was rumoured to be high-born and was accorded great respect as she shuffled about the streets, bare feet and in her threadbare black clothes. Whenever she caught sight of me, she would amble over and firmly demand 'Omai seniti!', which means 'Give me some money!' Given her great size and overbearing manner, I usually gave her sixpence but I disliked her peremptory tone. To my great shame, on one occasion when I spied Mele before she saw me, I went up to her and said 'Omai seniti, Mele!' She was not best pleased.

Clive and Margaret would take John and me to town on a Sunday evening to attend the English language church service in the king's chapel, a magnificent white-washed wooden building situated on the seashore next to the royal palace. It was delightfully cool inside. This was the building in which Tongan coronations had traditionally been held. The service, a good opportunity to catch up with other volunteers and friends, would be conducted by the Reverend George Harris or Reverend Jeff Cummins, the principal of Tupou High School, or by Clive.

The Reverend Harris was fluent in Tongan. He would frequently conduct the large public service on Sunday mornings in the main Centenary church. The king, who often attended, would sit at the front of the church, on a raised dais well above the rest of the congregation. When our own Sunday evening service concluded, we would come out into the warm tropical night air and be confronted by the glistening moonlit sea in front of us. It was a magical beauty. As the service ended, we would often hear the sound of a whirring Bell & Howell movie projector starting up on the porch of the king's palace next door and we would know that His Majesty was about to watch a new movie. Sadly, this magnificent wooden chapel also burnt down some years later.

On occasion, the Reverend and Mrs Harris would invite some of the VSA volunteers working for the Wesleyan Church to join them for afternoon tea in their lovely old red-roofed colonial Residence. As I sat nervously at a long dining table, Mrs Harris — with some formality — rang a little bell as a signal that afternoon tea was to be served. In came the Tongan staff to serve tea and cake. I had never been waited on in such fashion before. This little bell reminded me of Granny's bell on the stairs at Little Water Farm, when she would summon Miss Hood for her meal. I felt uncomfortable. While in my later career I have of necessity attended many formal state occasions, and been waited upon at meals, I have never rung a bell to summon anyone.

Sometimes when we were in Nuku'alofa, a cruise ship would be visiting. We would relish the fine Tongan dancing (lakalaka) put on for the visitors. A sumptuous meal would be laid out for them on the mala'e not far from the main Centenary Church. The P&O cruise ships, *Himalaya* or *Canberra*, similar to the *Orcades*, came on visits, disgorging their passengers who would invade the town to explore and buy local artefacts. Nuku'alofa was a town abuzz on cruise ship days.

On one occasion, when the ship *Kuala Lumpur* visited, Glen Carruthers and I wandered around admiring the sumptuous feast laid out for the tourists. Suddenly we were hastily dragged off by one lady who insisted we sit and eat at her pola. She thought we were tourists. While the real tourists, afraid to eat the food, picked at this and that, Glen and I tucked in royally. Neither of us felt we were fraudulent guests.

I made my first trip off the mainland, Tongatapu, in early April at Easter, when Lopini's brother, Taumoeha'apai Felisi, took John and me to meet his family on 'Eua, a large island to the east of Tongatapu, usually two hours away by boat. Unlike Tongatapu, which is flat and has no rivers, 'Eua is hilly and has streams of flowing water and hilltops.

Clive gave us a lift to town. An incident on the way gave everyone a fright. Clive was overtaking four Japanese tourists who were cruising along nicely in a three-wheeled taxi, when four pigs suddenly ran across the road in front of the car. Clive slammed on his brakes and stalled the car in the middle of the road. The three-wheeler just missed our car by inches, by a violent swerve to the right and was nearly upended. This gave the tourists and us a huge fright. Screams everywhere!

The following is based on my diary.

Taumoeha'apai and several of his friends, schoolboys at Tupou College, woke us up at 5am and told us to pack up. It was moonlight and people were still asleep — even the early-rising Tongans.

We sat at the wharf waiting for the departure of our boat to 'Eua at 7am. We came early to assure ourselves of a passage. By 7am, scores of people had arrived and were duly packed aboard the small 40-footer taking us across the open waters to the island. We got a good view of Tongatapu from the boat, but the sea was so rough — crossing the Waitemata in Auckland was nothing in comparison. The boat rolled, slithered, tossed, twisted, turned in mountainous waves. All the Tongans were sick. There was a thunderstorm and it poured with rain. The boat had only 10 square feet of canvas cover for 60 people so we all got soaked to the skin.

We arrived three hours later at about 10am. The captain worked his little boat skilfully through the reef into the small harbour. We met Eric Calvert at the wharf but only to say hello. Eric was supervising an agricultural project on the island. Taumoeha'apai took us and another boy, Mafua, who became a good friend, to the home of his relative, Siale Tafakula. He was chief of Ohonua, the main village on 'Eua. Tafakula, we were told, means 'Red Surgeon'. The chief was very pleased to have us stay and let us sleep in his own room and that of his sons while he slept on the floor. The chief, his wife and sons could speak no English so we spoke to them through our friends, Taumoeha'apai and Mafua. Our meals were presented to us in the main room while the family ate out the back. For three days, we lived on good Tongan food. After each meal, John and I thanked the old chief for his hospitality.

On the first night, we had a welcoming kava ceremony and from somewhere a beautiful girl came to prepare the kava, seated on a mat behind a large, circular kava bowl. The chief sat with us. It was late when we went to bed and I was very tired. The next morning, we had a drink of cocoa before setting out for a walk. I didn't feel too well because of the heat and kava but I insisted on going so as not to miss out on anything. The sun got hotter and hotter and I got sicker and sicker. I was very glad when, much to the disgust of my Tongan companions, I was allowed to ride on a horse while they walked. I rode many miles on that horse, through hot sun, drenching downpours, poor villages and varying vegetation.

Eventually we reached the highest point of 'Eua. The boys were very interested in the view from the cliffs of the sea far below, the running streams and erosion on the hills, all of which they had never seen before. We went nearly 15 miles. I cannot describe the agony I went through getting home, riding double on that horse. I nearly died of exhaustion and of course I felt such a fool. When, thank God, we did arrive home, I went straight to bed after a shower. During the next 12 hours I went to the toilet about eight times! I missed food for 18 hours and that night slept while the others had another 'fai kava'. Mafua slept on the floor in my room. The outside toilet, an odoriferous little hut, lay in full view of the whole village. Inside there was no paper so I made do with some of John's writing paper. The Tongans used coconut husk.

The people on 'Eua were poorer than those on Tongatapu but we were treated very hospitably by Tafakula and his family. He addressed us in the Tongan way for addressing chiefs and gave us the best food they had — yams, sipi, manioc, breadfruit. On Sunday morning I felt much better and very ashamed of the day before. We dressed for church but arrived late and had to squeeze in at the back. It was a small church and packed out. I understood not a word of the service. After church, I was feeling very hungry so I ate quite a big kai. As it was Sunday, the chief presented us with a big suckling pig, roasted on a spit. The previous day he had been fishing and from a very good catch he presented us with the biggest fish (which the others enjoyed).

After lunch the boys went out for another walk but were skeptical, in a nice way, about taking me. I assured them I was very fit. This time we walked in the opposite direction from our trip the previous day. Then we took a path off the road leading to the top of the hills. We walked for miles along a muddy track with tall bush on either side, stopping to drink coconuts. As we climbed upwards, the vegetation changed and the temperature dropped. In the cooler climate it was soon just like the bush in New Zealand.

We came across a mountain stream and deep pool. In we dived, clothes and all, lovely clear water and had a great time. We enjoyed clambering over the vines and creepers and soft undergrowth. In one place we found a perfect slide, a watery rock slope fifteen metres long covered in moss. In one village we were given some horsemeat, cooked in an umu. We also tried dog. Both tasted very gamey and I did not particularly enjoy eating them. We arrived home after dark and apologised to Tafakula for being tardy. We did not tell him we had been swimming on a Sunday.

That evening the same girl whom I had much admired came again to make a final kava. I had the honour of sitting next to her as she crushed the kava and mixed it in the wooden bowl. The boys were joking and told me to speak to the girl. Using rudimentary Tongan, I asked her for a date. She accepted. Even Tafakula laughed.

The next morning we packed early and had a final meal. We paid our respects to Tafakula and his family and then took photos of everyone. 'Ane, the girl who had made the kava for us the previous evenings, gave me a necklace made of shells. When the boat arrived, they came to the wharf with us. We got on board, saying goodbye to Tafakula and his son. Then I said goodbye to 'Ane with a traditional Tongan farewell, with words Mafua had laughingly told me to use: 'Heikai ngalo koe iateau', I shall never forget you. He was right about that but I never saw her again.

The boat left and our new father and his family were soon out of sight. 'Eua sank into the distance. Two hours later, after a good crossing, mildly rough, but on a beautiful clear day, we arrived back at Nuku'alofa.

King Taufa'ahau Tupou IV was born in 1918 and died in 2006. He was the eldest son of Queen Salote Tupou. He became king in late 1965 on the death of his mother. Queen Salote had stood out magnificently, riding an open carriage in the rain, at the coronation of Queen Elizabeth in 1953 and afterwards everyone knew where Tonga was. Once a lithe and athletic surfing champion in the South Pacific, Taufa'ahau was now the largest monarch in the world. He had been king only three years when I arrived in Tonga.

On 19 June a new session of the Tongan Parliament was opened. We dressed early. I put on my black suit, worn only on special occasions as it was far too uncomfortable to wear in the humid Tongan climate.

We waited for the school truck to take us into town and arriving there found our school and others marching very impressively down the main street, Taufa'ahau Road. John and I had been given passes to attend the opening. There were about a hundred people with us in the small room, waiting for the king to arrive. A royal guard formed up outside the Parliament building, the Chief Justice entered bedecked in red, then the British Consul, formally dressed complete with tails. Guns then began booming out a 21-gun salute. Four boys laid out fine mats and carpets for the king to walk over.

Eventually His Majesty arrived, an impressively big man, and emerged from his black limousine while the national anthem played. Everyone inside the Parliament building stood as he entered and walked over the mats to the throne. After seating himself amid a tangle of microphones, actually only two, he was handed his reading glasses and then a copy of his speech. His muffled voice was barely audible as he delivered it and of course I understood not a jot.

He spoke for 15 minutes, abruptly finished, was handed his sunglasses and regally walked out, to the playing of the national anthem and *'Three cheers for His Majesty'*. He then left in his big shiny limousine. I had just been privileged to witness the opening of the 69th Session of the Legislative Assembly of the Kingdom of Tonga. Tonga has a lovely national anthem, more like a hymn, which of course is entirely appropriate for a deeply religious country.

One memorable afternoon, King Taufa'ahau and Queen Mata'aho invited a group of us VSA volunteers to meet them at the king's rural retreat, Kauvai. This was a magnificent large building thatched with coconut palms and was more private than the prominent royal palace on the waterfront in Nuku'alofa. The king was hosting a feast for a visiting church dignitary. Clive drove John and me to the retreat. I had never met a king before and no one was sure of the protocol. We need not have worried. Arrayed around the sides of the very big fale, we listened to the king, sitting at the head of the room in a large chair, as he discussed phonetics and the use of the abacus and a few other topics I no longer recall.

As we were about to tuck into a sumptuous buffet meal, the king suggested we try to eat the rice with chopsticks. I had never eaten anything with chopsticks before. My Malaysian pen friend, Bee Koon, had sent me a pair as a present some years before but I had never really used them. Now the king deftly showed us exactly how to use them and to this day, I have always been grateful to him and often use chopsticks when eating Asian food. For some reason, rice tastes much better when eaten with chopsticks, than when shovelled into your mouth with a fork. This demonstration of the art of eating with chopsticks was an instance of Taufa'ahau's eclectic interests. He had a fascination for new technology and was himself an inveterate global traveller, making it on one occasion even to the Chatham Islands of New Zealand.

But it wasn't the rice that interested me that day as on the table before us, among much else, was a lovely dish of mashed potatoes. Potatoes do not grow in the tropical Tongan climate. They had to be imported on the cargo vessel which came each month from New Zealand. They soon spoiled in the humid climate. I had not eaten potatoes since leaving New Zealand several months before and was eager to have some. Unfortunately, the mash was very sticky. As I flicked some on to my plate, the potato fell in a messy heap onto the floor at the feet of Queen Mata'aho who was standing next to me. She very graciously took little notice of this bout of *lèse-majesté* from an 18-year-old boy.

I visited Kauvai on only one other occasion. In mid-September, HMNZS *Taranaki* berthed at Vuna Wharf in Nuku'alofa. The Governor-General of New Zealand, Arthur Porritt, was on an official visit to Tonga. I again wore my uncomfortably hot suit and after lining up at Kauvai with other VSAs to shake Porritt's hand, we tucked into a grand feast. The only problem was that I was sitting on the end of the pola, exposed to the hot sun. I suffered and sweated streams in my suit. Back in town later that day, after I had changed into more sensible attire, Mairi, Pat and I visited the *Taranaki* and were shown over the vessel by two sailors. We were given liberal amounts of rum and other drinks as part of the on-board hospitality. I left feeling very merry and quite dizzy.

Even this magnificent retreat at Kauvai burnt down some years later, a victim of its construction in very flammable local materials.

On another occasion His Majesty visited Tupou College to attend a feast of welcome for some church dignitary whose name I have forgotten. A 'pola taumafa', or feast befitting a King, was laid out on the school verandah and the VSA volunteers were invited along. At the conclusion Clive escorted the king to his limousine. Because of his great size His Majesty sat alone at the back of the car, in the middle, filling the vehicle. But to Clive's dismay his hyped-up dog Domino scuttled into the back of the limousine just before the king got in. A definite 'no-no' in protocol terms. Clive smiled in helpless embarrassment.

Rev Clive Skewes farewells His Majesty King Taufa'ahau Tupou, after a visit to Tupou College

CHAPTER 10

VSA IN TONGA — PART TWO

EACH YEAR, THE FREE WESLEYAN CHURCH HELD AN ANNUAL Conference of church leaders. This provided an opportunity to discuss church policy and to raise money to support church activities in Tonga. I was fortunate to be able to attend the 1969 Conference which was held in the middle island group of Ha'apai. I did not attend the conference meetings but was able to take part in the associated festivities.

Ha'apai, lying 180 km north of the main island Tongatapu, was rural and underdeveloped. People lived their daily lives unencumbered by much of the outside world. This is why I found it such a magical place, like 'Eua. I was billeted with a Tongan family and treated very kindly. My daily washing always turned up cleaned and ironed after a few hours. In those days Europeans, or 'palangi' as they are called, were still an unusual phenomenon in many Tongan villages. We would attract attention and interest wherever we went — especially from the children. They would follow us down the road, shouting in excitement 'Palangi, palangi!'

To raise money for the church, village women donated for sale the fine mats and tapa cloth they had made during the course of the previous year. Each village would try to outdo the other in demonstrating the quality of its mats. A boisterous competition threatened to become unruly but eventually order was restored and the donations gratefully received by the church authorities.

Evenings were spent sitting around a kava bowl where the men drank kava, smoked and talked over the day's events. I enjoyed drinking kava. Sitting on the floor in a wooden fale, with almost no furniture but the soft woven floor mats, talking long into the cool night, by the bright glow of a kerosene lantern, beside a warm, tropical, moonlit sea, was an experience I have never forgotten.

The next day I awoke early, although it was already daylight, and headed off to have a cold shower in a little room next to the house. To my surprise, as I opened the shower door, I caught sight of somebody already in the shower so I beat a hasty retreat. The event did not go unnoticed in a community where every event is noticed. I was informed that I had disrupted the morning ablutions of a certain young lady.

The news soon went out, virally as we would say today, that Peter had committed the sin of '*sio kaukau*' — Tongan for spying on a female as she bathes. It was evidently not conceivable that I had done this in error. My reputation badly damaged, I thought nothing of it until later that afternoon, as I was walking with a friend on a nearby beach, a young boy's voice called out to me from the undergrowth in the coconut trees, using my name: 'Pita, you wanna fux?'

I was naturally taken aback by this question and in confusion failed to answer and walked away. Looking back, I am not sure what precisely was on offer or what might have happened if I had said yes. Clearly, my mistake in not first checking whether the shower room was empty had had all sorts of unintended consequences.

After the conference some of us sailed back to the main island, Tongatapu, in a tiny tub of a boat that held perhaps 30 people sitting outside on the deck. Our first problem occurred when the vessel, overloaded, ran aground as it left harbour. By some deft manoeuvring and engine revving by the captain, we were soon free and on our way. Halfway home about midnight, we were struck by a violent storm which tossed our little tub mercilessly and drenched everyone.

I was very sick, dry-retching over the side and wishing for it all to end. The Tongan passengers began praying fervently to God for deliverance and I for one sincerely hoped he was listening. It was an unnerving experience and, like the crossing to 'Eua, showed just how 'unpacific' the Pacific could be. Fortunately, the prayers were answered and we arrived back exhausted in Nuku'alofa as dawn broke on the horizon.

One day news arrived that the Australian Broadcasting Corporation was coming to Tonga to complete a documentary called *Infinite Pacific* on the life of Captain Cook. Although Cook was killed in Hawaii, there were not enough Hawaiians readily available to make up the extras needed for the murder scene. Tongans would be asked to be Hawaiians for the purpose of the documentary.

The producers needed some European boys to be Cook's crew. John, Steve and I were delighted to be asked to turn up at Monotapu Beach, one of the northwest beaches of Tongatapu, for a film shoot. A taxi came to the college to collect us. We were fitted out with 18th-century seamen's uniforms in a nearby village before being bussed to the beach location. I had to remove my glasses and I felt slightly underdressed as there were no socks to wear with my buckled shoes. About 80 Tongan extras had been brought in from nearby villages to make up the Hawaiian contingent.

We had to do several takes of the violent murder scene as, to the frustration and annoyance of the ABC film crew, the Tongans could not stop laughing, once battle was engaged, such fun was being had by all. The Tongans were exhorted not to laugh and joke as they brandished their clubs. Eventually a wrap was made and the film completed. I really enjoyed my one and only film acting experience. The packed lunches provided by the ABC were delicious, as we did not always eat good food in our little fale at the college.

The film was duly shown on TV in Australia and New Zealand in 1970. I made a point of watching it. To my intense disappointment, the whole murder scene amounted to about 30 seconds in the documentary and I wondered at the effort and expense the ABC had gone to, just for 30 seconds of film footage.

I gave little thought to this film until, over 45 years later, I was watching another, modern, TV documentary about Captain Cook and his search for the Northwest Passage. This was well done and very enjoyable. When it came to the inevitable murder scene at Kealakekua Bay in Hawaii on 14 February 1779, it looked vaguely familiar to me. With the invention of a screen freeze and replay facility on the TV, which was not available in 1970, there it was — our old ABC murder scene, resurrected from the archives after nearly 50 years and re-run. I could even locate myself on the crowded beach as one of James Cook's sailors about to be murdered, a young 18-year-old, with no glasses, a good crop of hair and I knew, although no one else did, buckled shoes with no socks. And yes, there were those same Tongan (or Hawaiian) chiefs, many of whom had not been able to stop laughing so much at the whole murderous turmoil on their beach.

One Friday I was tasked with acting as a track and field umpire at an inter-school sports competition in Nuku'alofa. I thoroughly enjoyed myself. My tutor colleague, George Pahulu, was there with me on the Friday morning but then, to my surprise, didn't show up in the afternoon for the rest of the competition. Everyone got very excited during the races, screaming and shouting. The Tongan Defence Force, which also acted as a police force, was deployed to keep order. I needed an umbrella in the sun and girls from Tonga High School gave me very welcome refreshments every two hours. At the end of the day all the teams paraded about the field and the winners received their trophies from the king's brother, Prince Tu'ipelehake. Sheer bedlam broke out in our own ranks when Tupou College won the senior shield for the seventh time.

That night, Mairi, Dorothy, John and I sneaked away to see the floor show at the Dateline Hotel, then Nuku'alofa's only tourist hotel. We watched some lovely girls dancing and danced our feet off too. I had three gin and lemonades at the princely price of 50c each and smoked lots of cigarettes. We came home at midnight to Jeff and Glen's house, having spent $3 of my hard-earned money (our living allowance at Tupou College was only $5 per week). But it was worth it. We slept soundly that night on the hard floor. Of course, such adventures were not reported to the Reverend Skewes.

On Monday morning, back at the college, the news spread like wildfire that George Pahulu had secretly got married on Friday night. This explained his sudden disappearance after the Friday morning sports events. It transpired that he had run away with a Mormon girl. This news gave Clive what I described in my diary as 'chronic diarrhoea' until he learnt that the girl was going to convert to the right faith — Methodism. Siupeli, the head tutor, held a feast at his house for George, to congratulate him on his marriage.

The head girl at Tupou High School was a nice young lady about my age who became a friend of Dorothy and Mairi. Her name was Lesieli Ikatonga Kupu. I enjoyed her company and talking to her, although she never introduced me to her family. In 1970, I met her again unexpectedly when she enrolled at Auckland University. We lost touch after that but sometime later she married an American and moved to Palmerston North.

I got to know and liked Mohenoa Puloka's younger sister, Mele'ana, who went on to have a senior role in Tongan public and religious life. She became principal of Queen Salote College and an ordained Minister of the Free Wesleyan Church of Tonga. Mele'ana was the same age as me and had a kind and compassionate personality. I had a great admiration for her and knew even then that she would become a respected and loved leader of her community.

Volunteer Service Abroad in Tonga, with John Dunckley, Mele'ana Puloka and friend, 1969

I enjoyed cycling through the Tongan countryside in the weekends. The air was always warm and the bush vegetation had a lovely tangy smell. The land was flat so there were no hills to negotiate. On the coastal roads, the warm sea breezes would mingle with the tropical scent of the land, from the fluttering taro and yam plantations, and the glistening banana and coconut trees. One afternoon, as four of us VSA volunteers cycled on the remote northeast road, deserted except for us, along came a car with the king's brother, Prince Tu'ipelehake. He was showing the island to an American visitor.

We dismounted from our bikes, as a sign of courtesy, as any Tongan would normally sit on the roadside if royalty happened to be passing. Tu'ipelehake stopped his car to chat with us. He said we looked thirsty and because he knew we could not climb coconut trees like Tongan boys, he gave us each a very refreshing can of cold soft drink, which was just what we needed on that long, hot afternoon ride. I never learnt to climb a coconut tree, unless it was a short one with a lean on it. But I became adept at splitting open coconuts with a ground spike or machete, whenever we needed a cool drink or something to eat. Coconuts lay on the ground all around the island, free for the taking.

I wrote several long letters to Budge. I am told he read them to the school at assembly. He wrote to me too. Victor's brother Noel wrote to tell me that Hamilton Boys' High School had undertaken some fundraising activities to assist the college. This was welcome news. Receiving mail from home was always a high point of the week. Even my brother Stuart managed to write. He wrote one letter which was hilariously funny.

A burly policeman knocked on the door of my classroom one afternoon as I was teaching, to ask if I had a relative called Jenny Roper. The sudden appearance of a policeman caused quite a stir among the boys who must have wondered what I had been up to. Jenny, married to my father's cousin Mike, was on an agricultural study tour of the South Pacific and had detoured while in Tonga to see me at Toloa. She was able to give a full report to my parents on her return to New Zealand.

Sometimes film evenings would be held for the boys in the tractor shed, the film projected on to a huge white cloth. They loved action movies and whenever there were any scenes involving physical violence, they screamed with uncontrolled excitement. One evening a schoolboy turned up at our fale with a short note: 'Picture evening will start at 7:30 and no later than 8:00. Bring your wives and children'.

Tongans are not usually violent people but when aroused or inebriated could become very angry. I remember watching a teenage boy fleeing his angry father as he chased him through his banana plantation, brandishing a machete, the boy weaving desperately in and out of the banana trees, trying to escape the paternal wrath. Perhaps he had been lazy in his work in the gardens. Clearly, he had annoyed his father to such an extent that the latter's patience had snapped.

The Tongan rugby team was the pride of the nation. We would watch them practising on the open field mala'e in Nuku'alofa. The king would show up in his limousine to encourage them. Big beefy lads, there was no doubting their enthusiasm even if their ball-handling skills were not the best. To improve these, the king devised a new game, which he called 'Socris'— soccer played on a tennis court. This involved kicking the ball nimbly and with some skill over a tennis net, but with the requirement that it did not go outside the boundary of the court. Socris was all the rage for a while but the players gradually lost interest as, frustratingly, the ball always went far outside the confines of the tennis court whenever they kicked it.

One Saturday afternoon our VSA friend, Mairi McPhee, came to Toloa for a visit. We decided to walk to the prison farm as a friend, Isaleili, was to preach to the prisoners. The prison farm, known as Luatolitoli, was next to Toloa. The prisoners had much more freedom than their counterparts in New Zealand. There were few bars, fences or locks — just some friendly guards. The prisoners worked on the farm. If any did escape, they could not go far on a small island.

As we passed one prisoner, he evidently took a dislike to the 'palangi' walking by. He called out to me 'Usi lemu, usi lemu!' I had no idea what it meant but found out later this was a choice Tongan obscenity which seemed to have the import of 'Piss off, prick!' in English. I could understand his frustration at being disturbed by unannounced visitors. Apart from occasions such as this it was not easy to learn Tongan swear words, as no one would teach them to me.

Some years later, in 1982, Luatolitoli was the scene of the last executions in Tonga, when three men were hanged for murder.

I guessed something was wrong one Monday morning when the boys' assembly was very late in coming out. I hadn't gone, despite Clive's stricture, as I had been too tired. The previous night somebody had burgled Steve's fale and made off with $100 of his money and some possessions. This caused great excitement. No lessons were held that day. The school searched for the money everywhere. All the boys were questioned and the dormitories searched. Footprints were taken of suspects to see if they matched those left by the thief.

The boys were required to sit for hours, many speeches were given and the thief was enjoined to identify himself. Despite a search of the school grounds, nothing was ever found and Steve gave up on getting his money back. The police were informed of the theft. It reminded me of a certain episode, six years earlier, involving some bent tin snips. John and I were never burgled, if one excludes the loaf of bread that one day mysteriously disappeared from our kitchen, perhaps because we had nothing of value in our fale. Certainly, we never had much money.

Coming back from Nuku'alofa one day by bus — buses had no glass in the windows so they were always pleasantly cool — I was the only palangi on board. I called out to the driver to please stop at the end of the Toloa road. I shouted out '*Tu'u iheni*!' which I understood was Tongan for 'Stop here'. The whole bus started chuckling. Well, '*Tu'u iheni*' is indeed Tongan for 'Stop here' but to the literal Tongans, that is a physical impossibility for the bus driver, as he had already passed that spot ('here') by the time he heard my request. You have to say '*Tu'u ihena*' which means 'Stop *over there*'. I didn't make that mistake again.

I came up with the great idea of starting a garden as a means of raising money for the college, by growing tomatoes in my spare time and selling them in New Zealand. Siupeli gave me a tract of land in the bush and with the help of some boys, we planted 350 tomato plants. I had grossly underestimated the amount of labour involved in tending this garden, keeping it tidy, picking off the unwanted nodules and staking and watering the plants, but I had help from the boys and in particular our house boys. When it came time to pick, the garden produced dozens of baskets of lovely tomatoes but few of them made it to New Zealand because of problems with shipping schedules and because tonnes of tomatoes from other gardens on Tongatapu were competing for cargo space.

After much expense and effort by the college, the day arrived when the school's first concrete block showers and toilets could be dedicated. The whole school assembled before the new block. Hymns and prayers were followed by speeches by Faiva — whose team had built them — and Clive, the principal. Then we inspected the new block of 30 showers and 12 communal toilets. For some reason, the new facility did not include any urinals but it is hard to overestimate the health value of having good washing and toilet facilities in a school where the boys were daily dirty and sweaty from their work in the gardens.

I organised a 'Tutors' Club' at the college when once a week college staff would meet to discuss topics of interest in English. It helped the tutors improve their English and was a lot of fun. A grand debate was held when two teams of tutors addressed the topic: 'That oil would have adverse effects on our way of life' (how prescient!). About 80 boys came to listen in and although nothing radical or novel was said, we all enjoyed it. The tutors took participation in the Club seriously. When Tevita Talikai could not attend one evening, he kindly sent me a note saying: 'An unexpected visitor is here at home and he will spend the night here. This is an apology, as I wouldn't be able to attend our meeting (very sorry) tonight. T Talikai'.

Often at club evenings John and I would do a slide show of photos we had taken in Tonga or show films. These events were hugely popular. As good teaching materials were hard to come by, I wrote out some notes explaining the intricacies of English grammar. These were run off on the old Gestetner copying machine and were much in demand by students and tutors.

One of the people I most admired at Toloa was the Reverend Samiu Tupou, the head preacher, a deeply religious and pious man who was widely respected in Tonga. One Sunday we were invited to the 21st birthday celebration of his lovely daughter, Ana. Girls from Tupou High School attended, including Lesieli, so it was an enjoyable occasion. A lengthy prayer session conducted by the Reverend Cummins was followed by a magnificent feast laid out in the college tractor shed. I took many photos, of Ana speaking, Ana cutting her cake and Ana weeping floods of tears. She later married a lawyer and moved to Fiji.

On the occasions we did not go into town in the weekends, we would visit our Peace Corps colleagues, Sandy and Judy MacIntosh. A favourite pastime was to play cards, hearts or poker. Sometimes we would be so engrossed we would play outside in the warm night air until sunrise and then go home to sleep. I did quite a lot of reading at Toloa, *Hawaii* by James A Michener, *The Black Arrow* by Robert Louis Stevenson and *The Cardinal* by Henry Morton Robinson. Michener's magnificent description of the emergence of the Hawaiian Islands from the depths of the boundless Pacific Ocean is an unparalleled piece of descriptive writing.

Saturday, 28 June was my 18th birthday. According to my diary, the 27th was not a good day at school. I was glad when it finished and the weekend arrived. I went to town by bus — John came later after killing a pig for Clive. With John, Jeff Hocking, Mairi, Pat and Dorothy, I walked about two miles to a house where a feast was in progress, to celebrate the 21st of an Australian girl whom we knew. After the feast, things livened up and we danced to a guitar and played party games in-between.

We were all having a great time, dancing and laughing. At midnight, Mairi and Dorothy rushed out amidst the dancing to give me a birthday kiss and the band, just arrived, played 'Happy Birthday'. I danced with all the girls, not missing a dance. It was 5am before I went home.

Although I had never lived in a tropical climate before, I felt well and relished the warm weather. I was glad that we usually did not have to wear heavy clothing. It was great never to feel cold, unlike those winter days at Hamilton Boys' High School when we had frozen in our school shorts. After a while, the mosquitoes didn't bother me. The only illness I suffered was a bout of acute diarrhoea from eating some pork at a Tongan feast which had not been properly cooked. For about two weeks severe stomach cramp would strike at the most inopportune moments, especially when I was in full flight in class, mid English lesson. There was no alternative but to abandon the class abruptly and flee the 100 metres back to our fale and the relief of the outside dunny. My sudden unexplained departures must have puzzled my young charges.

It was while I was teaching an English class that the exciting news came through that Neil Armstrong had become the first person to walk on the moon. It was 20 July 1969.

During the August school holidays, I visited Tonga's northernmost island group, Vava'u, which lies just over 300 km from Tongatapu. We had arranged to travel on Peter Warner's relatively new little boat, the 'Ata. Peter had named his boat the 'Ata after an uninhabited island of the same name, located about 150 km south of Tongatapu. There, sailing past one day in 1966, he had stumbled across six young Tongan boys who were marooned on the island.

They had run away from their strict Catholic boarding school in Nuku'alofa and stolen a little boat. This had broken down in a storm and drifted off course, eventually landing them on 'Ata, where they survived for over a year using their own wits. Their families had given them up for dead. The story is interesting as it shows how the boys, culturally disposed to help each other, could survive such an ordeal in stark contrast to the young English boys depicted in Golding's famous novel *Lord of the Flies*, whose culture conditioned them to compete, often violently, against each other.

We departed Nuku'alofa on the 'Ata at 5pm, just as it was getting dark. Jeff, John and Pat came with me. We shared a small cabin on this little vessel, about three by four metres. Pat and Jeff became very sick. The sea wasn't too rough and I had taken a good dose of seasick pills to make sure I didn't have a repetition of the seasickness I had had returning from Ha'apai. Morning saw us well past Ha'apai, in beautiful weather and calm seas. Eventually, the land form of Vava'u came into view and in a few hours we were steaming past lush, uninhabited tropical islands. We went on top of the cabin roof and had a beautiful view of Vava'u, the sun streaming down on deep blue waters.

Just as we rounded one island a school of porpoises played alongside the ship for a minute or two, then lost interest and disappeared. We drew close up to 'Swallow's Cave', a famous natural limestone cave which can only be approached by boat. According to legend, an ancient Tui Tonga (high chief) had concealed himself there during a civil war.

Eventually we berthed at Nei'afu, a beautiful little town which overlooked the harbour. We were immediately aware of some influence which was not evident in Ha'apai or Tongatapu. All the roads were tarsealed and well-paved, everything was clean and neat. The whole place gave the impression of permanence. This was the result of the German influence in Vava'u before the First World War.

We took a church truck to the house where we were to stay. This was the residence of Reverend Justin Gooderham, before he was appointed President of the Wesleyan Church in Tonga. It was a long, Victorian-style house with an unpainted, rusty tin roof, surrounded by a beautiful garden. Four other VSAs were already there and they had decided not to go on to Pago Pago, which was the *'Ata's* main destination. I had the option of going on to Samoa but decided I would rather stay in Vava'u than face another long sea voyage. So Ian Lockie took my berth and after fixing up everything with Captain Warner, John and Ian sailed for Samoa.

One evening we went to the local cinema where *Warlord of Crete* was showing. When we arrived, there was a great throng milling about the door, all eager to get in, while one or two ushers strained to admit only those with tickets. We were jostled about just as much as anybody. Eventually we got to our seats, upstairs on 30-cent wooden seats with backs as opposed to downstairs, which was 20 cents and only a bench.

The film commenced and soon all the children were shouting with excitement as the two armies of Crete and Greece fought it out in bloody battles. Neighbours at home were soon attracted by the excitement and there was a flood of new arrivals in the cinema. For about 15 minutes we could not see or hear anything of the film while people continually pushed past us to get to their seats around the theatre. The film projector broke down once or twice and once the power failed. All you could see was the glow of cigarettes in the darkness around the theatre.

Not having been to any other village except Nei'afu, several of us decided to walk to Makave, a neighbouring village, to see a minister friend of mine whom I had met at the church Conference in Ha'apai. Makave hadn't seen any palangi for ages so it was quite a day when three turned up. Children tailed us wherever we went, watching our every move. Another day we tried to catch the bus — Vava'u had only one bus — to see the other villages but its schedule was irregular and it never turned up. Eventually the 'Ata arrived back from Samoa and we said goodbye to Nei'afu.

The trip back to Nuku'alofa took over 30 hours. During this time I had only one loaf of bread to eat. The reason for the slow trip was that we had to call in at Ha'apai for about 12 hours while the captain and the US Peace Corps did some business. We were all rather fed up with this, especially since we were eager to be home.

After calling at the islands of Ha'ano, Uiha and Nomuka (the 'Mutiny of the *Bounty*' took place just after the ship had sailed from Nomuka), we eventually set sail for home at 3.30pm, having already been on the sea for about 26 hours with little food and no sleep. The seas from Nomuka to Tongatapu were particularly rough, so rough that we had to close the portals and the doors of the cabin to avoid being washed out. Every time somebody came inside we would get flooded by a wave of spray. After two magnificent sunsets on the 'Ata, we were well and truly eager for the voyage to end.

Eventually, with the moon high in the sky, the boat stopped rolling and we reached calmer waters. At midnight we berthed in Nuku'alofa and as soon as we could we went ashore with our luggage. I spent a very dizzy night sleeping on the floor at Jeff and

Glen's place, after a cup of coffee and some toast, my first meal for nearly 40 hours.

Towards the end of my year in Tonga, Tevita Va'ivaka's parents prepared a farewell feast for us on a secluded beach. John and I caught a bus with Tevita to their village of Ha'ateiho accompanied by Tevita Tupou and Na'asoni Tui'ile'ila, our other houseboys. We walked a long way in the bush to reach the beach. When we arrived, we met Tevita's elderly parents, Filimone and Salote, preparing an umu on the seashore. We swam in the sea and had games of athletics on the beach. Then we went up for the feast, known in Tongan as 'kai me'a kai'. This we ate seated in the shade of a leafy tree while the sun beat down. The food was delicious.

Tevita's parents had travelled a long way in their horse and cart to prepare the meal for us. After we had eaten, John and I made a speech of thanks. The boys in turn stood up to apologise for 'the bad things we have done' while we were at Toloa — I could not think of any. After a rest in the shade of a tree, we had a small snack of tea and biscuits. Salote had brought her most precious china tea service for the occasion. Everyone was pleased when I wore a Tongan tupenu (wrap-around) instead of my normal attire.

The time for my return to New Zealand drew near. I felt very sorry to be leaving. My diary ended about three weeks before I left Tonga, no doubt reflecting the fact that we were very busy finishing our class lessons and preparing to depart. I left Tonga, the 'Friendly Islands', in December 1969 to tearful farewells, hardly believing our year as volunteers was over. For a while I felt very deflated.

Tongan was the first Polynesian language I had tried to speak. I have forgotten a lot of the language now, but I still love to hear Tongan spoken. When I do, I try to remember as much as possible. It always sounds such a bright and beautiful language, so different from the French and German I had grappled with at school.

I have been back to Tonga twice since I left, once in 1982, when we had completed our first posting with Foreign Affairs in nearby Fiji and again in 1999, en route home from Samoa, after my posting there as High Commissioner. Several of my colleagues on the teaching staff at Tupou College were now in senior positions: Dr Mohenoa Puloka was principal of Tupou College and my old friend Lopini Felisi was a high school principal in Nuku'alofa. A Tongan was now head of the Free Wesleyan Church of Tonga. Methodism is still the state religion. The Reverend Harris and the Reverend Skewes had long since returned to Australia.

Many of the people I had known and admired have now passed away but others continue to play active and senior roles in Tongan society. In 2018, the Reverend Dr Mohenoa Puloka was appointed by the King to be Governor of Ha'apai, the middle island group, where I had attended the annual Wesleyan Church Conference. I was privileged to have known them.

Tonga, despite all its challenges, is a magical place.

CHAPTER 11

AUCKLAND UNIVERSITY (1970 —1974)

COMING BACK TO SUBURBAN NEW ZEALAND AFTER A YEAR OF independence, living on a tropical island as a tutor at Tupou College, was as much a culture shock as I had experienced on first arriving in Tonga. As a country boy at heart, I did not like living in Auckland. City life was such a contrast to the idyll of a Tongan island or rural New Zealand.

I had little idea about the subjects that I would most enjoy studying at university or which would prove most useful in my later career. As I was at that point planning to be a high school teacher, it seemed natural to continue studying German, French and History. I did not feel proficient enough to study Latin at tertiary level. Instead, I kept up my Latin reading privately and have never lost my love for that difficult but fascinating language of Cicero, Caesar, Caligula and Constantine. Some people like Sudoku or crossword puzzles. I like to try to read Latin.

The subjects I found interesting and valuable in later life were unfamiliar to me at the age of nineteen. I had little experience of economics, politics or philosophy. It is of course often difficult at that age to know what one would really like to do as a career. When a friend talked to me about his passion for political science, I felt I could not imagine a more boring subject. I came to see the error of that view. I wish in retrospect that my university studies had been broader in scope.

The German teaching staff at the university were predominately Jewish, most of whom had left Germany before or during the Second World War to escape Hitler's tyranny. The founder of the Department of Germanic Languages and Literature at Auckland University was a New Zealander — Professor John Asher, a legendary figure in academic circles. He had made German studies respectable again only a few short years after the Second World War. Many of the French academic staff adopted a rather supercilious attitude towards their students whom they seem to regard as quintessential representatives of an uninspired New Zealand 'bourgeoisie'. Our history lecturers — to me at least — seemed more down-to-earth, as their presentations were grounded in topics which really interested me, such as the history of Anglo-Saxon England, the Middle Ages and the Crusades.

I spent my first year, 1970, boarding at the boys-only Saint Stevens' Hall of Residence affiliated to the Anglican Church. Located at the top of Parnell Rise in Auckland, it was a series of ramshackle two-storey wooden buildings, near the imposing red-brick Anglican Cathedral. We were housed three to a room.

There was nothing particularly appealing about this form of student accommodation other than that, at the end of a long day, a hot meal was always ready in the communal dining hall. Meals were presided over by the Reverend RK Dobson, who had been a regular force army chaplain, a kindly and long-suffering gentleman. Somehow, he had been inveigled into taking on the task of supervising a Hall of Residence for 60 young men. He never spoke of his war experiences. Perhaps he thought we were too immature to have understood them. Mrs Winifred Lang, the hostel manager, was a surrogate mother to us all, until she retired to run a motel on the foreshore in Paihia. Huia was the main chef and therefore very popular with the students.

Middle High German

In our second year, Professor Asher introduced us to Middle High German, the language and literature of Germany in the Middle Ages, about AD 1100–1300. This was his own academic focus. He had become a noted scholar, recognised in Germany for his research and publication of an authentic text of the famous medieval story of Der Guote Gêrhart ('Gerhart the Good') by Rudolf von Ems.

At first I was resistant to the idea of learning a whole new Germanic language, one which seemed to be of little value and for which I had not signed up. It did however coincide with my interest in the Middle Ages generally. In my second year of studying Middle High German, I grew to like it immensely, particularly some of the literary masterpieces such as the *Nibelungenlied* (from which Wagner developed his epic drama, *The Ring of the Nibelung*), the *Kaiserchronik*, the works of Gottfried von Strassburg, Wolfram von Eschenbach and many others.

Many of Wagner's operas, such as *Parsifal, Tannhäuser, Lohengrin* and *Tristan and Isolde* have medieval themes taken from the literature of this era. I later developed a great liking for Wagner's music.

The 12th-century love poems of the wandering troubadours, known in Germany as the Minnesänger, such as Walther von der Vogelweide, were particularly bright and fresh, heralding a reawakening of poetry and literature in Europe after the slumber of the Dark Ages since the fall of the Roman Empire. Here is one of the simpler poems from that time, which can still have meaning today, 800 years later:

> Dû bist mîn, ich bin dîn.
> Des solt dû gewis sîn.
> Dû bist beslozzen in mînem herzen,
> Verlorn ist das sluzzelîn.
> Dû muost immêr drinne sîn.

> (You are mine, I am yours,

Of this you can be sure.
You are locked in my heart,
And the key is lost.
You must remain there forever.)

One of the highlights of the academic year was the Middle High
German dinner which Professor Asher promoted and organised,
where we could all dress up in medieval costume and enjoy food
based on medieval recipes.

The Peat Farm at Moanatuatua

By 1970 my parents had rented out the little house at 226 Old Farm
Road in Hamilton and later sold it. They had lived in it for only six
or seven years before they moved to a farm south of Hamilton at
Ohaupo. The farm — called Moanatuatua — was attached to the
Rukuhia Soil Research Station, then part of the government's
Department of Agriculture. It comprised 100 hectares of flat peat
land, established to study ways of improving the fertility of New
Zealand's peat areas then being brought into agricultural production.
Dad was delighted to be back on the land and managed this farm for
15 years until he retired.

The farm had three full-time staff in addition to my father. Each was
a wonderful character. John Corby, who was Catholic, had never
married and lived with his parents in Hamilton. He worked with
Dad on grass field trials and selenium experiments on peat and
volcanic soils all over the central North Island (at Kinloch,
Rerewhakaaitu, Rangitaiki and Lochinver Station). Dad would often
be away days at a time doing grassland trial work with John in these
places. They were good work colleagues, although on occasion,
privately to us, Dad would evince some frustration with John's
comfortable Catholicism. In this he took after his father, my
grandfather, who once lambasted the Pope to me as 'that silly man in
his silly hat'.

Arthur Brassington worked full-time bulldozing, digging and tractoring, as did Tui Burling, a rotund, cheerful individual who loved his beer. They were retired farmers and worked at Moanatuatua for the extra income. John Corby was the best educated of the three. He took a keen interest in world politics and history and was something of a bibliophile. On my return visits to Moanatuatua from Auckland University, he would engage me in long discussions on topics of historical or current political interest. Dad on several occasions would admonish me not to talk so much to John, as 'it kept him from his work'.

In those days, the salaries of all New Zealand Government employees were published regularly in a great tome, the *Public Service Salaries* book. John regularly obtained the latest version and would carefully scrutinise where he stood in relation to his colleagues in terms of salary. Discussions on this could occupy the lunch and tea breaks for days. Nowadays such salary information is kept confidential to the individual recipient, which has meant that other topics of burning interest have had to be unearthed, for dissection during public service tea breaks across the nation.

Arthur proficiently did his work on his bulldozer and showed no interest in anything else. No matter where they were working on the farm, they would down tools and amble back to the shearing shed for morning and afternoon smoko and lunch. By the time afternoon smoko had finished it was almost time to pack up for the day at 4.30pm. Arthur and John lived in Hamilton, 15 km distant and needed time to get home. Tui lived locally in Ohaupo. They remain in my memory as the Three Musketeers of the swamp land.

Dad had two dogs to help him on the farm. He was very fond of the first one, a shaggy long-haired sheepdog called Toi. Toi worked hard for Dad but he met an unfortunate end when a steer he was herding stepped on him and crushed him. Dad was disconsolate. Toi's successor was a less-intelligent, but hyperactive, animal of dubious parentage, called Flip.

First Return to Little Water

At the end of 1971, our parents took Stuart and me on a six-week trip back to England, to spend Christmas at Little Water Farm. This was the first visit to my grandparents in over 10 years. It was with great excitement that we boarded the Air New Zealand DC8 flight in Auckland to Los Angeles where we spent a very enjoyable two days en route, lapping up the adventures at Disneyland. Christmas at Little Water was great fun and despite the winter weather, we were able to catch up with most of the family including Dad's brother Peter, his wife Mary, and his parents. The meeting with my paternal grandparents was strained, but at least Dad did meet his parents again, 14 years after he had left Speccott Barton.

For me, a highlight of this visit was being permitted to drive Grandad Dyer's little Austin 1100 on my own for day trips to historical places such as the Roman baths at Aquae Sulis (Bath), Berkeley Castle, where the deposed King Edward II was murdered in 1327, and Glastonbury Tor and Glastonbury Abbey.

The magnificent Abbey, now a ruin thanks to Henry VIII's dissolution of the monasteries in the 16th century, is the reputed burial place of the mythical King Arthur. I have never forgotten the solitude of the Abbey ruin with its magnificent broken walls, the abbot's house and the large fish pond which for centuries fed the monks. I had the whole place to myself on the wintery day I visited. In the little modern chapel, I thought I would make a concerted effort to see if the Almighty still inhabited this sacred place. Despite my earnest private endeavour to reach the deity, there was no answering my prayers so my skepticism about organised religion was increased.

After leaving the Abbey, I climbed up to the nearby Glastonbury Tor. It was late afternoon and I was completely alone as the freezing-cold winter wind blew over the Tor. The view was magnificent, but the place inhospitable. I thought of poor Richard Whiting, the elderly last abbot of Glastonbury Abbey who, on such a winter's day in 1539, was hung, drawn and quartered on the Tor on a spurious charge of treason worked up by Thomas Cromwell. His sin had been to remain loyal to the Church of Rome and he had been dilatory in surrendering the riches of the Abbey into the king's grasping hands. It could be risky to upset Henry VIII. There is something moving about being completely alone in a place where so much history has happened.

On another occasion, again alone in the late afternoon winter sun, I clambered up the grassy slopes of Cadbury Castle, one of the legendary sites of King Arthur's Camelot. It is probably nothing more than a rudimentary Bronze and Iron Age hill fort. King Arthur never set foot on it. But just as I reached the top of the hill, a peal of six bells rang out from the little village church in the distance below, an entrancing sound which broke the stillness of the evening as the sun set over this timeless and lonely place.

At Little Water Farm, my brother Stuart and I slept in the outside barn in a tiny caravan which belonged to our teacher at East Quantoxhead School, Aunty Frances and her husband Walter Napper. It was un-winterised, freezing cold and soon dripping damp. Stuart and I quickly decamped to inside the farmhouse, to the only bedroom still available — the tiny room under the stairs which could accommodate two small beds but nothing else. It was here that Pos, the Italian prisoner of war, had slept during the war.

Fox Hunting

The fox-hunting season, a rural winter tradition for centuries, was then in full swing. We went to several meetings of riders and fox hounds, in the brisk air of a wan winter sunshine. My uncle Terry Chidgey was a passionate fox hunter. As he was a Master of the West Somerset Vale Hunt, he would attend every gathering, known as 'the Meet', resplendent in his red Master's tunic. My cousin Sarah often 'rode to hounds' with her father, immaculately attired in her riding habit.

A strong community spirit united those who took part in a fox hunt. Everyone enjoyed the thrill of the chase across miles of marvellous

Somerset countryside, fields and woodland. The 'Meet' would begin at the farm of the host for that day's event. It was a great social occasion as riders turned up, greeted each other, chatted and gossiped, milled about on their horses and downed some warming liquid refreshment provided by the host farmer. As some point the Master would blow his hunting horn to call everyone to order. The eager yelping hounds and accompanying riders would 'move off' together to begin the search for the scent of a fox they could chase.

Those unfortunates who did not ride horses would endeavour to follow the chase in their private cars or on motorbike. There was always a mad scramble to try to second-guess where the hounds, or more accurately the poor fox being pursued, were headed next. A sighting or glimpse of the fox racing across the countryside as it fled for its life, away from the baying pack of hounds, was always most satisfying. The surrounding rural roads were a chaotic jam on such occasions.

The Masters of the Hunt had to have a very clear idea of whose land they were permitted to access or, more importantly, whose land they could not cross during the chase. Most farmers were happy for the hunt to cross their land, provided the horses and hounds did not do any damage to hedgerows or fields. Excited shouting echoed around the countryside from riders and foot traffic alike, reporting sightings of the fleeing fox. This was known as 'hollering'. If you heard an excited 'holler' some way off, you knew the fox had been sighted and you would endeavour to move yourself as quickly as possible in the direction of the holler. The Master's shrill hunting horn, as he sought to control and encourage the pack of hounds, reverberated around the countryside. It was a great spectacle.

Any sensible fox, once scented, would try to outrun the hounds or hide underground well out of their reach. When it did hide, the refrain would go out that the fox had 'gone to ground'. At this point the shovels and spades would suddenly materialise, in an effort to dig the fox out. If it was well hidden deep in the root system of a hedgerow or tree, Jack Burge would unleash his nasty little fox terrier, quivering in anticipation, to flush the fox out of its hole.

Either way, the fox's demise was a foregone conclusion: to be torn apart limb from limb by the pack of baying hounds if they caught the little critter in full flight, or by a *coup de grâce* from a pistol shot if it was unearthed by the terrier. It was a disappointing day if no kill was chalked up. The better specimens, once subjected to the gentle hands of a taxidermist, might adorn the hallowed halls of country houses, as eternal taxidermy mounts. There were several fox heads on the walls of Uncle Terry's home at Colepool Farm.

What this poor little critter felt — the object of such demented fury from the attacking hounds and the equally hyped human followers — one can only imagine. Even then, in 1971, opposition to fox hunting, and stag hunting which took place on nearby Exmoor, as a cruel blood sport, was beginning to mount, pitching town and country folk into a fierce national debate. This led to its eventual ban in the United Kingdom in 2004 (except Northern Ireland). No one knows, of course, how often this ban is breached.

Supporters of hunting did assert that country folk know best how to manage farm land and protect the countryside. Fox hunting, they argued, was a legitimate means of control, as foxes could be vicious killers of poultry and other small animals on the surrounding farms. I think though that the ancient English cultural phenomenon of the fox hunt was less about biological control of a rural pest than a lame excuse for a jolly good day out, on horseback or on foot, rollicking around the beautiful countryside.

Mum, as a young girl in the 1930s, had been inducted into the hunting community by being 'bloodied' — a pagan ceremony whereby the blood of a freshly killed fox is smeared on the forehead of children initiates, in a form of baptism. That she should undergo this ceremony was, she recalls, very important to her father, Grandad Dyer. I am embarrassed to admit, with apologies to the foxes, that I greatly enjoyed being outdoors in the fresh air and winter sunshine with Grandad, driving around the countryside on Meet Days.

Lordy, or to give him his full title, Lord Alexander Peregrine Fuller-Acland-Hood, 2nd Baron St Audries, had died in October 1971, aged 77, just a few months before our visit. He is buried in the churchyard of the lovely little country church at East Quantoxhead, near where Stuart and I had gone to school.

With his death, his UK barony became extinct. His two sisters, Hon Audrey Mildred and Hon Maud Isabel, the legendary Misses Audrey and Maud, born in 1889 and 1892 respectively, were still living as elderly spinsters at Fairfield House. Audrey and Maud very kindly invited me to visit their Fairfield home. I had never been inside a real Elizabethan manor house before and was overawed by the huge rooms, the high ceilings, the huge windows, the old furniture and musty faded carpets, the antiques and the large paintings of their ancestors which looked down defiantly from the walls.

Dame Elizabeth Gass inherited the Fairfield Estate from her uncle, after Lord St Audries died. Lady Gass very kindly permitted my grandmother to stay on at Little Water, on a peppercorn rent, for a further 22 years after Grandad Dyer had died and the adjoining land allocated to another tenant farmer. We think this was in recognition of the service Granny had rendered to the Acland-Hood family by looking after the Honourable Dorothy for so many years.

One day we heard that the new Concorde aircraft was going to be landing at Filton Airbase near Bristol. Grandad and I decided I would drive him the two hours to Bristol to catch a glimpse of this amazing aircraft, the product of British and French joint collaboration. Disappointingly, we did not see the aircraft but this was one of the few occasions when my grandfather and I spent time together on our own when we could talk about anything and everything and just get to know each other. He had only a short time to live before he collapsed in that gateway one afternoon.

It was very sad leaving Little Water after such a short visit. As we drove back to Heathrow Airport, my father said: 'I think we'll see your mother again but I don't think we'll see your father'. I thought this was a very cold observation, but as it turned out, he was right.

Back in New Zealand

Throughout my university years, I loved the periodic visits home to Moanatuatua, where I could help out on the farm and get my hands dirty assisting Dad with calving, feeding out to the animals, picking blueberries from the blueberry trials, or digging potatoes. I learnt how to help pull a calf from a cow in difficulty giving birth and I got to bury the calves that were sickly and died.

I was fortunate that my university studies were being subsidised by the Department of Education as I had committed myself to becoming a high school teacher on leaving university. By today's standards, the studentship gave me a very generous allowance and meant I did not need to ask my parents to pay for my tertiary education. To make travelling about easier, they presented me with a new Honda 175 motorcycle, not the fastest machine in the motorcycle pantheon, but I loved the freedom that came with motorcycling on the open road.

To earn a little bit of extra money over the summer holidays, it was then *de rigueur* for male university students to take on a labouring holiday job. As I rode my motorbike south from Auckland to Moanatuatua for the summer break, I thought I should investigate employment options for myself.

The first opportunity was the Horotiu Freezing Works (abattoir) just north of Hamilton. As I rode into the carpark with the intention of asking for a job on the gut table, I was decidedly unenthusiastic. Those working on the gut table earned very good money but it involved the dirtiest of jobs cleaning the innards of slaughtered cows and sheep. The work was messy, smelly and hot. I have a great admiration for those who do this work, an essential component of New Zealand's food-processing industry. I was not too put out to be told by the employment manager that all the jobs on the gut table had been filled for that season.

I headed off again towards Hamilton. By chance nearby I came across the new and ultra-modern Te Rapa Dairy Factory, which processed vast amounts of raw milk, collected each day from

Waikato dairy farms, into whole milk and skim milk powder for export.

I was immediately offered a nine-to-five job on the bagging line. This involved filling large 20 kg bags of whole milk or skim milk powder from a giant overhead hopper on a weighing machine and then placing the open bag on a moving conveyor belt so it could be mechanically sewn up. Working the hopper head required some skill. Overfilling the bags could lead to them falling over, with clouds of sticky white milk powder bursting out all over the packing room. This would cause a huge mess and was almost impossible to clean up.

After a few weeks, dressed in my white cap and overalls, I was able to fill the bags faster than some of the permanent staff. I was miffed that I earned only 60 cents an hour for my efforts whereas they earned 85 cents an hour. Perhaps, though, they had families to support and needed the extra money more than I did. On only one occasion did I cause chaos on the packing floor: I lost my balance and hit my head on the 'On' button. Suddenly a huge cloud of sticky white powder flew out of the hopper, all over the room. The supervisor was less than impressed.

I worked at the Te Rapa Dairy Factory for a second time during the summer holidays, this time not on the packing floor but underneath the main building where my job had the grandiose title of CIP, or 'Cleaner in Place'. This involved keeping all the pipelines of the huge factory flushed clean when necessary, through the application of appropriate solutions of chemicals. It was hot, humid and lonely. Both the packing head and CIP jobs have long since been automated.

One day a party of teenage schoolgirls came to the factory for a supervised tour of the facility. This created quite a stir among the younger workers. I did not see them, as the basement was not a suitable place for factory tours by young ladies. Later I asked a friend, who had seen the tour, who the teacher was leading the group. 'I don't know', he replied, 'some woman with big tits!' I duly related this comment to my mother that evening and it became a family joke. Because, of course, the teacher leading the tour had been my mother.

After leaving Fairfield College, Mum had taken up a Home Economics position at Te Awamutu College, 10 km south from Moanatuatua. She would drive there and back each day in her little old Morris Oxford. In due course she became Deputy Principal of the college, until her retirement in 1987, one of the few women in such a senior position in New Zealand at the time.

To help with household chores she decided to get some home help. One Saturday morning Mrs Letitia Beaumont, an elderly widow from Ohaupo, arrived in her beat-up old Škoda to start work. Stuart, who was then living at home, espied Mrs Beaumont alighting from her car and was amazed to see her first pass two crutches out of her car. He ran to Mum and in blunt language, apprised her of Mrs Beaumont's disability, which he felt sure would prevent her from doing the household cleaning

She became a dear family friend up to the time of her death several years later. She loved to tell the story of when she drove too fast one day (which she always did) and ended up in a ditch, causing a small accident. The traffic officer who attended the accident did a double-take when she thrust her crutches at him through the car window. She never let her disability get in the way of a full and positive life.

One afternoon in October 1972 when I was home on study break, the phone rang and the contents of an international telegram were read out: 'Dad died this afternoon!' That was all the message said. It was puzzling: did it refer to Grandad Dyer or Father Hamilton? We assumed it must be Grandad Dyer as Father Hamilton would not have been referred to as 'Dad'. Mum was not yet home from Te Awamutu College but she soon drove up and cheerily came inside. Dad said to me 'She won't be quite so happy soon'. Mum rang Granny Dyer later that evening, when it was morning time in the UK, to find out what had happened.

At university, I noticed an attractive young lady called Louise Ayling. We were in the same French and German classes and had several friends in common. We decided to get engaged in mid-1972, but had no money for an elaborate wedding.

Louise is a great-great-granddaughter of the Reverend James Hamlin, one of New Zealand's early missionaries. He too came from Somerset, in 1826. We had great fun on my motorbike exploring Northland off the beaten track, where Hamlin had worked, before he was transferred to the Waikato and Hawke's Bay. Hamlin had helped to build the Waimate North Mission Station, near Kerikeri. We also visited the historic Maori pa at Ruapekapeka, which features in the little poem at the end of this memoir.

Louise and I had wanted to avoid the fuss of a family wedding so we decided to spend the 1972/73 summer holidays in Noumea (New Caledonia). We hoped it might be possible to work there and get married as well as practise our French. Well, there were certainly opportunities to work but not of the paid sort. We duly turned up at the Noumea Labour Exchange, the *'Bureau d'Embauche'*, and got a casual job each — Louise at a café on Anse Vata Beach which turned out to be virtual slave labour, and me erecting a wire fence at the nickel factory and cleaning up a new house ready for hand-over to its purchaser. Only problem was that the boss man disappeared on the second day so I worked for nothing. He must have seen me coming. *Vive la France!*

We were camped in a little tent at the euphemistically named Noumea Camping Ground, which was a bare patch of rough land on a hillside, with few facilities. It transpired that we could not get married in Noumea. French law required us to post banns three weeks in advance so we could not meet the residency requirement.

Disillusioned, we headed off to Poindimié, a little settlement on the northeast coast of the island, where two friends from Auckland, Heather Craig and Rosemary Smith, had secured jobs working at the local, indeed only, hotel.

We pitched our tent on a beach near the hotel, in a secluded spot under the palm trees. An idyllic place on the edge of the wide blue ocean, with a fringing reef not far distant. We were soon investigated by the chief of the local tribe, Chief Poisdo Neophyte, who was clearly none too amused that two Europeans had plonked themselves on his beach.

Assuming we were French and, as tensions between the local Kanak population and the colonising French were very high at that time, he was all prepared to send us packing but as soon as he found out we were from New Zealand, his attitude changed and he became very hospitable. Each morning at sunrise he would go diving on the nearby reef and would present us with a large plate of assorted live shellfish or *'coquillages'*. This proved embarrassing, as the mere thought of eating them made me feel sick in the extreme. As we could not risk offending our generous host, I pretended somehow to eat one and pronounced the offered delicacy to be delicious. We buried the rest of the platter in the bushes once Chief Poisdo had departed.

Our idyllic stay on the beach was interrupted by the announcement that a hurricane was about to make landfall. We had a bit of money left over so we booked a modest room in the hotel for shelter. We could not afford to buy meals and were dependent on the bits and pieces Heather and Rosemary could surreptitiously lift (that is, steal) from the hotel kitchen. Hearing Heather's shoes clattering in haste along the concrete corridor outside our room meant that a welcome ham-filled 'casse-croûte' sandwich was about to come hurtling through our bedroom window.

Rosemary and Heather got to know the local representative of the French Government's agency charged with organising youth and sport activities, *'Jeunesse et Sports'*, for the local Kanak young people. The youthful Monsieur Falicon decided to take us on a road tour one afternoon but his little 'Deux Chevaux' Citroën car (which means literally 'two horses') had difficulty fitting all five of us in. Monsieur Falicon let me drive some of the way. If you have ever driven a Deux Chevaux you will know it is not a piece of cake. I can still hear his plaintive cries whenever I drove too fast and his little car would crash and shudder into another huge pothole in the road: 'Oh, ma pauvre voiture, ma pauvre voiture!'

Despite Chief Poisdo's generosity and Heather and Rosemary's valiant efforts to prevent us from starving, we soon ran out of money and had to go home earlier than we had planned. We arrived back in Auckland penniless.

Fortunately, thanks to my father who pulled a few strings, I managed to get a casual job picking blueberries at Moanatuatua. Louise worked as a cleaner at the Riverina Hotel in Melville, Hamilton — demolished long ago. She was not particularly impressed by the Governor-General, Denis Blundell, whose room she had to clean one morning.

Louise and I were married in the Maclaurin Chapel, attached to Auckland University, on 10 March 1973. Louise's mother, Marie, hosted a small wedding reception in her home in Meadowbank. Stuart turned up to the wedding, almost late, but he rode in dramatically and noisily on his big Triumph motorcycle. The most prominent feature was his black helmet to which he had attached two large cow horns, Viking style. Dorothy Williams, my VSA friend in Tonga, found herself wearing the same style of dress as my mother, but fortunately of a different colour.

The unintended spoiler of the day was Len Cannon who undertook to take photographs of the event, as we could not afford a professional photographer. His photos, to our disappointment, all turned out to be blurred. We had no money for a honeymoon.

Sitting several three-hour university exams was a necessary conclusion to a relatively painless year of study. In those days, exam results were posted publicly on a board at the university. There was always a mad scramble to check the board once they were published. In addition to your own mark, you could see everyone else's too. I was generally happy with my results in German and History. In the second year I, and many others, fell horribly foul of one of the French lecturers, who marked us well below what our expectations had been. Madame Murch had clearly formed no high opinion of our academic prowess in her literature course and we dubbed her results 'the Murch murders'.

In 1973, I studied with Louise at Auckland's Secondary Teachers' College in Epsom, as part of my academic bond to the Department of Education. This, for the most part, was an entirely forgettable experience although I undertook month-long teaching secondments to three high schools: Penrose, Manurewa, and Tauranga Boys' College. This meant that for three months of the year I was away from the Auckland campus. At Tauranga Boys' College, the Labour Prime Minister, Norman Kirk, a larger-than-life man, joined the staff one morning for a cup of tea. This was the only time I met him, the second Prime Minister I had come across, after Keith Holyoake five years earlier.

One of the highlights of our time at Secondary Teachers' College was a long weekend bus trip to the home marae of our Maori studies tutor, Dr Tamati Reedy from Ngati Porou. We stayed at Hiruharama, on the East Coast north of Gisborne with two kaumatua, Eruera Stirling and his wife Amiria Stirling. Both were later made famous in Anne Salmond's two delightful books about each of them.

This trip had special meaning as we learnt about Maori attitudes to land, the land confiscations and efforts to seek redress. The Waitangi Tribunal had not yet been established but soon would be. Eruera, who spoke halting English, had been a close friend of that great leader, Sir Apirana Ngata. Eruera told us about the hardship experienced by the Maori people dispossessed after the land wars. I began to understand how that poor Saxon thane, Brixi, must have felt, nearly a thousand years earlier, when he was rudely booted off his land around Stogursey to make way for invading Norman plutocrats.

Our dear old kuia Amiria would sit prominently at the front of the bus and all the way recite aloud Moteatea, centuries-old traditional Maori song-poetry.

On the way back from Hiruharama we stopped briefly at a tangi being held on a marae near Opotiki. I was deputed to give a speech on behalf of the visiting students (manuhiri). I had no idea who the funeral was for but felt very inadequate at my inability to speak fluent Maori as the occasion really demanded.

Dr Reedy went on to have a distinguished career as Head of the Maori Affairs Department from 1983 to 1988 in Wellington and was knighted in 2011 for his services to education.

I was not at that point much interested in politics and not very politically aware so I did not take part in the growing demonstrations against the Vietnam War. Without much conviction, but encouraged by a friend, I did attend one street march.

I had no experience of drugs and have never smoked marijuana. I did at one point, as a puerile affectation, smoke a pipe on the basis that if Grandad Dyer could enjoy his pipe so much, there must be something to it. I smoked the pipe for a couple of weeks but then one day rather overdid it and puffed too hard and long. It made me extremely ill. From that time on I have never shown any interest in smoking, cigarettes, pipe or anything else.

While at Teachers' College I was permitted to learn Spanish, an easy and enjoyable language. At the end of the year, I was reasonably fluent in it. My university years were relatively uneventful apart from marrying Louise, which was the highlight. I was keen to finish my studies and begin earning an income. It would still be several years before I could do so.

At the end of 1973, I taught for a month as a relief teacher at Arahanga Intermediate School in Mangere. The school no longer exists and I am sure my charges found me quite a novice, despite my year at Tupou College. I was obliged one day to take part in an inter-class softball competition but was reluctant to do so — for good reason. I missed the first ball launched at me and the class groaned. My reputation was taking a tumble. I missed the second ball and my reputation was now in free fall. Third and last ball before an embarrassing walk: the third ball hit true. I sent it miles into the distance, so far it got lost. Reputation saved. The pupils were mightily impressed. I, for my part, was just relieved at an acute embarrassment so narrowly avoided.

CHAPTER 12

A STUDENT IN DIVIDED
GERMANY (1975–1976)

IN 1974 I SIGNED UP TO COMPLETE A MASTER OF ARTS DEGREE AT Auckland University. I wanted to do this in History but I had not completed the requisite Stage 3 in History because of my year at the Teachers' College. It was German that I studied for my major — a mixture of German language, Middle High German literature and German philosophy. This was a very enjoyable year but even more enjoyable was the prospect of being granted a scholarship by the German Academic Exchange Service (DAAD) to study for a year at a German university. Dr Kathryn Smits, then a senior lecturer, helped me complete my application form. She told me that New Zealand students were always far too modest in describing their academic and personal attributes, compared to German students who would often accentuate their most modest achievements.

I completed 1974 with a Master of Arts degree (First Class) in German. The thought of spending the next year in Germany at the invitation and expense of the German Government was tantalising and I was very lucky to be awarded a one-year scholarship. Thanks to Professor Asher's personal connection to Professor Kurt Ruh, a noted Middle High German expert and medievalist at the University of Würzburg not far from Frankfurt, Ruh accepted me into his

Faculty. Louise was able to accompany me. While I studied at the university, she would attend lectures in German language as a guest student.

I thought seriously about doing a PhD in German. Dr Smits helped me pick out a possible research topic (the origins of 'Deutschland' in medieval German literature such as 'in tiutscheme lande') and I was given a PhD scholarship. I decided on reflection that I did not want to spend another long period of study at university which would have been quite narrow in terms of the employment opportunities it made possible afterwards. But I never lost my love for Middle High German literature and still frequently read it.

At Würzburg

Würzburg is a delightful old medieval town located in a valley on the banks of the river Main, upriver from Frankfurt, in a very Catholic part of Franconia. Administratively it is part of the Federal State of Bavaria, which has Munich as its capital. An ecclesiastical principality of the Holy Roman Empire, until the Empire was abolished by Napoleon in 1803, Würzburg was ruled by a Prince-Bishop who resided in the magnificent 18th-century baroque palace known as the Residenz, now one of the city's main tourist attractions. The other main attraction is an even older fortress, the Festung, which towers over the city on the other side of the river Main.

The citizens of Würzburg had not all acquitted themselves well during the Nazi period. On 16 March 1945, Bomber Harris unleashed the Royal Air Force on the city following the destruction of Dresden. In a 20-minute raid, incendiary bombs destroyed 90% of the old city and killed 5000 people. At one point, consideration was given to not rebuilding the city at all but by the time we arrived in 1975, 30 years later, reconstruction was in full swing. There were still cranes everywhere. Many buildings sported a roof with bright red tiles which distinguished them from the much darker roof tiles of pre-war buildings. The Residenz and the Festung had fortunately sustained only minor bomb damage but parts of these buildings were off limits and not yet fully restored.

Louise and I arrived at Frankfurt Airport after a long flight from New Zealand via Jakarta, where we had picked up a Lufthansa connection to Germany. We were dead tired but still needed to get to Würzburg, over an hour away from Frankfurt by train. On the train journey we got to try out our German with real locals for the first time and managed to be understood. We had booked two nights at the quaint Hotel Franziskaner in the town centre and collapsed exhausted into bed. It was midwinter but not too cold outside.

Next morning, starving, we went down to the dining room to get breakfast. Having had nothing to eat for over 24 hours, I felt a darn good fried eggs and bacon would not go amiss. The problem was that I did not quite know the conversational German for 'fried eggs and bacon', as obviously the phrase had not featured too prominently in Middle High German literature. I knew the word for bacon was 'Speck' and the word for egg was 'Ei'. I asked politely, and in eager anticipation, for 'Speck und Ei, bitte'. I was very disappointed to be served a slice of salami and a hard-boiled egg.

There was no time to waste as we had to find somewhere to live. The scholarship provided generous funds to live on but we had to find our own accommodation. We turned up at the Foreign Students' Office (Auswärtiges Amt) of the University of Würzburg as required, to report our arrival. We were warmly received by a bespectacled, homely and efficient Frau Anne-Marie Drexler. She could do little to solve our accommodation worries however, other than give us the local newspaper and suggest we look in the 'Accommodation to Let' section.

We spent the first day walking around the town chasing rental possibilities. There was nothing available in the inner town but eventually we found a one-room concrete flat in a little village called Gerbrunn, located on a rise above the city. The room, on the second level, was one of eight in a block of flats owned by a youthful Herr Bürger, who ran a delightful little café and pâtisserie in the same building. The small room had a shower and toilet, a little balcony and a 'Kochgelegenheit' (literally, 'cooking opportunity'). We had no idea what a 'Kochgelegenheit' was but it turned out to be a German euphemism for a small corner of the room with a paltry stove and tiny sink masquerading as a kitchen.

Herr Bürger was friendly and we were desperate so we signed up for a year's tenancy. The only problem was that letting furnished apartments is not a German practice. We now had a quandary: how could we furnish this one room when we could not afford to buy furniture? Back we traipsed to Frau Drexler and I was a little annoyed that she had not alerted us to this problem and been more helpful.

Frau Drexler had clearly encountered this problem before. She suggested we might try the 'Caritas Verband', as it might have furniture which could be loaned to us for the duration of our stay. I had never heard of the Caritas Verband before but it is the Catholic Church's welfare agency to help those in need. Würzburg is a decidedly Catholic city, and we were in need! We located the agency and were amazed to find it in a giant warehouse stuffed full to the rafters with used furniture and old home appliances. This was 1975 and the German 'Wirtschaftswunder' was in full swing. German households could now afford to upgrade their home furnishings, and unwanted items, often pre-war, were donated to welfare agencies.

We were greeted by an elderly gentleman whose name I have never forgotten: Herr Wohlfahrt. He was probably in his late seventies, very frail and gaunt. We explained in our best German that Frau Drexler had sent us and that we needed to furnish a one-room apartment for the year of our stay in Würzburg. He looked at us slightly quizzically and I could see that he was probably thinking: 'How come these two can afford a year at the University but can't furnish their accommodation?' Perhaps, too, he did not want the Caritas Verband to become the 'go-to' agency for Würzburg's growing population of foreign students.

I was intrigued by Herr Wohlfahrt and could not help wondering what this nice old gentleman had done during the war. Perhaps he had opposed Hitler and suffered for it, or perhaps he had, as a good Catholic, just kept quiet and ridden out the storm, or would he have acquiesced when the Nazis started marching the Jews of Würzburg off to the death camps? We were very privileged to have been given the scholarship but I could not help wondering sometimes what the Germans we met had done during the Hitler period. It was a common enough sight to see men in wheelchairs or limbless or disabled. The war was not *that* far away.

Scrutinising us, Herr Wohlfahrt asked me what my father did for a living. I was completely thrown by this question as I could not see its relevance to our present predicament. I searched for a suitable German explanation and came up with 'Er ist Bauer'. I didn't have enough conversational German at that point to explain that Dad managed a large farm in the North Island of New Zealand that was part of the government's extensive agricultural soil research programme so I just said 'He's a farmer'. At least that is what I thought I said, but farming, New Zealand style, cannot be translated adequately by 'Bauer', which in German has overtones of rusticity and rural poverty.

But it did the trick. Herr Wohlfahrt looked at us sympathetically, immediately understanding that our parents were too poor to assist with our education. He signalled that we might help ourselves to whatever we needed and that we could bring it back after a year. We found a small table and two chairs, a camp bed for Louise, an old broken sofa, hard as nails, for my bed, a small clothes wardrobe and an old TV. Herr Wohlfahrt said we could borrow the agency's little van to cart our new possessions. Even though I had never driven on the right (or more accurately for me the wrong) side of the road before, by late afternoon we were ensconced at Gregor-Mendel Strasse 9, Gerbrunn, just two days after our arrival.

We had a whole year ahead of us and were determined to see as much of Germany as we could, when university commitments permitted. Fortunately, the university campus 'Am Hubland' was within walking distance of Café Bürger. I presented myself at the Middle High German Faculty and was received by an avuncular Herr Professor Kurt Ruh, who welcomed me and asked after his friend John Asher in New Zealand. Herr or Frau Professors in Germany, of whatever discipline, are divinities in their respective faculties and Professor Ruh was no exception. I loved every minute of my time there and his lecturing staff, in particular Wolfgang von Hinten, were very welcoming once they realised they had an antipodean oddity in their midst. Wolfgang's Greek wife, Vassiley, studied German language with Louise and became her good friend.

Early on, Louise and I discovered the Mensa. I knew the word meant 'table' in Latin but in German it means the students' dining hall. Here, if we did not feel like using our little Kochgelegenheit, which was very often, we could get a cheap subsidised meal of rice and a meat dish, washed down with a very agreeable Apfelsaft or apple juice, all for a couple of Deutsch marks. The Mensa was our life-saver during the year.

We had to undergo that very German requirement of 'Anmeldung', which meant we had to go to the local civic chambers to register formally our arrival in the community. We had to have a perfunctory medical check, presumably to make sure that we were not carrying any infectious New Zealand or Southern Hemisphere diseases. It was the only time we had to visit a doctor while we were in Germany. After we filled out all the paperwork, the German authorities would be able to keep a good track of us, as indeed they can with all their citizens. When it was time to leave, we had to go back there again to do an 'Abmeldung', or deregister.

We had just enough funds to buy a second-hand car. We found a promising-looking prospect, an old Volkswagen, in a used car yard, but there was a hitch in getting our funds transferred to the bank account of the seller. It took three days and each time we went back to inquire if he had received our money transfer, his anger mounted: 'Those damn banks are just playing with my money!' he moaned.

Eventually we took possession of the car and drove off. I had no mechanical knowledge and had no idea if it would last out our year. The rumbling from the gearbox did not sound too promising. I liked the car registration though: Wü R1876. In Germany, all car registrations begin with the abbreviation of the community in which they are registered, so 'Wü' for Würzburg, 'HH' for Hamburg, 'M' for Munich, 'B' for Berlin and so on. We had great fun trying to work out where the cars came from which we saw on the roads.

On our trek each day from Café Bürger to university classes, we had to walk past a US army base, which then still formed part of the post-war occupation army. With the advent of the Cold War, US troops, and British and French troops in other sectors, were now less an army of occupation than a NATO guarantee of Federal German independence against the threat of Russian invasion from the Warsaw Pact countries.

The US base was heavily wired off. The US soldiers and their families lived a separate existence remote from the wider German community. We often used to see an earnest-looking, uniformed young man exit the base, driving his big saloon car at speed as he passed us, smoking a pipe. He was *always* smoking a pipe. I never knew who he was or where he was going, but I called him Colonel Pipe.

The Trip to a Divided Berlin

Every so often, the Auswärtiges Amt (the University's Foreign Students' Office) would organise subsidised bus trips to enable DAAD scholarship holders to see something of the rest of Germany. Herr Jovanovich, the organiser, worked in the same office as Frau Drexler. This was a very generous programme and there was always a mad scramble to sign up for trips whenever they were announced. By this means Louise and I visited Munich and its marvellous Alte Pinakothek art gallery, as well as Stuttgart and Hamburg. The highlight was a four-day trip to Berlin, still then a divided city.

Our bus left Würzburg early one morning for the long trip north to West Berlin. We had to cross 'enemy territory' as the only way to access West Berlin by road was via a land corridor through the communist East German Democratic Republic. Vehicles from West Germany were permitted by the GDR authorities to travel on designated land bridges, provided they did not leave the allocated highway and did not stop. Their fear was that we might pick up dissidents seeking to leave the GDR and try to smuggle them into West Berlin.

As we crossed at Hof into East Germany, the tension on the bus increased noticeably. Humourless East German border guards came onboard and closely scrutinised both us and our passports. Very 'in your face'! I guess they then radioed ahead to the East German border authorities controlling access into West Berlin to let them know how many were on the bus so that we could not smuggle anyone by stopping en route in GDR territory.

The autumn weather was bleak, the landscape treeless and dull. This matched the dour mood of the East German border guards. After a couple of hours, we reached the crossing from the GDR into West Berlin. We had to go through the same excruciating scrutiny from East German border guards who eventually let us through. Entering West Berlin was relatively simple. After a cursory check, we were waved through on the basis that the West Berlin authorities had no real interest in examining too closely who 'made it' into the West.

We spent several fascinating days exploring West Berlin. This included the Kurfürstendamm, the lovely baroque palace of Charlottenburg and the Schöneberg city hall where President Kennedy had made his famous, but grammatically incorrect, speech 'Ich bin ein Berliner', 12 years earlier.

We toured the domeless former German Parliament, the Reichstag. The Russians had captured it and largely destroyed it in bloody fighting in the final stages of the war, scribbling anti-German graffiti all over the ruins. Some of these graffiti have been left by the German authorities as a poignant reminder of the past. It was a cold, empty and uninviting building. Occasionally, committee meetings of parliamentarians from the Federal German capital in Bonn would be held there to make the symbolic point, to the communist East, that West Berlin was an integral part of the German Federal Republic.

The Reichstag had been the venue for Göring and Hitler's infamous Nürnberg race laws in 1935, but now, since reunification, cleansed of all past evil, with a magnificent new glass dome and renamed the Bundestag, it is once more the Parliament of a unified Germany.

One dark evening Louise and I walked several kilometres from our hotel past the Siegessäule (Berlin's landmark Victory Column) along the lengthy 'Strasse des 17. Juni'. This tree-lined avenue was named after the 17 June 1953 uprising in communist East Germany which had been brutally suppressed by Soviet tanks. We wanted to see the Berlin Wall located at the far end of this avenue. The wall blocked off access to the Brandenburg Gate just inside East Berlin, across a hundred metres of No-Man's Land. We climbed the observation platform and peered over the wall into the eastern part of the city. It looked heavily fortified, foreboding and lifeless.

It was here that President Ronald Reagan, in June 1987, called on the General Secretary of the Soviet Communist Party, Mikhail Gorbachev, to 'tear down this wall'. It did come down, just over two years later, in 1989. Along the 17th of June Avenue, however, there was no hint of any political activity at the time of our visit but intercourse of a different sort: a large number of Berlin's ladies of the night lurked in the shadows, waiting for clients to drive along and pick them up. They were scantily clad and it was a freezing-cold night. Since German reunification, the 17th of June Avenue is now far too public a place for such activity.

We were keen to visit East Berlin to see for ourselves what it was like. One morning Herr Jovanovich got us back onto our bus to cross over to East Berlin at Checkpoint Charlie. Once more the unsmiling guards came on board and stared into our faces as they checked our passports. They carefully checked the underneath of the bus with large mirrors. For the life of me I could not understand why they needed to check the underneath of the bus as no one in their right mind, I thought, would want to leave West Berlin and enter the East in that manner. Perhaps I am being naïve and they weren't looking for people but for drugs.

Having been given permission to proceed, we drove up Friedrichstrasse — right past the place where the New Zealand Embassy would be located after reunification and where, 30 years later, I would spend four years of my posting as Ambassador to Germany. Herr Jovanovich had procured tickets for us to attend a production of *Swan Lake* at the East Berlin Staatsoper on Unter den Linden. This was an excellent performance, as it was intended to be, to demonstrate the superiority of East German culture.

We were then taken to an art gallery somewhere to see the latest in East German art. I say 'art' but it was basically a collection of horrid socialist realist poster propaganda, with smiling men and women with sickles bringing in the harvest, beefy sweating steel workers with heavy hammers enjoying the challenges of building communism at their furnaces, with exhortations to 'create the workers' paradise' and 'smash capitalism'.

It was all so boring and I wonder where all this stuff is now. I asked our gallery guide, an engaging young man who didn't seem to have met anyone from New Zealand before, what role the Berlin Wall played in GDR life. I wish I could remember his reply but I have forgotten it. I probably had difficulty understanding his German. At any rate, he seemed happy enough with the whole set-up.

At one point I found myself at a men's urinal next to our bus driver from Würzburg, a stocky, no-nonsense Bavarian, of the sort you expect to see rollicking at an Oktoberfest in Munich. He was beside himself with anger at the way he and his bus had been treated by the East German border guards and he had the choicest expletives to describe his East German cousins. Clearly, the divisions ran deep.

We left East Berlin back to the western half of the city, this time not by bus through Checkpoint Charlie, but on the Underground just up the road at Friedrichstrasse Station. The Underground in West

Berlin still followed its pre-war route, before the city was divided and therefore ran for a part of the way under East Berlin. Friedrichstrasse was the only East Berlin station where trains from the West were allowed to drop off or pick up West Berliners visiting the East for the day. Of course, East Germans were not allowed to access it.

We had to go through the same excruciating border checks leaving the East, but to my surprise, the East German border guard checking my passport was very chatty and had a conversation with me — where was I from, what was I doing in Germany? He said he thought from the way I spoke German that I might be Dutch, which I took as a compliment.

After I was well past the West Berlin border control, I realised that I had left my umbrella propped up at the booth of the friendly East German guard. Without thinking, I ran all the way back from the West kiosk to the East, about 30 metres. This was a very dangerous manoeuvre and could have got me shot, but I guess both the West and East border guards were so astonished to see someone running *into* East Berlin, as distinct from fleeing it, that they didn't know quite what to do. I grabbed the umbrella and took off back to the West before any questions could be asked.

As we left on the train, we passed a number of Underground stations which were once busy places but which were now located under East Berlin and closed off. Our train was not allowed to stop there. On each platform, East German border guards with sub-machine guns made sure no one from the East tried to get onto our westbound train as it passed. It would be nearly 30 years before I would be back in East Berlin again, under very different circumstances.

Our little VW would cruise nicely along the German autobahn and we managed to make a number of trips away from Würzburg to explore around. On a trip to Fulda, we were surprised to come across the mummified head of St Boniface, displayed in the abbey/cathedral. Born, like me, in the west country of England, he was a leading figure in the Anglo-Saxon mission to Christianise parts of the Frankish empire. He was brutally martyred in 754 but fortunately they kept his head. Julius Caesar could have given him a pointer or two about how to handle recalcitrant locals. This was my first experience of a religious relic. It was crude and grotesque.

I was very careful driving and rarely drove above 90 km an hour. There was no speed limit on the autobahn so we would often be overtaken by big Mercedes or Audis. These, travelling at great velocity, would suddenly appear from nowhere behind us, flashing their headlights and disappear in seconds into the distance. It was disconcerting. But not as disconcerting as one day to find ourselves alongside a lengthy motorised tank unit, part of a NATO contingent on manoeuvres, driving at over 90 km an hour. I guess we had just witnessed a rapid deployment.

Family Visits

During our year in Germany, my parents were spending some time at Little Water Farm to be with Granny Dyer, a few years after Grandad had died. My brother, Stuart, was also in England at the time. He had agreed to go to Stogursey to live with Granny for a year or two and to study agriculture at the nearby well-known Cannington Farm Institute. He and Granny became very close and she was very grateful he came to live with her. His amazing adventures in England — gaining a reputation for himself and the nickname 'Kiwi' in the village and beyond — would fill a book.

Mum and Dad bravely decided to visit us in Würzburg, driving Granny's little Morris. Since Grandad had died some three years earlier, the car had stood largely unused in the barn at Little Water. They crossed the Channel on the car ferry and drove into Belgium, to meet us at Aachen, the place where Charlemagne had had his palace. Somehow, with difficulty in an age with no GPS, Dad negotiated his way through Belgium and Brussels. Having asked in English at one point for directions he was lucky to find a helpful local driver who escorted him to the right road for Germany. 'Aachen is that way, sir'!

I have three main memories of their visit. Dad was decidedly unimpressed by Würzburg's magnificent baroque buildings, the high domes, the ornate twisting columns, sculptured angels and gold-painted walls. We took him to view the splendid 18th-century baroque church attached to the Residenz, which had not been much damaged in the bombing of the city in March 1945. He said little about the church but on leaving said that it looked to him more like a Toby Jug shop. His Protestant upbringing went deep.

On another excursion we visited Rothenburg ob der Tauber, one of the best-preserved medieval villages in Europe. I had long wanted to visit it. Its battlements are still intact and one can walk kilometres around the encircling wall. Rothenburg is famous for its wooden medieval church altar, carved by Tilman Riemenschneider in 1501. Riemenschneider, who came from Würzburg, was a prolific sculptor. It is amazing that over a hundred of his great works still survive, despite the vicissitudes of German history. One does not have to be religious to appreciate the depth of religious devotion that led him to create these amazing works. It was a bitterly cold day and Mum remembers more about the weather than Riemenschneider's masterpieces.

During their visit, Mum wanted to visited the historic little village of Staufen in Baden-Württemberg to see a pupil from her school, Te Awamutu College, who was on a year's exchange programme there. Her hosts received us warmly, as is the German custom when dealing with a teacher. We had a thoroughly enjoyable afternoon tea, talking about the medieval history of Staufen Castle — now a ruin. Keen historians themselves, they were surprised that I knew quite a bit about the famous Habsburg Holy Roman Emperor, Charles V (1500–1558), whose aunt was Henry VIII's unfortunate Catherine of Aragon. The only jarring note was a photo displayed of our host's brother killed in the war, resplendent in his black SS uniform. Dad did not comment.

Stuart too, aged 21, took time off from his studies at Cannington Farm Institute and popped over the Channel to see us. Three in our little VW was a bit of a squash but we did a relaxed road tour of southeast Germany. We came across the magnificent square castle at Saldenburg, dating from the 14th century, which was now a Youth Hostel. We spent a magical night within its old walls. Stuart was so impressed by the place that, for the first hour or two after we left the next morning, he would wind down the back window of the car and shout out loudly, to no one in particular, 'Saaaaaldenbuuurg!'. It became a standing joke. Less funny was when we discovered he had pinched a very nice blanket off his bed in the Youth Hostel as a souvenir.

We stayed in Wunsiedel, the Bavarian town near the Czech border where Hitler's deputy, Rudolf Hess, was later buried after he died in 1987. It became the venue for neo-Nazi marches, until they were banned in 1991. Our own memory of the place is less dramatic. Since the age of 15, I had been wearing glasses to counter short-sightedness but I had decided to give contact lenses a try while we were in Germany. But I hated putting them on my eyes each morning and taking them out every night.

At the Wunsiedel Youth Hostel, I dropped a lens on the dirty floor of the bathroom. Stuart, Louise and I spent the next hour on our knees gingerly trying to locate it. In vain. I gave up, feeling very annoyed. We drove on our way. Fortunately, I had an old pair of spectacles to wear. After an hour or two, as I was driving along, I felt an irritation in my eye and to my surprise, the missing lens popped back onto my eye. It hadn't fallen onto the floor but had become lodged deeply at the back of my eyeball. I gave up on contact lenses after that.

One excursion took us to the Flossenbürg concentration camp, one of the smaller KZ's, as the Germans call them, but a harrowing experience all the same of Nazi barbarity. The ovens were still preserved. Here, on 9 April 1945 in the closing stages of the war, the Nazis, out of spite, hanged the prominent anti-Nazi pastor, Dietrich Bonhöffer, and Admiral Wilhelm Canaris, the hapless Head of the Abwehr, the German military intelligence service. Unlike the

Japanese, who often try to pretend that war atrocities never happened, Germany and the German Government are very open and honest about the past. Concentration camps are now public memorials to the misdeeds of a rogue regime and as a stark reminder to all the world.

Nearby was the West German border with communist Czechoslovakia. Out of curiosity we decided to see what it looked like. We found an isolated rural spot, marked every few metres by six-foot concrete posts, delimiting the border. On the Czech side was a wide strip of ploughed land which would make visible the footprints of anyone who tried to cross it.

Every few hundred metres there were large guard towers but these didn't seem to be manned in all cases. They were far less fearsome than their East German counterparts. Taking a risk, I decided to walk a few paces into Czechoslovakia to see what would happen. No shots rang out, as of course, I suppose, the guards were more focused on those leaving the East to escape to the West, not the other way around. I did not hang around long on the communist side.

In 2003, when I presented my credentials to the democratically elected Czech President, Václav Klaus, as New Zealand's Ambassador to the Czech Republic, I did not tell him that I had in fact visited his country once before, as a student, very illegally. Years later Donald Trump in 2019 would do something similar by crossing the DMZ line to step into North Korea, but, unlike me, he had an invitation from the dictator.

As it was midsummer, we took Stuart to a pub in a village near Gerbrunn for a beer. Three girls — our friends — joined us at a table outside. Two were on DAAD scholarships like us, one from Denmark and one from Finland. The third had a boyfriend, Udo, who was doing his compulsory military service in the German Bundeswehr. As it was a hot evening, Stuart and one of the girls decided to take an impromptu swim, fully clothed, in the fountain of the village square. When they came back to our table, they were dripping wet and they left large pools of water ponding under the seats where we were sitting.

Mein Host saw what was happening and flew out in a rage to tell us all off. He could tell we were foreigners and that made him even more angry, as no German would be so unruly as to swim in the village fountain. 'Deutsche sind anständige Leute!' he screamed at us, meaning 'Germans are decent people', unlike you rabble from wherever you come from. It was especially embarrassing for Udo, who was dead scared he would be identified as a Bundeswehr soldier on leave and be reported by Mein Host. We slunk off and never went back there again. By this means, I learnt a useful new German word: 'anständig', meaning decent.

Bayreuth and Wagner

We badly wanted to see an opera at the famous Festspielhaus, which Wagner had built in Bayreuth in 1876, but we didn't have any tickets. Performances are sold out years in advance. Taking a punt, we heard that sometimes on the day of a performance, ticket holders unable to attend that evening might come by to resell their tickets, at hugely inflated prices. Louise and I loitered around outside the Festspielhaus to see whether anyone would come by with tickets.

That evening was a performance of *Tristan and Isolde*. It looked unlikely that we would be lucky enough to get two tickets. But after several hours trading tickets for differing performances, we did end up with two tickets for that evening, having spent a fortune to procure them. We could not sit together but beggars could not be choosers. The performance was magical, but the narrow seats the most uncomfortable I ever sat on apart, that is, from that old settle in Granny Dyer's dining room.

Composed in 1859, *Tristan and Isolde* was the opera that Nietzsche had admired in the early years of his close friendship with Wagner, before their relationship soured.

Since we were in Bayreuth, we wanted to make a pilgrimage to Wagner's home, Villa Wahnfried, in a leafy suburb of the town. We duly found it and walked up the garden path to the ornate front of the building but were amazed to discover that the rest of the house, apart from that front facade, was completely missing. Villa Wahnfried had scored a direct hit during a bombing raid on Bayreuth, in the closing stages of the war, like Würzburg. We visited Wagner's grave in the garden, where he is buried next to his wife Cosima, Liszt's daughter, with his pet dog Russ. It was a moving experience.

We visited Villa Wahnfried again nearly 20 years later, with Louise's mother Marie, herself a great Wagner fan. To our astonishment, the whole house had been completely rebuilt according to its original plans and is now a museum dedicated to his music. Wagner, I came to discover, was a very flawed individual. His anti-Semitism was clearly fascist. Much of his music and his operas are magnificent and, while I do not pardon his transgressions, I am grateful for his music.

Another highlight in our search for Wagner was to visit all three of the fantasy castles south of Munich, built by mad King Ludwig II, King of Bavaria from 1864 to 1886. He was a devotee and sponsor of Wagner and his music. To honour Wagner, he built the magnificent castle Neuschwanstein, perched on a rocky hillside with the Alps in the background, as well as Schloss Herrenchiemsee inspired by Versailles in Paris, and the smaller and more intimate Linderhof Palace.

At one point, our Middle High German faculty organised a study trip to Alsace in France to examine its medieval links with Germany and the rise of humanism there. We enjoyed the famous wines and visited Strasbourg and the European Parliament, Colmar and then Sélestat. I had never really thought about the origins of humanism but, despite its narrow and controlling introspection, the Catholic Church had not been able to prevent great thinkers like Erasmus and others, even in small out-of-the-way places like Sélestat, from reflecting more openly about life and human existence.

In early summer we went to the famous Mozart Festival, held annually in the magnificent Würzburg Residenz. It is the oldest festival in Germany dedicated to Mozart's music. The baroque setting in which it is held is sublime.

On evenings spent in our cramped little apartment, the black and white television set that Herr Wohlfahrt had kindly loaned us proved a godsend. We tried to learn as much about German politics as we could. At the time, Helmut Schmidt was the Social Democratic (SPD) Federal German Chancellor, in a coalition with the Free Democratic Party (FDP) whose leader, Hans-Dietrich Genscher, was Foreign Minister.

Genscher, with his FDP colleague Otto Graf Lambsdorff, the Federal Minister of Economics, were key players when it came to addressing New Zealand's case for improved butter and sheepmeat access to the EEC — sheepmeat being the rather inelegant international trade term for lamb and mutton. Walter Scheel, a former leader of the FDP, was the federal German President. Later, in 1978, I would organise his State visit to New Zealand, the first ever high-level visit from Germany.

When it came time to leave Germany, we took our furniture back to the 'Caritas Verband' and went to say farewell and thank you to Professor Ruh. We trudged several times to his office, but he was never there, his secretary was nowhere to be seen and we had no means of contacting him. Students who wish to see the august Professor are expected to make an appointment during his Sprechstunden (consultation hours). These are published on his door and are a very German device for rationing the Herr Professor's time.

Our problem was that Herr Professor Ruh did not seem to be adhering to any Sprechstunden, so we left Würzburg without taking our formal leave. Months later, back in New Zealand, Professor Asher asked me pointedly if we had said goodbye to Professor Ruh on leaving. He had obviously received a communication to the effect that we had departed without the courtesy of an 'Abmeldung'. I told him a fib, if not exactly a white lie, that we had indeed said goodbye — but just not in person. I was annoyed that Professor Ruh had put me in this position through his chronic unavailability.

After we left Germany, we spent a few weeks at Little Water Farm and got to know Granny Dyer's older sister, my great-aunt Lily Davis. Widowed long ago, she was living at Little Water so that Granny could look after her and they could be company for each other. Aunt Lil had been a strict, prim and proper head teacher all her professional career at Yarde primary school in Somerset, but now in her late eighties she was a meek and loveable little old lady.

Louise and I went on several outings with her and Granny, including a day trip back to our old Devon farm at Speccott Barton, heavy with many memories. On the drive home we could see that Aunt Lil was growing increasingly uncomfortable in the backseat. Finally, she had to admit that she badly needed to 'spend a penny'. In the countryside it took some time to find a secluded spot in a private field, but I have never forgotten the sight of this dear old lady rushing off to spend her coinage, as fast as decorum would allow.

We went blackberry picking with her in the hedgerows at Little Water. Aunt Lil was a sound sleeper at night and could be seen guiltily smuggling a bottle of whisky upstairs to her bedroom for her night cap, with a new Mills & Boon novel tucked under her arm.

One winter's evening, as they sat by the fire, a large log rolled out of the grate and on to Granny's hearth rug, which suffered some minor damage. Granny was of the view that she would be able to make an insurance claim to get a new rug, but Aunt Lil was not convinced the insurance company would pay up on the basis of the damage it had sustained. Her sound advice to her youngest sister, to make the claim more compelling, was: 'Burn it some more, May, burn it some more!' Aunt Lil's favourite expression, when commenting on something of which she disapproved, was 'Have you ever heard of anything so ridikalas?'

Granny would keep in regular contact with her sisters by telephone, or more accurately, they with her. They were all hard of hearing so the conversations involved a lot of repetition and shouting and 'What was that, dear?'

Uncle Fred Besley had died and Aunty Daisy now lived on her own at 6 Anchor Street, in the picturesque Somerset coastal town of Watchet. Watchet is the likely inspiration for the start of Coleridge's poem *The Rime of the Ancient Mariner*. Aunty Daisy had no telephone in her home so in all weathers she would have to traipse to the nearest red telephone box, armed with a fistful of coins which she would insert into the phone every few minutes to keep the line open. Granny sometimes got tired of the chat, or it was too long. She would tell Aunty Daisy: 'Don't put in any more coins, dear!'

Aunty Daisy had a heart of gold and a warm, enfolding personality. She lived a simple life and never complained about anything. She would often send us Christmas cards and usually they would include the phrase 'sending later' at the bottom. We knew this meant that Aunty Daisy fully intended to send us a Yuletide gift, but hadn't quite got around to it. Sometimes, she never did. It's the thought that counts.

The *Taras Shevchenko*

In early 1976, when it came time to return to New Zealand, it was still possible to travel quite cheaply by ship. Louise and I bought tickets on a Russian cruise vessel, the *Taras Shevchenko*. This boat was owned by the Soviet Union's Black Sea Shipping Company, which left from Southampton for New Zealand via Panama and Tahiti. I liked the idea of transiting the Panama Canal, having been through the Suez Canal 15 years earlier. At that time, Russian cruise ships, based out of Odessa, operated from western ports to earn hard cash from the cash-strapped Russian economy. It was a shorter journey to New Zealand than via Suez, only three weeks and fewer ports of call, but at least we would get to see the Panama Canal and Tahiti.

I was surprised to find an old friend from my class at Hamilton Boys' High School on the same voyage. John Waugh, with his future wife Ingrid, were also returning to New Zealand from Europe. John went on to have a prominent career in the Department of Trade and Industry and its successors. Our paths crossed again years later when he was senior Trade Commissioner in London while I was posted to Berlin.

The voyage on the *Taras Shevchenko* had its unusual moments. Working on such a vessel was a privilege for the Russian crew and to ensure none of them defected in the first western port they called at, crew members were obliged to have family members at home in Russia (a husband or wife) as guarantees of their political reliability. The crew was reserved and unfriendly, it was not a happy place, but we did get to know Svetlana, who could often be found vacuuming the hallway outside our little cabin at all hours, indeed sometimes at 2am.

To pass the time on board we were offered Russian lessons. The only Russian I have ever learned came from those classes: *Ochin karasho, tovarisch!* There was a film theatre but the films were all socialist realism, like the East Berlin art gallery, on themes such as the fight against capitalism, the wonderful socialist brotherhood of mankind and how everybody wanted to go to Moscow and be welcomed as a socialist comrade.

We asked the purser if we could do a tour of the engine room. He kindly undertook to investigate this possibility, but he never seemed to make any progress in his investigations. Eventually we stopped asking. I realised later that that was a very good way of turning aside unwelcome requests from Westerners — never saying 'no' outright, but never saying 'yes' either, until you got tired of asking.

One night we were awakened suddenly by the intercom system blaring out in Russian 'Vnimaniye, Vnimaniye', which means 'Attention, Attention', but we did not understand the message. We sensed the ship had stopped moving and had turned around. It circled in the dark for several hours and we wondered why. All we could see by the light of the ship, after we dressed and went up on deck, was a deck chair floating in the water. Next day, trying to piece together what had happened, we were told that a male crew member had jumped overboard and committed suicide. We could only begin to imagine what had led him to do so.

Another unusual event occurred in the Caribbean, just before we got to Panama. Eating breakfast in the dining room one morning, we sensed, from the way the sun came in through the portholes, that the ship had started going in circles. We went on deck to find out why.

No explanation was given to the passengers, but we could see nearby what looked like the top of a missile floating in the water. It had written on it plainly 'Property of the USSR'. What this was we never found out, perhaps a weather measuring device, but it was exciting to imagine it was actually a missile launched as part of some Soviet rocket test. We continued circling much of the morning until another vessel on the horizon steamed in our direction. We assumed it must be Russian, as our own vessel resumed its normal course soon after.

Going through the Gatun Lake and the locks on the Panama Canal and visiting the historic Fort San Lorenzo was a fun experience and a distraction from the dull routine of the Russian boat. Tahiti too was beautiful. We explored Point Venus, where in 1769 Captain Cook observed the Transit of Venus on his first voyage around the world. We were back in the South Pacific and nearly home.

We said goodbye to the *Taras Shevchenko* in Auckland but not to any of the crew, as none had bothered to get to know us. Today, no Russian boat would be called 'Taras Shevchenko' as the vessel was named after a 19th-century Ukrainian poet and artist. Since the demise of the Soviet empire, Russia has had to cast off its imperial claims to the Ukraine. Some of Shevchenko's work was however written in Russian, so he is recognised in Russia for that. Built in 1966, the ship was scrapped in 2005 in India.

The sister ship of the *Taras Shevchenko* was the unfortunate *Mikhail Lermontov*, which ran aground and sank off Point Jackson in the South Island of New Zealand, in February 1986.

After we arrived back in New Zealand, Granny Dyer made her first trip out of the UK and her only trip to New Zealand, at the age of

76. She was accompanied by her niece Marion Hughes and Marion's husband Don, who lived in Gillingham, Dorset. Marion was Great-uncle Fred Watts' daughter, Granny's older brother (we would celebrate his 100th birthday in 1988). She was terribly jetlagged by the flight and disoriented when she first arrived, but soon got back on her feet. She spent most of her time at Moanatuatua Farm.

A highlight for her was a visit to a nearby dairy factory, managed by a family friend who was originally from Somerset. Granny had to dress up in large white overalls and a white hair-cap, an attire which almost smothered her. She looked hilariously out of place in the stainless-steel confusion of a New Zealand dairy factory but she seems to have enjoyed it.

PART II
DIPLOMATIC LIFE

CHAPTER 13

PREPARING FOR A DIPLOMATIC CAREER

BEFORE WE LEFT GERMANY, I WROTE TO THE NEW ZEALAND Embassy in Bonn to inquire about possible positions in the Ministry of Foreign Affairs in Wellington. I had little idea what a diplomatic career might entail but I had pretty much decided I did not want to become a high school teacher. Ira Buckingham, Counsellor at the Embassy, replied that I was welcome to apply and he would forward my expression of interest to Wellington. I could get in touch with the Ministry directly on my return to New Zealand, to ask about the recruitment process. If I was successful, I would still have to wait until February 1977, as that would be when the next annual intake of diplomatic trainees would occur. We had nine months to wait, during which time I would undergo a recruitment and selection process in Wellington.

We decided to base ourselves in Auckland. Louise undertook a valuable training course in Pitman shorthand. I found a job managing the forecourt of a self-service petrol station in Kingsland, a suburb of Auckland. It was great to be earning some money at last.

The petrol station, which had a car wash attached to it, has long disappeared. It was leased by an entrepreneurial businessman, Ross Armstrong, who also had a fish export business. He drove around in a big Jaguar and had very good connections to the National Party, which was then in government under the leadership of the feisty Robert Muldoon. Ross did not take much interest in the running of the service station and car wash, apart from its profit and loss situation. He left day-to-day operations to an efficient Mrs Bushell, herself an English migrant, and members of her family. Her daughter-in-law, Bubbles, managed the car wash.

My job was to manage the forecourt and make sure people paid for their petrol and any spare parts they bought, as well as for the warm meat pies which the shop sold. It was a routine existence. I used to enjoy talking to the young Cook Island girls who came every lunch time from the Kiwi Bacon Factory up the road to buy a pie for their lunch, because unlike other customers they had time to stop for a chat.

Every few days a battered old Bentley would drive up. A greatly overweight young man, in his mid-thirties, would ease himself out of his car and fill it up with petrol. He would then amble into the shop to sign for his petrol, on account. After a few mumbled words of greeting, he repositioned himself back in his car, which visibly groaned under his weight.

Mrs Bushell told me that he was an up-and-coming Auckland lawyer who did a lot of *pro bono* work for people who could not afford legal representation. Within two years, he would be elected to Parliament as MP for Mangere in Auckland. By 1984 he was Prime Minister of New Zealand. A meteoric political rise. Eight years later I found myself seconded as the Foreign Ministry representative on his staff. I always regretted that I did not remind David Lange how we had first met. He would, I think, have had a good laugh.

One night someone broke into the service station and stole the few meagre dollars that we kept hidden on the premises to use as a float for the till each morning. It was only a small amount, about $15, but a few weeks later I was summoned to court to give evidence in the trial of the supposed thief. I was surprised that the police had arrested anyone for the theft and even more surprised that it resulted in a judge-alone court case.

The judge asked me a few probing questions about the cash float and where it was kept, but I disliked the way in which he fixed his stare on me. He looked at me in a decidedly odd manner. Afterwards, it occurred to me that he might well have thought that I had stolen the float myself, in a classic insider's job, and had shifted the blame to some unlikely nocturnal prowler who just happened to discover where the money was hidden. I can't remember what happened to the thief.

During my time at Kingsland Service Station, I was required to go to Wellington for an interview as a follow-up to my application to join the Ministry of Foreign Affairs. There was no formal entrance examination for New Zealand's diplomatic service, unlike some other countries. The Ministry bosses preferred to rely on their own intuition and personal assessment of individual applicants. Professor Asher told me that he received a visit from a senior Ministry official, Assistant Secretary Tim Francis, who asked him about my suitability for a diplomatic role. I have no idea what Asher told him.

In Wellington, I undertook some psychological and language aptitude tests. The odd thing about the latter was that it determined that I had no facility at all for acquiring foreign languages, despite my knowledge of German, French and some Tongan. This test was ditched soon after as unreliable.

I was invited to meet the CEO of the Ministry, that is the Secretary of Foreign Affairs, the legendary, white-haired Frank Corner, who had two other senior staff with him to constitute an interview panel. I had no idea who Corner was and was totally ignorant of Wellington departmental hierarchies. I can recollect little of the interview. The fact that I had survived, at the age of 18, a year in Tonga as a volunteer teacher and had undertaken a scholarship year in Germany at least demonstrated that I was not fazed by hard work or the prospect of living and working in other cultures.

Frank Corner, I later came to appreciate, was a shy and remote figure who did not spend much time mentoring junior officers. He had, however, had a major influence in shaping an independent New Zealand foreign policy. As a junior officer, he had been outraged when Britain, under Anthony Eden's leadership, with France, had colluded with Israel to invade Egypt during the 1956 Suez Crisis and had taken it for granted that New Zealand would support its actions. He had striven for a foreign policy which did not blindly follow Britain under the old imperial mantra of 'where Britain goes, we go, and where Britain stands, we stand'. Under his leadership of the Foreign Ministry, the ties of 'blood and empire' were loosened as New Zealand looked to its relationships with the US, Asia and the rest of Europe.

Corner had been closely involved in the design of Tonga's constitution so it is likely he thought the Ministry needed staff who were familiar with the Pacific Islands. This may have worked to my advantage, as I was offered a permanent position in the Ministry, commencing with 11 others, on 14 February 1977 with a princely salary of $5000 a year. Louise and I made preparations to move from Auckland to Wellington.

CHAPTER 14

DIPLOMACY — LEARNING THE ROPES (1977–1980)

THE MINISTRY OF FOREIGN AFFAIRS WAS ACCOMMODATED IN TWO cramped, non-descript buildings on the Terrace, about 10 minutes' walk from Parliament Buildings in Wellington. When the conservative National Party leader Robert Muldoon became Prime Minister in 1975, he removed the Ministry from Parliament Buildings where it had been a component of his own department. Muldoon thought the Foreign Affairs leadership was left leaning — it had been very supportive of the internationalist foreign policy espoused by his predecessor, the Labour Prime Minister Norman Kirk, and when Kirk died in 1974, by his successor Bill Rowling.

Separating Foreign Affairs from the Prime Minister's Department made sense for another, more cogent reason. In the aftermath of the Vietnam War and tough negotiations expected on our trade access to the UK market consequent on Britain's entry into the EEC, New Zealand needed to expand its global reach. This was easier to achieve if the Ministry was separated from the Prime Minister's domestic responsibilities and was established with its own separate Cabinet Minister. My first political boss was Brian Talboys, who came from Winton in the South Island. A soft-spoken gentleman and a safe pair of hands, he had the unenviable task of also serving as

Deputy Prime Minister and as a foil to the feisty and at times unpredictable Prime Minister.

MFA, like most foreign ministries, was divided into functional divisions to handle our external responsibilities and objectives. There were separate divisions headed each by a director for Australia, Europe, the Americas, Asia, Legal, Economic, the South Pacific, as well as corporate divisions such as Personnel (handling human resources and overseas postings), Finance and Security. I arrived in Wellington unfamiliar with the Ministry's mode of operating and had quickly to learn the hierarchy of responsibility. The Secretary of Foreign Affairs, Frank Corner, had two senior deputies, who were served by four assistant secretaries. The director of each of the regional or corporate divisions would report in the first instance to one of the assistant secretaries.

The Ministry had been heavily influenced in its establishment by the British Foreign and Commonwealth Office, not surprising given the close relationship which then existed between the two countries. Senior New Zealand diplomats modelled themselves on their British counterparts in their diplomatic practice.

I quickly learnt that senior staff in the Ministry took very seriously their relative place in the pecking order. There was an outward collegiality among staff — operationally necessary because you might find yourself having to work together for years at a time in the same New Zealand Embassy or High Commission overseas — but this masked, as in any bureaucracy, a strong and at times visceral competition for the best postings and promotion within the organisation.

A measure of status was to be allocated an office of one's own. This enabled doors to be shut and a barrier erected to control ingress of staff. In this present age of open-planning, where even the CEO sits in an open-plan office, it is sobering to think what a dead weight was represented by the closed-door policy. An added advantage for smokers was that they could smoke unhindered in their own office, until smoking was banned throughout government premises.

Training for new recruits was on the job, apart from a short course to introduce us to the way the Ministry operated and its key relationships in the Wellington bureaucracy. We undertook a short visit to important economic areas around the North Island. Training junior staff placed a heavy burden on more senior officers, who were expected to mentor new recruits in addition to their normal responsibilities. Some were better at this than others. This was a time before senior staff were given any training in managing and motivating junior staff. It was rather hit and miss.

The practice of gathering around the tea trolley for morning and afternoon tea enabled staff to catch up with each other. It was a useful way for junior staff to find out what was going on outside their immediate area of responsibility. The eventual demise of the public service tea trolley, as a cost-cutting measure, did mean there was less informal communication among staff.

I was assigned to the Defence Division, run by a mid-level officer named David Atkins. One had to arrive no later than 8.30am each day and sign the attendance book. This was ruled off by a senior staff member precisely at 8.30am to identify and embarrass latecomers. An idiotic practice, it was soon discarded because staff routinely worked late into the evening, much longer than any putative public service 40-hour week.

Defence Division had been one of the Ministry's lead divisions in the heady days of the Vietnam War, but this had ended two years previously and the Division was now a shadow of its former self. It had just two staff, David and me. The Division acted as the main point of contact between our overseas missions (diplomatic offices) and the separate Ministry of Defence in Wellington. It was, in effect, a post box for communications from foreign governments to the Defence Ministry, if any formal defence-related response was required — for example, on joint military training exercises, or granting diplomatic clearance for a foreign military aircraft or naval vessel to visit New Zealand.

I was new to the whole business of departmental operations and had to learn the difference between encrypted inwards and outwards messages: telegrams printed on yellow and blue paper respectively. In those days, before the advent of desktop computers, yellow paper messages were incoming messages from our Embassies and High Commissions, providing a report on developments overseas, or requiring some form of official response, and blue paper ones represented communications or instructions that had been sent to our overseas missions. A sealed diplomatic bag was couriered each week to and from each of our Embassies and High Commissions overseas. These could contain reports and information or instructions that did not need to be sent by the hugely more expensive encrypted diplomatic telegram. Highly classified material such as diplomatic encryption codes and classified reports or instructions would however be carried by hand by couriers who had the necessary security clearances.

A team of secretaries, in those days always women, typed us replies to yellow inwards messages from written drafts or dictation, for onward approval and dispatch via the classified communications system. This was then located on the top floor of Parliament Buildings. The banks of clacking computers encrypted out-going classified messages or decoded incoming messages, churning out screeds of paper tape.

A separate team, usually women, was responsible for giving a filing number to all communications and memoranda. The Ministry's files were paper-based and required huge storage facilities. I marvelled at their ability to remember where each piece of paper should be filed and instantly retrieve it if needed.

Responses to yellow messages normally required the sign-off of the Divisional Director or, if more important, of the Assistant Secretary or Deputy Secretary. Very important messages dealing with key aspects of government foreign policy might require a written submission to the Minister if his instructions were needed, for example on voting in the UN, or to determine a new element in our foreign policy, or to decide which high-level visitors might be invited to visit New Zealand. On occasion, the Prime Minister's concurrence or views had to be obtained. To facilitate this the Ministry had one of its officers seconded to the Prime Minister's Department. Muldoon kept a close eye on foreign policy issues.

The key relationship was that between the Minister (Talboys), whose office was located in the main Parliament Buildings, and the Secretary (Corner) — a relationship that needed to be based on mutual respect, trust and confidentiality to work smoothly. For the most part, until towards the end of my career, these relationships generally functioned well.

Getting used to the Ministry's modus operandi took some time. On my second day, David encouragingly suggested he should introduce me to 'our' assistant secretary, responsible for Defence Division, Gray Thorp. Mr Thorp had had a number of overseas postings, in Samoa and the Philippines. He was now responsible for corporate divisions, which then included our division.

He occupied a little office of his own. It felt like we were entering an inner sanctum, as David gingerly knocked on the door and went in, saying he would like to introduce his new divisional trainee. Thorp shook my hand but said immediately: 'Sorry, I can't stop as I am doing something for the Minister.' We beat a hasty retreat. I was mightily impressed — I had just met someone who was doing something very important for the Minister!

Thorp never did get around to meeting me again. Most of the senior staff had come up through the disciplined hierarchy of the military in the war years, or they had fought it out in the Wellington School of Hard Knocks and had never learned the finer points of interpersonal relations. They could be excellent overseas on the formal diplomatic circuit, dealing with foreign government representatives, writing reports and pushing papers, but they were, many of them, less successful in motivating their own staff. Whether I myself was any better in my later career is, of course, for others to judge!

After a few weeks in Defence Division I began to be horribly bored and feared I had made a terrible mistake in joining the Ministry, if all jobs were going to be as mundane as the one I had been given. David helpfully suggested a little project: I was asked to probe the files to write a report on how the US viewed the ANZUS relationship, the trilateral pact signed in 1951 which linked the US with Australia and New Zealand in security guarantees.

The US always described ANZUS in formulaic terms: ANZUS was a 'cornerstone' of US foreign policy. President Nixon referred to it on several occasions in this way. I don't think my little report would have been very useful. Robert Muldoon was a committed adherent of ANZUS. ANZUS would, however, become inoperative between New Zealand and the US, when David Lange became Prime Minister and New Zealand became nuclear free.

Another little project I was given was to procure a First World War soldier's uniform, complete with lemon squeezer hat. With the help of the Ministry of Defence, we found a generous family who were willing to donate their ancestor's uniform. It was sent to Le Quesnoy in France for display in the ANZAC War Memorial Museum there. The museum commemorates the capture of this town by New Zealand soldiers in the First World War, an action which contributed to opening the route to Belgium and eventual German defeat.

Our division was co-located with the Asian Division, which handled our relationship with all of Asia from Pakistan to China, Japan and Korea. As our relations with Asia developed it would later be split into two, one handling South and South East Asia and the other, North Asia covering Japan, Korea and China. The Director was Brian Lendrum, who was a strong advocate of expanding our relationship with India, a fellow Commonwealth member with a burgeoning middle class.

Lendrum had been High Commissioner to India but he had great difficulty getting his views accepted by the senior hierarchy of the Ministry. With David Atkins' agreement, I offered to help out in Asia Division. I was very happy to be allocated responsibility for our relations with India, Sri Lanka and Pakistan.

This opened up an exciting and unfamiliar world to me. I was keen to understand developments in the sub-continent and read eagerly copies of the *Times of India* which were routinely sent to us by our High Commission in New Delhi. At one stage, I was the point person in the division when Ed Hillary made his famous journey by jet boat up India's holy river, the Ganges, to its source.

On 5 July 1977 the surprising news arrived that the Prime Minister of Pakistan, Zulfikar Ali Bhutto, had been deposed in a military coup. Bhutto, the father of the better-known, and later also Prime Minister of Pakistan, Benazir Bhutto, was a contentious figure. Although his party, the Pakistan People's Party, had easily won national elections earlier in the year, the Opposition alleged widespread vote rigging. Violence escalated across the country, culminating eventually in a coup d'état by the army and his removal from office.

Our High Commissioner to Pakistan, Bruce Brown, who was based in Tehran as Ambassador to the repressive Shah of Iran, sent a message (a yellow one) to Wellington asking whether he was to consider himself still accredited to Pakistan in light of the coup and change of government. New Zealand's representatives in Commonwealth countries are styled 'High Commissioner' but 'Ambassador' if in a non-Commonwealth country. This is why Bruce was Ambassador to Iran but at the same time High Commissioner to Pakistan. Confusing but the roles are exactly the same.

Bruce's query landed on my desk for reply. New Zealand's very sensible policy is that we do not 'recognise' individual governments as such but deal rather with 'countries'. I drafted up a brief message, thanking Bruce for his inquiry and confirming that he was still to regard himself as New Zealand's accredited High Commissioner to Pakistan.

I now had to get this short message approved up the hierarchy before it could be officially dispatched. I showed it to Denis Dunlop, the Deputy Director, for his approval. Denis had had a career in the old Department of Maori and Island Affairs before Island Affairs —

that is, our relations with the South Pacific — was merged with Foreign Affairs. He had transferred to the larger Ministry but had little experience of international diplomacy. Denis took my draft and, sensing a novice in me, said dismissively: 'This is not good enough, it needs to be much tighter.'

The message that went back to Bruce was an abrasive: 'Of course you are still accredited to Pakistan. If you were not, we would have told you.'. I thought this reply was unnecessarily rude and, indeed, Bruce came back with a final bleat: 'Thanks, but I thought it best to ask.' His question had been entirely appropriate and did not merit the response he received. I mention this little incident because it highlights the crucial role that 'wordsmithing' has in any foreign service. My first few years as a trainee diplomat involved a steep learning curve to grasp the finer points of correct writing, succinct drafting and clear messaging. It is a learned skill.

All messages, like that one to Bruce and any others to our overseas posts, are deemed to be sent in the name of the Minister. The CEO is responsible to the Minister for whatever the Ministry does in his name. I lost some respect for Denis after that incident. Even if instructions to our offices overseas have to be couched in clear and firm language, there is never a need for gratuitous rudeness. The incident did however reveal a tendency on the part of some in the Ministry to want to 'get one over' their colleagues.

Being at that point somewhat Machiavellian, I did wonder if Bhutto had engineered his own temporary removal from office, with the aim of reasserting his authority later with army support, when he had disarmed his opposition. It displayed a naïve understanding on my part of Pakistani internal politics and my theory, which I had prudently not mentioned to anyone, was dashed two years later, when Bhutto was hanged. If that had been his plan, it had gone spectacularly wrong.

At the end of the year I was transferred to the Europe Division and, not surprisingly perhaps, was given responsibility for our relations with Germany, Switzerland and Ireland. Given the growing importance of our trade and economic relationship with Germany, a key member of the EEC, I worked closely with the director of the division, Bryce Harland. Bryce had served as our first Ambassador to China and had a reputation for driving his staff hard and suffering no fools.

No one in the Ministry taught me as much about diplomatic trade craft as Bryce. He must have found me slow on the uptake as he sought to mentor me into my work. I respected him but did not particularly like him. He often took my written work, discarded it as inadequate and then, perfect wordsmith that he was, he would tediously dictate something to his secretary that was word perfect, like a report to the Minister, which required few changes. Bryce was rapid fire and very demanding. His office was just around the corner from my desk, where I was located with five or six others in an open-plan division. His chair had a distinctive squeak whenever he jumped up from it. I knew I had several seconds to compose myself when I heard it, before Bryce would descend with his next demand.

A piece of invaluable advice Bryce gave us was about the cocktail circuit, a necessary 'evil' of diplomacy. Bryce said it was important to come away from any cocktail function with at least one piece of information that would be to New Zealand's advantage. This good insight I never forgot through the innumerable functions I would be duty bound to attend in the years to come.

He could become impatient if things did not go exactly as he wanted and he could be highly critical of those who fell short of his exacting standards. I remember him venting his frustration one day about the Parliamentary Clerk of the House, describing him as the 'lowest form of bureaucratic life'. Much later, I came to appreciate what a crucial role the Clerk of the House plays in the smooth running of a democratic parliament. Bryce's colourful observation had been wide of the mark.

Two colleagues in Europe Division, Derek Leask and Maarten Wevers, went on to have prominent careers in the public service. Derek handled our market access negotiations with the UK and the

EEC after the UK joined the EEC on 1 January 1973, a key role which required good international trade experience. He was Deputy High Commissioner while I was on my first posting in Fiji. Later he was on the senior management team with me after which he became High Commissioner to the UK. Maarten went on to be Ambassador to Japan and then headed the Prime Minister's Department under Prime Minister John Key, a very senior role.

When Pope Paul VI died in August 1978, Maarten drafted up a nice letter of condolences to the Vatican to be sent on behalf of the government and people of New Zealand. When his successor, Pope Jean Paul I, died suddenly after only 33 days in office, Maarten dusted off his earlier message. No doubt he had to revise the text of the second message somewhat to ensure it wasn't an exact replica of the message sent only a month previously on the death of Pope Paul. A good drafter, as Maarten was, is very capable of writing a formal message to say exactly the same thing as a previous message, but this time in entirely different wording to make it look original.

Note-taking — the art of writing up a succinct summary of diplomatic meetings or conversations — is another learned skill. My first experience was to take the note of a diplomatic call which the Irish Ambassador made on the Minister, Brian Talboys. For a junior officer it was exciting to listen in on the discussion and then write up a report of the encounter for wider circulation within the Ministry.

Each week senior staff and divisional directors met to review global developments affecting New Zealand, to brief each other on key issues in their particular areas, or to be given a report by a returning Ambassador or High Commissioner on completion of their assignment. This was a principal means by which staff could find out what was happening in the wider Ministry beyond their immediate areas of responsibility and was important in enabling coordination and transparency. A junior staff member, sometimes me, would be asked to sit in on the meeting to prepare a summary of the issues discussed.

It then became a laborious task to circulate my draft report to everyone who had spoken at the meeting to ensure their remarks had been captured correctly. I say laborious because they would always use the opportunity to completely rewrite their remarks. What was eventually published and circulated to ministry staff was not what they had actually said in the meeting but what they wished they had said. Somewhere in MFAT's archives are years of 'Notes of Divisional Directors Meetings', which provide a fascinating insight into the day-to-day workings of the Ministry and New Zealand's foreign policy.

First Visit by a German President

Part of my responsibility was to work closely with the staff of the German Embassy in Wellington and to ensure our own Embassy in Bonn was appropriately assisted in its work. I got to know the German Ambassador, Dr Karl Döring, well. Several German diplomats, like Klaas Knoop, became friends although there is always a formality which necessarily attaches to diplomatic interactions between the Ministry and a foreign Embassy or High Commission. There were rumours about Döring's past which were never clarified.

Our Embassy in Bonn informed us that the Federal German President, Walter Scheel, wished to pay a State visit to New Zealand. This would be the first high-level visit from Germany since the war and marked a new stage in our growing trade and economic relationship. With Britain's entry into the EEC in 1973, German support for our continued access to the EEC market for our butter, cheese and sheepmeat became crucial.

The German Government asked for a formal letter of invitation from our Governor-General for Scheel's visit and I duly presented my draft of this letter to Bryce. Not surprisingly, he found it inadequate and dictated — off his own bat — a letter of invitation which he forwarded to the Governor-General, Keith Holyoake, for signature. Holyoake's signed letter was then dispatched to Bonn via the diplomatic bag for delivery. A week later, in comes a yellow telegram from the Ambassador in Bonn, Basil Bolt, to say the letter could not be handed over to the German Government because it had misspelt Scheel's first name 'Walter' as 'Walther'.

I comforted myself that my initial draft had not made this error. It was entirely of Bryce's own making. He taught me a great deal about the art of drafting and the importance of getting the name right of foreign dignitaries. Bryce used to drum into us that no one gives a damn about someone else's name and title but it was very important to the recipient to be correctly addressed — sage advice which he had failed to follow himself in this instance. A second, corrected letter went to Holyoake for signature. I wondered if the Governor-General realised he had signed the same letter twice.

My next task, and it was a major one, was to make all the arrangements for Scheel's visit to New Zealand, under Bryce's watchful supervision. Organising a high-level visit is a huge undertaking. It requires meticulous attention to detail and excellent coordination to put an official programme together. Scheel would arrive in Christchurch, be met officially by the Prime Minister, attend a gala concert in his honour given by the New Zealand Symphony Orchestra, visit Wellington for a state dinner hosted by the Governor-General and Lady Holyoake, then see something of New Zealand's agriculture (a display of aerial top-dressing and a lunch at a farm at Whatawhata near Hamilton), a visit to a German rowing team then competing at Lake Karapiro, then a visit to Whakarewarewa and a Maori welcome in Rotorua.

My German professor at Auckland University, John Asher, was keen to have the university award Scheel an honorary doctorate. Getting this added to the official programme was one small way I could express my appreciation to Asher for all he had done for me. Putting all this in place was a full-time task for several months, in addition to my normal workload, to ensure there was no scope for embarrassing 'stuff-ups' and to ensure everyone, including the Germans, agreed with the choreography.

A large number of New Zealand Government agencies now got involved in the preparations: the Prime Minister's Department to ensure the Prime Minister was involved and approved the overall programme, Government House for the state dinner, Police to provide security, Defence to assist with transport logistics, Agriculture to arrange the display at Whatawhata, Tourism to showcase Rotorua, and Maori Affairs to coordinate the programme of welcome in Rotorua. I even had to arrange for two high-quality sheepskin jackets to be tailor-made for Scheel and his wife so that the Governor-General could present them as official gifts from New Zealand.

The Scheel visit was a stressful but excellent introduction for me of the importance of high-level visits for developing bilateral relationships and furthering our trade and economic interests. The coverage of the visit back in Germany was valuable exposure for New Zealand in a population already disposed to view New Zealand as a dream holiday destination. During my career I organised many visits to New Zealand for overseas dignitaries or from New Zealand, such as the Prime Minister, Foreign Minister, the Governor-General and the Maori Queen. Having cut my teeth on the Scheel visit, these later visits became far less daunting although all required the same close attention to detail.

Scheel was accompanied by his wife, Dr Mildred Scheel, a noted cancer specialist, and by a large delegation of officials and reporters. He travelled in an aircraft of the German *Luftwaffe* and was to spend a night in Rarotonga en route to New Zealand. To facilitate the visit to New Zealand and to ensure everything went according to plan, I was dispatched to Rarotonga to meet the German delegation, to act as liaison. I then travelled on Scheel's aircraft to Christchurch. Mildred Scheel questioned me on why New Zealand's biosecurity regulations were so stringent.

Scheel played a round of golf with the Cook Islands' Premier, Tom Davis. To my amazement, one of the members of the Rarotongan dancing troupe which put on a lively and colourful concert for Scheel that evening was an attractive young lady who had worked at the Kiwi Bacon Factory and bought her pies from me at the Kingsland Service Station two years earlier.

After our *Luftwaffe* aircraft was en route to Christchurch from Rarotonga, Mildred Scheel asked for a last-minute change to be made to her programme in Christchurch. The only way to convey this information to the waiting officials in Christchurch was for me to go into the cockpit and use the pilot's radio link to Christchurch Airport. This was the only time in my life that I conveyed instructions from a German military aircraft.

Ensuring the German delegation kept together throughout the visit was like herding cats, as the motorcade would not wait for dilatory officials or journalists. The visit was a great success and over the years has been followed by further visits by the German Federal President in office. We have reciprocated only once, when our then Governor-General, Dame Silvia Cartwright, visited Germany in 2004 (see Chapter Twenty-three).

During the official welcome lunch in Rotorua, the master of ceremonies, the legendary entertainer and singer Howard Morrison, started telling a joke to enliven proceedings, told in his best imitation of a German accent:

'A Lufthansa aircraft is preparing to land at Kowloon Airport in Hong Kong, but overshoots the runway and lands in the water. The German pilot comes over the intercom:

'Achtung, Achtung, we haf landed in ze water but do not panik. All zose passengers who kan swim, pleze go to ze right ving. Zose passengers who kan not swim, pleze go to ze left ving.' Then after they do so: 'Zose passengers on ze right ving, who kan swim, you haf one kilometre to swim to Kowloon. Good luck! Zose passengers on ze left ving, [pregnant pause] zank you for flying Lufthansa!'

I thought the Germans would be most upset by this particular joke and his accent, but they showed no evident distaste. Even Scheel laughed, or perhaps he was just being polite.

I have to admit to a bit of naughtiness on my part. During the Maori welcome at Whakarewarewa village, two fierce warriors emerged, brandishing their 'taiaha' — the traditional Maori weapon used as a close-quarters staff weapon — to challenge Scheel, according to Maori tradition for visiting dignitaries. The German delegation was mightily impressed by the whole ceremony.

When some of the accompanying German media asked me to explain its significance, I mischievously said that, as a measure of the importance attached to this first visit by a German President, two warriors had challenged Scheel, whereas for a recent visit by Queen Elizabeth only one warrior had emerged. Of course, this bit of 'fake' news was duly reported in the German newspapers, but fortunately no one in New Zealand noticed the egregious deception.

The Scheel visit had a sequel many years later when I was Ambassador to Germany. I went to meet him in retirement at his little office in Berlin and took along an album of photographs, from our archives, of his visit to New Zealand 26 years earlier. Scheel leafed through the album without comment until he came to a photo of himself with the Prime Minister, Robert Muldoon — the legendary 'Piggy' Muldoon. He thought for a moment and then exclaimed: 'Ah, yes, I remember him.'

Many New Zealanders of my generation remember Muldoon well, our feisty and dictatorial Prime Minister. But it is a sobering thought that our daughter, Rachel, born in 1980, has absolutely no recollection of him. Scheel laughingly said he also remembered his golf game on Rarotonga — as he was teeing off for a good shot, a large porker had crashed out from the undergrowth right in front of him, putting him off his stride. He loudly imitated the rough grunt of the pig for me. Such things would never happen on a German golf course. But I suspect German golfers are the poorer for it.

Bryce Harland moved to another senior position soon after. My next director was a completely different individual, called Ross Craig. I say different because, in stark contrast to Bryce, Ross was laidback and bureaucratic. I remember that he took me seriously to task one day because, he said, I was evincing far too much enthusiasm for a particular project involving our relations with Germany. I needed to moderate my natural inclination to want to push the project along.

To develop good relationships with key decision-makers overseas, an

essential part of protecting and pursuing our overseas interests, New Zealand implements an active programme of inviting senior leaders to visit New Zealand, at our expense as a guest of the New Zealand Government. My last official visitor from Germany, before I left Europe Division, was the hard-driving Mayor of Bremen, Hans Koschnick. As Bremen was an important port for offloading New Zealand's exports destined for Europe, it was obviously desirable to have a good relationship with the leadership of this Free Hanseatic City.

Walter Scheel, Federal German President from 1977–82, whose golf game on Rarotonga was rudely interrupted (Credit: Bundesarchiv, Bild 146-1989-047-20)

There was some prospect that Koschnick, who was Mayor of Bremen from 1967 to 1985, might be a future Chancellor of Germany. This did not happen but he was a senior member of the German Bundestag until 1998. I sat in on the discussion which Koschnick had with the Prime Minister, Muldoon, and several key Economic Ministers. Muldoon again trotted out what was by now his favourite argument when dealing with representatives from EEC countries, about how much butter we needed to export to the EEC in order to import just one farm tractor.

A large part of the Wellington daily routine involved writing memoranda, known as 'submissions', seeking the Minister's views on, or approval of, a particular line of action that the Ministry wished to pursue in response to developments overseas. This might mean seeking instructions on how New Zealand should vote in the UN in New York or in Geneva, or on a political or trade development overseas which had implications for New Zealand. Background papers or 'briefs' were prepared for the Minister for an upcoming meeting, for example if he was to meet a local ambassador, or a visiting politician or delegation, or to prepare him, or the Prime Minister, for an important visit overseas.

Writing briefs was a learned art too as one had to be able to convey important information in a concise, well-written and well-argued document of only a page or two. Bryce used to say that the purpose of the Ministry was not just to tell the Minister what the Ministry wanted him to hear about a difficult topic but also to tell the Minister things he wanted to hear. There was a balance to be struck.

If a delegation was to attend an international overseas meeting, at the UN, or perhaps a trade access negotiation dealing with New Zealand's meat and dairy access to the EEC, or bilateral consultations with key partners, the various briefs would have to be assembled into a single volume. Because it contained sensitive material on New Zealand's negotiating positions, this volume would often be classified 'confidential' or less often 'secret' and require special handling.

Getting multiple copies made of a brief was a nightmare, because the Ministry had only one Xerox photocopying machine. This had recently been installed and was a massive, cumbersome piece of clunky equipment, one metre high, one metre wide and two metres long. Like any technological innovation, demand for it soon became overwhelming. There were always queues and jostling for priority work to be done first.

The Xerox machine was the personal fiefdom of a redoubtable Mrs Palmer, who had to fend off demands from all quarters for urgent copying and keep the breakdown-prone machine operational. Mrs Palmer could be feisty and brusque, as she had every right to be when demands on her time became too onerous, so one approached her with caution and deference. Behind every good foreign ministry there are always legions of people, like Mrs Palmer — secretaries, support staff, couriers, drivers and security staff —

without whom we could not operate. They are the unsung heroes of the place.

To work in MFAT one had to have New Zealand citizenship — I had become a New Zealand citizen in 1975. There was often a debate about the level of classification to be accorded to Ministry information. On occasion, to reduce the amount of extra handing that highly classified documents required, we would be told not to default to a confidential classification if a lesser one would do.

Information which had little or no national security implication could be left unclassified. If it involved sensitive information, it might be accorded a lesser 'restricted' classification or, for really sensitive material, a 'confidential' classification. On occasion a report might be marked 'secret', but this was rare. Sometimes we would joke that it was a secret that we had secrets.

There were strict handling instructions, like not leaving classified papers out on your desk overnight. Staff naturally feared being the cause or source of an unauthorised leak of classified information. No one wanted to be embarrassed by reading about it in the newspaper. This was dubbed the 'front page of the *Dominion*' test. When classified material, such as details of a New Zealand negotiating position, got mislaid in public, the consequences could be hugely embarrassing for the individual concerned.

To read material that was obtained by signals intelligence, or passed to us by our Five Eyes partners, the US, UK, Australia or Canada, one had to have an extra, special clearance. This was coordinated by a very secretive gentleman whose grossly untidy office, with the blinds drawn, was like Fort Knox. It was his job to work closely with other New Zealand intelligence agencies, the Security Intelligence Service (SIS), the Government Communications Security Bureau (GCSB), or the Ministry of Defence, to ensure relevant staff background checks were undertaken for those to be given a clearance to see such material. This clearance process was called 'indoctrination'.

A clearance was valid for five years and then had to be renewed. For the appropriately cleared staff of the Ministry, a 'bag lady' would come around periodically and in a locked room, one-on-one, she would present a folder for your perusal of the latest interesting intelligence. Staff cleared to read such material were able to read intelligence directly related to their immediate responsibilities. Even now, although I have been 'de-indoctrinated' for many years, there are still certain things I am not permitted to talk about.

At about this time an enlightened Director of Personnel agreed to my request that I undertake a six-week Maori language and cultural course at Wellington Polytechnic. Building on my knowledge of Tongan as a VSA volunteer, I lapped up this opportunity to learn te Reo. Maori is New Zealand's first language, a point often overlooked by non-speakers of Maori, and unlike every other language spoken in New Zealand, it is at home *only* in New Zealand.

I was fortunate to have two great tutors of te Reo, Teariki (Derek) Mei and Te Huirangi Waikerepuru. Huirangi, of Taranaki and Ngapuhi descent, became a prominent Maori language activist and radio and TV personality. He had great mana and a commanding presence. He died in April 2020 during the national Covid-19 emergency lockdown.

Senior Ministry officials understood that the Ministry needed to increase the number of Maori diplomats on the staff and to increase the understanding of Maoritanga among non-Maori diplomats. Noted New Zealand author and writer, Witi Ihimaera, who at the time was a member of the Ministry's staff, led the way.

Europe Division was co-located with the Pacific Division. I was asked to go to Wellington Airport one evening to meet and facilitate the arrival of the President of Nauru, Hammer DeRoburt. He was coming to talk to Muldoon's Minister of Transport, Colin McLachlan, about air links. Nauru in those days was quite wealthy and ran a heavily subsidised airline thanks to the sale of its nitrogen-rich phosphate as a much-needed fertiliser for farming in New Zealand and Australia. Intensive mining of phosphate has caused permanent environmental damage to Nauru. McLachlan was a close mate of Muldoon's, one of his few — they owned a race horse together — and Hammer liked to drop in from time to time in his own airplane, for a chat with Colin over a whisky.

When I got to the airport, the government limousine was waiting for the President and flying the Nauru flag. Just a few seconds before DeRoburt arrived, I realised the driver had the flag upside down so we hurriedly corrected it. Diplomatic *faux pas* averted. DeRoburt had a good conversation with McLachlan. When he left, he presented me with a bottle of whisky and a small pocket calculator. I soon disposed of the whisky, which I did not drink, but the calculator lasted for years and years and I always thought of the President of Nauru when I used it.

I became involved in what was called the Pacific Islands Industrial Development Scheme, or PIIDS. This scheme provided often sizeable amounts of start-up capital to encourage small-scale industrial development in the Pacific Islands. One particular project was controversial at the time but nevertheless went ahead - subsidising Rothmans to establish a tobacco-processing industry in Tonga and Samoa. This was approved by the Minister, Brian Talboys, on the basis of the good employment opportunities the project would encourage in both countries. Of course, such a project today would not get to the starter's line.

CHAPTER 15

FIRST POSTING — FIJI AND TUVALU (1980–1982)

IN 1979 I WAS BACK IN THE SOUTH PACIFIC ON MY FIRST POSTING as Third Secretary — the bottom rung of the diplomatic ladder — on a three-year assignment at our High Commission in Suva, Fiji. Louise gave up her good position with Wrightson NMA and we headed off to the unknown. For me, Fiji required little adjustment. My responsibilities in the High Commission included managing the bilateral aid programme under which New Zealand gave increasing funds for Fiji's agricultural development, including the dairy development scheme in the Rewa Delta and a beef development scheme at Uluisaivou.

I thoroughly enjoyed overseeing these projects as they took me out of the office into rural Fiji. An efficient and indulgent Kate Lackey, the First Secretary, helped me settle into the role and was a great and supportive colleague. Later, Kate was Deputy High Commissioner in Ottawa when I arrived there on my second posting.

Another task was to maintain a general oversight of our long-term sugar agreement with Fiji, under which New Zealand had agreed to take a specified annual quantity of Fiji's raw sugar. This required me to familiarise myself with the general operation of the sugar industry and to visit several of the sugar mills around Fiji which crushed the cane, extracted the juice and dried the raw sugar. I was amazed to see at one mill a huge mound of 75,000 tonnes of raw sugar, piled 20 metres high to the rafters in a dry depot, waiting to be transported to markets. In Fiji's humid and tropical climate, it was a challenge to keep the sugar dry before it could be shipped overseas.

Cutting the fields of sugar cane by hand is a hot, hard and exhausting task. The long trains that wound their way from the cane fields to the nearest sugar mill were picturesque, but Fiji's sugar industry suffered from chronic underinvestment so the annual tonnages of sugar produced began to fall. Cane growing was a crucial means of livelihood for many of Fiji's poorer people, in particular the Indian population who leased land from the Fijian landowners. Security of land tenure was a major political problem at the time.

New Zealand's aid programme, called 'development assistance' — a more acceptable description politically — was expanding rapidly, as New Zealand recognised a growing responsibility to assist its Pacific neighbours. The large-scale beef development project at Uluisaivou was located in the northeast of the main island, Viti Levu. I used to attend regular board meetings with the farm management and the local landowners where key issues would be debated. The Chairman of the Board was a well-connected Fijian, Tomasi Vuetilovoni, who later became a cabinet minister in Laisenia Qarase's government, until that government was deposed in a coup in 2006.

Board meetings at Uluisaivou involved a three-hour drive from the capital, Suva, over very rough roads. The New Zealand Government had spent many millions of dollars setting up the scheme, importing cattle and supplying farm infrastructure and competent farm managers. Volunteer Service Abroad provided volunteers for small-scale projects such as beekeeping and honey production.

There was a lively debate inside the Ministry in Wellington about New Zealand's role in developing tropical agricultural farming, with some arguing that New Zealand's temperate farming experience ill-suited us to be involved in tropical agricultural projects. Bryce

Harland, who was now in charge of our External Aid Division, then known as EAD, was one who was decidedly unenthusiastic.

There were those who wanted to push ahead to make the beef scheme a profitable and viable enterprise for the landowners and those who felt the landowners themselves needed to take much greater control of the project, if it was to succeed longer term. The beef scheme did fold after a few years, suggesting that it was perhaps not the wisest use of our aid funds. Cattle rustling did not help either and was not unheard of, even in Fiji.

More successful was the development of a dairy industry in the Rewa Delta, near Suva, and the establishment of a milk chilling centre at Naluwai — a major project overseen by a very capable New Zealander, Mel Eden, and later by Mike White. There were frustrating delays and hold-ups getting the needed chilling equipment from New Zealand but it eventually began operation. This was a boon to local farmers, mostly Indian families, who could now send their milk to the centre for prompt chilling, essential in Fiji's hot tropical climate, before it was sent on to the dairy factory in Suva for processing. I also arranged for a huge steel cheese vat to be imported from New Zealand so that the Rewa Cooperative Dairy Company could begin making cheese for local consumption.

Rachel is Born

On 11 July 1980 our first child, Rachel Alisa, was born in Auckland. Louise had gone back to Auckland several weeks previously to stay with her mother, Marie Ayling, to give birth in Auckland Hospital. I was due to go back to Auckland a week before the expected arrival, but Rachel, as unpredictable as ever, decided to come two weeks early so I missed out.

Rachel spent the first two years of her life in a Fijian environment. She became very close to her Fijian nanny, Milika Naidole, and her partner Maika Raburau. Maika worked in the Lautoka sugar mill and introduced us to his extended family who lived in the village of Muana, in the Rewa River delta near Suva. Maika's father, who was also called Maika, was the chief of the village. We called him 'Taitai', a term of respect and endearment for an elderly male.

Little Rachel was formally adopted into Taitai's extended family in a colourful traditional ceremony called in Fijian 'Me Taura na Mata ni Gone', or 'Showing the Eyes of the Child'. This ceremony must be performed after the first-born to ensure the children have access and rights to the village. On the day of the ceremony, young Maika and I went early to town to buy the necessary gifts to be presented to the village during the ceremony: one bolt of cloth (42 yards), two four-gallon drums of kerosene and two pounds of yaqona (kava) root. After dressing little Rachel in her best frock, we drove to Muana and were ferried across the river by punt (there is a bridge now over the river).

We went to the chief's bure (traditional hut or home) and little Rachel was wrapped in folds of masi (tapa cloth). The kava root, in a time-honoured Fijian ceremony called a 'sevusevu', was formally presented. Then the bolt of cloth, kerosene and a highly prized whale's tooth (tabua, pronounced *tambua*) were formally presented to the senior lady of the village, Waqa (pronounced *wanga*). The kava root was crushed and we drank copious rounds out of a coconut shell. Then traditional dancing began. Rachel, the star attraction, was very well behaved and was passed around by everyone. After several hours, we made farewell speeches and thanked the village for the honour done to Rachel. I felt exhausted after drinking 10 or 12 large bowls of kava and once home I slept for 12 hours.

Maika senior, Taitai, died while we were in Suva. His traditional funeral in the village was a very sad occasion. This was the first time I had ever seen a deceased person. Maika had had little formal education but I have never met a more dignified and upright gentleman. On his visits to Suva, he would often stay in our house and was always a welcome guest.

Rachel learns to dance in Fiji

Tuvalu

The New Zealand High Commission in Suva was responsible for our bilateral relationship with two other countries, Kiribati and Tuvalu. My colleague Des Rowe covered Kiribati. It was my task to oversee the delivery of our fledgling aid programme for Tuvalu.

Tuvalu had become independent only a year or two before, in 1978, but still has Queen Elizabeth as its Head of State. Formerly administered together by the British as the Crown Colony of Gilbert and Ellice Islands, Kiribati and Tuvalu as separate countries now faced the challenge of setting up the whole apparatus of government as befits an independent country and member of the United Nations. With a population of less than 10,000 and no ready sources of income other than fishing licence fees, it was a tough road for Tuvalu.

Tuvalu (pronounced *tu-va-lu*, not **too-va-loo** as many Americans and British mistakenly call it), could be reached once a week by airplane after a three-hour flight from Nadi in Fiji. The aircraft immediately turned around and went back to Fiji. It was always sobering to fly over such a vast expanse of ocean, knowing that if there was ever a serious malfunction in the aircraft, the chances of making it to any landing place were slim indeed.

One had the option of staying in Funafuti, the capital, for one hour or for a week until the next flight. The runway was grass, covering beaten coral. It had been built in the Second World War as an American base in the war against Japan. Given the small size of the atoll, the runway doubled as a soccer field. It needed to be cleared of all goal posts and other extraneous material before any aircraft could land. A versatile Peter McQuarrie ran Tuvalu's telecoms with the outside world and ensured the runway was safe for in-coming aircraft.

The large, circular Funafuti atoll was flat and only a couple of metres above sea level. Tuvaluans were already worried about the impacts of climate change although the issue had yet to grab the global headlines. In a storm, or hurricane, it was not uncommon for the ocean waves to wash right over the atoll, inundating homes and plantations. The porous coral made it difficult to build up a layer of soil for plant cultivation. It was a fragile and precarious environment. Getting rid of inorganic rubbish was impossible so there was a gradual build-up of polluting waste.

New Zealand's aid programme became substantial in subsequent years but was then only about $50,000 a year. It did not go very far. I loved my periodic visits to Funafuti as I was able to meet the Prime

Minister and other senior cabinet ministers (unusual for a junior diplomat) and report back to Wellington on developments affecting the country. The first post-independence Prime Minister, Toaripi Lauti, always received me warmly in his small and spartan office. He had few international visitors. There was of course the occasional carpetbagger, who came armed with harebrained 'get rich quick' schemes.

One of the ingenious ways of creating revenue for the cash-strapped country was the sale of bright postage stamps. There was a little cottage industry on the island, sticking stamps on envelopes for first-day covers, for sale to philatelists around the world. The British manager used to complain that his staff ripped or damaged too many of the stamps as they stuck them on the envelopes but it was a profitable enterprise. Prime Minister Lauti proudly gave me several handsome presentational first-day covers, which he autographed for me.

Essential supplies would reach Tuvalu via an infrequent shipping service from Fiji. The vessel was often unreliable and occasionally would run aground on a reef so the country would run out of basic commodities. While I was posted to Fiji, a New Zealand company, Sea Bee Air, operated a sea plane service between Funafuti and the main outer Tuvalu islands but it was expensive to run and spare parts were hard to come by. It did not last long.

But by means of the sea plane I was able to visit two of Tuvalu's other islands, Vaitupu and Nukufetau. Landing a sea plane in the troughs of an ocean swell is a hair-raising adventure. Vaitupu was the home island of Tuvalu's second Prime Minister, Dr (now Sir) Tomasi Puapua. He received me warmly and showed me over Vaitupu. He defeated Toaripi Lauti in the first post-independence elections held in September 1981. He served as Prime Minister until 1989 and was Governor-General of Tuvalu from 1998 to 2003.

On one visit to Tuvalu we flew in on a cumbersome New Zealand Air Force C-130 Hercules. It was a bumpy landing with no room for error. Michael Powles had recently taken over as New Zealand's

High Commissioner to Fiji, Tuvalu and Kiribati from David McDowell. I accompanied Michael on his first visit to Tuvalu to formally present his credentials as High Commissioner. We held a drinks reception for the Tuvalu Government Ministers and officials at the Vaiaku Langi Hotel — then Funafuti's only hotel — and paid a courtesy call on the Prime Minister and then the elderly Governor-General, Sir Fiatau Penitala Teo. He was Tuvalu's first post-independence Governor-General. The task was a big challenge for him, as no one had previously undertaken the role. He found it difficult to sustain a conversation.

Another source of income for the fledgling country was licence fees from international fishing in Tuvalu's huge Exclusive Economic Zone. Taiwan, Japan and Korea were involved, but it proved impossible to regulate their fishing, as Tuvalu had no independent means of checking who was fishing in its zone and whether or not they were abiding by the terms of their fisheries licence. Taiwan in particular was suspected of substantial and ongoing breaches. New Zealand Air Force Orions could sometimes check on suspected illegal fishing activity but it proved for the most part impossible to apprehend transgressors.

The redoubtable Henry Naisali, who was then Tuvalu's Finance Minister, showed evident anger at this activity: 'There is no such thing as an honest fisherman', he moaned to us. Naisali was a competent administrator, having been appointed Financial Secretary of the British Crown Colony in 1977. Later he became Deputy Prime Minister. Naisali was instrumental in establishing the Tuvalu Trust Fund, which was a sensible initiative to provide a regular income for the fledgling democracy.

One of the major projects which New Zealand undertook was a regional reef-blasting project, run by a resilient and indefatigable Peter Asher and his team of enthusiastic young engineers. Since many of the atolls had fringing reefs, it was impossible for small boats to access land from the ocean without often being tipped over as they crossed the turbulent bar.

Peter's task was to cut a channel in the reef so that the boats could enter smoothly. This involved blasting and digging a shallow channel out of the coral reef rock and removing it with a tractor. Working in such hot, tough and salty conditions was hard. Equipment failures were frequent. But Peter, undaunted, persevered. While the environmental impacts of such a project would be questioned today, there is no doubting the satisfaction which the island residents derived from the project.

One strange incident occurred when I was meeting the elders of Nukufetau in their 'maneapa', or open village meeting house. Some of the locals were concerned at the vibrations caused by the reef-blasting work. Peter was at pains to assure them there was no serious risk of collateral damage to buildings onshore. One elder then stood up and started querying me in the following manner. My friend and host, who was the local MP for the island, acted as interpreter. The elder asked me about my predecessor, a lawyer, whom I had taken over from in Fiji. Was he alive or dead? he asked. I knew he was very much alive, in Wellington. If he was dead, then the island wished to extend its condolences to his family. If, however, he was alive, the island wanted to know when he was going to come good on the project for the island he had promised to assist with.

I was completely taken aback by this, as I had no idea what he was talking about. No one had ever mentioned it. But after a while it became clear. My predecessor had visited Nukufetau several years before me. The islanders had asked him to provide some hand-held two-way radios so that they could communicate with an offshore islet about three kilometres away. This islet had a pig farm on it. The women of Nukufetau would row out to the islet each day to tend the animals, but there was no way of keeping in touch with home base while they were away. A radio link would be invaluable. They had been waiting patiently for several years for the radios to arrive.

I duly undertook to investigate and in due course two radio sets were delivered to Nukufetau. No doubt a better communications link has since been established with the pig farm, but it taught me a lesson:

Don't undertake to do something and then not deliver on your promise.

Peter and his team had a satellite radio communications link with the outside world so it was a great joy one afternoon to be able to speak to Louise back in Suva, with baby Rachel. Nukufetau felt a long way from home.

While I was on Vaitupu and Nukufetau, remote Pacific Islands, I could not help but think of the remarkable Tom Neale who gave up a good career in the New Zealand Navy to travel the Pacific. In 1952, Tom settled alone on an uninhabited island, part of Suwarrow atoll in the Northern Cooks, a modern-day Robinson Crusoe. He wrote an amazing book called *An Island to Oneself* in 1966 which told of his experiences. It captivated me as soon as I read it. Tom died in 1977 and is buried in Rarotonga. Although his life was not always happy and his exile was self-imposed, he was a free spirit. On Vaitupu and Nukufetau, I tried to appreciate what his life of solitude and loneliness might have been like.

Occasionally I would come across European men, like Tom, who had decided to make Tuvalu, or another small Pacific island, their home. They lived very simply, in open-sided thatched houses with few material possessions, beside the great ocean or a tranquil lagoon. In the history of the South Pacific there have been many such people who turn their back on the materialism of the modern world, preferring a precarious existence as a beachcomber, or trans-culturite. Sometimes, I envied them.

Taniwharau Comes to Fiji

In 1981, Taniwharau won the Polynesian Kapa Haka Festival in New Zealand. In recognition of their success their patron, the Maori Queen, Dame Te Atairangikaahu, accompanied by her husband, Whatumoana Paki, brought the group on a visit to Fiji. I had met Dame Te Ata before and immediately liked her, her quiet dignity, gracefulness, concern for others and her great mana. It was my job to organise their visit to Fiji, a unique occasion when two great Pacific cultures would meet.

The Kapa Haka group gave a wonderful concert performance to a packed audience in Suva and also visited the island of Kadavu. The well-known guitarist Napi Waaka was in charge of the group and it was a great opportunity to showcase Maori culture in Fiji. Both the visitors and the Fijians loved every minute.

Dame Te Ata was received warmly by the Tui Vuda (pronounced *vunða*), paramount chief of the Vuda district of northwest Fiji. He put on a fine reception for the group. The whole visit went off smoothly. Only on one occasion did we lose Dame Te Ata and her husband for several hours. No one knew where they had gone. The Fijians began to be worried, as did I.

Losing a prominent visitor can have embarrassing consequences. Eventually Dame Te Ata and her husband turned up. They had snuck away to do some family duty-free shopping in Lautoka. In those days Fiji did a roaring trade selling duty-free goods to New Zealanders on holiday — watches, cameras, tape recorders, TVs, perfumes, jewellery, all items which were hugely expensive in New Zealand behind a high tariff wall. New Zealand's decision some years later to remove import duties on such items, as part of New Zealand's domestic economic reforms, effectively destroyed Fiji's duty-free tourism industry.

The Fiji Ruck Sack Club

Every spare moment, Louise and I would try to explore as much of Fiji as we could. We joined the Fiji Ruck Sack Club and were able to visit some of the less accessible places. One adventure involved a bus ride into the interior of Viti Levu to stay overnight in a small village. The village chief was delighted at the unexpected income derived from our visit. I recall seeing him sitting on the floor of his bure (Fijian thatched house) eagerly counting out the pile of cash he had just received from us. On this occasion, my parents and their friends Laurie and Cushla Neal from Te Awamutu joined us.

We left baby Rachel in the capable hands of her nanny, Milika Naidole. Staying overnight in the village was hard for my parents, who did not sleep a wink on the hard, wooden beds of the traditional Fijian bure. Next morning was great fun, however, as we headed off downriver, each on our own four-metre-long bamboo raft poled by a capable lad from the village. There was spectacular scenery but after an hour we came to a narrow gorge. It proved difficult to squeeze the long cumbersome rafts through it.

We all made it except unfortunately Cushla, a large lady, who fell off into the river as her raft upended. Everyone panicked until it became clear the river was not overly deep at that point. Cushla managed by hard paddling in the swirling waters to hold on to the raft until a deft Fijian lad was able to rescue her. She was soaked through but undaunted and managed to laugh. Her main concern was to ensure her cigarettes did not get wet as she was a heavy smoker. Fortunately, she had thought to wrap these in a plastic bag and she held it high above her head as she bobbed in the water.

Another trip took me to Vanua Balavu, in the Lau islands east of Fiji. This was the home island of Laisenia Qarase who was then Head of the Fiji Public Service Commission. Lai had become a good friend, with his wife Leba (pronounced *lemba*), and it was a privilege to stay in his home village, Mavana. This beautiful island had an airstrip so we were able to fly there in a de Havilland Twin Otter. Our friends, John and Mary Scott, joined us on many of our trips. At one point, John joked that Lai and I would both become Prime Ministers of our respective countries.

John was very wrong as far as I was concerned but Lai did become Prime Minister of Fiji, from 2000 to 2006, until he was toppled in yet another of Fiji's debilitating coups d'état, this one orchestrated by a soldier, Frank Bainimarama, who, as I write, is still Fiji's Prime Minister. Lai died in April 2020. There is no doubting his love and passion for Fiji, whatever the political upheaval he encountered.

New Zealand engineers had recently constructed a runway on Rotuma, an island 600 km to the north of Fiji. Many Rotumans lived and worked in Fiji but until then had few opportunities to go home. The advent of an airstrip was a major development and I was fortunate to travel on the first aircraft to land on Rotuma — a New Zealand Air Force plane. We included on our passenger list some prominent Rotumans who had not been able to visit their home for years. It was a great and festive occasion. We spent only a few hours on the ground before the aircraft had to depart again. But it meant the island could now be connected to the rest of Fiji by regular flights. The dirt runway has now been sealed.

During my posting, our relationship with Fiji, at the government-to-government level, was not without its tensions. Fiji's patrician Prime Minister, Ratu Sir Kamisese Mara, himself from the Lau islands like Laisenia Qarase, was quick to take offence at any perceived slight, even if unintended, from New Zealand officials or politicians. Any sense that New Zealand was insufficiently sensitive to Fiji's concerns or developmental aspirations could give rise to annoyance, or irritation, on his part. I was amazed to discover on our files a copy of a three-page rambling, handwritten letter which the Labour Prime Minister Bill Rowling had written to Mara in the mid-1970s to apologise for any misunderstandings that might have arisen in the relationship and seeking to establish a positive personal rapport with him.

Rob Muldoon, who was National Prime Minister at the time I was posted to Fiji, would never have put his hand to such a personal letter. Mara and Muldoon had a difficult and at times tense relationship. This did not affect me in my day-to-day work as I was too junior in the High Commission. Brian Talboys, our Foreign Minister and Muldoon's deputy, did come to Fiji to keep open the lines of communication with Mara, something that Muldoon himself was not overly interested in doing. I left Fiji well before any of the coups occurred.

Writing assessments of key developments in a host country and their implications for New Zealand is part and parcel of a diplomat's work. One incident occurred which taught me a valuable lesson. It was at the time of the 1981 rugby union tour of New Zealand by

South Africa. Muldoon had insisted the tour take place on the flimsy basis that politics — in this case South Africa's racist apartheid policies — should not interfere with international sport. The tour bitterly divided New Zealand, leading to violent protests at rugby matches. We were tasked by head office in Wellington to ascertain what the Fiji rugby authorities thought of the 1981 tour and whether or not it might affect their attitude to engaging in future sports events with New Zealand.

I spoke to the secretary of the Fiji Rugby Union, Hari Pal Singh, who was a good friend. He gave me a very positive assurance that the 1981 tour would not negatively impact on Fiji's attitude to playing sport with New Zealand. I relied far too heavily on HP's comments, which resulted in my preparing a one-sided, overly positive report for Wellington.

It turned out from separate discussions which Derek Leask, the Deputy High Commissioner, had with other senior administrators in the rugby union that their view was a good deal more nuanced and decidedly less understanding of the New Zealand Government's position. A follow-up, more accurate report had to be sent to Wellington. The episode taught me to be very careful in preparing assessments on controversial subjects and to avoid overreliance on the views of one individual with seemingly positive, but perhaps not widely shared, opinions.

While my parents were visiting us in Fiji, we received a phone call from Dad's youngest brother, Peter, in England, to say Mimi, my grandmother, had died, aged 81. Her funeral was held in early June 1982. Father Hamilton, who was ten years older, died not long after. They are both buried in St. George's Churchyard, in Saham Toney in Norfolk. Given the circumstances under which we had left England in 1961 to emigrate to New Zealand, Dad was philosophical about the death of his parents. Speccott Barton seemed a long way away.

CHAPTER 16

FISHING AND FLYING (1982–1984)

AFTER PACKING UP AND SAYING GOODBYE TO FIJI, WE RETURNED to New Zealand via Tonga, where after 13 years I was able to show Tupou College to Louise and baby Rachel and to say hello to some old friends. John Brady, our High Commissioner to Tonga, and his wife Sonia allowed us to stay in their home, the New Zealand Residence, perched atop one of the few hillocks on the Nuku'alofa foreshore, while they were on leave out of Tonga.

Sonia had been a good friend as she had been working in the External Aid Division in Wellington on the Fiji desk while I was grappling with the problems of the beef development project at Uluisaivou. Sadly, John died several years later. Sonia, who was from the Philippines, left New Zealand diplomacy to return to her home country. She became Philippines' Ambassador to China, a very senior role.

Tonga had not changed much and had yet to experience the Chinese influx and civil unrest which Nuku'alofa underwent some years later. The little white-painted fale at Tupou College which John and I had lived in for a year was still there and the school looked pretty much unchanged, apart from the grand old thatch church which had burned down. We visited the famous blowholes at Houma as well as

Monotapu Beach where I had been 'murdered' as a member of Captain Cook's crew by a mob of laughing Tongans.

Back in Wellington we bought our first home, at 8 Erris Street in Johnsonville. Christopher joined our family on 5 September 1983, a brother for Rachel. We gave him William as his middle name after his grandfather and great-grandfathers. For Rachel's fourth birthday we arranged for a little message of congratulations to be broadcast over the local radio on a children's programme. I will never forget her look of pleasure and surprise when she heard her name on the radio.

I was assigned to the Economic Division with responsibility for the international aspects of fisheries, civil aviation and maritime issues. I knew very little about any of these subjects but had to learn quickly. There was keen interest by the Soviet Union, Japan and Korea to secure access to our fisheries resources. It was my job to notify them formally each year of the quantities of a particular fish species they were permitted to catch in our Exclusive Economic Zone (EEZ) and how much the licence fee was for the tonnage allocated. They were particularly interested in high-value species such as terakihi, hoki, ling and orange roughy. Japan and Korea also wanted access to squid.

It was the responsibility of the Ministry of Agriculture and Fisheries to determine each year the size of the total fish stock and how much might be allocated to foreign fishing vessels from the total allowable catch (TAC). Once the Minister of Fisheries, based on MAF's advice, had made decisions on quota limits and set fee levels, I had to notify the countries concerned via a third-person note, commonly referred to as a TPN. This is an archaic device, standard in any diplomatic service, which formally conveys the views or decisions of one government to another. Such TPNs are very common and usually open with a formulaic phrase such as:

'The Ministry of Foreign Affairs presents its compliments to the Embassy of Japan [or the Republic of Korea, or the Union of Soviet Socialist Republics] and has the honour to inform the Embassy of decisions taken by the Government of New Zealand in respect of fishing quotas in New Zealand's EEZ for 1982.'

Such notes usually conclude with another formulaic phrase such as:

'The Ministry of Foreign Affairs renews to the Embassy of Japan the assurances of its highest consideration.'

The language is hackneyed but since everyone understands it and uses it, it does not need to be reinvented each time a TPN is dispatched. It is not elegant, but it is easy to comprehend and the recipient knows the body of the message contains important information.

Once I had prepared such TPNs, I had to call in the official responsible for fisheries matters in each embassy, formally hand over the note and answer any initial questions. No fishing was allowed before the licence fees had been paid in full to MAF and they had to pay the full fees, whether or not they actually caught all the allocated amounts. Preference was given to New Zealand companies which were then in the process of expanding their fishing fleets and growing their catching capacity, sometimes in joint ventures with overseas partners.

This work required me to work closely with each embassy concerned. I enjoyed working with the Soviet Embassy the most. The Prime Minister, Robert Muldoon, had expelled the Soviet Ambassador, Vsevolod Sofinsky, in 1980 while I was in Fiji, after Sofinsky allegedly gave money to the pro-Soviet Socialist Unity Party in New Zealand. The Soviet Union in turn expelled our own ambassador in Moscow. There was therefore a perceptible tension in our relationship with the Soviet Embassy, which was located in Messines Road, Karori. Muldoon achieved political advantage from one of his campaign slogans of '*Reds under the Bed*' and a TV advert of '*Dancing Cossacks*', to prove he could be tough on the Soviets, a move welcomed by the US, then our ANZUS ally.

These problems did not affect me unduly as the Soviets were still keen to access our fisheries resource. I got to know the Soviet

Fisheries Representative, Sergei Kornev, well. Several times I was invited to receptions at the Soviet Embassy. These would be rather dour affairs with stilted conversations, burnished with caviar (which I could not eat) and vodka. I never had to admit that I could not countenance eating any of the fish they were so eager to catch.

I had to notify my superiors of any contacts with the Soviet Embassy. On one occasion after a late evening reception, the Embassy driver gave me a ride in one of the official cars back to my home in Johnsonville, as I had no other means of transport. It did occur to me later that spending time alone in a Russian Embassy car at night might have looked suspicious to others, but I can report that the ride was quite uneventful.

Sometime later our Security Intelligence Service asked to interview me as they had suspicions that one of the staff at the Soviet Embassy might be a KGB agent. After being given clearance to speak to the SIS, I was grilled about what I knew of the individual concerned and what I knew of his relationship to others in the Soviet Embassy. Did others defer to him, despite his relatively low diplomatic rank, did he seem to take the leading role in conversations? I answered the questions to the best of my ability. The individual concerned did leave New Zealand soon after, but I never knew if this was the result of a normal posting rotation or something more complicated.

A large Soviet fisheries vessel docked in Wellington. The captain invited me to lunch on board, along with my MAF Fisheries colleagues. I had never been on a Russian fishing boat before, but its spartan nature reminded me of the *Taras Shevchenko*. It was a pleasant enough lunch despite the language barrier. Somehow I managed to get around the problem that I could not eat the fish or the caviar on the menu.

Russia was for some years an important market for New Zealand butter. We produced large quantities but could not sell it easily as international dairy markets, like the EEC, were heavily protected. To pay for the butter, the Russians wanted to sell us their Lada cars, in a counter-trade arrangement. Little Ladas could in due course be seen skittling around the roads of New Zealand.

There was a joke at the time that a shipment of Ladas arrived on the wharf in Wellington and was proudly inspected by the Russian Ambassador and a New Zealand Cabinet minister. The Ambassador opened the front bonnet of one car to show off the latest in Soviet engineering, but was embarrassed to find a bird's nest sitting atop the engine.

The work on civil aviation introduced me to the arcane world of international air traffic rights, civil aviation negotiations and the many 'Freedoms of the Sky' by which international air traffic is regulated. These are unbelievably complex commercial aviation rights and I have to thank my good friend, Yvonne Lucas, for teaching them to me.

At its simplest, the First Freedom grants, to Air New Zealand for example, the right to fly and carry traffic over another country (e.g. Australia) without landing. The Third Freedom grants the right of an airline of Country A (e.g. Air New Zealand) to land in and carry traffic to Country B (e.g. Australia). They get progressively more complicated. The Ninth Freedom grants the right to fly within a foreign country without continuing to one's own country, for example a flight between Auckland and Christchurch by an Australian airline.

When I arrived on the desk, Air New Zealand was expanding its international network so we urgently needed the various permissions from other countries, to overfly, land, drop off and pick up passengers. To obtain such rights we would need to grant reciprocal rights to other countries and foreign airlines. This resulted in complex, protracted and often mean-spirited negotiations as one country sought to advance the interests of its own national carriers at the expense of its rivals. I worked closely with the Ministry of Transport which had day-to-day responsibility for civil aviation matters.

I took part in several such negotiations in Wellington and overseas. Air New Zealand was always most obliging when it came to our travel arrangements. It often gave us free First Class travel, something that would not be countenanced nowadays. Brian Lynch, a senior MFAT official, led the negotiations and we visited Singapore and Japan for a series of detailed talks about exchanging aviation rights.

We made a trip too to Apia to talk to the Samoan Government about landing rights. I met the legendary Aggie Grey and stayed at her hotel in Apia. She and her sister Mary were widely believed to have been the models for James A Michener's character 'Bloody Mary' in his 1946 book *Tales of the South Pacific*, which was adapted by Rodgers and Hammerstein for their hit Broadway musical *South Pacific*. Aggie had died by the time of my own posting to Apia, 15 years later.

Some countries advocated doing away with such negotiations, preferring an 'open skies' policy which in essence removed all such restrictions on airlines and would permit a fully competitive international aviation market. But protectionist instincts are still strong in many countries even today as they seek to advance and protect the interest of their national flag carriers. During the 2020/21 Covid-19 pandemic, the skies were for the moment largely empty of passenger flights.

Junior staff took it in turns to be comms duty officer for a week at a time, responsible for handling any emergency communications that might come in from our overseas posts and need action out of office hours. During one of my stints, I received a call late one evening from Geneva. Jim Bolger, the Minister of Labour in Rob Muldoon's National Government, was attending an International Labour Organization (ILO) meeting there and wanted to have a copy of the controversial draft legislation on voluntary unionism which he had recently introduced into our Parliament.

I could not for the life of me figure out why Bolger had not taken a copy of such an important piece of legislation with him to Geneva. I had no idea where to get a copy so late at night. In desperation, I rang up the Secretary of Labour, Gavin Jackson, who fortunately had a copy of the draft law with him at his home. In the dead of night, I got on my motorbike, went to Gavin's house, and then took a copy to the comms section in Foreign Affairs, which had someone on standby to fax it to Geneva. That was the only way of getting the Bill to Bolger. It was well after 2am before I got home. I mention this little episode lest those who are so used to email and instant desktop communications forget what communications were like only 35 years ago.

In mid-1983, I was asked to be the Ministry's representative in the Prime Minister's Department. This required me to move to the Beehive and involved regular contact with the Prime Minister, Rob Muldoon. I was immediately struck by his capacity for work — papers submitted to him would come back with his comments or instructions in short order. Even when he was away at his holiday home at Hatfields Beach, near Auckland, a suitcase of official papers would be sent to him each evening by special courier. It would be back in Wellington, all papers actioned, early the next day. He can't have been having much of a holiday. He was of course a workaholic. He would dictate his speeches into a dictaphone for typing up by a secretary. The speeches were word perfect and rarely needed any editing.

Muldoon was also Minister of Finance and gave a great many speeches on his pet project of reforming the international trade and payments system. No one today remembers any of them. Despite his deserved reputation for abrasiveness, he was always unfailingly polite to his own staff. He was a short and dumpy, quite small man. I still have this image of him sitting in his chair at our staff meeting, holding forth, but his feet not quite touching the ground.

While I was working in Muldoon's Department, in December 1983, former Prime Minister and Governor-General Sir Keith Holyoake died. Holyoake had been Prime Minister from 1960 to 1972. In 1977 Muldoon controversially had him appointed Governor-General. He was Governor-General during the Scheel visit. I went to see his coffin lying in state in the red Legislative Chamber of Parliament Buildings one lunch hour but was surprised to find myself the only visitor in the room at the time. It was 15 years since he had invited me, as a young VSA volunteer, to think of him as my father.

'Kiwi Keith', as he was affectionately known, had, like General Monck, been awarded the prestigious Order of the Garter by the monarch. On his death a commemoration of his life was therefore to be held at Windsor Castle. Muldoon asked me to handle the arrangements for Keith's wife, Lady Norma Holyoake, to travel to London accompanied by their eldest son, Roger, who was a farmer at Kinloch near Taupo. I had several long conversations with Lady Norma who was worried about the trip and very grateful for my help in arranging it.

In July 1984 Muldoon lost the surprise general election. David Lange, my customer at Kingsland Service Station, became Prime Minister. These were fascinating times to be in working in Parliament as he settled into office and grappled with the requirements of political leadership, office management and pushing paper. He found it difficult to deal appropriately with highly classified material which sometimes could be found mislaid under his bed. There was confusion and exhilaration, and a falling out with the United States following the banning of nuclear-armed and nuclear-powered ship visits to New Zealand. That put paid to the ANZUS alliance. Like the rest of New Zealand, I loved Lange's brilliant wit and eloquence.

As well as being Prime Minister he took on the role of Minister of Foreign Affairs, a huge workload but this was where his real interest lay. He had no relish for the economic portfolios, which he left to others. Now that Lange was Minister of Foreign Affairs, the Ministry had direct access to him so there was no need for me to duplicate the role as Foreign Affairs representative on his staff. After a few months I went back to the Ministry and prepared for my second posting, as Second Secretary at our High Commission in Ottawa, Canada.

The first formal note which I prepared for Lange after he became Prime Minister was on Air New Zealand's pending purchase of new aircraft for its fleet. In his final year in office Muldoon had been trying to convince Air New Zealand to re-equip using Airbus aircraft purchased from Europe, as a way of signalling to EEC countries that we were prepared to purchase expensive aircraft from them in return for our exports of sheepmeat and dairy products. Air New Zealand was inclined to opt for Boeing. I felt that the decision should be one for Air New Zealand to make, based on its own assessment of the commercial and operational factors involved and should not be influenced by trade access considerations. Lange readily agreed.

CHAPTER 17

BILINGUAL OTTAWA IN
CANADA (1985–1988)

OUR POSTING TO OTTAWA WAS A COMPLETE CONTRAST TO OUR time in Fiji. I knew little about Canada other than that it was a Commonwealth country, is huge in land area and had the Queen as its Head of State like New Zealand. It has a history of political, economic and language competition between the French-speaking Francophones, primarily in Quebec, and the English-speaking Anglophones in most of the rest of Canada. I remembered de Gaulle's famous meddling in Canadian internal politics in 1967, when on an official visit to Montreal, he had said *'Vive le Québec libre'*, which made Anglophone Canadians apoplectic with rage. One book I read about Canadian politics said that Canadian voters tended to avoid far right or far left politics and usually voted for the 'extreme center'.

From a small country like New Zealand, Canada immediately struck us by its vastness and great open spaces. Ottawa is a picturesque city on the banks of the Ottawa River and by the Rideau Canal. Queen Victoria decided to make Ottawa the capital of a united Canada based solely on a painting she had seen of the location. It didn't seem to be placed in a very strategic location. Perhaps Toronto was considered too close to the US border and therefore vulnerable to Yankee expansionist tendencies. Montreal, on the St Lawrence River in Quebec, was too Francophone. Ottawa was sufficiently distant from both places to be an ideal political compromise.

Within a few months of our arrival, Ed Latter, the High Commissioner, departed and was replaced by John Wybrow, who was accompanied by his wife, Nora. I need at this point to digress somewhat and explain what a political appointee is.

The usual practice is for a country to staff its embassies or high commissions overseas with professional diplomats, trained for the job and well-versed in international diplomacy. Occasionally, however, a country might appoint someone to be ambassador or high commissioner from outside the ranks of professional diplomats. They would be regarded as a 'political appointee'.

There could be good reasons for such an appointment. The government of the day might want to appoint to a key embassy someone in whom it had particular confidence, had particular attributes, or who had a brief to undertake a particularly difficult assignment. Less validly, it might appoint someone as a reward for past political service (a 'job for the boy - or girl!') or as a means of easing them out of the domestic political equation.

US presidents routinely make such appointments from outside the ranks of the US State Department as a means of thanking financial donors to their election campaign or to reward political supporters. US ambassadors have to resign the moment the president who appointed them leaves office. This is highly disruptive and weakens US influence during the time of the change-over from one ambassador to another. It is a practice New Zealand sensibly does not follow, as its professional diplomats are apolitical. In New Zealand's case, political appointments are the exception, not the rule as in the US.

National and Labour governments had both made political appointments as High Commissioner to Canada. Dean Eyre, whom I got to know, was High Commissioner from 1968 to 1973. He had been MP for North Shore and Minister of Defence in Keith Holyoake's National Government from 1960 to 1966. Ed Latter was a competent MP for Marlborough. Ill health forced him to retire from politics so he was offered a position as High Commissioner to Canada. He left Canada in 1984, just as we arrived.

Canada tended to be a favoured and uncontroversial destination for political appointees from New Zealand, although Canberra, London and Washington have also featured. David Lange sent former Prime Minister Bill Rowling to Washington as Ambassador in a forlorn attempt to smooth the troubled waters over our nuclear-free policy and withdrawal from ANZUS. Former National Prime Minister Jim Bolger also went as Ambassador to Washington. In recent years, New Zealand has sent a former Foreign Minister, Russell Marshall, as well as former Speakers of Parliament like Jonathan Hunt and Lockwood Smith and even a former Governor-General, Jerry Mateparae, to London as High Commissioner to continue the task of grappling with the colonial motherland.

Political appointees may be unfamiliar with the nuts and bolts of international diplomacy, may not be used to writing diplomatic assessments or cannot be bothered with the day-to-day running of the Embassy or High Commission, so the Mission has to have a very competent and supportive professional deputy. They oversee the bulk of the Mission's work, leaving the political appointee to undertake necessary constituency building, opening doors at a high level in the host government that a professional diplomat might be less successful at doing. A good example is David Lange's appointment of Sir Edmund Hillary as High Commissioner to India from 1985 to 1988, in a determined effort to repair the damage done by his predecessor, Rob Muldoon, who had disliked Prime Minister Indira Gandhi and had closed our High Commission in New Delhi.

A country is always asked to give its concurrence to the appointment of a foreign representative, a process known as seeking 'agrément'. Approval is usually given. I can think of only a couple of instances affecting New Zealand where approval was withheld. New Zealand does not follow the US practice of requiring its ambassadors to undergo political level confirmation hearings. Instead, appointments are made by the Governor-General on the advice of the Minister of

Foreign Affairs and Trade. Such appointments used to require the Queen's formal approval as our Head of State. Now the Governor-General does the paperwork without reference to the British monarch.

John Wybrow had been General Secretary of the Labour Party and a close confidante of Prime Ministers Norman Kirk and Bill Rowling. When David Lange became Prime Minister in 1984, he wanted new talent in the Labour Party machinery, more attuned to his own flamboyant approach to politics, so he offered to elevate John up and out of his role as General Secretary of the Labour Party. An appointment as High Commissioner to Canada provided the perfect means of facilitating his exit, in a face-saving manner.

John and Nora were engaging and warm-hearted but had no familiarity with diplomatic practice or the nuances involved in being New Zealand's lead representative in a major partner country. It was a difficult and at times sensitive assignment, particularly as we had to explain to the Canadian Government the finer points of our decision to become nuclear free, ending the long-standing defence relationship with the US under ANZUS. This required tact and diplomatic skill. The task fell to the very capable deputy High Commissioner, Kate Lackey, to ensure the Canadians received an accurate appreciation of the New Zealand Government's position. It was not a foregone conclusion that Canada, itself closely linked to the US in security ties, would understand New Zealand's reasons for its actions.

A key task of mine was to follow and report to Wellington on the intricacies of Canada's negotiations with the US on its free trade agreement, NAFTA. I was fortunate to be given good insights by Canada's lead negotiator, Simon Reisman. New Zealand wanted to know what Canada would sign up to with the US, especially on dairy products, because we had an interest in trade liberalisation in agriculture and were actively pursuing a new round of multilateral trade negotiations in Geneva.

The GATT, or General Agreement on Tariffs and Trade, was an international agreement designed to liberalise trade between member countries. It became the WTO, the World Trade Organization, in 1994. The main focus had been on industrial goods, and highly protected agricultural sectors had largely been excluded. Australia, with New Zealand's ready support, called together a group of agricultural exporting countries to press for a new round of negotiations to cover agriculture. We wanted to limit or remove the damaging domestic production and export subsidies which impeded trade opportunities in our key markets such as the EEC.

The group of countries which Australia brought together met for the first time in Cairns, Australia in 1986. Besides New Zealand and Canada, it included South American agricultural exporters such as Argentina, Brazil, Uruguay, Chile and, in South East Asia, Indonesia, Malaysia, the Philippines, Thailand and several others. The group became known as the Cairns Group. Canada was an active supporter of trade liberalisation for its grain exports but it had a very protectionist attitude towards its own supply managed industries of dairy, pork and poultry. Given New Zealand's interest in reforming the international dairy trade, Canada's very ambivalent position became a major cause of friction in the Cairns Group. This required careful political management.

The second meeting of the Cairns Group, which I attended in Ottawa, almost resulted in physical blows but certainly very choice words between Australia's rough diamond Trade Minister, John Dawkins, and Canada's patrician Minister for International Trade, Pat Carney, with New Zealand's Trade Minister, Mike Moore, trying to referee.

One of the issues which bruised egos all round was whether Australia should be the permanent chair of the group or whether chairmanship should be exercised by whichever country was hosting the meeting. After a few meetings it was accepted that Australia should undertake this responsibility, with the host country representative as co-chair.

To New Zealand's disappointment, Canada was largely successful in isolating its dairy producers from US competition under *the North American Free Trade Agreement* (NAFTA), something which US President Donald Trump would find objectionable years later when he sought to renegotiate NAFTA with Canada. Protecting its dairy farmers is a holy grail for Canadian politicians. I once visited a Quebec dairy farm in the middle of winter. The poor cows were stuck inside for months on end in a hot steamy barn, while the pastures outside lay frozen under metres of snow and ice. Only an optimist could be a dairy farmer in Canada.

Our main contacts in the Canadian Department of Foreign Affairs and International Trade, DFAIT, were André Simard, Ed Grant and Michael Martin. They looked after Canada's relations with Australia, New Zealand and the South Pacific. André was French Canadian. Ed was an Anglophone very proud of his Scots heritage. Michael was a very capable young diplomat who went on to have a stellar career in the Canadian Public Service, culminating as head of Canada's important Ministry of the Environment and Climate Change.

Canada did not have major interests in our part of the world, the South Pacific, but it was Michael who phoned me in May 1987 to give me the astonishing news that Sitiveni Rabuka had staged a military coup in Fiji, to assert Fijian supremacy after the 1987 elections produced a government dominated by ethnic Indo-Fijians. Clearly, during my time in Fiji I had not understood just what its military might be capable of. So began the whole sorry saga of coup after coup which has bedevilled Fiji's politics until recent times.

As Canada is a close friend and Commonwealth member, we had instituted a process of regular information exchange so that we could benefit from each other's diplomatic reporting from areas of the world where we were not well represented. We provided information on developments in Asia and the South Pacific. Canada shared with us its insights on developments in Afghanistan, Africa, South America and elsewhere. The information was usually exchanged in hard copy via the diplomatic bag.

To my great annoyance I discovered one day that the Ministry in Wellington had handed over to the Canadian High Commission in Wellington a report, prepared by our Embassy in Paris, of an OECD meeting that had been chaired by Canada's representative, Sylvia Ostry.

Ostry was a no-nonsense, hard-hitting Canadian official who frequently rubbed other countries up the wrong way. She was Canada's lead Sherpa, which meant she was the senior official responsible for Canada's input into the annual G7 Economic Summits of Heads of Government. Her views were influential. The OECD report in question was however highly critical of Ostry's performance at the meeting. Its authors had not intended that the report be shared outside Wellington official circles and certainly not with the Canadians.

Sheepishly, I phoned Ed Grant, explained the embarrassing situation and asked if he might intercept the offending report before it was circulated within the Canadian bureaucracy and possibly to Ostry herself. Ed thought it was a great joke and said, after he had read the report in question, that he shared many of its observations. He agreed to suppress it and a diplomatic incident was averted.

Twenty-five years later Ed's daughter was Canada's High Commissioner to Singapore during my own time there, although sadly Ed had recently died. I told her about the lifeline her father had once thrown his New Zealand colleagues.

Mike Moore, Trade Minister in the 1984–89 Lange Labour Government, came to Canada on several occasions to pursue the Cairns Group agenda and our trade interests. A committed free trader, Mike's first Canadian counterpart was an avuncular Jim Kelleher, the Minister for International Trade in Brian Mulroney's Progressive Conservative Government. Kelleher, with transparent insincerity, professed to be a great fan of New Zealand lamb but he did not evince the same liking for New Zealand dairy products.

A while later a feisty John Crosbie became Canada's Trade Minister. He had had a distinguished career in Newfoundland provincial politics before he entered national politics. A strong supporter of free trade (except, that is, for dairy products, pork and poultry), Crosbie hit it off with Mike Moore. We had to travel on one occasion to his remote home patch of St. John's in Newfoundland on the Atlantic seaboard for a bilateral meeting. He plied us with the local delicacy, fried cods' tongues and rum. Cod fishing was a mainstay industry in Newfoundland until irresponsible overfishing of North Atlantic fish stocks caused the fishery to collapse. The rum I could drink but I avoided the cods' tongues.

Mike came to a GATT Ministerial review conference in Montreal, in 1988, as part of the Uruguay Round of Multilateral Trade Negotiations then under way in Geneva. In his hurry to check out of his hotel after the conference he omitted to pay his hotel bill. The manager duly cornered me and it was left to me to pay it, with my personal credit card, including the adult videos Mike had been watching. I insisted on being reimbursed officially for the full amount when I got back to the office in Ottawa.

After he left Parliament, and in keeping with his free trade principles, Mike became the third Director-General of the World Trade Organization, serving from 1999 to 2002, the only New Zealander to have held this important position. He died on 2 February 2020, aged 71, after a lifelong battle with cancer.

Family Visits

Rachel and Christopher started their schooling in Canada. They were taught in both French and English, reflecting Ottawa's bilingual character. On her first day of school Rachel marched off with her little backpack and packed lunch as if it were the most natural thing she had ever done. Within a very short time she was reading and speaking French effortlessly. Chris, who was always a very happy little fellow, would greet me warmly at the door whenever I returned from work. In the depths of a Canadian winter, wrapped up snugly, at the age of two, he would help me shovel the large piles of snow off the driveway each morning, after a heavy snowfall overnight, trudging up and down the driveway with his little spade, full of enthusiasm for the task in hand.

Occasionally the temperature was so cold that school would be cancelled, but on warmer days — when it was only zero or minus five degrees Celsius outside — Rachel would happily walk the 300 metres from home to school, dwarfed by the great mounds of snow piled all along the pathway. The only way to keep track of her progress, to ensure she got safely to school, was to follow her little Red Riding Hood coat as it wended its way through the dazzling white snow.

It was great fun in winter to go tobogganing down the slopes or skating on the frozen Rideau Canal. I managed to become a reasonably good ice-skater, in the sense that I did not immediately fall over whenever I had ice skates on. Rachel became a proficient ice-skater and was learning to play ice hockey by the time she was eight. She was well on the way to becoming a little Canadian when we left to return to Wellington. Both Chris and Rachel had their first piano lessons in Ottawa, learning the Suzuki method. Christopher has never lost the great gift he has of being able to improvise the most amazing pieces on the piano.

Rachel learns to ice skate in Ottawa

At breakfast one morning Rachel, aged six, presented herself clutching an empty gin bottle. This would be a perplexing apparition for any parent, but Rachel said she had found it under the bed in the guest bedroom. Evidently a recent visitor had discarded it, and forgotten about it, after liberally enjoying its contents.

The tentative arrival of spring in Ottawa meant we could go sugar bushing. This is a lovely Canadian tradition when the sap begins to flow again in the maple trees, in the spring thaw. Canadians celebrate it with a huge cooked breakfast of pancakes and fried bacon doused with the new maple syrup, sitting outdoors in the woods in the still near-freezing temperatures.

Travelling to and from Ottawa meant the children were able to visit Disneyland in Los Angeles. In San Francisco they had the privilege of being locked up in a prison cell on Alcatraz Island. Another memorable trip to escape the Canadian winter took us to Florida, to Cape Canaveral, to Disney World and the Epcot Center. The taxi ride from Orlando Airport was particularly hair-raising. The taxi driver called himself Cowboy Martin and fancied himself a real cowboy, complete with spurs on his boots and leather tassels. His driving was erratic in the extreme. He would weave dangerously in and out of the traffic, making liberal use of his horn, giving the fingers to everyone and swearing profanely out of the window at any other driver who displeased him. The children were spellbound. Only in America!

It was particularly special that their great-grandmother, Granny Dyer, aged 85, came to visit us in Ottawa. This was only her second trip out of the UK, after her visit to New Zealand in late 1976. Rachel and Christopher had never met anyone so old before, took to her instantly and had great fun playing with her. She stayed several weeks, accompanied by her niece Marjorie Williams, daughter of her oldest sister, Annie. It was Marjorie who had given me the tortoise at Speccott Barton all those years before and who had thrown Grandad Dyer that punch.

Marjorie's son John, a bachelor, accompanied them both as chaperone, but he soon went off to attend a conference in Toronto. Granny arrived at Ottawa Airport, tired and dishevelled after her eight-hour flight from Heathrow Airport. Her glasses were all askew on her face so she looked endearingly comical.

Christopher with his great–grandmother, Granny Dyer

We went on several outings with them both, six in the car. Aunty Marjorie was a noted flower arranger back in Somerset. She delighted in plucking bulrushes from the Algonquin River to make a superb dried flower arrangement. This lasted for years after she had left. Another trip took us down to the St Lawrence River where we crossed over to the United States for the afternoon, the only time Granny visited the US.

As we left the US to return across the St Lawrence River back to Canada, the US border official omitted to remove the entry visa card from Marjorie's passport. We discovered this omission later. I endeavoured to return the card to the US immigration authorities as I feared Marjorie might otherwise be listed in their records as an overstayer. Aunty Marjorie Williams died in Taunton, Somerset in 2013, aged 101. Knowing how chaotic US government systems are, I fully expect that, 35 years after her visit, she is still regarded as an overstayer although hopefully she was not on Donald Trump's list of really bad hombres (or in her case, bad mujeres).

My parents came for a visit. Mum and Dad had both recently retired from their work in New Zealand — Dad from managing the research farm at Moanatuatua, Mum as deputy principal of Te Awamutu College.

We took them on a tour of Canada's Maritime Provinces, visiting Quebec City (a piece of old France in North America), New

Brunswick, Prince Edward Island and Nova Scotia, before coming back to Ottawa via Maine in the US.

Canada has several little villages which recreate, authentically, life in rural Canada as it was in the mid-1800s. At Upper Canada Village in Ontario and at Kings Landing in New Brunswick, staff dress in period costumes and carry out their lives as if they were back in the

19th century. They are major tourist attractions, set in the quiet countryside of rural Canada. There are horses, cows, sheep and vegetable patches, with rustic cottages and farm industries with produce which you can sample and drink. It was great for the children to experience something of a bygone era. Another highlight was to visit the fictional setting of *Anne of Green Gables*, Lucy Maud Montgomery's classic children's novel, set in Prince Edward Island. Rachel was a huge fan of Anne Shirley.

On a visit to England from Ottawa, Rachel and Christopher catch up with an old friend at Madame Tussauds

We visited the French-built fortress of Louisbourg, on Cape Breton Island in Nova Scotia. Here two seaborne sieges had taken place in the mid 18th century, as Britain sought to expel the French from Canada. The fortress was destroyed but is now being lovingly recreated. It was a freezing-cold Canadian summer's day when we visited and Mum did not enjoy the experience. Given that she did not like Rothenburg ob der Tauber either during her visit to Germany — for similar reasons of inclement weather — she has not had much luck visiting ancient fortresses and walled cities.

Andy Weston was one of our office drivers. Andy's real passion was not driving, but taking part in colourful historical re-enactments. During his free time, he would dress in the resplendent red uniform of an early 19th-century British soldier. Relocating in his Tardis to Fort Henry, near Kingston in Ontario and the War of 1812 with the

United States, Andy would stand ready to defend Canada from any Yankee invasion across the St Lawrence River. These military re-enactments brought alive the history of the period. Andy in his period costume, now a completely different persona, marched boldly in formation. He engaged in mock battles with all the sound and fury of real encounters but in which fortunately no one was injured.

Canada is such a vast land. It is impossible for any Canadian to fully know their own country. We met Canadians in Ontario who had never been east to Newfoundland or west to Vancouver in British Columbia. Sometimes Canadian friends would joke that they understood how difficult it was for New Zealand to live next door to an economically larger country like Australia, as they had the same experience with the US.

The land border between Canada and the US is 8900 km long. We stumbled one day on the border posts in a deserted forest — miles of concrete posts stretching into the distance that delimited the two countries. There was nothing to prevent anyone from crossing from Canada into the US totally unobserved. Nowadays, every metre is no doubt covered by video surveillance.

At the time of our posting to Ottawa, Ronald Reagan was the often bumbling, but sometimes likeable, Republican President of the United States. Canada's Prime Minister Brian Mulroney, like Reagan a conservative, did not always find it easy to retain the interest and attention of his US neighbour.

I found out one day just how hard it was for Mulroney to build a constituency in Washington when I was watching a TV report of his various meetings on the Capitol. There he was, with some crusty old US senator. The latter proceeded to explain to the cameras that he had had a very good meeting with the Canadian Prime Minister and that it was always a pleasure to welcome Prime Minister Muldoon to Washington. Clearly, our former Prime Minister had been in Washington sometime previously and had made a more lasting impression.

While I was in Ottawa, I was promoted to First Secretary. After two years the Prime Minister, David Lange, decided not to extend John Wybrow's assignment and he and Nora left. I never saw them again. John passed away in 2019. Kate and David Lackey departed. Sarah Dennis arrived as Deputy High Commissioner, with her husband Dominic Santini.

John was replaced as High Commissioner by Bruce Brown, the same Bruce Brown who had asked if he was to consider himself High Commissioner to Pakistan when Bhutto had been ousted in that coup d'état in 1977. I liked working with a professional diplomat again.

Bruce had in his early career been a principal private secretary to Walter Nash, New Zealand's second Labour Prime Minister from 1957 to 1960. Nash had left office just three months before we had arrived in New Zealand at Puketarata Road. Bruce clearly had a great affection for 'dear old Walter', as he called him. He told me Nash was a born procrastinator. Walter's in-tray was always overflowing, as he liked to micro-manage every Cabinet portfolio. His secret was that if a file stayed long enough in his in-tray, the problem would solve itself anyway. The file could then be safely transferred to his out-tray. Great story, if perhaps not completely accurate.

Bruce's wife Mary fell ill with cancer and passed away while we were in Ottawa. It is so hard to be seriously ill on an overseas assignment, far from the care and support of family and friends in New Zealand. I was amazed at Bruce's total dedication to his work. He refused to take any time off and kept himself focused on his role.

One highlight of our time in Canada was the opening of the magnificent Te Maori Exhibition in Chicago. Louise and I decided we just had to drive to Chicago to take part. Leaving six-year-old Rachel with Kate and David Lackey and their daughter Jenny, we headed south with three-year-old Christopher on the 1100 km drive to Chicago, past Toronto, Detroit and Ann Arbor. It was a huge shock to drive past the poverty-stricken and run-down neighbourhoods of South Chicago.

Dame Te Atairangikaahu, the Maori Queen, was leading the delegation, accompanied by Maori Affairs Minister Koro Wetere. It was good to see Dame Te Ata again. The exhibition went on to several US cities and was a great success, showcasing some magnificent pieces of ancient Maori art, weaving and carving. What most impressed Christopher, however, was sitting in a booth next to a Chicago cop at breakfast and being shown his gun.

The long drive home to Ottawa was not uneventful. We struck a heavy snowstorm on the Canadian border. After seeing the wreckage of numerous large trucks down embankments where they had slid off the icy roads, we prudently decided to halt for the night in a motel. The motel was as cold inside as it was outside.

In 1986, René Lévesque, the founder of the Parti Québécois and ardent proponent of political independence for the French-speaking province of Quebec, published his memoirs. He had recently resigned as Premier of Quebec and, a chain smoker, died not long after in 1987, aged only 65. I am glad I went to the Ottawa launch of his memoirs as I was able to have a good conversation with him in French. I suggested that he might visit New Zealand, which he had never been to. He thought this was a great idea. After our conversation, he inscribed my copy of his memoirs in French, as follows: 'To Peter Hamilton, a New Zealander who speaks better French than Anglo-Canadians'. He was overly generous!

CHAPTER 18

TRADE NEGOTIATIONS AND A POSTING TO GENEVA (1988–1994)

WHEN WE ARRIVED BACK IN WELLINGTON FROM OTTAWA, WE sold our little home in Johnsonville and bought a house in Pinehaven, in Upper Hutt. We loved its more rural setting. Rachel and Christopher were enrolled in Pinehaven Primary School, within easy walking distance of our home.

I was asked to join the Ministry's Multilateral Trade Division (MTD). Apart from some courses on economics and public policy which I had undertaken at Victoria University, I did not consider myself economically literate and was hesitant about undertaking complex trade access negotiations. I need not have worried. It turned out to be among the most interesting and rewarding work I ever did in my diplomatic career.

In 1988 desktop computers first appeared in the Ministry. They were clunky and cumbersome machines compared to today's portable versions but it heralded a dramatic shift in the way everyone went about their work. Up to that point I had to write any report, telegram or submission by longhand. As, like most people, I could think much faster than I could write, my written work was largely unintelligible to any of the long-suffering typists who had painstakingly to decipher my handwriting and type up a clean version. Now we were responsible for our own written work and it meant learning to type on a computer. The clacking of the stenographers' typewriters fell silent except that a few old die-hards liked to continue dictating what they drafted.

Despite courses at government expense, I never progressed beyond the two-fingered approach to the keyboard and always envied those who were keyboard proficient. But now we could send emails to individual colleagues overseas or internally, which meant instant communications. Much time and effort had to be spent to develop appropriate protocols for the use of classified and unclassified emails and viable formats for Ministry messaging. The system in its first few years had major operational and even security weakness. Many bugs had to be ironed out or 'patched'. It was nearly another 10 years before Ministry staff had access to Nokia cellphones, although the odd Blackberry began to make an appearance.

At first, trade policy work was a complete mystery, especially for someone who had left university without the faintest inkling of what a tariff, excise duty, import licence, import quota, subsidy or anti-dumping duty was, let alone the GATT, the General Agreement on Tariffs and Trade. But the Ministry excelled in providing opportunities for its staff to learn on the job. I needed to educate myself about New Zealand's industry protection policy and the Labour Government's decision, after 1984, to open up the New Zealand economy to international competition by reducing import tariffs and removing quantitative import licensing.

The New Zealand *Tariff Book*, a voluminous tome detailing how much duty an importer had to pay on each of thousands of imported items, was split into two parts. Part One listed the standard rates applied to imported products. Part Two listed thousands of exceptions to the high standard rates. This reflected successful industry lobbying of the government of the day to have lower than normal duty rates applied to specific items imported for agricultural and manufacturing inputs, as a means of advantaging certain New Zealand industries.

The *Tariff Book* was a mind-boggling, complex array and a mish-mash of differing import protection policies. The Labour Government was attempting to reduce and rationalise import protection and to subject New Zealand industry to greater international competition. This over time would reduce input costs for New Zealand industry and agriculture. The legal maintenance of the *Tariff Book* was the responsibility of the Department of Trade and Industry (DTI). Despite the Labour Government's policy after 1984, DTI still had senior staff who were not completely reconciled to opening up the New Zealand economy to import competition.

There was at times a keen debate between the senior staff of DTI and MFA over aspects of New Zealand's international trade policy, especially when it came to dealing with the EEC on our critical dairy and sheepmeat access problems. When I joined the Multilateral Trade Division, the government decided to merge the International Trade Policy Directorate of DTI with the Ministry of Foreign Affairs, which henceforth became the Ministry of Foreign Affairs and Trade, or MFAT. Combining the trade negotiations expertise of DTI officials with the diplomatic skills of MFA staff was a sensible move and made much better use of New Zealand's scarce trade negotiations resources by combining the strengths of both departments.

MFAT acquired new expertise and new staff in the trade negotiations area. Staff in MFAT had to become proficient in trade access and trade negotiation work, especially on their overseas assignments. It made for much more satisfying careers and, importantly, a stronger *'New Zealand Inc'* effort in international trade negotiations.

I needed to immerse myself in the arcane articles of the General Agreement on Tariffs and Trade, the GATT, as New Zealand was preparing for a new round of multilateral trade negotiations in Geneva to bring agriculture under GATT rules, to tackle distorting farm production subsidies, agricultural export subsidies and import quotas. I had seen some of the preparatory activity for this in the Cairns Group work which I had covered in Ottawa. For the first time, too, there were to be comprehensive negotiations on international trade in services.

The most famous GATT article is Article One, the non-discriminatory Most Favoured Nation (MFN) clause which requires a member country to offer to all members any tariff concession it grants to any one member. There are a host of other rules dealing with subsidies, anti-dumping, trade facilitation and free trade agreements, covering our CER with Australia. There are side agreements dealing with economic assistance to least developed countries.

It had been agreed internationally that a new round of GATT negotiations would get under way, deliberately called the 'Uruguay Round' to signal that the market access concerns of developing countries would, for the first time, be front and centre of the negotiations. All previous GATT rounds, the last of which had been the Tokyo Round in 1977, had primarily involved industrialised countries.

New Zealand now had to table its own comprehensive offer of tariff reductions in Geneva to start the negotiating process. The goal of the Uruguay Round negotiations was to achieve at least a one-third average cut in each country's national tariffs. This required me to undertake detailed consultations with the tariff policy experts in DTI and Customs. These were often difficult and tetchy as some in DTI wanted to minimise what New Zealand should offer in Geneva, despite the requests for large tariff reductions and agricultural policy adjustments we presented to other countries.

Mercantilism, a beggar-thy-neighbour approach to trade policy, was still alive in some quarters. I had to focus on each of thousands of tariff lines in our schedule to prepare our offer of tariff reductions for tabling in Geneva. It took me days and even late nights of calculation, but once the GATT Secretariat had assessed our offer, we were delighted that it turned out to be exactly the required one-third cut.

I accompanied Alastair Bisley, like me a former pupil of Hamilton Boys' High School, on a lengthy tour of South East Asian countries, Singapore, Thailand, Malaysia, Indonesia and the Philippines to encourage their support for the Uruguay Round. Our meetings were productive and all eventually came on board. It helped that, apart from Singapore, these countries were already members of the Cairns Group. In New Zealand we conducted extensive consultations with New Zealand exporters to find out what products they would like us to target for tariff reductions in our export markets.

So began a five-year association for our family with Switzerland and the GATT. The GATT building is located on the banks of Lake Geneva, not far from where the abortive League of Nations had been housed after the First World War. I was posted to Geneva as Deputy Permanent Representative of the New Zealand Mission headed initially by Tim Hannah, then Alastair Bisley and, in my last year, by Wade Armstrong.

The GATT conference room, where we held the regular meetings of the 100 member countries, was a dull, uninspiring edifice, with four 20-metre-long tables placed at right angles to the chairman's raised podium. Member nations positioned themselves on each side of the tables and whenever you wanted to intervene in a meeting you would attract the attention of the Chair, the Gauloises-chain-smoking Swiss, Director-General Arthur Dunkel, by upending your country name plate. Interpretation was simultaneous in English, French, Arabic and later Chinese, when China joined the World Trade Organization, the successor to the GATT.

It was not possible to script in advance your interventions on a particular topic. It was essential to be able to 'ad lib', to be spontaneous, but what you said in a meeting on behalf of New Zealand would be recorded in the minutes. You could decide what you said in a meeting but were answerable for your comments to head office in Wellington. I had learned to give speeches as a VSA volunteer in Tonga so was not fazed by needing to speak on complex trade matters in international meetings.

In addition to bilateral (one-on-one) negotiations to secure market access improvements for New Zealand's exports, we took part in general meetings to discuss global trade issues, trade disputes and other trade-related issues. There was no ban on smoking. Unfortunately, the New Zealand delegation sat downwind from the Japanese who were chain smokers. Meetings usually ran for three hours at a stretch. Afterwards my clothes stank of cigarette smoke and I had a splitting headache.

The work of GATT and WTO negotiators is little known in New Zealand. For the most part, it appears arcane and opaque. But in the smoky haze of these closed-door negotiations, New Zealand exporters stood to gain economically and financially from improved conditions of international trade. New Zealand conducted individual market access negotiations with about 35 key trading partners, including the US and EEC. There was always a lot of preparation. I shared this heavy workload with Crawford Falconer, who went on to become a prominent international trade negotiator — most recently providing advice to the UK government on its bilateral trade strategy post-Brexit.

Ad hoc groups of like-minded countries would also be formed to pursue their interests in particular sectors. New Zealand was heavily involved in a fish exporters group which aimed to open fish export markets in the EEC, Japan and Korea. We had a keen interest in improved access to overseas markets for our forestry exports, especially sawn timber, so we were active in the group of countries pursuing trade liberalisation in that sector.

The US pushed its own export interests in forestry and steel very hard. It expected others to fall into line, but the US was not above cutting secret bilateral deals and leaving others high and dry once they had concluded they had got what they were going to get from a particular negotiation. The Japanese were tough negotiators too but once they had reached a deal, for example on reducing the tariff on our sawn timber exports, they would faithfully abide by the results. The Koreans, on the other hand, could seek to modify agreements even when concluded if they thought more could still be extracted to their advantage. At one point Korean negotiators complained to my superiors in Wellington that I was being too tough on them in our bilateral market access negotiations. This did not result in any rebuke of me from Wellington.

The Tokyo Round of negotiations in the 1970s had failed to deal with agricultural subsidies but it did establish a mechanism to mitigate the impact of the EEC's trade distorting domestic and export subsidies for dairy products. The International Dairy Products Council, IDPC, on which I was New Zealand's representative, was principally a device for New Zealand, Australia and a few other dairy exporters like Uruguay to interact with the EEC to regulate international dairy trades. It set minimum export prices for butter, cheese, skim milk powder and whole milk powder. This was a limited membership club, an agreement not to sell product at below the agreed minimum prices to avoid undercutting each other in international markets.

The minimum prices for dairy powders and cheese were adjusted from time to time by mutual agreement. By the mid-1990s the Dairy Board paid just under NZ$4 a kilogram of butterfat to its suppliers. It hasn't increased much in real terms over the years, since now, 25 years later, it is paying about $7 a kilo. The EEC, which became the European Union in 1993, spoke and negotiated on behalf of all member countries of the Union. It valued the IDPC as a means of keeping an eye on dairy production, pricing and export trends in New Zealand and Australia. We, for our part, valued the IDPC as it at least put some disciplines on the EEC's egregious trade distorting dairy export subsidies.

As New Zealand had large surpluses of butter, it wanted to dispose of them on the Russian market in countertrade deals. (This is the reason little Ladas started to turn up on New Zealand roads.) An IDPC waiver was required to enable us to sell the butter to Russia at below the agreed global minimum price. It was my job to obtain it. Formal meetings were held every quarter, serviced by the GATT Secretariat.

We were dependent on the New Zealand Dairy Board, the precursor of Fonterra, for the accuracy of the production and export pricing information we tabled in the IDPC. I often felt that I was not given the full picture of what the Dairy Board was up to in international markets. It clearly did not want to reveal more than necessary of its marketing strategies, especially as it was the EU's huge subsidies which were responsible for distorting international dairy trades in the first place.

The humorous definition of a diplomat in the 18th century was someone who is sent abroad to lie for their country. I used to joke that a New Zealand diplomat was someone sent overseas to lie for the Dairy Board. I doubt that I was deliberately misled, just not told the whole truth sometimes.

Another trade mechanism with the EU was the International Meat Council (IMC). This did not set minimum prices for beef and sheepmeat so was less effective. But the international meat marketing information presented to the IMC was always useful to our own industry. Some meetings would be conducted in French. I had quickly to learn the relevant vocabulary.

Both the IDPC and the IMC were discarded once the World Trade Organization was established in 1995. For the first time, agriculture was brought fully under the umbrella of international trade rules, thanks to the hard work of our agriculture negotiators, Tim Groser, Alastair Bisley, George Rutherford and Chris Carson. David Walker too had a prominent role in bringing international trade in services under WTO rules.

The GATT provided, as the WTO still does, a mechanism to investigate a complaint by a member country if it considered another member was in breach of its obligations to it under international trade rules. Staff at Geneva Missions would be routinely asked to take part on panels as trade experts to examine and rule on the complaint.

One of the most controversial while I was in Geneva was a dispute raised by banana-exporting countries in Central and South America, the so-called 'dollar banana' exporters whose industries were often owned and operated by major US companies. They complained that former British and French colonies in the Caribbean and Africa were being given unfair preferential access for their banana exports on the UK and other EU markets.

A GATT panel was duly established, chaired by IG Patel, a former Governor of the Reserve Bank of India, who it was felt would bring an appropriate developing country perspective to the problem. I was asked to join the panel with a colleague from Japan. We three conducted numerous closed-door meetings with the affected parties, with the GATT Secretariat acting as secretariat to our panel.

The French, acting on behalf of their former African colonies, were outraged that the US-controlled 'dollar banana' exporters were trying to remove the access preferences which France accorded to its former colonies on its domestic banana market. The dispute became heated and the panel was faced with a difficult choice — was it fair for former French and UK colonies, all developing countries, to enjoy trade advantages on the EU market over other developing country exporters, just because they happened to have past colonial ties to certain member countries of the EU?

The French followed the deliberations of our panel closely, as did the UK. I wondered how it was that the French always seemed to be so well informed about our internal deliberations. Were they listening in on our meetings? Or was somebody briefing them? We were keenly aware of the unpalatable implications of our decision for one side or other in the dispute. We eventually found that France and the UK, consistent with GATT rules of non-discrimination, were not justified in giving trade access preferences to their former colonies and that the 'dollar banana' countries should not be disadvantaged on EU markets.

Once tabled in the full GATT Council for consideration, our panel report caused a huge fracas. The European Commission, UK, France and their affected former colonies damned the panel's findings. A fatal weakness in the GATT's then dispute resolution process was

that any panel report needed to be adopted by consensus in the
GATT Council for its recommendations to be implemented. There
was of course no consensus to adopt our report so it was not made
public. I did not enjoy the personal abuse hurled at me by the
Jamaican representative in the Council meeting. More to my liking
was the unexpected warm embrace I received from the (female)
Foreign Minister of Guatemala, one of the Latin American
complaining countries.

We had failed to resolve the dispute. It was, however, only the first in
a long series of further panels on the international banana trade, all
of which I believe reached the same basic conclusions as our panel. A
resolution was eventually achieved but long after I had left Geneva.

One of my main roles was to work with other members of the Cairns
Group, chaired by Australia, to prepare the agenda for subsequent
Ministerial-level meetings of the Group. There was a remarkable
camaraderie among the officials concerned as we all had a common
goal. We met regularly for a working lunch to plan and agree on our
negotiating positions and strategies. I was fortunate to attend two
significant Cairns Group meetings, one in Manaus on the banks of
the Amazon River in Brazil and one in Montevideo, Uruguay.

After a couple of years breathing in the smoke of Arthur Dunkel's
Gauloises and Japanese cigarettes at GATT Council meetings, my
Australian colleague, John Buckley, and I decided it was high time
that crusty old trade diplomats joined the real world and established
a smoke-free workplace. We had to get a proposal to this effect on to
the GATT Council agenda. To ensure we could get a consensus, we
had first to consult far and wide among GATT member countries in a
series of preparatory meetings.

We knew that Dunkel, the Japanese and other smokers would
vigorously reject any paper which was headed 'Proposal to Ban
Smoking in the GATT'. Instead, we tabled a cunning little paper
headed 'Proposal on Air Quality in the GATT', which was less easy
to torpedo. The paper was duly adopted and the GATT became
smoke-free. It made for much more pleasant meetings and work

environment. There ought to be a plaque somewhere in the WTO building to record our victory!

In addition to being deputy in the New Zealand Permanent Mission in Geneva, I was New Zealand's Consul-General to the Canton of Geneva. Despite its incorporation into the Swiss Confederation in 1815, Geneva liked to maintain its former status as a republic, which the Protestant reformer John Calvin had proclaimed in 1541. I duly went to City Hall to present my credentials and was received by several of Geneva's city councillors in a little ceremony where I handed over my formal letter appointing me as Consul-General. It was a quaint occasion, not least because of the large, but incongruous, portrait of the unfortunate Louis XVI which hung near our proceedings, a royal gift no doubt to the Genevan Republic, presumably sent before His Majesty lost his head in the French Revolution.

The final act of the Uruguay Round negotiations was to be signed at a gala meeting of all the participating countries. Morocco had agreed to host this in Marrakesh. Choosing Morocco for this final meeting was designed to highlight once more that this round of negotiations was intended primarily to advantage developing countries.

I flew from Geneva to Madrid to catch a connecting flight to Marrakesh, several days in advance of the arrival of the delegation from New Zealand, to ensure arrangements were in place. To my embarrassment, when I was about to board my connecting flight to Morocco, an eagle-eyed Spanish passport control officer noticed that my diplomatic passport had expired. He refused to let me board the flight.

Upset at this turn of events and surprised that the Swiss authorities had not noticed this when I had left Geneva, I was forced to cancel my onward connection. Fortunately, Paul Tipping, our Ambassador to Spain, was able to extend the validity of my passport (something which would not be possible nowadays). I made good use of the enforced stay in Madrid by visiting the magnificent Prado art museum and marvelling at the many famous paintings familiar to me from art books.

The Moroccan authorities had done a major clean-up of the dusty Marrakesh city in advance of the meeting. Thousands of beggars had been rounded up and shipped off to a temporary 'camp' somewhere outside the city for the duration of the conference. Since most of the negotiations had now concluded, there was not a lot of work remaining for us to do in Marrakesh. We enjoyed the Moroccan hospitality, hosted by King Hassan II, visited the local souk (bazaar) and took the New Zealand Trade Minister, Philip Burdon, for a car trip up into the nearby Atlas Mountains. We were surprised to find the mountains shrouded in thick fog which made driving very hazardous. I wondered how I could explain things back in Wellington if Philip Burdon's car vanished in the fog of the Moroccan mountains.

Family Life in Geneva

Once the Uruguay Round of negotiations got seriously under way, it was full on. Long days, late nights and work on weekends took a toll on the family. We did get away from Geneva as much as possible to climb the lovely Jura mountains behind Geneva, or the Swiss Alps. Louise and the children could sometimes go skiing while I sat in the smoke-filled rooms of the GATT.

As it was easy for her to obtain a security clearance, Louise was able to work part-time in our office undertaking classified admin tasks. It seemed an easy transition for Rachel and Christopher moving from Pinehaven School to an international school in Geneva. Rachel once more went to a bilingual French and English school at La Châtaigneraie in Founex. This was a short bike ride from our home at 11 chemin des Pommiers, in the quaint village of Mies on the outskirts of Geneva. Christopher was enrolled at Pregny-Rigaud International school, which was en route to the New Zealand Mission in Geneva where I worked. I loved the daily morning ride to school with him when we could talk about every and any thing. At the age of seven or eight, he would become extremely agitated if the car clock showed 8.20am, which meant he risked being late for school. There was no alternative but to cover the clock to ensure a more relaxed morning ride.

We rarely had to rebuke the children. Reaching her teenage years, Rachel started to assert her independence. Her stubbornness and bad language sometimes became difficult to bear. At her school, she studied some eight or ten subjects, far more than the New Zealand curriculum. The academic pressure on her was severe. She acquired a taste for kick boxing, which proved a great personal defence mechanism in later years, but she eventually grew out of it.

Sometimes Christopher would show a stubborn side too. One time that he did was when we had guests to lunch. He decided to misbehave and took himself off in high dudgeon to the cloakroom, slamming the door loudly and locking himself in. I let him stay there for a while until I heard him playing with the fire extinguishers and letting off clouds of carbon dioxide in the enclosed small room. When he refused to answer, I was unsure whether or not he was still conscious. I panicked and decided I had to break the door down.

The sound of this certainly perplexed our lunch guests who assumed I must be some sort of modern Wackford Squeers. Christopher eventually decided to relent and tell us he was still alive. I was more relieved than angry with the little monkey. Our lunch guests did not grace us with their presence again. I am quite proud of the fact that I never once, as he was growing up, gave him a hiding. I was well in advance of Green MP Sue Bradford's Anti-Smacking Law.

Aged 14, Rachel agreed to act as babysitter for Christopher when we had to go out to an official function one evening. This was on a trial basis as we had not left the two of them alone before without a babysitter. When we returned later, Rachel was sound asleep in her bed and Christopher was, too, in his. Except that his desktop lamp, which he had been using to read by, was now starting to burn a big hole in the duvet cover of his bed. A few minutes more and the bedclothes would have burst into flame. It was a narrow escape from what might have been a tragedy, and a sobering reminder of the dangers of leaving young children at home on their own.

Return to Little Water, with Granny Dyer

From our little village of Mies we could visit many places of historical interest. The bare and spartan Cathédrale de St-Pierre in Geneva, Calvin's home church, was cold and uninviting, just like Calvin's brand of Protestantism. Just over the border, in France, lay Ferney-Voltaire, where Voltaire had lived from 1759 to 1778, or as Fordy at high school had called him, Monsieur Arouet.

Near Mies was the Château de Coppet, the former home of Germaine de Staël. She hosted the intellectual elite of Europe there shortly after the French Revolution. Napoleon persecuted her for her public criticism of him and forced her into exile. Her father, Jacques Necker, Louis XVI's finance minister, had tried unsuccessfully to reform the chaotic public finances of France on the eve of the Revolution. Necker had been greatly admired by Alexander Hamilton, the architect of the United States' public financial institutions.

We stumbled by chance on the grave of Richard Burton, the famous Welsh actor. He had had a mellifluous baritone voice. Far from his beloved Wales, he died in 1984 and reposes in the obscure Vieux cemetery in the village of Céligny. I loved his play for voices *Under*

Milk Wood and his fine film portrayal of another Richard, Wagner. Who remembers today his tumultuous love affair with Elizabeth Taylor? To our surprise, near Richard Burton lies Alistair MacLean, the author of *The Guns of Navarone*, turned in 1961 into a popular film starring Gregory Peck. Strange that these two should have chosen to lie in exile so far from their native lands.

We loved walking in the French and the Swiss Alps and staying in the romantic village of Grindelwald. Paris was a favourite destination, only four hours away by the TGV, the high-speed train. We visited the Eiffel Tower, Notre Dame, the Arc de Triomphe, Montmartre and explored the 'Conciergerie', where Marie Antoinette was imprisoned before her execution in 1793. After paying our respects to Napoleon at his marble tomb in Les Invalides, we spent a great time exploring Versailles, the Hall of Mirrors, the Grand and Petit Trianon and Le Nôtre's amazing gardens.

On a visit to the Louvre, we saw the *Mona Lisa* — what a small painting! We had imagined it would be much larger. And I was finally able to make the acquaintance of the Venus de Milo, that armless lady in marble from ancient Greece who had caused such disruption to Gaston's art appreciation class at Hamilton Boys' High School.

Rome was a magical place too. Wandering the Forum, we could imagine Julius Caesar and Cicero holding forth. The Colosseum and the Vatican, the Church of Santa Maria Maggiore, the Sistine Chapel and the Pantheon made Europe's history come alive. We walked along the Appian Way to see the tomb of Caecilia Metella and visited some of the catacombs.

I loved the third century AD public baths of the Emperor Caracalla, a magnificent building even now as a ruin. We could imagine the citizens of Rome enjoying a nice cleansing bath after watching a good day's human blood sport in the Colosseum, while my ancestors in Somerset were likely still painting themselves with woad. I enjoyed my second trip to Pompeii. I am not sure whether Rachel and Christopher were able to fully appreciate its tragic past.

Rachel did surprise us one day in Rome by violently chasing away a band of Romanian gypsy women who accosted us in a street near the main train station, all ready to fleece me. They backed off very quickly. I was impressed by her quick and spontaneous, even aggressive, action in confronting them. Ever after she likes to tell me how she had saved me from being robbed in Rome.

One fine weekend, I made a day trip with two work colleagues, Heather Carew and Trevor Hughes, to Beaune in the Burgundy wine-making region of France. Beaune is a marvellous walled city with a magnificent medieval hospice, the Hôtel-Dieu. We sampled the great local wines over a relaxed lunch but were puzzled by the last entry on the menu which offered 'une voiture de fromages'. I thought of Monsieur Falicon in New Caledonia and his 'pauvre voiture' but on this occasion we were not being offered a car of cheeses but simply, as it turned out, a small cheese trolley. The French do exaggerate things sometimes.

With the conclusion of the Uruguay Round of negotiations, my assignment was over. Louise, Rachel and Christopher left Geneva a few weeks before me to visit friends in Ottawa. I took the opportunity to visit Granny Dyer in Somerset. She was now, at 94, living with her daughter, my Aunty Betty, and her husband Terry Chidgey at Colepool Farm. This was a huge extra burden of care for my Aunty. Terry was still very much focused on his hunting interests. He avoided his mother-in-law as much as possible, unless Granny needed to be turned or propped up in her bed, in which case she usually insisted that Terry undertake the task.

Granny was not the easiest person to look after in her old age and she missed her beloved home at Little Water. To ensure she could summon help whenever she needed it, she was given a little bell. The arrangement worked well for a while until she began to ring it a little too often. The little bell was duly removed, much to Granny's annoyance.

Like her older sister Aunt Lil, Granny liked to read light fiction, sometimes a Mills and Boon. She would also read the local newspapers. When she was no longer able to visit a library herself, a very kind librarian in the Nether Stowey village library, the nearest library to Colepool, would select books which she thought my grandmother and my Aunty Betty might like to read.

One day my cousin Sarah discovered that her grandmother was reading a novel with graphic narrations of sexual activity. Such reading interest appeared to be unusual in a nonagenarian so she showed the book to her mother. At dinner that evening, Terry asked innocently of his mother-in-law what book she was currently reading. Granny, without looking up from her dinner plate, said she was reading a very good book but it appeared to have been taken from her room. After a short pause, she said perhaps that was because it used the word 'fuck' in it.

When the book was taken back to the Nether Stowey library, the librarian nearly had heart failure when she realised what book she had unwittingly selected for Mrs Dyer to enjoy.

When, after my arrival, I knocked on the door of her bedroom I could hear Granny inside telling my Aunty Betty 'not to let me come in just yet', as she needed to compose herself, adjust her pillows and sit up in bed. We had a lovely family Christmas lunch at Colepool Farm but immediately after I had to leave to drive to Heathrow Airport to catch my flight back to New Zealand. It was a hurried goodbye. There was something about her close embrace as I left. We both knew it might be the last time that we would meet. She died just over a year later, aged 96. She had always been such a large part of our lives even though we had migrated to New Zealand 35 years previously and had missed out on so many years together.

CHAPTER 19

DEVELOPING TRADE LINKS WITH SOUTH EAST ASIA (1995–1996)

BACK IN WELLINGTON AFTER GENEVA, I FOUND MYSELF ASSIGNED to the South and South East Asian Division as deputy director, working with Win Cochrane, the director. East Timor was struggling to gain its independence from Indonesia and Win handled the tortuous political ramifications, involving sensitive dealings with Indonesia and frequent lobbying visits to Wellington by the East Timorese leader, José Ramos-Horta.

This left me to focus on developing New Zealand's trade and economic links with the South East Asian countries Thailand, Malaysia, Singapore, the Philippines and Indonesia and, some years later, Vietnam. With Britain's entry into the EEC in 1973, New Zealand was forced to diversify its markets. South East Asia was a natural focus given the burgeoning economies in this region. Following the conclusion of the Vietnam War in 1975, South East Asian countries were discovering the advantages for themselves of trade liberalisation and closer political cooperation. They had established ASEAN, *the Association of South East Asian Nations*, and its economic arm, AFTA, *the ASEAN Free Trade Area*. Their progress was uneven given their highly protected markets and different languages and cultures, but New Zealand worked hard to develop its links with ASEAN, with annual meetings at the level of Foreign Minister.

After discussions with Australia, we decided to promote the concept of an AFTA and CER free trade link. The ASEAN member countries agreed to hold exploratory discussion with us to see if the idea had merit. Dick Nottage and I travelled to Jakarta for the first of what proved to be a series of very fruitful discussions, culminating some years later in an AFTA-CER free trade agreement. Dick was Secretary of Foreign Affairs and Trade. His presence at that first meeting demonstrated to the ASEAN countries the seriousness with which we took the initiative.

As part of its development assistance to South East Asian countries, New Zealand assisted financially in the running of the Mekong Institute in Khon Kaen, Thailand. The Institute is an inter-governmental institution owned and operated by the Governments of Cambodia, Thailand, Vietnam, China (Yunnan Province and Guangxi), Laos and Myanmar. Its principal aim was to assist the skills development of senior officials and to promote regional cooperation and integration. I was very pleased to be asked by David Gamble to conduct a 10-day trade policy course with him at the Institute, for about 15 nominated trade policy officials from each of the six member countries. David coordinated the course. He had been a senior trade policy official in the New Zealand Department of Trade and Industry before transferring to MFAT in 1988.

Given my GATT experience I focused my lectures on multilateral trade policy and the GATT/WTO. I thoroughly enjoyed being back in the classroom but what impressed me most was the calibre of the young officials attending the course. Most had never been outside their own countries before so their trip to Thailand was a new experience. I was amazed at the quality of their English. They were fluent speakers. Two of them, Han Ching from Kunming in Yunnan and Tu Thu Hien from Hanoi, spoke English with almost no accent. I marvelled at their English language capability especially when I compared it to my own far from fluent French and German.

In 1995, New Zealand hosted the Commonwealth Heads of Government meeting in Auckland. MFAT officials were tasked to help with the logistics. This was the meeting when I escorted the unfortunate Foreign Minister of Sri Lanka, Lakshman Kadirgamar, who later was assassinated in Colombo. These meetings are held every two years in different Commonwealth countries. Although the Commonwealth does not rate highly in the day-to-day lives of New Zealanders, I have always thought it is a valuable organisation. Its programmes of cooperation and development assistance and the political forum it provides for dialogue on regional and global issues are worth fostering. Successive New Zealand Prime Ministers and Foreign Ministers have on occasion had difficult relationships with the Commonwealth, or with the Commonwealth Secretary-General in London, especially when it tackled controversial issues like apartheid or Mugabe's wrecking of the Zimbabwe economy.

As I argue below, I believe New Zealand should, like the majority of Commonwealth countries, become a republic within the Commonwealth. Becoming a republic would not mean that we have to leave the Commonwealth as some have mistakenly suggested. If anything, we should intensify our involvement in the Commonwealth and its activities. The Auckland meeting saw both Nelson Mandela and Robert Mugabe take part, as well as the British Prime Minister, John Major. What an impressive man Mandela was.

I used to joke that the relationship between New Zealand and the UK is so close that New Zealanders don't even notice that the UK Prime Minister never comes to visit. In 1995, John Major was the first UK Prime Minister to visit New Zealand since Harold Macmillan, 40 years earlier. Mrs Thatcher as Prime Minister never made it to New Zealand despite her supposed close relationship with Muldoon, cemented by our assistance to the UK during the 1982 Falklands War. (Thatcher did make one visit, but as Leader of the Opposition in 1976, before she became Prime Minister.) British Prime Ministers know that the Queen is our Head of State, so they have been very happy to leave it to her and her family to develop the bilateral relationship with New Zealand, leaving them to focus on other, more important, relationships like the US and the EU.

Rachel and Christopher once more made the adjustment back to life in New Zealand. Louise went to work again, like me, in Wellington.

Christopher attended the newly opened Hutt International Boys' School in Trentham, while Rachel was enrolled at Chilton St James in Lower Hutt. Christopher thoroughly enjoyed his time at HIBS. Rachel, used to the hyperactive multicultural environment of her Genevan high school, found the academic monoculture at Chilton St James much less appealing.

CHAPTER 20

BACK IN THE SOUTH PACIFIC: HIGH COMMISSIONER TO SAMOA (1997–1999)

IN 1996 I WAS ASKED TO GO TO SAMOA AS HIGH COMMISSIONER. This was my first posting as a Head of Mission.

I was determined to prepare carefully for this important assignment and read as much as I could about Samoa's complex history and politics and our close relationship based on the 1962 Treaty of Friendship. I set about learning Samoan, which I expected would be helped by the fact that I knew some Tongan and Maori. I am very grateful to Galumalemana Alfred Hunkin who painstakingly tried to teach me the basics of the Samoan language at Victoria University.

New Zealand's foreign service had few diplomats fluent in a Pacific language, quite an indictment given the importance to us of the South Pacific countries. I quickly learnt that despite a superficial similarity with Tongan as a sister Polynesian language, Samoan was quite different, both in vocabulary and in its predominant use of vowels over consonants. Perhaps because so few palangi (Europeans) speak fluent Samoan, Samoans themselves seem to prefer that you do not try to speak their language at all, unless you get it absolutely right.

I introduced myself to the High Commissioner of Samoa in Wellington, the patrician Masiofo La'ulu Fetauimalemau Mata'afa, who was the widow of Samoa's first post-independence Prime Minister, Fiame Mata'afa. The title Masiofo indicates the wife of the holder of one of the highest matai titles in Samoa, akin to royalty. She was very kind to me and gave me much useful advice and help in settling into my role.

She continued this when, sometime after, she retired back to Samoa while I was High Commissioner. Her daughter, Fiame Naomi Mata'afa, also a senior matai (high chief), became a good friend. Fiame was Deputy Prime Minister for many years, until she fell out with the Prime Minister, Tuilaepa, over an important constitutional issue in 2020. As I write, Fiame is poised to become Prime Minister of Samoa, after a constitutional crisis following the 2021 general election. While I was in Samoa, Fiame was Minister of Education.

Samoan friends told me that while other Polynesians might think they have come from somewhere else, such as the mythical Hawaiki, they, Samoans, had always been in Samoa! Samoa and Tonga share close linguistic and historical links, even occasional past wars, so much of Samoan culture was familiar to me from my year as a VSA volunteer in Tonga. Except that now I was not a junior school teacher but New Zealand's senior representative in a country which had close historical, social, trade and development assistance links to New Zealand. It was a daunting task.

New Zealand had expelled the German colonial administration from Samoa in 1914, at the start of the First World War but our own colonial administration of Samoa, under a League of Nations mandate, was at times heavy-handed. This was especially so in our mishandling of the deadly influenza epidemic in 1918 and the manner in which we dealt with the non-violent Mau movement in 1929. While the distance of time has healed many of the scars from those days, no one in Samoa has quite forgotten them. The experience of New Zealand's colonial administration continues as a backdrop to the current relationship. New Zealand's representatives in Samoa need, therefore, to be very mindful of the past when carrying out their role.

My first responsibility was to present my credentials to Samoa's Head of State, the elderly and greatly respected Malietoa Tanumafili II. Credentials, as was the case when I was Consul-General in Geneva, are formal documents appointing me in this case as High Commissioner of New Zealand to Samoa. They were addressed to Malietoa and signed by the Governor-General. It was a very warm and unpretentious ceremony in his Official Residence. At the formal presentation I was accompanied by my deputy, Penny Ridings, as well as Annelies Windmill and High Commission staff.

Thanks to Galumalemana Hunkin I was able to say a few words in Samoan in my speech of introduction to Malietoa. I remember his look of great surprise when I said them. I hoped I had not made some huge linguistic blunder. But they were replayed on the *TV Samoa* news that evening, as clearly few if any of my predecessors had addressed the Head of State in his own language.

Presenting credentials to Samoa's Head of State, His Highness Susuga Malietoa Tanumafili II in Apia, 1997

From then on, whenever asked to make a speech at a key event, such as an ANZAC Day commemoration or when presenting a new item of equipment to the Apia hospital donated by New Zealand, I would endeavour to speak Samoan. For this I owe a great debt of gratitude to Rachel Hunt, who was my very capable executive assistant during my time in Samoa. Rachel would patiently translate my speech into

Samoan and then ensure I pronounced it correctly. Samoans seemed to appreciate my efforts despite the many errors, or more likely, perhaps, they just quietly indulged me.

A posting in the South Pacific is a tremendous opportunity and a rich learning experience for a New Zealand diplomat. For younger diplomats today who might be reading this memoir, it is to be highly recommended. It brings important insights into who we are as a nation, situated in Polynesia and the South Pacific. I was very fortunate that I had the opportunity to live and work in Tonga, Fiji and now Samoa and visit other Pacific countries, such as Tuvalu and the Cook Islands.

Tonga had combined its most senior chiefly titles in the 19th century to create a monarchy but, despite one failed attempt to do something similar, Samoa's chiefly titles had not been united into one so there is no 'King' of Samoa. Malietoa was however one of the four most senior matai or 'tama a'aiga' as they are known in Samoa. Besides Malietoa, the other three senior titles are Mata'afa, Tamasese and Tuimaleali'ifano.

I got to know the last two well. The current holder of the Mata'afa title died shortly after my arrival and the title was left vacant. Although Malietoa was not 'King' of Samoa, he was styled Head of State. I was struck by the Samoan decision to avoid the use of the word President, but simply to use 'Head of State', or 'O le Ao o le Malo' in Samoan. Given that the title President can have negative connotations for many New Zealanders, because of the idiosyncrasies of US presidents like Donald Trump, I have always thought that New Zealand, when we become a republic, could follow the Samoan example.

Malietoa lived simply in a modest home and eschewed all pretension. His manner of living had increased the love and respect the Samoan people had for him. This was in stark contrast to the Tongan royal family which lived in several large and well-appointed palaces, maintaining a strict cultural separation from the rest of their people.

After presenting my credentials to Malietoa I went to call on the Prime Minister, Tofilau Eti Alesana, and each of his Cabinet Ministers. Tofilau was well known to successive New Zealand Prime Ministers and greatly respected by them. In addition to being Prime Minister he was Minister of Foreign Affairs. The High Commission had frequent contact with him and his staff.

Meeting the Prime Minister of Samoa, Tofilau Eti Alesana

Tofilau had a positive view of New Zealand. There was none of the edge to the relationship evident with Ratu Mara in Fiji. He had had a colourful, rumbunctious past before entering politics as a member of the Human Rights Protection Party (HRPP). I got to know Tofilau and his kind and gentle wife Pitolua well, right up to the point where his illness made it impossible for him to continue in office and he had to step down. He was replaced, just after I left Samoa, by his capable deputy, Tuilaepa Sailele Malielegaoi. Tuilaepa remained Prime Minister of Samoa for the next twenty years.

A new High Commissioner has to introduce him or herself quickly to political leaders, senior officials, business people, church leaders and many others. The first few weeks involved a lot of courtesy calls. Each member of Tofilau's Cabinet received me warmly. I worked closely with all of them, except for one, the Minister of Public Works, Leafa Vitale. There was something decidedly disquieting about Leafa, who seemed remote and disinterested.

It was a huge shock therefore, just after I left Samoa, to hear that Leafa had been dismissed by Prime Minister Tuilaepa from Cabinet for alleged embezzlement of public funds and had then had his son assassinate his successor as Public Works Minister, Luagalau Levaula Kamu. Luagalau and his wife Maiava Peteru, a New Zealand-trained lawyer, were personal friends of mine. Leafa was sentenced to death by hanging in 1999 but his sentence was commuted to life imprisonment by the Head of State. My successor as High Commissioner, Mac Price, had to deal with the serious fallout and ramifications of this major political scandal. When I heard that the instigator of the assassination was Leafa, I thought back to my own initial negative assessment of the man.

Samoan politics are not for the faint-hearted. The internal complexities are beyond the comprehension of most outsiders. The turmoil of the 2021 election has certainly proved that point. The Lands and Titles Court of Samoa is one of the busiest institutions in the country as Samoans fight legal battles, often acrimoniously, to sustain competing claims to land and the associated matai titles. Tofilau had helped form the Human Rights Protection Party (HRPP) which has been in government for much of the time since independence in 1962. The HRPP was on occasion criticised for heavy-handedness and its human rights label questioned. But Samoa was not a one-party state.

An Opposition party, the Samoan National Development Party, led by Tupua Tamasese Efi, a tama a'aiga, or high chief, ensured debates in Parliament were tense and often fractious, with ad hominem epithets not unusual between Tupua and Tofilau's then deputy, Tuilaepa. Tupua had been Prime Minister, under the title Tupuola Efi, from 1976 to 1982, until replaced by Tofilau. Tupua and Tuilaepa seemed to have a great affinity for locking horns with each other.

Tupua was educated at St Patrick's College in Silverstream and at Victoria University. He became a passionate advocate for Samoan cultural traditions. After the aged Malietoa died in 2007, Tupua was elected Head of State as Tui Atua Tupua Tamasese Efi.

He is the nephew of the Mau leader, Tupua Tamasese Lealofi III, who was killed on 28 December 1929 by New Zealand military police, along with other marchers, during the widespread Mau agitation for independence. The tragedy is known in Samoa as Black Saturday. It is not surprising, therefore, if he had mixed feelings about New Zealand. I last met Tupua when he made an official visit to New Zealand and the then Prime Minister, Helen Clark, hosted a very pleasant and relaxed dinner for him at Premier House in Wellington. He asked me how I was getting on with my Samoan language efforts. Fortunately, he did not put me to the test.

With Louise, Rachel and Christopher in Samoa, 1997

In preparing for my posting to Samoa I read JW Davidson's remarkable book *Samoa mo Samoa*, the history of Samoa before independence from New Zealand in 1962. This graphically outlined the complex relationship between Samoa and the German and then New Zealand colonial administrations.

Writing a comprehensive history of Samoa is no easy task. Anyone deeply versed in Samoan politics could be quickly criticised as partisan by one side or the other. An outside historian not knowing the language and culture could be labelled by the Samoans as lacking a true appreciation of Samoa. It is to be hoped that good and objective writers of Samoan history continue to emerge. Margaret Mead's book *Coming of Age in Samoa*, published in 1928, caused lasting divisions, if not outrage, which is still evident in some quarters. Derek Freeman sought comprehensively to ditch Mead's thesis of Samoan sexual laxity as an anthropological myth, in his own riposte to it in 1983.

The High Commission had a small staff but all were busy. New Zealand had a large and growing development assistance programme in Samoa, focused on education, health, agriculture, tourism and small business development. Samoa's annual development allocation was NZ$7.7million. It required frequent consultation with Head Office in Wellington on project implementation. I was grateful for the prompt and constructive assistance we always received, especially from Grant Robertson, manager of the Samoa aid programme in the Ministry's External Aid Division. Grant soon left the Ministry to pursue a career in politics and in late 2017 became New Zealand's Minister of Finance.

Immigration is a key element in New Zealand's relationship with Samoa. Under the 'Samoan Quota Resident Visa', New Zealand had agreed to permit 1100 Samoans to migrate to New Zealand each year, including partners and dependent children, provided the applicant or partner had a job offer in New Zealand sufficient to support them all. On arrival they could live, work or study in New Zealand indefinitely, a privilege granted to few other countries. It reflected the close relationship under the 1962 Treaty of Friendship and as settlement to the vexed problem in the 1970s, when Samoan overstayers were subjected to rough dawn raids by the New Zealand police. (The New Zealand Government has recently formally apologised for these raids.)

There was always a keen competition for the available places under the quota. There was on occasion criticism of the quota because of the negative impact in depleting Samoan villages of their labour force, but there is no doubting the value of the money transfers sent back to family, church and communities by Samoan families working in New Zealand.

To administer the quota and general immigration issues with Samoa, the New Zealand Immigration Service (NZIS) had two staff in Apia. They were co-located with the High Commission but in essence ran a separate operation. NZIS operated a 'first come, first served' approach to filling the quota. On the day the quota was opened each year, the High Commission would be besieged by applicants wanting to get their application lodged. Each application had to be carefully vetted and the job offer in New Zealand checked so it would be several months before any application was actually approved.

I was happy to leave the administration of the quota in the hands of the professional immigration officials but in my second year, the process nearly turned to disaster as those seeking to submit their application and be first in the queue started invading the High Commission premises, climbing the outer security railings and generally creating a public disturbance. I told NZIS back in New Zealand that we needed a better system of processing such applications and it agreed to my suggestion that we henceforth operate a ballot system. All applications would be entered into a ballot. Successful applications would be drawn from the ballot under Samoan Police supervision. In one step we had eliminated the need for an annual invasion of the High Commission offices.

I learnt my lesson the hard way about not interfering in the work of the Immigration Branch. One day I received a telephone call from the Minister of Education, Fiame Mata'afa, who said she had been approached by a community that wanted to send a group on a cultural tour of New Zealand to raise money for a village project. The problem was that two key members of the group were young boys who were regarded by NZIS as high risk of overstaying their visitor's visa in New Zealand. I duly interviewed the two families concerned and the two young men in question in my office and was given categorical assurances that the two boys would not overstay but would leave New Zealand on completion of the tour with the rest of the group.

On this basis I informed the Immigration Branch that I had been given such assurances. Because the office manager was away from Apia at the time, his staff approved visas for the two young men. I thought nothing more about it until several weeks later an irate office manager informed me that one of the boys had disappeared and was an overstayer in New Zealand — 'and this is what happens when you interfere in immigration decisions'. I was completely floored and upset to have been lied to in this way. Fiame was very apologetic but could do little to rectify the situation. I still do not know what happened to the lad in question. I had been warned by others not to take at face value such assurances, but it is hard not to trust the word of another person when they make a promise direct to your face. It was an embarrassing mistake which I did not make again.

I mention this episode because it was one of the few occasions in my career when I felt I had been taken advantage of. But I did not let it deflect me. It was a busy office and there was always something new happening each day. There were a lot of visitors to Samoa whom we had to assist — including the Governor-General, Michael Hardie Boys, and the Prime Minister, Jim Bolger. Every year, the Foreign Minister, Don McKinnon, commandeered an Air Force plane and brought a large delegation of Members of Parliament and their spouses on a familiarisation visit to South Pacific countries. Samoa was often on the itinerary.

Another visitor was the Queen's second son, Andrew, but I will leave comment on that to the chapter on why New Zealand should become a republic.

Prime Minister Jim Bolger visited to mark 35 years of the bilateral Treaty of Friendship and was given a matai title, Nanai. He had to attend an installation ceremony at the village in question. It was a colourful event. We faced two initial complications. Samoan tradition requires that a man being installed with a matai title has to be bare-chested and must sit cross-legged for several hours in the kava circle, during the installation ceremony.

Bolger made it clear that he would not be taking off his shirt for the ceremony, on the basis, I guess, of 'how would it look to the voters back home?' and furthermore that he was physically incapable of sitting crossed-legged for a second, let along several hours. The Samoans graciously conceded: he could wear a shirt and could cover his outstretched legs with a fine mat. I, for my part, have never had any problem sitting for hours crossed-legged at any Tongan or Samoan kava or Fijian yaqona ceremony, as Mrs Bamsey at Merton School had taught us to sit that way.

When I first arrived in Apia, Mata'afa had floated the suggestion that I be granted a matai title. I thought carefully about this and acknowledged that it was meant as a courtesy to the office of High Commissioner. But matai titles are a core element of Samoan culture and are not to be taken on lightly. Assuming a title obliges one to maintain a link, including through financial assistance, with the particular community which is granting the title. I felt it was inappropriate for New Zealand's representative to take on this responsibility.

There is the problem too of matai title 'inflation', such that there are now quite a number of people holding the Nanai title. In many cases awarding a matai title to a non-Samoan means the holder will have little ongoing contact with the community in question, once they have departed. I quietly did not pursue the proposal.

Tofilau's generosity of spirit was made plain to me one day when he called me to his office and put forward a suggestion. In recognition of New Zealand's action in establishing the annual quota for Samoans to migrate to New Zealand, he suggested Samoa reciprocate by establishing a similar, albeit smaller, quota for New Zealanders who would like to live in Samoa and become citizens. His offer was sincerely meant even though New Zealand had not sought such a quota. He persevered with the idea for several weeks but it clearly had little support in Samoan official circles beyond Tofilau himself. After a while, it was quietly dropped.

In 1997, the first cellphone towers were erected in Samoa. International telecoms by cellphone were now possible. To mark the occasion I arranged for the Prime Minister, Jim Bolger, to be on hand in his office in Wellington to receive the first international cellphone call from Samoa, from Tofilau. We had a little reception at the Tusitala Hotel. Then Tofilau dialled up Bolger waiting in his Beehive office in Wellington. It was an historic event.

I attended many church services and church events. I became close friends with the Reverend Oka Fauola, the Head of the Christian Congregational Church, the largest denomination in Samoa, and his wife So'o. They were my near neighbours at Vailima. Sundays are a day of church-going and rest. Women in their smart white dresses and white hats heading off to church are an abiding image of Samoa. The smoke fires of the family earth oven, the umu, slowly cooking the Sunday meal while everyone is at church, would waft over the town and up the valley to my house. The aroma reminded me of Walter Drayton's hawthorn fires at Speccott.

I made some good friends in Samoa, including Afamasaga Toleafoa who was a member of the governing HRPP in the Fono or Parliament. He had been Samoa's Ambassador to the EEC. His wife Phillipa was a New Zealander who, like me, had been a VSA volunteer, in her case in Thailand. They were very hospitable and helped me to understand local politics. Phillipa remains a family friend.

In addition to being High Commissioner to Samoa, I was Consul-General to American Samoa. This meant occasional official visits to Pago Pago. The relationship between the two Samoas is very close, sundered only by the accidents of colonial history. Tofilau had been born in American Samoa. His nephew, Tauese Sunia, was the Governor of American Samoa while I was there. The economic fortunes of American Samoa were very much dependent on the tuna canning factories, as well as infusions of US dollars.

Reflecting American influence, the Governor used to drive around Pago Pago township in a large official limo with police outriders and shrill sirens wailing so that everyone would know the Governor was approaching. In contrast, Uncle Tofilau in Apia drove around in a simple Land Cruiser, often unescorted, and certainly with no sirens. It did have an appropriate registration plate however: 'PM1'.

Not far from the New Zealand Official Residence at Vailima is a small hill, above Apia, called Mt Vaea. This can be reached by an easy walk through the tropical forest. On its slopes lies the grave of Robert Louis Stevenson, who died in Apia in 1894. His books *Treasure Island*, *Kidnapped*, and *Dr Jekyll and Mr Hyde* had fascinated me. On the side of his grave is a wonderful epitaph which I want to repeat here:

> Under the wide and starry sky,
> Dig the grave and let me lie.
> Glad did I live and gladly die,
> And I laid me down with a will.
>
> This be the verse you grave for me:
> Here he lies where he longed to be;
> Home is the sailor, home from sea,
> And the hunter home from the hill.

Tofilau's illness gradually worsened until he found it hard to carry out his Prime Ministerial duties. Ever the fighter he would force himself to go down to the Fono, even as he lapsed in and out of a coma, to keep a close eye on business. Eventually it became too much for him and he had to resign. He gave a valiant speech of resignation in the Fono — he struggled but could not finish it. He asked his deputy, Tuilaepa, to conclude his resignation speech for him. There was a very smooth handover, from the old to the new.

I visited him several times in his home where he and his wife, Pitolua, made me welcome. Tofilau seemed able to talk more freely to me in private and he was not above offering some very good insights into Samoan politics and his political colleagues. On my last visit, he asked me to kneel by his bedside while he said a quiet prayer of blessing and thanks.

I left Samoa a few days later and went to see my good friend Taito Phillip Field and his wife Maxine, in their home in Mangere. Taito Field was Labour MP for Otara and then Mangere from 1993 to 2008, succeeding former PM David Lange. He once secured the highest majority in a general election of any MP. Born in Apia, he had come to New Zealand in his teens but retained close links to Manase on Savai'i, the home of his matai title, Taito.

In 2002 Taito became Parliamentary Under-Secretary for Pacific Island Affairs in Helen Clark's Labour Government. Sadly, he would have a spectacular and very unfortunate fall from grace some years later through a great mish-mash of cultural misunderstandings and errors of judgement, ending in a six-year prison sentence of which he served two years.

During my time in Samoa, he and Maxine, her daughter Dorothy Hunter and their extended Samoan family, were very kind and hospitable to me. Taito gave me much helpful advice on life and politics in Samoa. Through him and his family I met June Hughes, who is the mother of my second daughter, Fiona, born in 1999.

After I left Samoa, I decided to drive from Auckland to Wellington for a few days' relaxation. I was out of phone contact but when I got to Hamilton, I received a message from John Hayes, then Head of the South Pacific Division in the Ministry (and later National MP for Wairarapa) to say that Tofilau had just died and his funeral was to be held the following day. This posed a dilemma. There would be a large contingent from New Zealand flying to Apia to attend the funeral including Jenny Shipley, the Prime Minister, as well as the Leader of the Opposition, Helen Clark, and a whole host of other politicians and people with Samoan links. They would all, about 60 of them, be arriving in a specially arranged Air Force plane early the next morning.

The problem was that my successor as High Commissioner, Mac Price, had not yet taken up his position. Officially I was still New Zealand's High Commissioner to Samoa. I needed to be on hand in Apia to help facilitate arrangements. There was no alternative but for me to turn around, go back to Auckland and catch the next flight that evening to Samoa. It felt odd going back having just said goodbye.

A more immediate problem was what to wear as all my luggage was still en route home. I could hardly go to the funeral in casual attire. At this point Taito Field came to the rescue. About the same build as me, if slightly bigger, he kindly lent me a suit to wear. It was Taito's wardrobe that I took back that evening to Samoa. The flight was a night one and landed in Apia about 5am. I had four hours at the Residence for a quick nap before heading back to the airport again to meet the incoming aircraft with the large New Zealand contingent on board. It was a sombre occasion as we went to see Tofilau lying in state in the Fono and attended his funeral. I treasure to this day the private moments we shared just before he died.

I went on my own on the posting to Apia although the family would join me as often as possible during school holidays. Being separated from the family in this way was the most difficult part. I missed the children as they were at high school in Wellington.

On one of his visits to me, I arranged for Christopher, with his close friend David McNabb, to play a game of soccer in a Samoan team on Savai'i. The humidity and heat got to them both. They were exhausted by half-time.

CHAPTER 21

NEGOTIATING FREE TRADE AGREEMENTS (1999–2003)

WHEN I RETURNED TO WELLINGTON AFTER MY POSTING TO Samoa, I was asked to head up the Trade and Economic Analysis Division (TEAD) which, as the name suggests, was the Ministry's division responsible for analysing and managing trade policy proposals and research issues. This brought me back into the area of work I had been covering in Geneva.

The division had a small but very capable staff. Each had specific areas of expertise and responsibility. Ron Sandrey had co-authored a seminal book, *Farming without Subsidies*, which had had a major positive impact on government policies to eliminate agricultural financial support in New Zealand, resulting in a much more internationally competitive agricultural sector. The elimination of production subsidies in the sheepmeat sector resulted not only in a sharp reduction in sheep numbers, from around 70 million to 40 million, but no reduction in the quantities of sheepmeat exported. It was a success story that I was later to use in Germany when talking to German farming groups. Ron was the division's analyst and ran computer programs which could assess the likely trade impacts of a particular proposal for a free trade agreement.

Carol Douglass, my deputy, spent much of her time as a member of an inter-departmental committee drawing up advice for the government on its proposal to ban genetic modification in New Zealand, the GM-Free concept. This was an inordinately complex minefield to negotiate. Carol's role was to ensure the international ramifications of New Zealand's proposed policy were fully assessed. The decisions which the Labour Government took on genetic modification have largely stood the test of time. I greatly admired Carol's ability to work with the other departments to pull it all together.

Peter Guinness represented the Ministry on an inter-departmental committee examining the possible impacts on government computers and communications systems of the new millennium. It was feared computers would automatically shut down irretrievably once they changed over from 31 December 1999 to 1 January 2000 (dubbed Y2K, or the 'Millennium Meltdown'). Nobody had much idea what would really happen but there was a lot of contingency planning that the Ministry had input into. As it transpired, Armageddon did not happen on 1 January 2000. I never understood if the threat was real and properly mitigated, or a beat–up that was never going to happen.

Mike Grace and I worked closely on what was called the Trade Access Support Programme, TASP. This comprised a small, but very valuable, departmental financial allocation devoted to supporting our diplomats and exporters in opening up new market access opportunities for New Zealand exports. The fund was flexible, the amounts allocated quite small but it was a useful support mechanism that was always heavily subscribed.

The Singapore Closer Economic Partnership Agreement

My principal preoccupation in these years was to lead New Zealand's free trade negotiations, first with Singapore, our first such negotiation since CER with Australia, then with Hong Kong and finally with the South Pacific.

CER with Australia had been completed in 1983. Despite the naysayers, in the trade unions and elsewhere, it had been a spectacular success. By the late 1990s, the Bolger/Shipley National Governments were keen to increase the number of our FTA agreements and to develop our markets in Asia. Singapore is an open economy and had a similarly positive approach to trade liberalisation as New Zealand. Singapore would be a good place to start and from there to build up our free trade relationships with other Asian partners, such as Hong Kong and eventually all of the key Asian economies.

Tim Groser had promoted the concept of new free trade agreements with the National Government and its Trade Minister Lockwood Smith. He conducted the first rounds of negotiations with Singapore but then moved on to other work. I was asked to pick up the reins and to complete the negotiations successfully. By the time I took over, the government had changed in New Zealand. Helen Clark's Labour Government came into office talking more about 'fair trade' than 'free trade'. We had to be mindful of the public presentation of this nuance as the negotiations progressed. I established a close rapport with Clark's Trade Negotiations Minister, Jim Sutton, a Canterbury farmer who, unusually for a farmer at that time, was a Labour supporter.

Once he had settled into office it became clear that Sutton was in favour of progressing the negotiations with Singapore. Although I was the lead negotiator for New Zealand and worked closely with my Singaporean counterpart, Pang Kin Keong, a negotiating team is only as good as its component parts. The New Zealand team comprised a large group of senior officials, with expertise in services trade, trade rules and remedies, legal aspects and customs tariffs, rules of origin and trade facilitation. David Kersey, our High Commissioner in Singapore, well versed in South East Asian politics, provided much-needed input. We set up a number of separate working groups which beavered away on their respective areas. It was Kin Keong's and my task to pull it all together to develop a legal treaty which could be submitted to both Governments for approval.

We held frequent meetings of the negotiating teams, alternating in Singapore and New Zealand. In addition, on the New Zealand side, we needed to consult widely with New Zealand business groups for their views, as well as with Maori representatives. There was widespread support for our efforts but the gainsayers, who opposed trade liberalisation as a matter of faith, were vigilant, including political parties such as the Alliance, New Zealand First and the Greens.

I spent a lot of time talking to the Combined Trade Unions (CTU), especially its President Ross Wilson and its chief economist Peter Conway. I greatly valued their perspectives. On the sidelines of the CTU was the ideological anti-free trader, Jane Kelsey, from Auckland University. There is no doubting Jane's commitment to opposing free trade agreements, but I have never seen any good, ex post facto, analysis from her of the outcomes, after a decade or two of the free trade agreements, as distinct from the preachy lectures she gave us *before* any negotiation. While the CTU was not a wholehearted supporter of what we were trying to do, they, apart from Kelsey, did not seek to torpedo it. It helped that there was a Labour Government in office.

In addition to making sure that the Minister, Jim Sutton, was happy with our progress each step of the way, I had to coordinate the drafting of numerous Cabinet papers to obtain formal government sign-off for what we planned to include in the agreement, especially in areas such as liberalisation of trade in services, investment and rules of origin. Early on I obtained Sutton's agreement to style our eventual agreement with Singapore *'the Agreement between New Zealand and Singapore on a Closer Economic Partnership'*, ANZSCEP or CEP for short. CEP it remains.

For the most part the negotiations proceeded amicably but were not without the occasional tense moments. We wrangled over finer points in services, or investment, or when Singapore realised it needed to eliminate its tariff or excise duty (it was never clear exactly what the impost was) on imports of New Zealand beer if the agreement was to be duty-free in both directions.

I enjoyed this negotiation and had a great respect for my colleagues on our team who dealt with complex and often arcane areas of the draft text. When we finally had a text ready to initial, Nigel Fyfe, one of the Ministry's international lawyers, and I went to Singapore for two days of painstaking review of the draft treaty, word by word, to ensure legal accuracy, a process quaintly called legal scrubbing or legal rectification.

On 31 August 2000 Pang Kin Keong and I initialled the draft Treaty, which was now ready for formal approval by both Governments. The CEP negotiations were comprehensively described by Professor Steve Hoadley of Auckland University in a book he prepared for the New Zealand Institute of International Affairs.

With Sutton's agreement, I included in the text what became known as the 'opt out' clause for the Treaty of Waitangi. This provision ensured that the Agreement with Singapore would not prevent New Zealand from taking any measures it deemed necessary to fulfil its obligations under the Treaty of Waitangi. The Opposition National Party under its leader, Jenny Shipley, objected to this clause.

When the implementing Bill came to a vote in Parliament, National voiced its opposition to the provision on the Treaty of Waitangi, but voted in favour of the whole Treaty. Labour could not have got the Treaty through Parliament in the face of combined opposition from all the other political parties, National, the Greens, New Zealand First and Jim Anderton's Alliance. The support of the National Party was therefore crucial. The Treaty of Waitangi opt-out clause then became a precedent and has been included in all our subsequent free trade agreements.

In some quarters there was opposition to the CEP agreement out of concern at Singapore's environmental and labour policies. National, as a strong supporter of free trade, could not bring itself to oppose the CEP just because a Labour Government had finalised it. I was asked to take part, as an advisor on the text of the proposed agreement, in a closed discussion between Helen Clark, the Prime Minister, with Jim Sutton, and Jenny Shipley as Leader of the

Opposition, to hammer out the basis upon which National would vote in favour of the Treaty.

On 18 December 2000, Cabinet ratified the CEP Agreement following a vote, 98 to 21, in Parliament in favour of a Bill to give effect to it. Our team was delighted that we had succeeded. New Zealand now had its second comprehensive bilateral trade agreement, after CER with Australia.

We continued the strategy of building New Zealand's trade and economic relationship with Asia by proposing a free trade link to Hong Kong. Hong Kong had reverted to China in 1997 as a Special Autonomous Region or SAR of China. It was a free port like Singapore. For New Zealand, having an FTA with Hong Kong would be a valuable entry point to China and a useful precedent for negotiating a free trade agreement with China. We could then pursue similar agreements with other key trading partners like Taiwan, Korea and Japan. I had not expected to be asked to lead the negotiations with Hong Kong.

The first step was to draw up a 'Heads of Agreement' with Hong Kong which set out what each side envisaged was the purpose of our FTA and what it would encompass. A delegation from Hong Kong led by Cherry Ling, a senior trade official, came to Wellington for this purpose. Charles Finny, one of the Ministry's senior trade officials, was closely involved in this process.

Once the 'Heads of Agreement' had been approved by both Governments, we were able to commence formal negotiations. As with Singapore, this required bringing together a team of experts to conduct sector negotiations on services, trade remedies, customs duties and other components of the FTA.

We held several rounds of negotiations in Hong Kong and Wellington. These proceeded very smoothly. The FTA with Hong Kong would be New Zealand's third FTA but Hong Kong's first. It wanted to use the example of concluding a quality FTA with New Zealand as a precedent for similar negotiations with their more important trading partners. The negotiations ran into a serious problem, however, over rules of origin: because of the close relationship between China and Hong Kong in the textiles sectors, any tariff advantage New Zealand might give to Hong Kong exports of textiles would actually accrue to China, thereby giving it an unintended trade advantage on the New Zealand market, representing a windfall gain for China.

Cherry Ling and I initial the Heads of Agreement which set in train New Zealand's free trade negotiations with Hong Kong

Try as we might, we could not get around the problem. It became clear that an FTA with Hong Kong would in essence mean duty-free access for Chinese textiles on the New Zealand market. We therefore had to put the Hong Kong negotiations on hold for several years, until the FTA negotiations with China were completed. Once we had secured an FTA with China, covering sectors like textiles, it would be relatively simple to finalise the agreement with Hong Kong. Unfortunately, I was moved to another assignment so I did not complete the negotiation with Hong Kong.

The other major trade negotiation which I led was the beginning of closer trade links with our important South Pacific Island neighbours. We conducted several exploratory rounds of negotiations in Fiji at the headquarters of the South Pacific Bureau for Economic Cooperation, SPEC, and in New Zealand, making good progress in the initial rounds. Understandably a key concern for the Island countries was the implications of duty-free trade for them because tariffs applied to their imports were an important component of overall government revenue. To give a name to the negotiations, I came up with the idea of 'PACER', *Pacific Agreement on Closer Economic Relations*. This name has stuck.

Twenty-five years after the end of the Vietnam War, Vietnam's communist government was interested in developing its trade links with the rest of the world. It was keen to join the World Trade Organization. New Zealand's interest in developing its trading links with South East Asia was still only slowly emerging but I thought it important that New Zealand respond to this interest. I went to Hanoi to conduct the first round of WTO accession negotiations. I was not able to see the negotiation to completion as I was posted soon after to Germany, but the Vietnamese clearly appreciated this initiative on New Zealand's part. One of the officials on the Vietnamese negotiating team was Tu Thu Hien, who had taken part in my WTO trade course at the Mekong Institute in Khon Kaen, Thailand, five years previously.

This was my first visit to Hanoi. Two things struck me. The first was the huge number of motorcycles on the streets, as most people could not afford private motor cars. These jostled each other all over the roadways. It was an exhilarating experience sitting on the back of one of these motor scooters. The riders are all pretty capable and there are few serious accidents. There is no point worrying about personal safety as a pillion passenger, you just have to go with the flow. When I later visited Ho Chi Minh City, Saigon, the ubiquitous motorcycles were just as chaotic there as in Hanoi.

The second was the apparent absence of any rancour towards foreigners as a result of the Vietnam War. Despite the horrific impacts the war had on the people and land of Vietnam, there was no evident animus towards those outsiders who had fought the communist government. But then again, as someone pointed out to me, the Vietnamese did not need to feel any such animus, as they had won the war.

CHAPTER 22

AMBASSADOR TO GERMANY
— PART ONE (2003–2006)

I JUMPED AT THE OPPORTUNITY TO RETURN TO GERMANY IN 2003 as New Zealand's Ambassador, although it was now a very different country from the divided nation we had seen as students in Würzburg, 28 years previously. The capital of the united Germany had gradually moved back to Berlin from Bonn in the decade since the Berlin Wall came down in 1989. The New Zealand Embassy was on the third floor of a new modern building on Friedrichstrasse, just up the road from Checkpoint Charlie, where we had crossed to East Berlin by bus all those years before.

I had rarely used my German since I had left Würzburg and it was rusty. I needed to get rapidly up to speed with my spoken and written German if I was to interact with senior politicians and business leaders. I enrolled at a two-month German language course at the Goethe Institute in Munich in October and November 2002, just as autumn gave way to a very cold winter. The other course participants came from all around the world. It was a great experience re-immersing myself in the language and culture.

Two young women on the course, one from Russia and one from Ukraine, stood out. Until recently Russia and the Ukraine had been part of the Soviet Union but were now separate countries. What struck me about these two was the love-hate relationship they had for each other. They both spoke Russian and were sometimes the best of friends in class, but then the Ukrainian woman would evince a visceral hatred for her Russian friend and some of the things she said. It revealed to me something of the relationship between these two countries which would turn toxic years later, when Vladimir Putin took the Crimea back into Russia from the Ukraine.

I spent the two months of the course living in a students' residence, just up the road from Hitler's favourite restaurant, the Osteria Bavaria (now renamed the Osteria Italiana — he would not have liked the name change!) on Schellingstrasse in Schwabing. Munich was of course the city in which the Nazis first came to prominence, calling it their '*Hauptstadt der Bewegung*' or Capital City of the Movement. Munich is a fascinating city to walk around. The Alte Pinakothek is one of the world's great art museums.

With my good friend Yichen Zhang, a senior lecturer in German at Shanghai University, who was then on the same Goethe Institute course as me, I made a pilgrimage to the Dachau concentration camp on the outskirts of the city, a grim and sobering memorial to barbarism personified.

A visit to Schloss Nymphenburg nearby made me think of home and I wrote the little poem which appears at the end of this narrative. This lovely palace was built in the late 17th century and became the summer residence of the kings of Bavaria.

While in Munich I was in frequent contact with Win Cochrane in Berlin, who was completing his posting as our Ambassador to Germany. Win had been my director in the South East Asian Division eight years earlier. When I arrived in Berlin from Munich by train, it was freezing cold, reminding me of a Canadian winter. I went to a crowded New Year's Eve fireworks display at the Brandenburg Gate and it was minus 10 degrees Celsius. Now one could freely walk through the Brandenburg Gate, which on our last visit in 1975 was located right beside the Berlin Wall, just inside the Communist Zone. Hitler ostentatiously had marched his Nazi troops through the Brandenburg Gate down Unter den Linden. Now the Gate was closed to all but pedestrians.

The Embassy staff were mainly Germans who had worked for the Embassy for many years in Bonn and had transferred when it relocated to Berlin in 2001. My executive assistant, Frau Dagmar Wilhelm, had a huge institutional knowledge, was very well connected in Berlin and had worked with six or more New Zealand ambassadors before me. She was therefore an indispensable member of the staff and was one of the longest-serving ambassadorial EAs in any of our Embassies.

The Governor-General, Dame Sylvia Cartwright, presents the Queen's Service Medal to Dagmar Wilhelm in Berlin. Dagmar was the longest serving Executive Assistant at any of New Zealand's numerous overseas diplomatic missions (photo: Mike Minehan).

It was thanks to Dagmar that I was able to get an early appointment with the German Federal President, Johannes Rau, to present my credentials as Ambassador to Germany. Dagmar helped me in a thousand ways with appointments, meetings and arranging diplomatic functions. In her retirement she remains a good friend. In recognition of her record of service, I nominated her for the award of a Queen's Service Medal (QSM). This was presented to her personally by the Governor-General, Dame Silvia Cartwright, when Dame Silvia paid an official visit to Germany in 2004. It was touching to see how greatly moved Dagmar was to receive this award.

I presented my credentials to President Rau on a freezing-cold morning in January 2003, at his official Residence, Schloss Bellevue. For this ceremony the Germans insisted that male Ambassadors wear formal long coat and tails, known as 'Frack' in German, but fortunately no silly top hat. I had to hire a suit especially for the occasion. I had to wear this same attire again during my Vienna credentials ceremony. In some things the Germans and Austrians could be as oddly traditional as the British.

At the appointed hour, an official car with police escort came to collect me from the famous Adlon Hotel, near the Brandenburg Gate. We drove the three kilometres to Schloss Bellevue, where an honour guard was drawn up outside for inspection. I did not have an overcoat to wear over the coat and tails and it was freezing cold.

After going inside the Residence, I was formally escorted upstairs to a reception room where my staff had gathered. President Rau came in. I presented my credentials to him formally and said a few words. Then he and I withdrew to a side room with one or two of his staff for a private conversation in German. I needed every day of that language brush-up course I had just done in Munich. Rau had recently visited New Zealand as the guest of the Governor-General, Dame Silvia Cartwright. He was interested to hear of developments since his visit.

Receiving credentials from newly appointed ambassadors is part and parcel of the role of a Head of State, just as it is for our own Governor-General in Wellington. As there are some 130 ambassadors accredited to Berlin and as these rotate every four years, the German President has to conduct 30 or so of these credentials ceremonies each year. For this reason and many others, it makes good sense to separate the representational function of Head of State from the executive function of Head of Government so that the latter can concentrate on the business of government. Some countries, like the US, combine both functions in the office of the President.

New Zealand's diplomatic service is small compared to other developed countries. Most of my diplomatic colleagues in Berlin focused their effort only on Germany. In my case, I was also ambassador to six other countries, Poland, Switzerland, Hungary, Slovakia, the Czech Republic and Austria. I had during the course of 2003 to present credentials to the Heads of State in each of these countries. This would mean that we at least had a formal diplomatic link with each of them via the Berlin Embassy. It was not possible to visit them more than once or twice a year. We did open an Embassy in Warsaw in late 2003, so I lost that responsibility. After I left Berlin, we opened an Embassy in Vienna too.

After completing the accreditation formalities with President Rau in Berlin, the way was clear for me to present my credentials in the six other countries. By diplomatic convention, I could not present my credentials in them before I had completed this task in the country where the Embassy is actually located, Germany. The formal ceremonies with the Head of State in each country were broadly similar in format: inspecting an honour guard before being taken to meet the Head of State, hand over my credentials, then have a brief 15 minutes' conversation with the President. In both Warsaw and Budapest, I laid a wreath, in a public ceremony, at their equivalent of the Tomb of the Unknown Soldier or Memorial to the Victims of War.

The ceremony in Bern, the Swiss capital, was the least formal of all. It involved no honour guard, but a formal meeting with the President of the Swiss Confederation, or the Swiss equivalent of the Head of State. Switzerland rotates this office each year among members of the Swiss Federal Council. In 2003, Pascal Couchepin was President and Head of the Federal Department of Economic Affairs. Couchepin had some time earlier had a verbal stoush with our then Minister of International Trade, Lockwood Smith, at an international meeting, on the topic of agricultural trade liberalisation. The Swiss agricultural sector is very heavily protected and Swiss politicians reacted very negatively to any suggestion that they should open the Swiss market to import competition, as Lockwood Smith had evidently suggested. But Couchepin passed over this piece of unpleasantness quite quickly and we had a good conversation on other bilateral and international issues.

The credentials ceremony in Vienna was held in the famous Hofburg, the former Palace of the Austro-Hungarian emperors. The spirit of the old emperor, Franz Josef, who died in 1916, still seemed to inhabit the place but it is now the official residence of a democratically chosen President. In my case this was President Thomas Klestil, who was clearly very unwell and died in office soon after. I had been to Vienna once before on holiday, with Louise and the children. I was keen to explore as much as possible of this historic city.

One of the most amazing places I came across, for anyone interested in the history of Europe, was the Habsburg Imperial Crypt, underneath the Capuchin Church in Vienna. Here are displayed the sarcophagi of generations of ruling Habsburg family members, including domineering old Kaiser Franz Josef, who took Austria into the First World War. Beside him lie his wife, Empress Elisabeth (Sisi) who was assassinated on a visit to Geneva in 1898, and their only son, Crown Prince Rudolf. Rudolf committed suicide at the Mayerling hunting lodge in 1889 with his mistress Mary Vetsera. Their apparent murder-suicide was the subject of a popular film in 1968 starring Omar Sharif and Catherine Deneuve. The Habsburgs, like the German Hohenzollerns and Kaiser Wilhelm II, were deposed after the First World War.

Most impressive of all in this crypt is the huge, ornate sarcophagus of Empress Maria Theresa who died in 1780, the Austrian Empress who had famously fought and lost to Frederick the Great of Prussia. Two other poignant sarcophagi remain in my memory. In stark contrast, Maria Theresa's son, Emperor Josef II, who tried unsuccessfully to reform the staid Austrian political system, is buried in a very simple tin coffin right at his mother's feet. He was the brother of the unfortunate Marie Antoinette, wife of Louis XVI, who were executed in the French revolution in 1793. For anyone who enjoyed the movie *Amadeus* on the life of Mozart, Josef was the Emperor who appeared in that movie and told Mozart that his music had 'too many notes' — apocryphal of course.

Finally, standing all alone is the simple coffin of Empress Marie Louise, Napoleon's second wife from 1810 to 1814, after he had ditched the legendary Josephine. When Napoleon was defeated in 1814 at the battle of Waterloo, followed by exile on St Helena, poor Marie Louise was unceremoniously packed off back to her family in Vienna and a minor role in Italy as Duchess of Parma. Her husband, in Les Invalides in Paris, has a much grander resting place.

The last Habsburg to enter the Imperial crypt was Otto von Habsburg, who died in 2011. As a child, he was the last Crown Prince of Austria-Hungary from 1916 until the dissolution in 1919. He considered himself the rightful emperor-king from 1922, as his father, Emperor Karl, had never abdicated. From the 1930s, he was active on the European political stage and was a fierce opponent of the Nazis. In 1938, on the Anschluss with Hitler's Germany, he fled to the US. After the war, he was a strong proponent of European integration and was elected to the European Parliament in 1979. I mention his life because in this one person is encapsulated the story and history of Europe, over the last hundred years, which has had such an impact on a distant country like New Zealand.

On one of my visits to Vienna, I walked the five kilometres to the St Marx cemetery on the outskirts of the city, to pay homage to Mozart who is buried there in an unmarked grave. I visited one of his Vienna homes and the magnificent Stephansdom where his funeral had been held. It has always struck me as odd that the wealthy aristocrats and burghers of Vienna, in 1791, had been prepared to consign to an unmarked grave Austria's most famous citizen, Mozart, who is still loved by countless millions today, whereas they, for the most part, are entirely forgotten.

One current joke was that the Austrians have been very good at convincing the world that Beethoven was Austrian and that Hitler was German. Beethoven of course was from Bonn in Germany and Hitler came from Braunau am Inn in Austria.

Unlike Empress Maria Theresa, reposing in her grand, ornate sarcophagus in a Viennese crypt, her arch nemesis, the legendary Frederick the Great of Prussia, who died in 1786, is buried in a simple, unremarkable grave covered by a stone slab, in the grounds of his beloved palace, Sanssouci, outside Berlin. Sanssouci, which survived the ravages of war, is the palace where Voltaire used to visit him. Alongside his simple grave are those of his favourite dogs.

Because we did not have New Zealand diplomatic staff on the ground in Austria, Poland, the Czech Republic and Hungary, we appointed local honorary Consuls-General. They were citizens of the country in question, but they had a formal mandate from New Zealand, approved by their own government, to assist New Zealand with consular and other activities. New Zealanders know little of the record of service to New Zealand undertaken by many of these Consuls and Consuls-General who provide a cost-effective means of ensuring a New Zealand presence in countries where there are no resident New Zealand diplomats.

We were fortunate to have Vera Egermayer in Prague, Peter Sunley in Vienna, Bob Sklar in Warsaw until we opened the Embassy there, and Rezsö Sárdi in Budapest. They were remunerated very little for their service but went out of their way to promote and assist New Zealand. Vera, as a young girl, had been incarcerated in the Theresienstadt concentration camp during the Nazi occupation of Czechoslovakia. I could only begin to imagine her experience.

Every ambassador's job is to promote and protect the interests of their own country in the country of posting. In Germany, I worked closely with the Trade Commissioner, Marta Mager, based in Hamburg, and would frequently travel to Hamburg, or elsewhere in Germany, where New Zealand-related trade promotion events were being held. Germany is the land of the 'Messe', or trade fair, a medieval institution which has survived to modern times.

New Zealand was particularly active in the annual ITB, the world's largest tourism fair held in Berlin. There was always a good turn-out of New Zealand tourism companies and airlines promoting tours and tourism products for New Zealand. At one gala dinner, Hayley Westenra sang for the German invitees. On another occasion, the London-based *'Moana and the Tribe'* gave a great concert, which the German audiences, disposed to view New Zealand as a dream destination, thoroughly enjoyed.

Another trade fair was CeBIT, an annual computer fair held in Hannover, showcasing the latest in office automation, information technology and telecommunications. It was always great to see how many New Zealand companies could display cutting-edge technology on the world stage.

The Australians at the time did not place much importance on CeBIT but usually some Australian technology exporters attended. At one CeBIT, New Zealand was the guest foreign country for that year. Phil Goff, then Minister of Foreign Affairs, now mayor of Auckland, met the Premier of the Federal State of Lower Saxony (Hannover is the capital) and hosted an informal drinks session for invited CeBIT guests.

One of the Australian invitees was clearly miffed at the prominence being accorded New Zealand that year in the CeBIT. We talked about some of the EU's problems with its neighbours, such as Russia. Far too generously, I said that New Zealanders realised we were lucky to live where we did in the South Pacific and have Australia as a neighbour. Quick as a flash, he said, 'Yes, you could have New Zealand as a neighbour'.

Over the years New Zealand has concluded a large number of reciprocal Working Holiday Schemes with other countries. These enable young people, usually aged between 18 and 30, to visit New Zealand as tourists for up to a year, but with the right to work to support themselves while they are here. The schemes have been spectacularly successful in allowing young people from around the world to get to know us. Some have become permanent migrants.

While I was in Germany I was able to get the annual quota raised from 200 to 5000. It was always fully subscribed. I often hear young backpackers speaking German as they go around New Zealand, unmindful of my role in facilitating their travel. The Covid-19 pandemic has put a hold on this travel — hopefully temporarily.

I negotiated a similar Working Holiday Scheme with the Czech Republic and went to Prague to sign the agreement on behalf of New Zealand. This was a tough negotiation as the Czechs had never entered into any such agreement before and were very worried about the impact on their labour market. They took some convincing that hordes of young New Zealanders were not going to descend on them and take jobs away from Czech workers.

Another treaty I signed was a double taxation agreement with Austria, in 2006, which required a trip to Vienna on behalf of the Minister of Revenue, Peter Dunne. Austria's oil and gas company, OMV, had for many years been active in oil exploration in New Zealand waters.

Promoting New Zealand exports to Germany required us to be vigilant about protectionist moves by the German Government. The Minister for Food, Agriculture and Consumer Protection, Renate Künast, a popular Green MP in Chancellor Gerhard Schröder's left-wing SPD coalition, began a campaign to promote local German Werder apples. We saw this as detrimental to our own export interests. I arranged for a nice case of New Zealand apples to be delivered to her office in Berlin to make the point that New Zealand apples could be even more delicious — it was obviously not politic for me to publicly criticise her policy. The campaign fizzled out after a while and did not really affect our exports to Germany. Whether that case of New Zealand apples had had any impact will remain one of life's mysteries.

Every year senior businessmen in Hamburg, in a tradition going back centuries, held a gala dinner called the '*Ostasiatisches Liebesmahl*', which celebrated Germany's economic and trade relationship with Asia. Male ambassadors from Asian and Pacific embassies in Berlin were invited. This was a smoked-filled, black tie occasion. I disliked as a matter of principle that it was a male-only event and thought it was counter to Hamburg's own commercial interests, as many ambassadors in Berlin from Asia were women. I made it clear after the first dinner that, tradition notwithstanding, it could not continue as a male-only event. Many others felt as I did, including on the Hamburg business side. The discrimination was soon ended.

During my time in Germany, New Zealand was looking to build new frigates for our navy. There was keen interest from international shipbuilders to bid for the tenders. Blohm und Voss, the famous Hamburg shipbuilder, was one of the bidders. I duly went to visit the company on the banks of the river Elbe, with a strict brief from our Ministry of Defence as to what I could and could not say about the tender process.

I was given a fascinating tour of the huge shipyard, followed by lunch in their boardroom. But what really blew me away happened after the lunch. I was escorted to a private room and, to my amazement, there on display was a 1/50 scale replica of the battleship *Bismarck*, about five metres long. The pride of the Nazi navy, the *Bismarck* was sunk in May 1941 after one of the most intensive naval manhunts in history.

The model of the *Bismarck* had been begun at the same time as the ship but not completed by the time the war ended. Justly proud of this ill-fated vessel, Blohm und Voss staff had hidden the model from the invading British who never found it. After the war it was completed and is now on display at their offices in Hamburg. I am no admirer of war machines, but I could not help recognising something special in this particular replica.

Shortly before her demise, the *Bismarck* had sunk HMS *Hood*, one of the British Navy's lead battleships, with the loss of over 1400 lives. Only three sailors survived. Some 17 years earlier, in May 1924, HMS *Hood* had visited Auckland as part of an imperial round-the-world cruise. She had sailed majestically into Auckland harbour, passing in front of where my Waiheke home is now.

Launched in 1918, HMS *Hood* was named after the famous 18th-century Admiral, Viscount Samuel Hood, the distinguished ancestor of the Honourable Dorothy.

CHAPTER 23

AMBASSADOR TO GERMANY
— PART TWO

After President Scheel visited New Zealand in 1978, two other German Presidents paid State visits to New Zealand, but New Zealand had never reciprocated. In diplomatic practice, this is unusual. It was high time that New Zealand paid a reciprocal high-level visit to Germany. Over the years our Prime Ministers and Foreign Ministers visit key relationship countries regularly. Helen Clark came twice. Phil Goff and Winston Peters as Foreign Minister came during my time in Germany but such visits are deemed working visits. They do not have the same status in protocol terms as a visit by a Head of State. New Zealand's Head of State is currently Queen Elizabeth II, but she was never going to visit Germany officially on our behalf.

It had not been common practice for the Governor-General to make overseas visits, other than to Tokelau and Niue, or some Pacific Island countries (like Arthur Porritt's visit to Tonga while I was a VSA volunteer there). That policy had begun to change. Overseas travel by the Governor-General is controlled by the Prime Minister of the day. It is to Helen Clark's credit that she recognised a need to make better use of the Office of the Governor-General in promoting New Zealand overseas. While I was in Germany, Dame Silvia

Cartwright, then Governor-General, paid two State visits, one to Germany and a second to Hungary and the Czech Republic.

The Germans were very pleased that Dame Silvia was proposing to visit but they were unsure of the protocol. They had not had to receive a Governor-General before. The question arose whether Dame Silvia should be received as if she were our Head of State, or as the deputy to the real Head of State, Queen Elizabeth, which is what she was. It made a big difference in the level of courtesies to be extended to the visitor. This might sound arcane, but it is still today very much a component of the manner in which countries relate to each other.

Governor-General Dame Silvia Cartwright lays a wreath at the Neue Wache on Unter den Linden in Berlin, the first by a New Zealand Governor-General since the war

The Germans did quietly ask Buckingham Palace if there would be any objection to receiving Dame Silvia *as if* she were a Head of State. The Palace quite properly voiced no objection, since the Queen could not carry out this part of her assigned role. Dame Silvia's visit, over five days, involved an official welcome with full ceremonial honours and a gala dinner hosted by President Johannes Rau at the magnificent Schloss Charlottenburg in Berlin, a lunch with

Chancellor Schröder, meetings with other political leaders and visits to Hamburg, Heidelberg and Munich, with good local media coverage.

A poignant moment was when Dame Silvia laid a wreath at the 'Neue Wache', on Unter den Linden in Berlin. This is the Federal German Republic's central memorial to all the victims of war and dictatorship. The symbolism of our Governor-General laying this wreath in final reconciliation with Germany after the Second World War was completely lost to the New Zealand public because the New Zealand media deemed it not of sufficient interest or they did not have enough funds to send a stringer over from London to cover the event. Either way, I felt they did a great disservice to the New Zealand men and women who had fought and sacrificed so much in the war.

The visit required a lot of careful preparation, but how proud we were in the Embassy to see a New Zealander treated to such high-level courtesies and for the first time, to see the New Zealand flag flying over the German Parliament and on all the main flagpoles of Berlin.

During Dame Silvia's official visit to Hamburg, we were taken to the Airbus factory which was then building part of the first of the A380 aircraft. I had never seen a commercial aircraft being built before and was amazed by the total jumble of parts and wiring everywhere, as the interior of the aircraft was fitted out. I could not understand how anyone could possibly know where each of the thousands of wires had to be fitted. Sometime later, I went to an airshow near Berlin to inspect the completed aircraft and to see the first A380 take off and land. It needed very little of the runway before that great bird became airborne. Although its longer-term use as a commercial aircraft now seems to be in question, it is an amazing piece of engineering.

Some might question the importance of such high-level State visits but in my experience they can have a significant positive impact in branding yourself in the country in question and getting your country featured and promoted. I have always believed that we make too little use of the Office of Governor-General to promote New Zealand overseas.

The role is not just to sign into law Acts of Parliament, hold the occasional investiture, host visitors, or visit hospitals and kindergartens, important though these functions are. There is an international role to play. Some of our Prime Ministers have not always been comfortable with this, as they no doubt have felt it could detract from their own international profile.

In Berlin the New Zealand Embassy was active in establishing links with prominent Germans, business leaders and politicians who had an interest in the New Zealand market. That required us too to get to know as many members as possible of the German Government and the Bundestag. Given the heavy demands on their time, the Chancellor and Cabinet Ministers were hard to get hold of. We encouraged New Zealand Cabinet Ministers to visit Berlin to meet their German counterparts.

Prime Minister Helen Clark on an official visit to Berlin (photo: Mike Minehan)

Helen Clark as Prime Minister got on well with Chancellor Schröder, who was an SPD left-of-centre politician like her. Clark and Angela Merkel also got on well together, after Merkel replaced Schröder. Partly no doubt this was because Merkel, who was a conservative Christian Democrat, enjoyed meeting a fellow woman leader despite their differing politics. Merkel hosted several lunches for New Zealand visitors while I was there. Merkel's English is good but of course speaking to the international media, she did not use it.

The Bundestag had established an Australian-New Zealand Friendship Group, which brought together members of the German Parliament from across political parties who had an interest in promoting Germany's links with us. I worked closely with members of this group who were always keen to meet visiting New Zealand Cabinet Ministers, or members of our own Parliament. It was useful to have in the Bundestag a group of politicians who were sympathetic to New Zealand's concerns, such as our trade links with the EU.

I would be questioned closely on our policy towards Iraq after the US invasion. Explaining the finer points of this policy in German to senior members of the Bundestag was sometimes a stretch. Some tended to assume that New Zealand would unquestioningly follow the British lead on a major foreign policy issue (hadn't we, in the past, said as much?). It was no easy task to convince them that we were not just Anglo-Saxons transported to the Antipodes.

I had had a great admiration for the SPD leader, Willy Brandt, a former Mayor of West Berlin, who had been Germany's Chancellor while it was still a divided nation, from 1969 to 1974. Brandt did much to strengthen cooperation in Western Europe and improve relations with Eastern Europe, in his Neue Ostpolitik (new Eastern policy) initiative. He was an opponent of the Hitler regime and in exile for much of the war years. In 1970, in a magnificent act, he knelt at a memorial to the Warsaw Ghetto Uprising, while he was visiting communist Poland to sign the Treaty of Warsaw. This treaty guaranteed German acceptance of the new borders of Poland. Such symbolic acts can have great force.

Brandt had died by the time I was Ambassador but I got to know Egon Bahr, the main architect of Brandt's Ostpolitik. Bahr was a member of the Bundestag and Cabinet Minister in Brandt's government. A humble and unassuming man, he was doyen of the German Social Democratic Party. I always appreciated his keen and well-informed insights into current European political questions. He died in 2015.

Freya Klier is a German author and film-maker who wrote an amazing book on the experiences of Jewish refugees in New Zealand. I got to know Freya well and helped to launch her book in Berlin, *Gelobtes Neuseeland*, which was translated into English by an old university colleague of mine, Jenny Rawlings. Freya's own personal history was amazing too: born in 1950, she grew up in communist East Germany, but was expelled from East Germany in 1988 as a dissident.

Her book canvasses the life experiences of many Jews who fled Germany in the 1930s and 1940s to safety in New Zealand. This included the philosopher Karl Popper who wrote much of his famous *The Open Society and its Enemies* while in lonely exile at Canterbury University, and the poet Karl Wolfskehl. I had the privilege of meeting some of those described in her book, when she launched the English-language version in Auckland some years after I had returned from Berlin. There are many harrowing accounts of individual sufferings. Fred Silberstein, as a 14-year-old, was forced to work for the SS at the Wannsee House where the Conference to decide the Final Solution to the Jewish 'problem' was held. He was then carted off to Auschwitz in 1944 and after miraculously surviving, made it to New Zealand after the war.

Shortly after I retired from the New Zealand Foreign Ministry, I was able to meet up again with Gerti Blumenfeld, who had been one of my German language tutors at the University of Auckland, 50 years before. She was now in her nineties. As a young Jewish teenager, she had grown up in Nazi Germany. Her family had a jewellery business in Montabaur, in the Rhineland-Palatinate.

Prudently, they had sent her to England for her schooling to escape Nazi oppression.

Gerti eventually found her way to New Zealand, married and settled in Opotiki, before moving to Auckland. Many of her family members were not so fortunate however and had died in the Holocaust. On my visits to her, we discussed her childhood experiences, and whether or not there could ever be forgiveness for those who had committed such crimes. She was firmly of the view that they could not be pardoned, whereas I said I felt it was important to forgive and move on. She died shortly after our conversations.

Reflecting on what we had discussed, I wished I had made myself clearer to her. My view is that the crimes of the past cannot be laid to the account of those who were not involved in them. Those who were unintentionally or unwillingly caught up in the Hitler regime could be forgiven for being fellow travellers. But there is no forgiveness for those who were willing accomplices in Nazi horrors and brutality. They can never be forgiven and no religious institution can absolve them of their actions. I often think of the film I once saw of a little girl, aged about seven or eight, holding her mother's hand, walking trustingly along as they headed off the cattle trucks into Auschwitz. There can never be forgiveness for those who injure a child.

I have never been able to understand the mentality of anyone who seeks to deny that the Holocaust took place.

Each year, on 20 July, the German Government commemorates the attempted assassination of Hitler on that day in 1944. The plot, led by Count Claus von Stauffenberg, failed and he was executed the next day along with many other plotters, who died horrible deaths as Hitler took his revenge. I had always been in two minds about von Stauffenberg who had fought for the Third Reich and the Wehrmacht in Tunisia and on the Russian front until he and others realised that Hitler was losing the war for them. Von Stauffenberg was no democrat, being a Prussian aristocrat, but the tragedy is that the failure of his plot ensured the war continued for another senseless eight months, costing so much waste in lives.

In 2005 I was invited to attend the 20 July commemoration at the Bendlerblock in Berlin, the army headquarters where von Stauffenberg had been executed. It was a sombre occasion. His wife, Nina, was still alive, but died the following year in 2006. The events of 20 July 1944 were made into an excellent film in 2008 called *Valkyrie*, starring Tom Cruise and Bill Nighy, in which Hollywood, unusually, took few liberties with the truth.

Despite my misgivings I realised that it is very important for modern Germany to acknowledge those who gave their lives in an effort to bring down a barbaric dictatorship. But my real heroes are people like the young university student, Sophie Scholl in Munich, who was never a fellow traveller of the Nazis but had opposed Hitler from the outset. This is why I list her in the introduction to this memoir.

Sophie was convicted of high treason by Nazi judge Roland Freisler, and was guillotined in 1943, aged only 21. If you have ever seen any film of Freisler let loose in his courtroom, trying the victims of the regime, you will know *to what depths of barbarism and depravity it is possible for supposedly civilised people to sink*. In that courtroom, the world of Martin Luther, Beethoven, Goethe and Schiller was very far away.

The New Zealand and Australian Embassies took it in turns to host the annual ANZAC Day commemoration held at the Heerstrasse Commonwealth War Graves cemetery in the west end of Berlin. The cemetery contains over 3500 graves. Eighty per cent are airmen who died in air raids over Berlin and Eastern Germany. The remainder were prisoners of war. Each April 25th, our commemoration was held in the warm sunshine of a spring dawn as the surrounding rhododendrons began to bloom.

We had representatives from many countries, including the Turkish, Indian and Pakistani Ambassadors, representatives of the German Armed Forces and Jewish, Christian and Muslim religious leaders, who were all given a role in the proceedings. This was a reflective and dignified ceremony which allowed Australians and New Zealanders living in Berlin to come together to share what our compatriots had shared back home, 12 hours earlier.

The annual ANZAC Day commemoration in Berlin was particularly poignant for my deputy, Stephen Harris, and his family. Stephen has a great-uncle, Colwyn Jones, who was killed in an air raid over Berlin in February 1944 when his Lancaster bomber was shot down. Stephen wrote an amazing book about his great-uncle: *Under a Bomber's Moon*.

I visited Dresden, the capital of the state of Saxony, on several occasions and saw the progress being made in rebuilding this beautiful city after it had been obliterated in aerial bombing by US and British bombers in March 1945. Symbolic of its phoenix-like re-emergence was the rededication of the magnificent Protestant church, the 'Frauenkirche'. Built in the 18th century, the church was left as a ruin by the communist East German Government, but plans to rebuild it according to its original design were quickly drawn up after German reunification.

Building commenced in 1992, using as much as possible of the rubble from the original church. I was invited to attend the opening of the rebuilt church. Edward, Duke of Kent, a cousin of the Queen, was a guest of honour. Britain had funded the creation of a magnificent new gold cupola to stand atop the church, as a sign of final reconciliation after the destruction of the war.

In Dresden I was invited to give the keynote address to the annual conference of the Saxony equivalent of Federated Farmers, on the topic of New Zealand's experience of farming without subsidies. The advantages of unsubsidised farming were a message we sought to convey as often as possible in our contacts with farmer organisations in Europe, to encourage the EU to reform its Common Agricultural Policy or CAP, which provided large trade distorting subsidies to EU farmers.

My address was in German — Jan Heyen from our Embassy staff had assisted me to write it. While delivering it in German was no problem for me, answering in German the many complex questions on agricultural economics after my speech was less easy to tackle. I found there was great interest in New Zealand's agricultural policies and gave numerous presentations on the topic while I was in Germany.

A memorable occasion was the expansion of the EU, on 1 May 2004, when 10 new countries simultaneously joined. Seven of these were part of the former communist Eastern Bloc, including Hungary, Poland, Slovakia and the Czech Republic. This event, as I reported to Wellington at the time, finally lifted the Iron Curtain which Churchill, in March 1946 in a speech at Fulton, Missouri, had dramatically brought down over a divided Europe.

We were invited to take part in a symbolic ceremony near the little East German town of Zittau, where the boundaries of Poland, Germany and the Czech Republic meet. We were able to walk through all three countries in only a few minutes on a circular path. The ease with which I crossed from Germany to the Czech Republic and to Poland that day was in stark contrast to the occasion, 30 years previously, when I had gingerly stepped a few metres into communist Czechoslovakia and had feared I might get shot at for my impudence.

Berlin is an attractive city for young New Zealanders. It is cheaper to live in than London or Paris. An annual 'Writers in Residence' award, granted by the New Zealand Ministry for Culture and Heritage, allowed promising New Zealand writers to spend a year in Germany on creative work. Musicians and artists often made Germany their home, like Hattie St John, who made a name for herself as a jazz singer. While I was in Berlin, New Zealand author Cathie Dunsford's work *Manawa Toa* was translated into German; and Philip Temple completed a magnificent history of the Wakefield family, *A Sort of Conscience*.

My former MFAT colleague and author Witi Ihimaera gave well-attended readings from his works. Berlin is a vibrant city culturally.

Young New Zealanders flocked to it. Our daughter Rachel was one of them and she stayed for 15 years.

I always regretted that New Zealand and Germany did not share a major national sporting interest. There is no doubting that the shared passion for rugby has helped in developing our relationship with France.

One day I was informed that the Berlin Zoo had successfully bred two kiwi chicks, one of only a handful of zoos around the world to have done this. The Director of the Zoo, Dr Jürgen Lange, wanted me to come to a media ceremony to name them. The Berlin Zoo is justly proud of its kiwi breeding programme and it has a thriving population of kiwi. Kura Hakaraia, the embassy's administration officer, accompanied me. Kura decided that the two chicks should be named Kia and Ora!

Kura Hakaraia, from our Embassy team, names Kia and Ora, the two new Kiwi additions to the Berlin Zoo

Later I arranged for noted New Zealand artist and sculptor Jeff Thomson to come to Berlin to build a giant-size kiwi out of his famous corrugated iron. Jeff and his wife stayed with me at the Residence for a week. The completed artwork, a kiwi in corrugated iron standing about two metres high, was presented to the zoo by the Prime Minister, Helen Clark, when she visited Berlin. Dr Lange was delighted and the sculpture is, as far as I know, still on display in the zoo.

One weekend I was taken on a visit to my old university, Würzburg, by my friend Rainer Schubert, a Berlin writer and publisher. It was lovely to revisit the beautiful baroque city, sample some of the famous Randersacker wine and the wines of the famous Juliusspital. Professor Kurt Ruh had died in 2002 so I was never able to apologise for my failure to say goodbye to him properly, 30 years previously.

We drove the 500 km from Würzburg back to Berlin in a large 7 Series BMW, which without too much effort would cruise at speeds of 250 km an hour on the straight and wide autobahn. I thought of that student driving along at a sedate 90 km an hour in a clapped-out VW and being overtaken by just such an annoyingly fast BMW.

In my last year, I was asked by our Ministry of Research, Science and Technology to go to Geneva to sign a Memorandum of Understanding to facilitate cooperation between New Zealand's Ministry of Research, Science and Technology (MORST) and CERN, the European Organization for Nuclear Research. CERN was in the process of constructing the huge Hadron Collider under the Geneva and French landscape, the world's largest and highest energy particle collider. I was taken underground to see the Collider being built. A complete ignoramus of the physics, I was overawed by this amazing project. The Collider started up in 2008. In 2012 it confirmed the existence of the Higgs boson.

In June 2006, Berlin hosted the final of the FIFA World Cup. Our Foreign Minister, Winston Peters, by very happy coincidence (!) was visiting Berlin at the same time. We arranged for him to have talks with his German counterpart, Frank-Walter Steinmeyer, who today is the Federal German President. I took him to a summer garden party and introduced him to Chancellor Merkel. We visited the site where Hitler's body had been burned in the final days of the war, outside the Führerbunker.

After the FIFA final match, Mr Peters and his partner Jan Trotman were booked to fly early the next day out of Hannover airport, to catch the NZ1 direct flight back to New Zealand from London. It had not been possible to secure flights from Berlin to London because of the FIFA event. Hannover, some 280 km distant, was the nearest airport offering the means for them to get to London.

We left Berlin early the next morning to catch the 11am flight from Hannover. I had not imagined that there would be much traffic on the Berlin–Hannover autobahn at that time of the morning. About 20 km from Hannover we suddenly struck heavy traffic and a complete 'Stau' as the Germans call it — traffic completely immobilised. It looked very likely that he would miss his Hannover-to-London flight and his flight to New Zealand as well.

Desperate situations require desperate measures. I asked our driver, Alan Jones, a capable Welshman who had spent many years in Berlin in the British Army, to put the New Zealand pennant on the car. We then drove, flag flying, the next 20 km up on the right-side verge of the motorway, passing two long streams of immobilised traffic. I feared we might be intercepted by the German police and have some explaining to do for illegally driving on the verge. I would then have to plead diplomatic immunity but in 20 km there wasn't a policeman in sight and the verge was clear of traffic all the way. Germans are so disciplined. In New Zealand, of course, lots of other drivers would be driving on the verge to get around the traffic jam. It was my decision to break the German road code in this manner but we got to Hannover just in time for their flight to London.

Christopher was at the time studying at Victoria University in Wellington. During one of his visits to Berlin I took him to the Dreifaltigkeit cemetery. He wondered why I was taking him to a Jewish graveyard until he realised I had brought him to the grave of Felix Mendelssohn, who died in 1847. He was the grandson of the prominent philosopher Moses Mendelssohn, well known in Berlin society in the early 19th century. I have always loved Felix Mendelssohn's music, especially his evocative *Scottish* symphony, the *Hebrides Overture* and his *Midsummer Night's Dream*. The Nazis did not disturb Mendelssohn's grave but banned performances of his work and even tried to rewrite his music to accord with Nazi tastes. The arrogance of small minds which try to improve on the already perfect!

Christopher and Rachel in Dresden

One winter's morning, when I was staying with friends in a Swiss Alpine village, I awoke and discovered I was half blind in my right eye. I had no idea what the problem was. I went immediately back to Berlin for a medical examination. I was informed that the retina at the back of my eye had become detached and needed to be reattached immediately or I would be permanently blind in that eye. I was most fortunate to end up in the care of a prominent professor and eye surgeon at the Benjamin Franklin University Hospital. Its name signifies that the US had funded its establishment after the war.

The Herr Professor, whose name I have forgotten, reattached the retina in my eye in a very painful operation under a local anesthetic. I am eternally grateful to him for that. I had to go to see him again perhaps six or eight times for a post-op check and was amazed by the formality that existed in his office. Reception staff and junior assistants treated him like a deity. It was not unusual for me to have to wait an hour or two, beyond the appointed time, before I was admitted to his august presence.

After the operation, I needed several days to recuperate at home. I was lucky that Ruth Piluden, the manager of the New Zealand Residence in Berlin, kept me well fed. Ruth, who is from the Philippines, had worked for many of my predecessors and had given unstintingly loyal service to New Zealand in managing and running the Residence.

Unlike most others in the Philippines, Ruth is Anglican, not Catholic. She comes from Baguio, which is a mountain town on the island of Luzon, north of Manila. Her first language was Igorot, the language of the mountain region, not the more widely used Tagalog (or Filipino). What amazed me was to discover how much this language, Igorot, has in common with New Zealand Maori. I discovered word after word that was *exactly* the same. This clearly demonstrates some linguistic connection going back before recorded history.

Ruth and her sister, Claire, who also worked for a Berlin Embassy, encapsulate the Philippines' global challenge — many of its people have to live and work overseas for decades, far away from home, in order to support family back in the Philippines.

The Murder of Birgit Brauer

The worst moment of my career came when news arrived in September 2005 that 28-year-old Birgit Brauer, a young German backpacker, had been murdered near Oakura, southwest of New Plymouth. She had innocently accepted a lift and the driver, Michael Wallace, had brutally killed her. This is a family's worst nightmare. Birgit's parents lived in East Germany, in Eberswalde, 55 km north of Berlin. Her trip to New Zealand was intended to be a voyage of discovery for their only child, who had long wanted to visit her dream destination.

There was widespread negative publicity in the German media, but the New Zealand police were outstanding in the manner in which they conducted the investigation and kept the family informed each step of the way through the German Embassy in Wellington.

Eventually Michael Wallace, 44, was found guilty of the murder and was sentenced in 2009 to life imprisonment, with an 18-year non-parole period. Wallace had a long list of previous convictions including for rape and abduction. It was Birgit's great misfortune that day to have trustingly hitched a ride with him.

Having obtained a large increase in the German working holiday quota, I was mindful of the risks many young backpackers take in being insufficiently cautious in our country. I hope that Birgit's story is a lesson on the need to be careful and wary at all times and not to suppose that everyone one meets in New Zealand, or anywhere else for that matter, is safe to be with. Unfortunately, in the history of backpacking in New Zealand, Birgit's case is not unique.

I assisted New Zealand Rotary, through the good offices of a former MFAT colleague, Brian Lynch, to bring Birgit's parents to New Zealand in 2006 so they could visit the place where Birgit had died and attend some of the court proceedings. I could not imagine the pain they suffered. The murder had a traumatic effect on the Taranaki community. A memorial to Birgit was unveiled in New Plymouth in 2008.

Hungary and the Czech Republic

The presentation of my credentials in Budapest, in 2003, to Hungary's President, Ferenc Mádl, at the Sándor Palace on the Buda side of the Danube, was special both for me and, as it turned out, for the Hungarians. Sándor Palace, built in 1803–1806, had been the official residence of successive Hungarian Prime Ministers, but the building had been completely destroyed by Allied bombers during the Second World War. The whole of Buda was destroyed as the retreating Nazis tried to hold off the advancing Russian troops.

The gleaming white Palace building had been painstakingly restored. I was one of the first ambassadors to present my credentials to the Hungarian President in the restored building. He had recently moved in and the credentials ceremonies that day were something of a prototype for all future such events. After the ceremony, on a beautiful sunny day, President Mádl took me onto the balcony of his Residence, which had a commanding view of the whole city of Pest below.

I was then taken in a convoy, roads cleared and with outriders, to lay a wreath at the Heroes' Square, one of the major squares in Budapest, with an iconic statue complex. It was a dignified and an impressive ceremony with slow-stepping military guards as an escort. To give the wreath a New Zealand colouring, we had arranged for the flowers to be in blue and red. Knowing how much Hungary had suffered in the war and since then under the communist dictatorship, it was a humbling experience.

With President Ferenc Mádl of Hungary on the balcony of the
Sándor Palace, with the River Danube and the city of Pest below
(Photo: Hungarian News Agency)

Sometime later, the Governor-General, Dame Silvia Cartwright, paid a State visit to Hungary — and on this occasion the Hungarians had no qualms about the level of courtesies to be extended to her. President Mádl and his wife were warm and generous hosts. Our Consul-General, Rezsö Sárdi, who was Air New Zealand's representative in Hungary, was a great help in putting the visit together. As in Germany, the visit served to increase our profile in Hungary. Particularly impressive was to see the New Zealand flag flying for the first time on the magnificent Hungarian Parliament and strung out along the Danube bridges.

In October 2006 Hungary commemorated the 50th anniversary of the 1956 Hungarian Revolution, a popular uprising brutally suppressed by the communist government and its Soviet masters. Hungary was keen that New Zealand be represented at the commemoration at senior level. After some delay in sorting out who would represent New Zealand, the government sent Rick Barker, a Labour list MP who was Minister of Internal Affairs and Minister of Veterans' Affairs. He brought his wife to Budapest and was accompanied by Nándor Tánczos, then a Green List MP well known for his trademark dreadlocks. Nándor's father came from London. He had fled Hungary in 1956 at the time of the Revolution.

All the heads of state, presidents and a few monarchs of Europe (King Juan Carlos of Spain), were there. New Zealand was a little overshadowed although Rick was made very welcome. He laid a wreath at the formal commemoration ceremony and attended a commemorative event held in the debating chamber of the Hungarian Parliament on the banks of the Danube.

On the first evening, the New Zealand delegation was invited to a big gala reception. Rick, not knowing anyone there, asked me to introduce him to some of the world leaders in the room. We bowled up to the German President, Horst Köhler, and one or two others and then button-holed the President of Poland, Lech Kaczyński. I had presented my credentials to his predecessor, Aleksander Kwaśniewski, as New Zealand Ambassador to Poland, but I had not met Kaczyński before because by then we had a separate Embassy in Warsaw.

Fourth President of the Republic of Poland, Kaczyński and his identical twin brother, Jarosław, the Prime Minister, between them dominated Polish politics at the time. Jarosław still does. I introduced Rick to him, but his English was poor. I expect he had little idea where New Zealand was and no concept of what a Minister of Internal Affairs did. Rick could not sustain the conversation. After inviting him to pay a visit to New Zealand, we moved on to someone else.

There was never any prospect that Kaczyński would be interested in visiting New Zealand — he had his hands full in Poland. In any case, he was killed in the crash of a Polish Air Force jet, on 10 April 2010, as it sought to land at a Smolensk airport. He was going there to commemorate, with Vladimir Putin, the Katyn massacre, the infamous Soviet mass execution of Polish army officers at the start of the Second World War, a heinous crime which for decades the Soviets had sought to blame on the Nazis until being forced to admit the truth.

For Nándor's father, though, the commemoration of the 1956 Hungarian Revolution held special meaning.

In Prague, I presented my credentials to President Václav Klaus, the Czech Republic's second President after he had taken over from Václav Havel in 2003. I had always admired Havel, a writer and anti-communist dissident who had steered Czechoslovakia through the difficult days after the Velvet Revolution in 1989 and was President of the separate Czech Republic when Czechoslovakia broke up into its component parts, Slovakia and the Czech Republic in 1993. Klaus told me he admired New Zealand's former Minister of Finance, Ruth Richardson, because she had been the first Finance Minister to have published a public sector balance sheet, something Klaus himself wanted to do as part of necessary economic reforms in the Czech Republic after decades of communist economic mismanagement.

Dame Silvia Cartwright paid a State visit to the Czech Republic in conjunction with her visit to Hungary. Klaus hosted her to a gala dinner in the historic Prague Castle, now the President's official Residence. In Prague, our Honorary Consul, Vera Egermayer, arranged a private visit to the home of the family of famed Czech artist Alfons Mucha (1860–1939), who was celebrated for his stylised theatrical posters, particularly that of Sarah Bernhardt. The home was full of his works, not normally seen by the public.

Formal wreath laying is frequently part of the credentials ceremony for a new ambassador. This one in Warsaw.

Please Excuse Us!

I worked closely in Berlin with former German ambassadors to New Zealand who shared with me the goal of promoting New Zealand-German links. One recent returnee from Wellington told me of an incident that occurred when he was presenting his credentials to the Governor-General, Dame Silvia Cartwright, at Government House in Wellington.

In the middle of the formal ceremony, a ground-floor window was suddenly thrust open from the outside and a group of protestors stuck their heads in, interrupting proceedings. Fortunately, they were unarmed. They had thought the ceremony involved the new US Ambassador to New Zealand and had mistaken the timing of his credentials ceremony. They did not have a beef with Germany. Despite the security at Government House, they had managed to get inside the grounds and across the lawns to the front of the Official Residence. They were soon removed by security staff, but Dame

Silvia, not batting an eyelid, continued the formal ceremony, with an apology to the ambassador: 'Please excuse us!'

I think this incident encapsulates nicely why it is that New Zealand is a popular posting for foreign diplomats, escaping the formalities of such ceremonies in most other countries.

CHAPTER 24

DEPUTY SECRETARY OF FOREIGN AFFAIRS AND TRADE (2007–2010)

TOWARDS THE END OF MY POSTING IN BERLIN, I APPLIED FOR A position as one of the four Wellington-based deputy secretaries, part of the Ministry's Senior Management Group, or SMG. This position, with the title of DSP4, meant that it was responsible for Programme Four in the Ministry, covering all the corporate service divisions as well as responsibility for our relations with Europe, the Middle East and Africa. The position was being vacated by John Larkindale, who was being posted to Canberra as High Commissioner.

I travelled back to Wellington for an interview for the position, chaired by MFAT's CEO, Simon Murdoch, who had the late Alan Williams with him and someone from the State Services Commission on the interview panel. Simon was one of New Zealand's foremost public servants, having headed the Prime Minister's Department and served as High Commissioner to Canberra. Since I was relatively untested in a senior management role, I knew he would be taking something of a risk in appointing me to this position.

The interview itself was pretty standard but I remember a question put to me by the State Services Commission representative. She asked me how I handled stress in my work. I have never had any problem with stress as I knew well how to completely switch off from work from time to time and relax, achieving what is the common objective for all public servants of a good 'work-life balance'. She was clearly unimpressed by my answer and said 'obviously, you have not had enough stress in your life'. She may well have been right but stress never was, nor ever became, a problem for me.

I was delighted and grateful to Simon when he informed me that he was giving me the job. I greatly enjoyed the nearly four years I undertook this role and was fortunate to have some very capable colleagues in each of the divisions which reported to me.

Just before I returned to Wellington, Winston Peters replaced Phil Goff as Minister of Foreign Affairs and Trade. There was some apprehension about having a new Minister after six years working with Goff. The key to a good departmental relationship with a Minister is mutual respect, where the Ministry and its staff recognise their responsibility to serve the Minister to the best of their ability. The Minister in turn treats the Ministry with a professional respect. This does not mean there aren't tensions in the relationship. There often are, as policy initiatives are proposed, debated, accepted or rejected. The Minister always makes the final decision and can expect to have it faithfully implemented. But there is no substitute for an underlying mutual respect to make the relationship work effectively.

Foreign Affairs and Trade is a senior portfolio of government. The Ministers who hold this portfolio have generally served a long apprenticeship in politics. It can be daunting for a Minister new to Cabinet to take on the task of overseeing a large department of state. There is really no training that can be given to a first-time Minister, who suddenly finds himself or herself responsible for the political leadership of a large entity, employing thousands of people and spending millions of dollars of taxpayers' money. The full support of their department in implementing government policies becomes crucial to their success in their portfolio. In the private or corporate sector, leaders come up through the corporate world and know the business well, or have the business skills to run big enterprises.

Ministers of the Crown usually do not have prior experience of the departments they are expected to run.

Both Goff and Peters interacted with the Foreign Ministry professionally throughout their time in office. The demarcation between the separate but linked responsibilities of the Minister and the Ministry were well established. Peters continued to focus on improving our relations with the US and the Pacific and established a good rapport with the US Secretary of State, Condoleezza Rice. He also had to grapple with the latest coup d'état in Fiji, led by Frank Bainimarama.

The Ministry's Senior Management Group met each week to examine and decide on policy initiatives and to review the operation of the Ministry. There was a good camaraderie, with colleagues who worked well together under Simon's leadership as CEO. My own responsibility, in addition to the whole of organisation responsibility that all SMG members shared, was to manage the Ministry's corporate affairs and promote our relationships with Europe, the Middle East and Africa.

The corporate services divisions included Finance, Audit, Human Resources, Security, Information Technology, Property, and Organisational Planning and Performance. Each division was headed by its own Director who in the first instance would report to me on key issues and through me to the CEO and the Minister.

The Organisational Planning and Performance unit, headed by a very capable wordsmith, Denise Almao, was responsible for ensuring each unit in the Ministry, including each of our overseas posts, completed its annual planning and reporting requirements — reports were updated quarterly. These were then considered by the SMG along with the new annual planning documents, in often multi-day sessions. I would then provide detailed feedback to each director or Head of Mission who reported to me. Denise also wrote and coordinated the Ministry's Annual Report to Parliament.

Each year, a promotions round was held to promote good staff in the organisation, or to provide small financial bonuses for outstanding achievement.

Alan Sainsbury ensured that the Ministry's IT systems were constantly updated and modernised. Alan bore my own ignorance of advanced IT systems with equanimity. To deal with his own stress levels, he engrossed himself in vintage car rallies. Phil Goulin, the Director of Finance, and his team ensured the Ministry's expenditure remained within budget — I was mightily impressed by the fact that on Phil's watch, we never overspent our approved budgetary allocation.

I was fortunate to have excellent executive assistants. A young Le Roy Taylor combined organisational skill with an ebullient personality. Later, he went on to work for Government House and more recently, Prime Minister Jacinda Ardern. If there is any substance to Plato's Theory of Ideas, Le Roy would be the ideal EA!

As part of my human resources responsibilities, with Simon's approval, I made regular recommendations to the Minister on who should be appointed to head our various Missions abroad. For the most part, Winston Peters recognised that trained professionals were best for the job and accepted our recommendations.

Peters did make one political appointment, Brian Donnelly, as High Commissioner to the Cook Islands. Brian had been a New Zealand First MP. Unfortunately, Brian fell ill while on assignment in Rarotonga and died soon after in New Zealand in 2008. To replace Brian in Rarotonga, Winston Peters accepted our nomination of Te Rongotoa 'Tia' Barrett, who was from Ngati Maniapoto/Tainui iwi. He did this despite strong pressure on him from a prominent Auckland businessman and local body politician who felt he had earned the right to the job.

Tia had been High Commissioner to Fiji while I was in Samoa and then head of the Ministry's Maori Policy Unit. He was instrumental in promoting a sharper awareness of Maoritanga and Maori perspectives in the Ministry and in our foreign policy. He served for a while as the Official Secretary at Government House but after a time found himself unexpectedly back in the Ministry.

In November 2009, Tia suffered a heart attack one weekend while playing golf in Rarotonga. It was nearly an hour before any medical assistance arrived. It proved difficult to organise an emergency evacuation. Commercial airlines could not handle it and no aircraft was available for the purpose in New Zealand. The French authorities in Tahiti kindly assisted by providing free of charge an aircraft to fly him back to New Zealand for treatment, but he died in Middlemore Hospital a week later. This highlighted once again the severe difficulties which MFAT staff face when they become seriously ill out of New Zealand.

Tia's funeral was held at Ngaruawahia marae, attended by the Maori King, Tuheitia, Tia's extended family and Ministry colleagues. I was a pallbearer. I recalled in my own eulogy on the marae that Tia and I were just two boys from Otorohanga, we had lived not far from each other and had become good friends. Tia was a big man: his coffin weighed a tonne and I almost could not manage it. We laid Tia to rest in the urupa of the beautiful Kahotea marae near Otorohanga. Haere, haere e hoa!

As part of my geographical responsibilities, I held official Foreign Ministry talks overseas with key partners, or important bilateral relationships. For these I travelled to Pretoria, Cairo, Riyadh, Tel Aviv, Ankara, Tehran and numerous EU countries. These provided an opportunity to touch base with our staff serving overseas, who on occasion might not see anyone from head office for a year at a time. Such visits were important in making sure staff out in the field felt fully connected back to the Ministry in Wellington. Desktop computers made instant contact with Wellington colleagues possible (no more blue and yellow telegrams) but there is no substitute for supportive visits to our staff at their workplaces overseas.

Foreign Ministry talks were hard work because of the wide range of issues that could be covered. I needed to be across all aspects of New

Zealand's foreign and domestic policy, not just those issues in my immediate areas of responsibility.

The talks I held in the Egyptian Foreign Ministry were in a surreal setting. Looking out from the windows of the meeting room, there stood the pyramids of Giza, some 20 km distant. A timeless setting. Later that afternoon our Ambassador, Rene Wilson, took me on a private tour of the pyramids after the gates had closed to the public. One of my most unforgettable experiences was climbing inside the pyramid of Khufu and coming back out just as the sun set behind the pyramids over the endless desert.

Suddenly, in the deep stillness of the evening, numerous muezzin started up in one mosque after the other, calling the faithful to prayer in the villages surrounding the delta below. Hauntingly, the old and the new mingled. It was for me very moving but quite alienating — being alone at the foot of the Sphinx and the ancient pyramids as darkness fell and being reminded dramatically of the history of the Arab conquest of this enchanting land.

Churchill and Roosevelt had visited the Sphinx during their meeting in Cairo in December 1943, to plan the invasion of Europe the following year. As Churchill describes it: 'I gazed at her for some minutes as the evening shadows fell. She told us nothing and maintained her inscrutable smile'.

Rene took me next day to visit the New Zealand Defence Force contingent which formed part of the 1100-strong international group Multinational Force and Observers (MFO) from 11 countries. This was established in 1982 and was located at North Camp in the isolated Sinai Desert. Its purpose is to monitor the peace agreement between Israel and Egypt. This has been an important, but little recognised, contribution by New Zealand to international peace-keeping in the region. The MFO cannot take action against breaches of the peace by either side but must report these to its HQ in Rome, which then advises the Israeli and Egyptian governments.

The Egyptian military authorities insisted on providing an armed escort for us as we drove through the desert to North Camp. The local Bedouin did not look friendly and I could not help noticing the mounds of inorganic rubbish scattered everywhere.

A big concern was the smuggling of rockets and ordnance via Egypt into Gaza. Smugglers' tunnels were often discovered and destroyed by the MFO but new means of getting ordnance into Gaza always seemed to materialise.

The battered little car in which our military escort (four soldiers) was driving soon ran out of petrol. We left it behind on the roadside and continued our journey unescorted. At the town of El-Arish, occupied by the Israelis from 1967 to 1979, we had a pleasant lunch in a deserted restaurant by the Mediterranean Sea, and watched ships in the distance. There were no tourists because of the security situation. We drove up to the Rafah Gate, the entrance from Egypt to Gaza. Because of the heightened security situation, the Gate was firmly closed as is often the case.

I was greeted at North Camp by the New Zealand contingent with a Maori welcome. I responded with a little speech in Maori which I think surprised them. The US Commander of the MFO expressed some concern about the capabilities of his newly elected Commander-in-Chief, one Barack Obama. He need not have worried.

On the way back to Cairo from North Camp, Rene took me across the Suez Canal by public barge. A strikingly beautiful little girl, aged about nine or ten, begged me for some coins which I gave her. She appeared to be a regular beggar on the canal barges.

We then popped unannounced into an Egyptian military camp by the Canal at Ismailia, to watch the international shipping ply the waterway. We were served a nice cup of local tea. Egyptians are famed for their hospitality — I just never expected to receive it in a military camp as an uninvited guest. I could not help but think of that boy, aged nine, who had transited the Canal 45 years earlier.

I visited Tehran twice. The Iranians saw New Zealand as a constructive partner with good links to the US at a time when they did not have their own diplomatic links to the US, as they still don't. We encouraged them to enter into an international agreement to limit the possibility of producing nuclear weapons. Hamish MacMaster, our ambassador, accompanied me on talks in the Iranian Foreign Ministry. I had a great respect for those I met.

I met the Iranian Foreign Minister, Manouchehr Mottaki, on two occasions. Iran appreciated this contact, for which I had a tight brief from the Minister in Wellington. We covered regional issues and raised our concerns about Iran's human rights record in a constructive manner. Our representations on human rights were noted but the advent of the conservative and more draconian Ahmadinejad regime in 2005 meant that Iranian moderates were being sidelined.

Hamish took me to the Tehran home of the Ayatollah Khomeini and the mosque where his tomb is. I visited the Shah's Palace where Bruce Brown had presented his credentials to the Shah just a short time before he was deposed. Despite his reputation for opulence and brutal suppression of dissidents, his palace was quite a modest building. The notorious and thuggish Basij, part of the Islamic Revolutionary Guard, designated a terrorist organisation by the US, do cast a shadow over any visit to Tehran, but I felt much freer walking around the streets of Tehran than on the streets of Riyadh. The heat of the day in Riyadh makes walking anywhere unpleasant, but it also has very tight security.

After talks with the Israeli Foreign Ministry in Jerusalem, I was taken to see the Church of the Holy Sepulchre, also known as the Church of the Resurrection, built over the site where, according to a fourth-century tradition, Jesus was crucified and laid to rest. The place was packed with pilgrims. I watched them touching in ecstasy the slab on which Jesus had supposedly been laid. They wiped items of clothing on the slab, relics to take back home for those who could not be present. It was a scene straight out of the Middle Ages. It was at once a fascinating but depressing sight. I was troubled by the naïve belief that led people to abase themselves in response to a tradition that is manifestly spurious.

Dozens of Jewish worshippers nodded up and down as they prayed at the Wailing Wall, part of the second temple which stood on the Temple Mount from 516 BCE to 70 CE. There is no doubting the amazing history that surrounds every inch of the city of Jerusalem, but I was depressed by the firm grip that unexamined tradition and religion still have on so many.

Thanks to the good offices of the Canadian Embassy in Israel, I was able to spend a day of talks with the Palestinian Authority in Ramallah. Getting there, through all the Israeli roadblocks, was a nightmare. I was warmly received and we had good discussions. How sad that the pervading atmosphere had to be so oppressive for all concerned, Israelis and Palestinians alike.

After formal talks in Ankara, I visited Istanbul, the legendary Constantinople. I was able to seek out the remnants of Byzantine influence before the Ottoman Turks conquered the city in 1453. A humbling experience is to stand within the walls of the Hagia Sophia with its massive dome. Opened in 537, it was the main Christian church of Constantinople until converted into a mosque by the Turks. It was made a museum in 1935 but in a retrograde move was recently restored as a mosque. What great events of history this magnificent building has borne witness to.

In the Istanbul Archaeological Museum, I discovered the so-called 'Alexander Sarcophagus.' Named after Alexander the Great, the sarcophagus was not his but probably that of a contemporary ruler of Sidon. Discovered by accident in an underground burial chamber in 1887, it is one of the most important and amazing works of classical archaeology, consisting of exquisitely carved small marble figures in very high relief. The colours have long faded (the ancients used to paint their sculptures) but the carvings are as fresh and vibrant as if they had been carved yesterday. It is a most beautiful piece of ancient sculpture. I was amazed that it has survived nearly 2500 years undamaged.

I visited another ancient Christian Church now used as a mosque. My guide had sought it out, at my request, as it is not on the usual tourist route. A small building, it had fallen into almost complete ruin since the 15th century. The bare walls and hard floors attested to a past glory. On the day of my visit, an Imam was giving lessons in the Koran to a small group of children, seated on mats at the head of the church where the altar would have been.

After the children left, the Imam invited me to have a look around the building, cold, sombre and dark, but still serving a religious purpose. As I left and thanked him, I gave him a small monetary donation. My guide looked askance at me and I wondered why. 'You gave him too much', he exclaimed as we left the church. 'Next time I take a visitor to this place, he will expect to get the same amount. I had been paying him much less.'

One of the important initiatives we undertook with the EU at this time was to commence exploratory talks on a possible NZ-EU free trade agreement. This was always going to be difficult because of the known opposition in some quarters, especially in France, to our exports of dairy products and sheepmeat. I conducted several meetings in Brussels and in New Zealand with EU delegations. These carefully and painstakingly laid the ground work for the bilateral FTA negotiations which are still under way. Our ambassador in Brussels, Peter Kennedy, and his successors in the role, worked very hard to promote the concept with the EU Commission.

I went to numerous EU capitals, Paris, Madrid, the Hague, Rome, Helsinki and Stockholm to pursue the initiative. As I write, some 12 years later, we still haven't achieved our objective, but the dialogue continues, complicated now perhaps by the UK's disastrous decision to leave the EU. We lose any positive impact we enjoyed on EU policy decision-making by having the UK, as a close ally, inside EU counsels.

I endeavoured to move our High Commission in London out of the expensive and half-empty New Zealand House in the Haymarket, to something smaller and more serviceable. I feared it did not have bomb blast-proof windows. At the time, this was a concern after a bomb went off in the neighbourhood of the High Commission building. The British, who owned the land on which the High Commission was built, were keen to get the land back but the Prime Minister, Helen Clark, saw it as an iconic building, so the proposal was stillborn.

I organised a meeting of all our Europe Heads of Mission, held in Rome, to review developments in our relationship with the EU and Russia and to plan our strategy for the next few years. Such regional meetings are important in making sure MFAT staff all operate 'on the same page' in their activities overseas. It helps to build and maintain camaraderie. Winston Peters, as Foreign Minister, came and gave political direction to the meeting.

Afterwards our ambassador to Italy, Julie MacKenzie, took Winston Peters and me to call on the head of the *Food and Agriculture Organization*, which has its headquarters in Rome. The FAO is an important international body for New Zealand even if at times we have not liked some of its policies. The long-standing Director-General of the FAO was then a Senegalese diplomat, Jacques Diouf. He had become more than a little comfortable in his role.

His whole office was lined with framed photographs of himself meeting world leaders: Mr Diouf with 'King This', Mr Diouf with 'President That', Mr Diouf with 'Prime Minister So and So'. It was an amazing collection. During our meeting, he asked no questions about New Zealand's agriculture and Winston Peters was not invited to have a photograph taken with him. Diouf died in August 2019. I wonder where all those photographs are now. The vanity of some international civil servants!

One visit to Brussels was especially memorable. Thanks to our ambassador, Peter Kennedy and his wife Demetra, I discovered that an old friend whom I hadn't seen for years, Heather Craig, was now living in Brussels. Heather, you may recall, had kept Louise and me from starving when we had visited New Caledonia as penniless students all those years ago. Heather was now married to an Australian, Doug Bartlett, who was working for the EU

Commission. Doug and Heather took me to an ANZAC Day commemoration in Flanders near Brussels, held in the mists of an early spring morning. We visited Ypres/Passchendaele, Messines, the Menin Gate, Tyne Cot and other World War One battle sites.

It was a very moving and humbling experience, to see the endless graves in the cemeteries, so well maintained by the Commonwealth War Graves Commission.

Winston Peters secured a large funding injection for the ministry, in tight negotiations with Labour's reluctant Finance Minister, Michael Cullen. (Cullen, born in the UK, later accepted the award of a knighthood for his services to New Zealand. British-style knighthoods were re-introduced by the John Key Government in 2010, despite the fact that Cullen had been part of the Labour Government, led by Helen Clark, which had abolished these titles.)

We were pleased that the importance of an active New Zealand foreign policy was being recognised by a new funding injection. We made extensive plans to ramp up our overseas effort to promote New Zealand overseas. Winston Peters instructed us to open three new embassies in short order, as part of an expansion he instigated in our foreign policy. We worked hard to achieve this and managed to have the new embassy in Stockholm up and running within six months. This was a record time frame. Mike Grace and his wife Pene, cross-posted from our embassy in Warsaw, did much of the hard preparation, along with Barbara Bridge, our first Ambassador to Sweden actually resident in Stockholm.

We were worried, however, rightly as it turned out, that the funding injection might be withdrawn by another government. This funding increase did indeed stall and was quickly wound back once the Labour Coalition Government lost office and John Key took over, appointing Murray McCully as Foreign Minister in 2008.

Restructuring the Ministry of Foreign Affairs and Trade

Murray McCully was a feisty personality. His reputation preceded him. In his first meeting with MFAT's senior management group on becoming Minister of Foreign Affairs and Trade, McCully introduced himself: 'My name is Murray', which of course everyone knew. We did not imagine he wanted us to address him in such a familiar manner. Paraphrasing Randolph Churchill's description of Gladstone, McCully said he was 'an old politician in a hurry'.

He had earned a reputation over many years as a difficult Minister to work for, a reputation I believe he himself thoroughly enjoyed and sought to promote. There is a weakness in New Zealand, or indeed Westminster-style, politics: a new Minister coming into office feels compelled to try to shine in their portfolio. It can never be admitted that any aspect of a previous Government's policies was sufficient or adequate — there is an irresistible urge to tinker, reform, change, revamp, undo, replace, even if the business case for such change is weak or unclear.

One of the first areas of tension was over McCully's wish to change the focus of our international development assistance (NZAID) from 'poverty alleviation', as pursued by the previous Labour Coalition government, to 'economic development'. This was in fact a sensible change, but it caused a lot of internal debate about the sorts of aid projects New Zealand should henceforth get involved in. I doubt the change made much actual difference to the recipient governments in the South Pacific. McCully continued the focus on assisting Pacific Islands development with an emphasis on infrastructure and energy projects and established good rapport with Pacific Island leaders, as had Winston Peters.

For some reason unclear to me, McCully insisted on closing the new Stockholm embassy and toyed with the idea of closing a few more of our embassies around the world. Having just opened it and now closing it in short order made us look indecisive to the Swedes — why couldn't New Zealand make up its mind on its foreign policy priorities? But the embassy was closed and we weakened our relationship with an important EU member state. The hard work of our Ambassador, Barbara Bridge, and her team, was undone and the public funds involved in opening it, wasted. The irony is that as soon as he came back to office again as Foreign Minister in 2017, Winston Peters re-established an embassy in Stockholm and opened one or two others.

I enjoyed the discussions I had with Russian counterparts. During a working visit which Murray McCully made to Moscow one winter, we had an interesting conversation over lunch with the Russian Foreign Minister, Sergei Lavrov, on the topic of Iran's nuclear capability. Twelve years later, Lavrov is still Russia's Foreign Minister. A visit to Moscow in midwinter is not to be recommended but it did give me an insight into the indomitable Russian character. I nearly missed my flight from Moscow because the Russian officials at the Domodedovo airport were infuriatingly slow and bureaucratic in checking the passports of departing passengers.

McCully initially did not seem overly interested in UN Human Rights activity, getting New Zealand to forgo its slot on the Human Rights Council to open a way for the US to return to it, a good move which President Trump later undid. McCully had a pro-Israeli stance at the outset (Dad approved), although the uncompromising positions of the Netanyahu Government and its blinkered Foreign Minister at the time, Avigdor Lieberman, tried the patience of any well-disposed partner. McCully did take strongly to task an MFAT staff member who failed to get proper sign-off from him for a vote which New Zealand cast on Israel in the UN. The individual concerned was put through a departmental wringer and censured.

McCully often declined to accept the Ministry's nominations for a Head of Mission position and would make his own appointments, either from within the Ministry or often from outside as political appointees — as was his right. He liked to keep people guessing whether he would approve their appointment. This could wreak havoc with the personal lives of staff and their families, including spouses who might have senior positions in Wellington which they would have to resign from, once the posting was approved. In contrast to Winston Peters, he became very much involved in the detail of such appointments and had very definite opinions on the suitability or otherwise of particular individuals nominated for appointment.

I am not sure why it is that some politicians who have a mandate from the people think they also have a mandate to be unnecessarily rude to their staff. I felt very sorry for his staff who had to suffer the persistent brusqueness and demands. No doubt it was occasioned by what he saw as a slow response to a particular instruction. His reaction was often to threaten that unless something was done immediately and to his satisfaction, he would get his own, non-Ministry, people to do the job.

I don't recall any instance where he actually carried out this threat. I never knew who exactly he had in mind. McCully, for the most part, placed himself on something of a war footing with the Ministry, which had an immediate negative impact on morale, as the Ministry sought to grapple with frequent difficulties in its relationship with its Minister.

This relationship was kept on an even keel while Simon Murdoch, a consummate professional diplomat, remained CEO. His retirement in mid-2009 was unfortunate. The government engineered the appointment of an outsider as CEO, someone who had had no training in running a large department of state and no background in diplomacy. The new CEO did have a penchant for public speaking and was given, so it was believed although it was never made clear, a mandate to change the Ministry's culture from that of a standard department of state to something more akin to a public listed company. He came, with the government's endorsement and that of former Prime Minister Jim Bolger, from running New Zealand Post.

It was a painful period for all concerned, not least I suspect for the new CEO himself, an experienced and engaging businessman, who had no background to enable him to become, suddenly, New Zealand's chief diplomat. A wholescale change process in the Ministry was implemented using expensive outside consultants, who for the most part had absolutely no idea what a diplomatic mission did. He oversaw a large shake-up which aimed to bring about a major change in the way the Ministry was run, appointments made, objectives set and divisions managed. The Ministry was not resistant to change. It had been through several successful restructures in the past, but the difference then was that the professional staff saw the value of the changes, actively owned them and were onside with implementation.

This time it was change from the top-down with very little staff input into key decisions, despite a supposed consultation process run by an army of consultants who were frustratingly vague on the long-term implications of their proposed changes. Wellington rotational positions were made permanent, requiring staff at the completion of an overseas posting to be made redundant unless they were successful in securing a Wellington position. These became available less often, because security of tenure in Wellington was henceforth very important to the incumbent.

It undermined the rationale for accepting the hard yards and family disruption of an overseas assignment if there was no guarantee of a job in head office once you had completed your tough assignment overseas. A name change from SMG to SLT (Senior Leadership Team) was not a huge change, but the implication was that, henceforth, only the SLT provided leadership to the organisation, whereas the Ministry's culture required all its staff to be leaders in one way or another, especially the numerous Ambassadors and High Commissioners running important posts overseas. It was disempowering.

This change process was a costly disaster from the start and underscored the risks of expecting outside experts to be able to revamp a department of state which they are unfamiliar with. Staff felt deflated, unsure of their positions and undervalued. Some resigned, depleting the Ministry's capabilities, especially in the crucial middle ranks from which are drawn future Heads of Mission.

Senior staff overseas felt out of touch with Wellington. Tried and true mechanisms to keep staff in touch with each other, like the weekly Directors' meetings, were disbanded as a waste of time. Staff rapidly felt cut off from the wider Ministry and decision-making processes. Having a hands-on Minister at the same time as the Ministry had a CEO unused to grappling with the interface between a department of state and its Minister meant the lines of responsibility were tested, as the Minister exercised his strong personality.

After four years in Wellington, I was looking forward to a final posting and wanted to go to Asia, which I had never served in before. I was very grateful to Murray McCully that he agreed to appoint me as High Commissioner to Singapore.

After I left for Singapore, my old position was disestablished and my particular clutch of responsibilities reallocated. The CEO decided to appoint only two deputy secretaries to handle all our global geographical effort offshore, instead of the previous four. This in my view was a retrograde step and impacted negatively on our profile in key markets, especially as the CEO himself was not in a position to represent New Zealand overseas diplomatically at key meetings.

The resulting problems in the Ministry have been widely canvassed, and at one point led senior staff and the heads of our offices offshore to register formally their concerns at the material damage being done to New Zealand's diplomatic effort. I opposed some of the structural changes as I could not in good conscience support them.

While I was High Commissioner in Singapore, a report I wrote detailing some of the negative effects the planned reforms would have on our bilateral relationship with Singapore was leaked to the former Foreign Minister, Phil Goff. He then asked questions about the Ministry's change process in Parliament, in an effort to embarrass the government.

In due course, a formal investigation was launched to identify the source of this and several other related leaks. The State Services Commission, which had failed to exert any real control over the 'root and branch' change process in the Ministry in the first place, now appointed someone with no knowledge of the Ministry and New Zealand's diplomatic effort to embark on the proverbial witch hunt. This wasted much time and effort and smeared the reputation of senior public servants in the process, to no ultimate purpose. A subsequent appeal to the Ombudsman found that the investigator, Paula Rebstock, had overstepped the mark in several of the key findings in her report, leading to the payment of large damages to several senior MFAT staff members.

This is all water under the bridge now. The Ministry has moved on, with the return of a professional diplomat as CEO. Morale and therefore the ability to pursue New Zealand's foreign policy interests has greatly improved.

CHAPTER 25

HIGH COMMISSIONER TO SINGAPORE AND THE MALDIVES (2010–2012)

AT THE AGE OF 59, I WANTED TO UNDERTAKE ONE LAST POSTING before retirement and had thought of Cairo, except that my lack of Arabic would have been a disadvantage. I had not had a posting to Asia despite the time I had spent in Asian capitals on trade access related issues. I knew Singapore quite well from previous visits and of course I had negotiated *the New Zealand-Singapore Free Trade Agreement*, ANZSCEP, nine years earlier.

I presented my credentials to Singapore's President, SR Nathan. Because of their shared Indian ancestry, he was a good friend of our Governor-General at the time, Anand Satyanand. The credentials presentation took place at the Istana, the former residence of the British Governor before independence and now the official residence of the President. The Istana includes the working offices of the Prime Minister, Lee Hsien Loong, the son of Lee Kuan Yew. I was able to wear one of the Ministry's wonderful 'korowai' or Maori cloaks, airfreighted to Singapore for the occasion.

Friends had told me that Singapore, a well-run but tightly managed democracy, was hardly Asia. In a sense that is correct but a misnomer. Singapore, thanks to Lee Kuan Yew, has demonstrated that a small country can become an economic powerhouse if it has good governance and uncorrupt, technocratic leadership. Of course, having a great geographical location helps too.

This was my final posting and involved a busy social life, with receptions and functions to attend almost every day. I assisted New Zealand businesses through the New Zealand-Singapore Chamber of Commerce, and worked with our South East Asian Regional Trade Commissioner, Alan Koziarski and his team, especially the Trade Commissioner for Singapore, Ziena Jalil, to develop trade links with Singapore. New Zealand universities, such as Massey, were keen to promote themselves to prospective Singaporean students or to develop joint courses in Singapore, for example in food technology and research.

Presenting credentials to the President of Singapore, His Excellency SR Nathan (Photo: Ministry of Communications and Information of Singapore)

Since Singapore is en route to Europe for New Zealanders, we had an endless stream of visitors, political figures, academics and business people. We would assist them where possible and make connections for them with Singaporean counterparts. In my office, I was fortunate to have Jacqui Caine as my Deputy. Guy Lewis looked after educational matters and consular activities. Guy on numerous occasions had to help out New Zealand travellers who found themselves stranded at Singapore airport after Singapore immigration authorities prevented their onward travel because their passport had less than the required six months' validity.

New Zealand is an active participant in *the Five Power Defence Arrangements* (FPDA) with Australia, UK, Singapore and Malaysia. These provide security-related cooperation with Singapore and Malaysia and involved quarterly meetings of high commissioners, in either Singapore or Malaysia, and annual meetings at ministerial level. The Minister of Defence, Wayne Mapp, attended.

Our High Commission team included a Defence Attaché, Gp. Capt. Tim Walshe, seconded from the Ministry of Defence in Wellington, to oversee the extensive defence cooperation with both countries. The Singaporeans valued the defence link with New Zealand and regularly exercised their armed forces in New Zealand. This offered them both space and terrain for training that they could not access at home. (Tim's predecessor as Defence Attaché, with whom I overlapped for a couple of months, was Steve Goodman, who later became Chief Executive of Volunteer Service Abroad. It was VSA which had sent me to Tonga so many moons ago as a school-leaver teacher.)

Jonah Lomu visited as a Rugby Ambassador, as did former All Black captain Sean Fitzpatrick, cricketer Richard Hadlee and actor Sam Neill. Jonah was treated as a hero by young Singaporean boys who, despite rugby not being a national sport, were very keen to learn ball-handling skills from Jonah. He willingly and engagingly obliged.

The Singapore Prime Minister and his Cabinet colleagues, especially the Ministers of Defence, Trade, Transport and the Environment/Natural Resources, always received me, or a visiting New Zealand Cabinet Minister, very cordially, if much more formally than is the New Zealand practice. We had regular contact with the Singaporean Ministry of Foreign Affairs, especially Siew Lin and her team and the Minister of Foreign Affairs, George Yeo.

Professor Tommy Koh was one of Singapore's prominent international lawyers and Ambassador at Large for the Singapore Government. He was a great admirer, he confessed, of our former Prime Minister, Helen Clark. Singapore's diplomats are an impressive group and excellent representatives. They know, as do New Zealand diplomats, that they represent a small country and need to be active when it comes to promoting and safeguarding Singapore's economic and security interests in their immediate region.

The only difficult issue I had to raise was New Zealand's concern at Singapore's retention of the death penalty, which it reserves for serious drug offences. I was told that the death penalty enjoyed wide public support although in the absence of extensive polling, I was unsure how the government knew this.

I called on the Speaker of the Singapore Parliament several times. He has a far less onerous job than his British or New Zealand counterpart. The Singapore Parliament has far fewer sitting days than in New Zealand. The corridors of the Parliament are all but empty, unlike the frenetic activity seen in Parliament in Wellington. The governing PAP, People's Action Party, has an overwhelming majority. There is never any doubt that the government can enact whatever legislation it chooses. Singapore is an impressive model, however, in the way it handles the racial mix of its society, with the majority Chinese but significant minority populations of Malays, Indians and Europeans. Other countries could learn much from it.

If Singapore's MPs do not have to spend much time in Parliament, they do interact constantly with their constituents, in regular 'Meet the People' workshops. In these, constituents can bring problems, of even the smallest sort, to the attention of the MP, who has on hand a bevy of volunteers to take appropriate action on the request and ensure follow-up by the relevant government ministry.

The diplomatic corps in Singapore was among the most active I had encountered, especially given the proximity of other Asian countries in the ASEAN relationship and the need to deal with sensitive regional issues such as China's encroachment in the South China Sea.

I got to know well many of the Asian ambassadors. Many were influential in their own governments. The Singaporeans retained the old practice of requiring the diplomatic corps to attend at the Istana to be formally presented whenever a foreign head of government or Head of State was paying an official visit to Singapore. In this way, I met a dozen or more world leaders, including Dr Merkel, the German Chancellor, who was surprised to see me there, and the youthful Thai Prime Minister, Yingluck Shinawatra, who in 2014 was turned out of office after a Constitutional Court decision.

The Christchurch earthquakes affected every New Zealander in Singapore and there was a strong desire among the New Zealand community to assist the people of Christchurch. One event I hosted was a well-attended barbecue at my home, which raised $5000 for Christchurch. The Mayor of Christchurch, Bob Parker, and his wife came to promote Christchurch and its rebuilding efforts to Singaporean investors. They stayed with me at the New Zealand Residence while they were in Singapore.

Singapore is a prime source of investment. I was amazed to find out just how much of New Zealand's hotel stock is owned by wealthy Singaporeans. Just about every major chain in New Zealand has a Singapore connection. John Key, the Prime Minister at the time, had earlier spent time in Singapore, making his money at Merrill Lynch in the foreign exchange market. Key visited Singapore several times and got on well with his Singaporean counterpart. He was well received at a business leaders' lunch we organised for him. He did however display a tendency not to brief himself well in advance of some of his more important meetings, and as many busy politicians do, preferred to wing it in some of his encounters.

At John Key's request we brought together *all* the top Singaporean investors including Ho Ching, the wife of the Prime Minister, who was Chief Executive Officer of Temasek Holdings, the main Singaporean Government overseas investment facility. Despite recommendations to do so, Key had not come with any specific initiatives or proposals for investment possibilities, which left the Singaporeans wondering why he had asked for the meeting. Singaporeans rarely engage in small talk and are very focused and transactional.

The US Ambassador to Singapore, David Edelman, a former member of the Georgia State Senate and a political appointee of Barack Obama, became a good friend. As Singapore was the staging post for many US military deployments in the Indian Ocean and South China Sea, we were invited on several occasions to tour visiting aircraft carriers, like the USS *Abraham Lincoln* and *Benjamin Franklin*. This made quite an impression on the rest of the family, who were invited along. An unforgettable experience was being flown way out to the South China Sea and landing on the USS *John C. Stennis*, the only time I have landed and taken off on an aircraft carrier. We were invited to view a military exercise of war planes taking off and landing — there was something both attracting and, at the same time, repelling at such a display of loud military might.

As Secretary of State, Hillary Clinton came to Singapore while I was there. In a speech I attended, she signalled a major change to US foreign policy, with a pivot from the Atlantic to one more focused on the US relationship with Asia. I thought she was an impressive woman and hoped she might become President. Only in the United States, which champions itself ad nauseam as the bastion of democracy, would it be possible for the majority of citizens to vote for her as President but to end up with someone else. No amount of explanation about States' Rights will convince me that the Electoral College, in this day and age, is not a great defect of the US political system.

While I was in Singapore, Barbara Bridge, my friend who was Ambassador to Sweden, invited me to her wedding to an Austrian, Wolfgang Mitterecker, held in Dürnstein village on the Danube River. It was a magnificent location. Dürnstein Castle is an imposing medieval ruin. It was once the prison of Richard the Lionheart, when he was captured and held for ransom by the Duke of Austria, with whom he had fallen out, when he was returning from the Third Crusade in 1192.

The Maldives

While I was in Singapore, I was accredited as New Zealand's High Commissioner to the Republic of the Maldives in the Indian Ocean. I presented my credentials to the young, reformist President Mohamed Nasheed, in Malé, the capital. Nasheed, the first democratically elected President of the Maldives, served as fourth President from 2008 to 2012. He was engaging and an activist. He had famously held a Cabinet meeting underwater to demonstrate the negative impacts that climate change would have on a country like the Maldives which consists entirely of low-lying coral atolls.

With President Nasheed of the Maldives

Nasheed was concerned at some of the fundamentalist tendencies emerging in the population, reflecting the impact of religious teachings in the madrassas of Pakistan. Being a reformer in a strongly conservative Muslim country was no easy task for him. I was sorry to learn that he was ousted from office in 2012 and arrested on trumped-up charges of abuse of office. He was sentenced to 13 years in prison, a conviction which drew strong international

condemnation, including from Amnesty International. The sentence
was finally overturned in 2018 by the Supreme Court of the
Maldives, which ruled that the charges against him were wrong and
should not have proceeded.

As I write, Nasheed has returned to Maldivian politics and is
Speaker of the People's Majlis (Parliament). He was however
recently injured in a bomb blast outside his home, an apparent
assassination attempt. It is difficult to be a reformer in some
countries. Nasheed's experience would require a whole book in itself.
I greatly admired him.

Our Honorary Consul in the Maldives at the time, businessman
Ahmed Saleem, was passionately pro-New Zealand. He had
undertaken his training as an architect in Dunedin and felt a lasting
debt of gratitude to New Zealand. He assisted New Zealand's
interests in the Maldives in many ways over the years. After I left, he
became involved, as a company director, in an employment dispute
with employees of the Conrad Hilton resort on Rangali Island, one of
the top Maldivian resorts. I do not know the details of the dispute,
which ended up in the High Court of the Maldives, but there is no
diminishing the record of service Ahmed gave to New Zealand.

PART III

REPUBLICANISM, RATIONALISM AND (MAYBE) OPTIMISM

CHAPTER 26

THE REPUBLIC OF NEW ZEALAND?

OVER THE COURSE OF MY CAREER, I HAD OFTEN REFLECTED ON our constitutional structure and wondered why New Zealand, as an independent country, did not have its own Head of State. It might seem odd that an impressionable nine-year-old boy from Somerset, who can name every king and queen of England since Edward the Confessor, should want to break the tie with the old colonial motherland. Simply put, I came to believe that a republic would be the final necessary and significant move, constitutionally, in our becoming a fully-fledged and sovereign nation.

The first member of the British royal family I met was the Queen's second son, Andrew, who visited Samoa while I was high commissioner. I was invited by the Samoan Government to a reception, followed by an official dinner in his honour. I am not sure why he was visiting Samoa, perhaps in his role as a UK Trade Ambassador. It was immediately clear that he was a shy individual and very uncomfortable 'circulating', as one has to do to meet the guests at an official reception. He stayed planted in one corner of the room and hardly moved. His minder, a pushy young woman, grew exasperated that people would not simply bowl up to him and engage him in conversation. She started shoving people, with a hard push from behind, towards HRH. I was not exempt from a rude shove.

The official dinner was held Samoan style — invitations had gone out far and wide, but as the Samoan practice is not to RSVP, one never knows who is actually going to turn up. There were numerous empty places at the dinner tables. I had no sense that Andrew felt he had any connection to New Zealand as the son of our Head of State.

While I was ambassador in Berlin, the Queen paid a State visit to Germany. The British ambassador kindly invited my Australian colleague and me to a gala black-tie dinner in her honour. As we joined the reception line to be presented to her and Prince Philip, I was not surprised that, for the Queen, this was just another of those rather boring reception lines which she is obliged to encounter. Prince Philip did joke with my Australian colleague and me, but the Queen looked tired and disengaged.

When the British national anthem was played, I wondered how many times the poor woman had been obliged to listen to this ponderous hymn — no one in history, I suspect, has been forced to listen to it more often than her. Of course, when it first began to be routinely sung in the 1740s, it might have sounded novel, and resonated as an expression of public loyalty to the foreign Hanoverian monarch at the time of the Jacobite rebellion of Bonnie Prince Charlie. Its words today in a secular world sound oddly misplaced. (New Zealand's own national anthem, which invokes the deity, also needs to be modernised.)

The next day the Queen went to a small village outside Berlin in East Germany to thank the villagers for taking good care of a Commonwealth War Graves cemetery in the village. The communist authorities of the German Democratic Republic had pointedly neglected and ignored it. She laid a wreath at the cenotaph in commemoration. I was invited, with my Australian and Indian colleagues, to do the same.

What amazed me was the staid manner in which the British Embassy, or the royal household, tried to script tightly the whole choreography. We were given in advance several pages of instructions, the 'do and don'ts' when meeting the Queen. We were told such things as not to talk to her unless she spoke to us first, to address her, if she did, as Ma'am as in 'arm' and not Ma'am as in 'jam'. And not to shake her hand unless she proffered hers. This last point I could readily understand, given the millions of hands she is expected to shake, but the rest of it was surreal. Here was our Head of State and yet she could in her international role only ever advocate for the UK, never New Zealand.

While I was in Singapore, I met William and Kate, an engaging and likeable couple and, unlike Uncle Andrew, socially very much at ease. Then I met Charles and Camilla, again in Singapore, when they were returning to the UK after a visit to New Zealand. What struck me was the rigid separation the royal household maintained between the couple and the rest of the official party. I did have a very good informal conversation with Charles, focused mainly on developments in the South Pacific, the impact of environmental pollution there and climate change. I liked him and admire his advocacy for environmental and heritage issues. Camilla, poor woman, suffered in the Singapore ambient temperature as she could not bear air-conditioning and the outside temperature was a humid 32 degrees Celsius.

Queen Elizabeth has an unparalleled record of public service. She will remain our Head of State until she dies but New Zealanders need to give careful thought to what happens when she has passed away. In my view, Charles and Camilla and the Windsor family generally do not fit the requirements.

New Zealanders are justly proud of their country although thankfully, unlike Americans, we do not wear our patriotism on our sleeves. We know, despite the many challenges we face, that this is one of the best countries to live in and I, for one, am very lucky that my father brought his family here.

We have in fact been embarked on a process of nation building since the Treaty of Waitangi was signed in 1840 with the Maori chiefs, the tangata whenua, the first people of the land. I had ensured this Treaty was enshrined in the free trade agreements we negotiated. It has been an uneven process, but like all other colonies in history, New Zealand has gradually sought to assert its independence from the motherland.

In my career I often had to try to explain to important overseas partners why we borrow the British monarch for the job and do not take on the role ourselves. It is of course a legacy issue, but they often found it hard to comprehend, as they for the most part had long ago ditched their colonial past. The accidents of history, while an explanation of why the British monarch is still our Head of State, will not suffice into the future.

We have had no say in choosing the British monarch as our Head of State. The Queen in turn has had no say in being required to fulfil this role in respect of New Zealand. Any initiative to change this will not come from her or her successors. It must come from New Zealanders.

Is New Zealand mature enough as a nation to have its own Head of State? Polling suggests that a majority of New Zealanders, when asked, think so.

The Governor-General is currently the monarch's representative in New Zealand but by definition, she or he is only ever 'vice-regal'. The term 'vice-regal' has fallen out of fashion but it means the Governor-General is the representative of the Queen, and can only ever be the deputy to the Head of State. The British monarch is Head of State of about 14 other countries, like Tuvalu. New Zealand makes no contribution to the huge expense involved in maintaining the extended British royal family in comfortable luxury. This falls to the British taxpayer. We are freeloaders.

Here is an example of how not having our own Head of State works to our disadvantage. Successive Dutch monarchs have paid high-level State visits to New Zealand and have been received warmly by New Zealanders, and not just by those of Dutch descent. But the Netherlands will never reciprocate these courtesies. Since our actual Head of State resides just across the Channel from The Hague, the Dutch will not accord equivalent courtesies to our Governor-General if they ever visited the Netherlands officially. The same approach is likely to apply in other countries which have a monarch as their Head of State. Queen Elizabeth or her successor are never going to visit these countries in their capacity as our Head of State, to promote New Zealand's interests. This creates an imbalance in our relationship with them.

As a diplomat representing New Zealand overseas, I was of course obliged to keep my views on this to myself but that constraint no longer applies. I joined the campaign for a New Zealand Head of State when I retired from MFAT. I believe that the Office of Governor-General should be transformed into that of our 'Head of State', using the Samoan example.

This would not require as big a change as some many imagine, or fear. Although constitutional questions do not loom large in the lives of New Zealanders — they never have — we will soon be required to face the question, 'After Elizabeth — what next?' I often wonder whether the British royal family itself is not surprised that Australia and New Zealand have not become republics long ago.

I don't think New Zealanders, on reflection, would want to have yet another election for the office of Head of State. It is a ceremonial position and not an executive one. The Head of State should in my view be chosen by consensus, or majority, among our elected representatives and serve for four years, with the possibility of renewal.

In 2013, I first publicly advocated for a New Zealander to be Head of State, which the *New Zealand Herald* reported under the misleading headline 'Queen holds New Zealand back'. It unleashed the expected debate among supporters and opponents.

Two criticisms of me I particularly liked. One said 'Who is this Peter Hamilton? I've never heard of him'. This critic little realised that they were paying me a compliment. Every serving MFAT officer strives not to develop a public profile in New Zealand as this detracts from the prominence rightly accorded to the Minister. Those former MFAT officials who have developed a public profile, Hugh

Templeton, Hekia Parata, David Cunliffe, Tim Groser, Grant Robertson, John Hayes and others have all had political ambitions. I was spared this.

Another criticism was that I must be annoyed with the Queen because I had failed to secure a knighthood for my public service. MFAT staff do not aspire to this. John Key had reintroduced the British honours system when he became Prime Minister and permitted himself to be given a knighthood. But former Prime Ministers Jim Bolger and Helen Clark, both supporters of New Zealand becoming a republic, had eschewed this. Canada and Australia have permanently abolished British-style knighthoods.

Committed monarchists can be heard saying: 'Who cares what people overseas think? If we want to retain the British monarchy, that's our choice!' It is a myopic view, but understandable for those who are captivated or entranced by the pageantry of monarchy.

The argument that the Treaty of Waitangi with Maori was signed by the British Crown and that Maori would not want Aotearoa to become a republic is spurious. The British Crown permitted decades of serious breaches of the Treaty and brutal land confiscations. It was a localised New Zealand Government, and not the British monarchy, which began the long process of rectifying these breaches through the Waitangi Tribunal.

Some argue that we need the British monarch to ensure political stability in New Zealand and that without it we would become a banana republic. Whether or not we become a banana republic is entirely in the hands of New Zealanders themselves, and the British monarch could not prevent this. Queen Elizabeth's powerlessness in the face of the recent Brexit turmoil has shown how little influence the British monarch can really exert over serious constitutional issues.

Another criticism was that, if we became a republic, we could have a controversial figure, such as a former Prime Minister, as our Head of State. Prime Minister Robert Muldoon did appoint his political ally and predecessor, Keith Holyoake, as Governor-General in 1977.

Who becomes our Head of State would be a matter for our elected representatives to determine. I have every confidence in their ability to choose someone suitable. Neither would we leave the Commonwealth — in fact, as I have argued, we should be more engaged than we are in Commonwealth activities.

I have worked closely with, or met, five or six Governors-General. In my view each of them would have been capable of carrying out the role of Head of State with distinction. I think it is inappropriate and discourteous to ask such prominent New Zealanders to undertake the role of Governor-General but to consign them to the B team of constitutional importance. New Zealanders need not fear that we do not have sufficiently good candidates for the Head of State role.

We have come a long way since 1840 in building this country. We still have to take some final steps to create a fully independent and sovereign nation.

CHAPTER 27

SOME FINAL THOUGHTS

DIPLOMATIC LIFE CAN PUT GREAT PRESSURE ON A FAMILY. WHEN I first joined the Ministry of Foreign Affairs in 1977, a diplomatic spouse was expected to subordinate their career or professional aspirations to that of the diplomatic officer who, in the early days of the Ministry, was predominately male. Wives of senior officers, like Mrs Lloyd White, would give training to young diplomatic female spouses on how to set a dinner table or host a cocktail function. Fortunately, that has now changed and whether or not a spouse is willing to assist the diplomatic officer in undertaking representational activities, such as hosting dinners or other functions, is entirely at the discretion of the spouse or partner.

Louise was a great help to me during the posting in Suva, Ottawa and Geneva. She did this on top of raising at first one then two children. The work of spouses at our overseas posts is unpaid and often unrecognised, certainly often under-appreciated. When I was Deputy Secretary responsible for human resources and overseas postings, I did look at ways of recompensing partners who undertook such work in support of an Embassy or High Commission. It proved impossible to find an equitable way to measure their contribution and to remunerate it appropriately and fairly. Many Ministry partners continue to put on hold their own professional careers in New Zealand to assist the work of promoting New Zealand's interests overseas. This needs to be better recognised.

My Goddaughter Kirsty

Our family friends, Helen and Len Cannon, had asked me to be godfather to their second daughter, Kirsty Lynne, born in 1970. Although I am not religious, I regarded this as a great privilege and kept in close touch with her as she grew into a young adult. One of my special memories of Kirsty, aged about 10, was sitting alone with her on the doorsteps of the farm cottage at Moanatuatua. Looking directly at me, she said, matter-of-factly: 'You know, if you weren't my godfather, I would not be spending so much time with you'. The honesty of children!

Kirsty was a popular young woman and was Head Girl at Fraser High School in Hamilton. Many years later, Kirsty, aged 22, was working in Auckland while we were posted to Geneva. One Saturday autumn morning (22 October 1992) after a busy week at the GATT, I woke early, at about 5.30am, while it was still dark. This was unusual for me as I am normally a late riser. Feeling quite unsettled and disconcerted, I decided to go for an early walk alone in the autumn mists of the apple orchards, which adjoined our house in Mies. Something I had never done before.

It was a huge shock to receive a telephone call from Kirsty's mother, Helen, a few hours later, to say that Kirsty had been injured in a car accident at Te Kauwhata, while her boyfriend James Chin was driving her from Auckland to Hamilton. Kirsty was flown to Waikato Hospital but died shortly after of her injuries. Although I am not a spiritualist, I have ever after wondered why I had felt the need to take that walk in the orchard so early in the morning, at the precise moment when Kirsty had her accident and passed away. Being so far away, I could not attend her funeral. She is buried in the Hamilton Park Cemetery. This is the kind of tragedy no family can ever recover from. It hit Kirsty's two siblings, her older sister Megan and younger sister Tracey, very hard. At Fraser High School, a puriri tree has been planted in her memory.

Sadly, Kirsty's mother, my 'babysitter' Helen, died suddenly at her home in Napier in February 2020. She had in later life specialised in reading recovery programmes and had helped hundreds of young children to improve their reading skills, teaching in New Zealand, Kenya, England and Wollongong in Australia. We once spent some time tracing the outlines of the old Berlin Wall when she visited me in Germany. She spent Christmas 2019 and New Year 2020 with our family on Waiheke Island. None of us could have imagined that would be the last time we would see her. She was an immensely popular, outgoing individual, with hundreds of friends.

I was also godfather to Peter Marchant, the son of one of my closest friends at university, Jeff Marchant and his wife Olivia. I always admired Jeff who went on to become a prominent engineer and construction designer. It is reassuring to know that many of the bridges I drive across around New Zealand have been designed by Jeff. Being out of New Zealand for many years meant it was difficult to keep in touch with Peter, a lovely young man who, like Kirsty, sadly passed away at far too early an age.

* * *

During my posting to Berlin, Chris and Rachel would come to visit. As I have mentioned, Rachel came, liked the place and stayed for 15 years. I took Christopher, aged 21, when I made an official visit to Warsaw during a freezing winter. He insisted on walking everywhere underdressed in a short-sleeved shirt and drew looks of surprise and suspicion from passing Poles.

While Rachel stayed on in Germany and Christopher began his university studies in tourism management at Victoria University of Wellington, my second daughter, Fiona, was born on 14 May 1999 in Honiara. She spent a year with me while I was posted to Singapore, attending the International Overseas Family School. Up to this point she had lived with her mother in Toowoomba, Queensland, in Anguilla in the Caribbean, and in Majuro in the Marshall Islands, so it was a special opportunity for me to get to know her. Fiona loved her time in Singapore, and likes to go back there as often as she can. After she left Singapore, Fiona went to Geelong College, in Victoria, for her high school years.

In Which I Meet an Australian 'Environmentalist'!

I loved my frequent visits (pre-Covid!) to Geelong, south of Melbourne, to see Fiona and her Australian family. Long walks along the meandering Barwon River are a favourite form of exercise for me. On one occasion, Fiona's younger sister, Isabella, an intelligent, inquisitive and imaginative eight-year-old, decided to join me. Along the river, we passed numerous glades, and small ponds teeming with bird life, including pelicans, ducks and parrots. There was a strong scent from the foxes which inhabit the banks of the river, a scent I recalled from my Stogursey childhood.

On this particular walk, Isabella suddenly ran on ahead and I lost sight of her. Turning a corner, I was surprised to encounter her standing alone, motionless and rigid in front of a large tree. I asked her what she was doing there. Adopting a new persona, she replied very formally that she was called Rose Tree-Guardian, and her job was to take care of all the trees and animals along the Barwon River. Playing along, I had a great conversation with Rose, who told me about her life as a river guardian. She had a clear understanding of the importance of protecting the natural environment and its inhabitants. Rose introduced me to some of her friends on the nearby pond, including Dr Phil Duck who swam about taking care of all the ducks, and Mag and Pie, a magpie couple who helped him out.

It was an impressive piece of theatrical role-play by an eight-year-old. When we reached home, she told her mother that on our walk we had encountered a lady called Rose, who was responsible for guarding all the trees along the river bank. 'Oh', said her mother, 'so you met an environmentalist!'

Ever after, Isabella, who is now an amazing young teenager, always laughingly updates me on Rose's latest activities, and what Dr Phil (who we realised was just a quack) and Mag and Pie have been up to all along the Barwon River.

Fiona, and her younger sister Isabella, with her grandfather and grandmother, shortly before Dad passed away

* * *

Diplomatic life offers pluses and minuses for a diplomatic family — great opportunities to travel and experience different cultures, but at the same time, missing family and friends and being absent on significant family occasions. Children miss out on growing up as Kiwi kids in New Zealand.

After my parents retired from the peat farm at Moanatuatua, they lived on Waiheke Island and converted their little summer bach into a three-bedroom home. My mother became a licensed Anglican Minister as part of the Waiheke Island church's shared ministry programme. This enabled her to take church services, christenings, marriages and funerals, but only on the island.

It was a very special occasion therefore when Christopher's grandmother was the officiating Minister at his wedding to Lindsay McPherson, held on Waiheke in February 2014. My first grandson, Alexander William Hamilton, was born on 14 July 2017. A second grandson, Coen Brae, was born on 8 October 2020, a few minutes before his twin sister, Isla Marie, in Hutt Hospital. Granny Dyer would have been immensely proud of her New Zealand great-great-grandchildren.

Chris's grandmother Joan officiates at his wedding to Lindsay McPherson on Waiheke Island, February 2014

Dad died on my 64th birthday. His funeral was held at the little Anglican Church of St Andrews by the Sea in Onetangi, on Waiheke on 4 July 2015. In my eulogy, I said that Dad had made two best decisions in his life: one was to marry my mother and the second to come to New Zealand. Fiona, aged 16, spoke words of endearment about her grandfather that moved everyone to tears, as did his grandson, Christopher. Rachel in Berlin was not able to be present for her grandfather's funeral, but was present in spirit.

Dad never did get to own his own farm, partly because he did not have the capital to break into the risky business of farm ownership, but also, I suspect, because he was unwilling to take on the substantial debt burden that this would have involved.

Was Dad happy in New Zealand? I think he was always disappointed that he never owned a farm of his own as that was his dream, but he took pride in his family. My parents visited me on each of my six postings overseas. Dad used to go back to the UK every few years to help his brother Peter on his farm in Cornwall or just to enjoy living there. Dad never lost his love for England and farming in England. This is not surprising as he was already 35 when he emigrated to New Zealand. As they got older my parents realised there was never any real possibility of them returning to the UK permanently.

It was my mother who became the more Kiwi of the two. My father had given her the ultimatum to come to New Zealand but he was always a reluctant Kiwi. Perhaps because she spent her professional life working with school children, starting with the opening given to her by that ANZ bank manager in Otorohanga, it was easier for her to adjust. She was always positive in her outlook, kind, generous and socially at ease. Although she had not wanted to

Dad, in a jovial moment. His great sense of humour carried him through the challenges he faced.

leave England, over time she grew to love New Zealand. After her parents had died, she could not bear the thought of going back to England permanently. That village girl who had refused to curtsey to Lady St Audries, 85 years ago, was a distant memory. For her England was no longer 'home'.

Since Dad passed away, Mum has lived happily in her apartment at a Retirement Home in Auckland. My brother Stuart, with his partner Karen Luxton, has established an amazing avocado orchard and honey business at Maungatapere near Whangarei, producing the best avocados and honey I have tasted. They are still both hard at work — Stuart, aged only six when we came to New Zealand, quickly imbibed the strong Kiwi 'can do' attitude. Unlike me, he can turn his hand to anything!

To conclude this chapter, I would like to quote someone else's observations on diplomatic life:

> 'There is a general theory that a diplomatic career is the most pleasant of all, especially when the rank of ambassador is reached. My acquaintance with the career is confined to its ambassadorial stage, and I pronounce it detestable. A man may work all night to report his achievements of the day, may succeed in a difficult and complicated negotiation, often hampered by clumsy instructions: the credit of the success is secured by the minister, whose ambiguous despatches have allowed his ambassador to guess his intentions, expressed with sufficient obscurity to enable him to disavow the negotiations if they should fail. On the other hand, if failure is the result, the minister shrugs his shoulders and the ambassador is pronounced to be wanting in tact, and as secrecy is the first law of the trade, self-justification is impossible.'

If these views sound modern, they are in fact those of the Comtesse de Boigne, writing about 1835. Her father was French ambassador to the Court of St James when the Bourbon monarchy was restored in France after the battle of Waterloo and the fall of Napoleon.

A little later in 1848, Lord Macaulay in his magnificent *History of England* colourfully described Lord Arlington, who was Charles II's Secretary of State, as suffering from a '*cosmopolitan indifference to constitutions and religions, which is often observable in persons whose life has been passed in vagrant diplomacy*'.

Few New Zealand diplomats would, I think, agree either with the Comtesse that diplomatic life is 'detestable' or with Lord Macaulay that diplomacy engenders vagrancy!

As I have said, diplomatic life can be hard, challenging, stressful, and the frequent changes of location disruptive of family life. But there is great professional satisfaction in undertaking, during the course of a career, so many new and challenging roles and responsibilities and being obliged to quickly get on top of a new confronting issue. There is the satisfaction that comes too from doing something useful for New Zealand, or to New Zealand's advantage. You will never become rich working as a New Zealand diplomat. You are, after all, working to promote your country, unlike private sector entrepreneurs who, for the most part, are focused on personal advantage.

Lasting friendships are forged through the shared experience of working together in Wellington and collaborating, often years at a time, at one of our overseas Embassies or High Commissions.

In 1977, 11 other diplomatic trainees joined MFA with me. One resigned quite quickly (the diplomatic life was not for him), and another, Atareta Poananga, early got offside with Ministry bosses over a policy matter relating to Maori, and pursued her career elsewhere, becoming a lawyer advocating for Maori rights (sadly, Atareta died in 2020 in Gisborne). A third colleague, Alastair Stewart, completed a posting to Ottawa and left to pursue a legal career in Canada.

The remaining eight, like me, all had careers in the New Zealand public service: Barbara Bridge, who now lives in Vienna, was Ambassador to Sweden; Mark Sinclair was Ambassador to Japan and Mexico; Yvonne Lucas held senior positions in the Department of Trade and Industry and was a great help to MFAT in our various free trade negotiations; Christine Bogle was most recently Ambassador to Mexico; Lynne Dovey held senior positions including in the Ministry of Social Development; Helen Fawthorpe became a senior adviser on human rights issues; James Kember was most recently Ambassador to France; Maarten Wevers had a stellar career as Ambassador to Japan, and then head of the Prime Minister's Department — he was conferred a knighthood for his public service when John Key was Prime Minister.

What different paths our professional lives have taken since that first year in 1977. We have remained colleagues. There are many other New Zealand public servants I worked alongside whose contributions should also be commended. They know who they are. I have a lasting admiration for their professionalism and dedication in the pursuit of New Zealand's interests.

Respect, as they say, to all of you!

CHAPTER 28

DISCOVERING RATIONALISM

It has taken a long time to work out my basic metaphysical beliefs. I studied and explored as much as I could about philosophy, religion, metaphysics, ethics, morality and history. I have had to reach the conclusions on my own but I was fortunate to have grown up in a culture where this was possible. Mr Luffett's Sunday school classes at Kio Kio School were of little assistance.

My quiet contemplation in the ruins of Glastonbury Abbey, in the Hagia Sophia in Istanbul, or the unforgettable experience of being alone at dusk at the base of the pyramids in Giza, have all had an influence on me, as have the many thousands of people I have met on the way.

In the end it was an article on humanism, 'The Power of Kindness', by New Zealander David Whitehead, a former senior lecturer and researcher in neuroscience in the US, which encapsulated neatly what I have come to believe (*Open Society Journal*, September 2019). Humanism has come a long way since its tentative 16th-century beginnings which I encountered during that trip to Alsace in 1975. These are the key points which David cites:

- there are no supernatural beings;

- the material universe is the only thing that exists;
- science provides the only reliable source of knowledge about this universe (and, I would add, we must continue to probe its mysteries);
- we live only this life — there is no after-life and no such thing as reincarnation;
- human beings can live ethically without religious beliefs;
- human beings derive their moral code from the lessons of history, personal experience and thought.

One wonders where the myriad deities have been all the while. In their time, they come and pass away. All religions offer hope to their adherents on life's journey. Some religionists evince a true humility and a pastoral care; others, corrupt evangelists, have found a way to enrich themselves from religious dogmas. They offer the excuse to put down life's burdens and to sit under a shady tree, as if the shady tree were the destination.

We cannot blame those who want to rest but the tree can offer no shade from the squalls of winter. As I came to realise, the universe is supremely indifferent to each personal pilgrimage along life's road. But there is majesty in undertaking it and feeling part of a great beauty and mystery.

We are all pilgrims, as Chaucer so brilliantly portrayed, and there is great fellowship on the journey. But unlike Chaucer's 'nyne and twenty in a compaignye of sondry folk', it is the journey that is our purpose, not the destination. Or as Cervantes put it, 'the journey is better than the inn'.

Those who believe in a benign deity may be comforted but are taking the easy way out of the human dilemma. They push off to the deity responsibility for their own strengths, weaknesses and shortcomings, when evil is a man-made creation. There is nothing more grotesque than St Augustine's pessimistic doctrine of Original Sin, by which newborn children bear the sins of Adam and Eve, or of predestination. The Garden of Eden did indeed exist, our world in its pristine form, before mankind began to diminish it.

Few religions give serious thought to the duty of care we have for this fragile world of ours. Christ, like all other prophets, neglected to mention that the earth is round and our world heliocentric. What later grief might have been spared us if he had shared such knowledge?

One suspects that the gentle, rambling, rebel Rabbi Jesus, 2000 years ago, had no knowledge of such things. There is no shame though in not knowing. True humility lies in admitting that we don't and can't know everything. But we do not acquiesce in our ignorance. We commit in this life to a constant search for new knowledge and understanding.

As I conclude this memoir, summer has returned to the island. The bright blue sea sparkles its optimism in the distance. A pod of five or six orcas splash about in the bay below, chasing the stingrays. The garden bursts forth with new growth and the tui and kereru help themselves to the fruit of the puriri and the banana trees.

What a road it has been from Little Water Farm. Great memories crowd in of people and places: the sweet scent of the summer meadows in Somerset and Devon as the hay is made; the gentle breezes rippling over the corn and barley in Grandad's fields; the tangled aroma of the sea-lapped tropical Pacific islands and the lonely expanse of the vast oceans; the deserted streets of Pompeii and a lost civilisation; the rotting dead sheep in John Elliott's orchard and the Sistine Chapel; the relentless pulsating of the milking machines on Wally's farm on a humid and lazy summer afternoon; Ringo, Fordy, Doc Ales, Gaston and Budge at High School; Christopher, aged two, shovelling the snows of a Canadian winter; Rachel chasing off a band of Romanian thieves on a Rome street; the sublimity of a Wagner opera at Bayreuth or a Mozart concert in Würzburg; the pyramids of Giza at dusk as the muezzin calls to prayer the faithful in the delta below; the unparalleled beauty of the New Zealand landscape.

Memories of a wonderful world, but beset with sadness, pain and ignorance. There is melancholy too as we remember those we have met and loved on the way but are no more. Each of us struggles to give meaning to our life. It is often lonely and difficult. There is a constant struggle between optimism and pessimism.

The American novelist, Gertrude Stein, who died in 1946, reportedly said: 'There ain't no answer, there ain't going to be an answer, there never has been an answer, that's the answer'.

But I think we can have great fun, in this magnificent life, trying to formulate the question. And who knows, we might one day, in our search, be rewarded with the answer that so eluded her.

What, I wonder, will my grandchildren, not yet five years old, make of their New Zealand, English and Scottish heritage, when they read this memoir which tells of so many amazing people and of times long ago?

POEM: THE FUNERAL BIER
AND THE TUI

On a visit in 2002 to Schloss Nymphenburg, Munich, not far from the Dachau concentration camp, I wrote this poem standing before the funeral bier of Queen Maria Theresa, last Queen of Bavaria. The coldness of the bier, empty a hundred years, made me think of a starkly different emptiness, the long deserted but beautiful slopes of Ruapekapeka, a Maori pa (a large fortified village) in Northland which was overrun by aggressive British colonial forces on 11 January 1846, at the start of the violent New Zealand wars.

The Funeral Bier and the Tui

Magnificent that special carriage
made with
hard cold steel and rusting now.
A sombre procession that last
mournful journey,
carried well to eternal rest
surely on a dull winter's day.
Who was this Queen for whom this bier was fashioned?
Forgotten now, but then revered
and maybe loved.

Emptied of its moulding cargo,
standing quiet,
and useless
forever now alone.
The day weighs heavy,
and suffocating.

Take me back to the bright green hills of
Ruapekapeka,
quiet now,
a place of rest, but
not oppressive here.
The gentle slopes,
where once they lived and loved,
stand silent too
in the warmth of a summer sun.
The cold steel cannons gone
and rusted now.
Sentinel to a fleeting, violent past.
Gaze at the far-off hills
and let the spirit roam.
Let's not, today, think
of death
and faded glories gone,
all but forgotten.
See,
the Tui
flies free
Majestically,
above the empty slopes,
swoops over the memories,
and gives us hope.
To go on...

Hauððum að finem itineris

For the journey has not yet ended.

ABOUT THE AUTHOR

Peter Hamilton is a former deputy-secretary in the New Zealand Ministry of Foreign Affairs and Trade. He worked as a New Zealand diplomat at MFAT's head office in Wellington and at postings overseas in Fiji, Canada, Geneva, Samoa, Germany and Singapore. He has three children and three grandchildren and lives in Auckland, New Zealand.

newmoonsforsam@outlook.com